The World of Football Encyclopedia

First published as *The World of Football* in 2017
This edition published in 2018 by Sevenoaks
An imprint of Carlton Books Limited
20 Mortimer Street
London W1T 3JW

A CIP catalogue record for this book is available from the British Library

ISBN: 978-1-78177-847-0

Project Editor: Chris Mitchell
Design: www.fogdog.co.uk and
Stephen Cary
Illustration: Tim Brown, Bill Donohoe, Paul Oakley,
icons supplied courtesy of The Noun Project
Production: Ena Matagic
Picture Research: Paul Langan

Printed in Italy

Some of the content of this book was previously published as *The Complete Encyclopedia of Football*

The World of Football Encyclopedia

SEVENOAKS

CONTENTS

Cristiano Ronaldo goes on a typical surging run during the 2018 UEFA Champions League final. He finished as the tournament's top scorer, with 15 goals, as Real Madrid won their third straight title.

INTRODUCTION

1

HISTORY OF THE GAME

2

MAJOR INTERNATIONAL COMPETITIONS

3

MAJOR MULTI-NATIONAL CLUB COMPETITIONS

4

FOOTBALL NATIONS

5

FAMOUS CLUBS FROM AROUND THE WORLD

6

GREAT PLAYERS

INDEX

CHERYSHEV
6
ALBURAYK

INTRODUCTION

by Keir Radnedge

Association football, also known since the late nineteenth century as soccer, has variously been labelled the "simplest game" and the "beautiful game" and the "people's game." But, above and beyond all that, it is the world's most popular game.

Politicians in newly independent nations ponder over which organization to join first: the United Nations or FIFA, and successive FIFA presidents have compared world football in global wealth and strength with the greatest multinational corporations.

But football is far more than a cold mess of financial statistics. The game appeals to peoples of all ages and social status from Afghanistan to Zimbabwe because of the passion it arouses: passion both for the player, whether in back street or Bernabeu, as much as for the spectator, whether on the sand of Copacabana or in the best seats in Berlin.

The basic concept is childishly easy to understand: for one team to score more goals than the other. A natural spirit of loyalty, along the way, picks up player adulation, club adherence and national team ambition.

This book seeks to weave those threads together while also examining the single strands. That is just as it should be. Football is, after all, a team game played by individuals.

← Denis Cheryshev of Russia takes aim in the opening game of the 2018 FIFA World Cup. The hosts ran out 5-0 winners over Saudi Arabia at Moscow's Luzhniki Stadium.

1

HISTORY OF THE GAME

Football is now the world's most popular game, and over the years its competitions have broken down barriers all around the globe. With evidence of football-like sports being played over 2,000 years ago, it is also one of the oldest games, and as such has a lengthy and delightful history.

The early history of football

Association football is the formal title awarded by the nineteenth-century school teachers who turned an unruly physical pursuit into the codified game that swept the world.

The likes of Lord Kinnaird, Charles Alcock and Ebenezer Morley had no idea how their part-time pastime would develop. The notion of billions of people around the world sitting down in front of a square screen to watch a match would have been beyond their comprehension.

Yet football had already conquered the world once. Ancient China, Japan, the Roman empire . . . all left fragments of their civilization etched or carved or embroidered with images of men kicking some sort of a ball around. Football may thus be described as a game almost as old as civilization itself.

China provides history's first football report, in the writings of the Han Dynasty 2,000 years ago. They made it a proud boast in support of their hosting of the Beijing Olympic Games in 2008. The rules may have changed through the centuries but the pursuit of what may be termed "soccer" or "football" has remained one of man's most consistent entertainments.

It was just so for the Greeks and the Romans. Pollux describes the pastime of harpastum in the following terms: "The players divided themselves into two bands. The ball was thrown upon the line in the middle. At the two ends behind the places where the players were stationed there were two other lines [which would seem to be equivalent to modern goal-lines], beyond which they tried to carry it, a feat that could not be done without pushing one another backward and forward."

This suggests that harpastum was the origin of both rugby football and association football.

Ball games in Britain seem to have started as annual events staged over Shrovetide. As a rule these contests began in the marketplace and involved two teams of unlimited numbers trying to propel a ball into the opposite side's goal, which was usually some convenieănt spot not too far from the centre of town.

It was very hostile, violent and extremely dangerous. Householders had to barricade their lower windows as the mobs did battle along the streets. The hero was the lucky player who eventually grounded the ball in goal. Not that it was always a ball. The followers of the rebel leader Jack Cade kicked a pig's bladder in the streets of London.

In Chester, the object of the boot was a little more distasteful. There the game originated as a celebration of victory over the marauding Danes, and the head of one of the vanquished army was used as a football. Later generations were content to boot a leather ball at their Shrove Tuesday festivals.

There is a record of London schoolboys playing organized football before Lent in 1175, and so popular had the game become in the streets of London in the reign of Edward II that the merchants, fearing this most robust and violent activity was affecting their trade, petitioned the king to prohibit the game.

Such a fate makes no sense in the twenty-first century. Football is established as the world's most popular game and its competitions are hailed for breaking down political barriers. The world governing body, FIFA – whatever its failings – is probably more effective in the administration of its sport than any other such global organization. Decisions on the way the game is played command remarkable universal obedience.

In the twenty-first century there is no sign of a relaxation of football's grip on the public's imagination. That various corners of the world should come to a virtual standstill for an intense series of matches every four years underlines the point. The football revolution is here to stay.

↑ One of the myriad early variations on the football theme survives to this day, in the Eton Wall Game.
← There were few, if any, "rules" for the mob football played throughout the towns and villages of England in the Middle Ages.

HAN DYNASTY CIRCA
255 BC
CHINA PLAYS **TSU CHU**, USING GOALS, NETS AND A BALL

GREEKS AND **ROMANS**
PLAY HARPASTUM

1349

EDWARD II
BANS FOOTBALL IN ENGLAND

20
SHILLINGS FINE AND 6 DAYS' IMPRISONMENT DECREED AS PUNISHMENT IN 1410

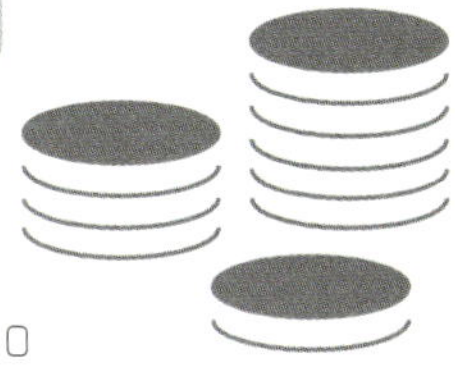

THE NINETEENTH CENTURY

On April 13, 1314, Edward II issued a proclamation forbidding football as a breach of the peace. Similar vain attempts to hold back the sporting tide were undertaken by Edward III, Richard II, Henry IV and James III. Only Lord Protector Oliver Cromwell had any success and that, like his Commonwealth, was temporary.

Yet football's early existence and subsequent image as the "working man's game" is misleading: it was the public schools, and Oxford and Cambridge Universities in particular, that brought shape and order out of the almost aimless fury of violence.

Nearly all the schools and numerous clubs that had mushroomed in the wake of the Industrial Revolution had their own sets of rules. By 1846, the overall situation was so chaotic that the first serious attempt to unify a code of rules was instigated at Cambridge University by Messrs Henry de Winton and John Charles Thring. They met representatives from the major public schools with a view to formulating a standard set of rules.

Their deliberations took seven hours and fifty-five minutes and were published as the Cambridge Rules. These were developed further by Thring in 1862, while he was an assistant master at Uppingham School.

Thring's rules served for what he termed "The Simplest Game". But they were not sufficient in themselves. Hence the creation of the Football Association on October 26, 1863, by a meeting of clubs at the Freemasons' Tavern in Great Queen Street, central London.

Arthur Pember was appointed chairman and Ebenezer Morley as honorary secretary. Morley sent further invitations to the leading schools but a second meeting heard that Harrow, Charterhouse and Westminster preferred their own rules.

Thring joined the FA after a third meeting to spark progress on unified laws which were published on December 1, 1863. An inaugural game using the new FA rules was initially scheduled for Battersea Park on January 2, 1864, but, as impatient members of the FA could not wait, an experimental game was played at Limes Field, Mortlake, on December 19, 1863, between Morley's Barnes and neighbours, Richmond.

Concessions were made to Richmond who were not members of the FA. The match was played with 15 players on each side (including Morley himself). After 90 minutes the game was declared a goalless draw. Richmond, unimpressed, decided to stick to rugby football; Barnes stuck with association football

➊ The FA Cup is the oldest football competition in the world, and over the years five different trophies have been awarded to the winners. The original was stolen in 1895 while under Aston Villa's care, and despite a £10 reward offered for information, it was never recovered.

➋ Royal Engineers were runners-up to Wanderers in the first FA Cup Final in 1872

➌ Clubs start to use co-ordinated kit, usually designed in hoops or blocks, such as the dark blue and maroon of the Royal Engineers

➍ Referee's whistle used for the first time at a Nottingham Forest match in 1878

1840-59

1848 First code of rules compiled at Cambridge University
1855 Sheffield FC, world's oldest club, formed

1860-69

1862 Notts County, world's oldest league club, formed
1863 The Football Association is formed in England, October 26

1870-79

1871 FA Cup inaugurated in England
1872 Size of ball standardized
▮ Scotland draw 0-0 with England in first official international at West of Scotland cricket ground
1874 Shinguards introduced by Sam Weller Widdowson of Nottingham Forest and England
1875 Crossbar replaces tape
1878 Almost 20,000 people watch first floodlit match, between two Sheffield teams, with lighting provided by four lamps on 30ft wooden towers

and would become founding competitors of the FA Cup.

The Association and the game both grew steadily in public popularity after the introduction of the FA Cup in 1871–72, and international fixtures in 1872. Such comparatively peaceful progress was then followed by a burst of major reforms, including the launch of the Football League in 1888–89.

This development prompted the first major crisis over the advent of the paid player: football's first professionals. The row came to a head early in 1884 when William Sudell, the chairman and manager of Preston admitted that they did pay their players and that nearly every other important club in Lancashire and the Midlands did likewise.

Sudell's confession brought home a need for the FA to face reality. Secretary Charles Alcock duly proposed "that the time has come for the legalization of professionalism", which was approved in July 1885.

Meanwhile, British sailors, soldiers, merchants, engineers, teachers, students and other professional classes had already taken their sports – football, but also cricket – around Europe. Curious locals joined in and were quickly entranced. The number of English-language club names across the continent proves the historic point. But Europe was not alone. Football, by the end of the nineteenth century, was being exported to all four corners of the world.

HOW IT ALL BEGAN
THE SIMPLEST GAME

1 Kick off from middle must be a place kick.
2 Kick out must not be from more than 25 yards out of goal.
3 Fair catch is a catch from any player, provided the ball has not touched the ground, or has not been thrown direct from touch, and entitles to a free kick.
4 Charging is fair in case of a place kick (with the exception of a kick off) as soon as the player offers to kick, but he may always draw back, unless he has actually touched the Ball with his foot.
5 Pushing with the hands is allowed, but no hacking or tripping up is fair under any circumstances whatsoever.
6 No player may be held or pulled over.
7 It is not lawful to take the ball off the ground (except in touch) for any purpose whatever.
8 The ball may be pushed or hit with the hand, but holding the ball (except in the case of a fair kick) is altogether disallowed.
9 A goal must be kicked, but not from touch, nor by a free kick from a catch.
10 A ball in touch is dead, consequently the side that touches it down must bring it to the edge of touch, and throw it straight out at least six yards from touch.
11 That each player must provide himself with a red and a dark blue flannel cap. One colour to be worn by each side during play.

THE PERFECT SEASON
THE INVINCIBLES

Preston North End, founded in 1881, won the first-ever Football League championship in 1888–89. They also completed the first League and FA Cup double that season. They defeated Wolverhampton Wanderers 3–0 in the final to secure their cup without conceding a goal. Preston also set an English goalscoring record when they thrashed Hyde 26–0 in the FA Cup; inside-forward James Ross set a First Division record by scoring seven goals in one match. Preston, who finished 11 points clear of Aston Villa, won the league again the following season. The inaugural season recorded 586 goals in 132 matches, an average of more than four goals per game.

➊ The nineteenth century saw leather studs used for the first time, which had to be hammered into the boots

1880-89

1882 International Board formed
1883 Two-handed throw-in introduced
1885 Professionalism legalized in England
1887 The first South American football club founded - Argentina's Club de Gimnasia y Esgrima La Plata
1888 Football League, brainchild of Aston Villa director, William McGregor, founded, and first matches played on September 8
▌Scottish Cup winners Renton beat English FA Cup winners West Bromwich for the "Championship of the World"
1889 Unbeaten Preston, "The Invincibles", become first club to win League and Cup double (above)

1890-99

1891 Goal nets and penalties introduced
▌Referees and linesmen replace umpires and referees
1892 Football League Second Division formed
1893 Genoa, oldest Italian League club, formed
1895 FA Cup, held by Aston Villa, stolen from Birmingham shop window and never seen again
1897 English players' union is formed
1898 Promotion and relegation introduced

1900–1919

Football had planted significant roots in South America by the start of the 20th century. In Argentina, although the game had been imported earlier by British residents of Buenos Aires, it had proved slow to catch on until after the migrant influx from Italy and Spain.

The British influence in South America remains clear to this day through the adopted names of clubs such as River Plate and Newell's Old Boys in Argentina, Liverpool and Wanderers in Uruguay, Everton and Rangers in Chile as well as the likes of Corinthians - after the great English amateur club - in Brazil, a nation respected, on merit, as the world's greatest football nation.

In Africa and Asia, not only the English but the French and, to a lesser extent, German and Portuguese colonial movements played predominant roles in introducing the game.

The worldwide momentum was reflected in the creation of the world federation governing body, the Fédération Internationale de Football Association (FIFA), in Paris on May 21, 1904. It could have been launched two years earlier but for the ponderous ways of the Football Association.

In the spring of that year the initial proposal for an international association was sent to Sir Frederick Wall, the FA secretary in London. The letter, posted on May 8, had been drafted by the secretary of the Dutch federation, Carl Hirschmann, and a French journalist, Robert Guerin of Le Matin who was also treasurer of the Union des Sociétes Françaises de Sports Athlétiques.

They believed that the fast-growing popularity of football throughout Europe deserved international co-ordination some 10 years after another Frenchman, Baron Pierre de Coubertin, had revived the Olympic Games.

Nothing came of either this or a second approach made to Wall. Therefore, on May 1, 1904, as France and Belgium played their first international, so Guerin and Belgian federation secretary Louis Muhlinghaus agreed to go ahead regardless.

Thus, on May 21, the USFSA offices at 229 rue Sainte-Honoré in Paris, saw a historic meeting between representatives of the fledgling associations of Belgium, Denmark, France, Holland, Sweden and Switzerland plus Spain's FC Madrid club (later Real Madrid). They voted for the foundation of FIFA and bestowed it with the power to organize a world championship.

Guerin was the first president. But a year later, on April 14, 1905, Baron Edouard de Laveleye, president of the Belgian federation, persuaded the FA to come aboard. England's Daniel DB Woolfall was elected to the presidency which he held until his death in 1918.

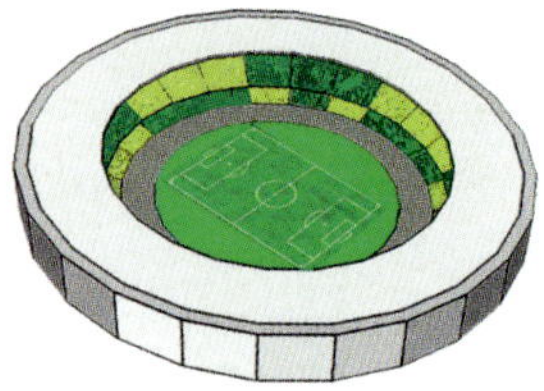

THE GREAT STADIUMS
Maracanã, Rio de Janeiro, Brazil. Capacity 78,838
Hosts: Brazil.
The Maracanã, Brazil's largest stadium, is named after the Rio suburb where it stands. Its official title is Estádio Jornalista Mário Filho, bestowed in 1966 on the death of the Brazilian journalist Mário Filho. The stadium was built for the 1950 World Cup, when a crowd of around 174,000 (probably many more) watched Brazil lose the final 2–1 to Uruguay. For the 2014 World Cup, the Maracanã was extensively rebuilt at a cost of more than $500 million.

The 1901 FA Cup Final between Tottenham Hotspur and Sheffield United was the first FA Cup Final to be filmed by Pathé News. Tottenham Hotspur remain the only non-League club to win the trophy

First £1,000 transfer sees Alf Common move from Sunderland to Middlesbrough in 1905

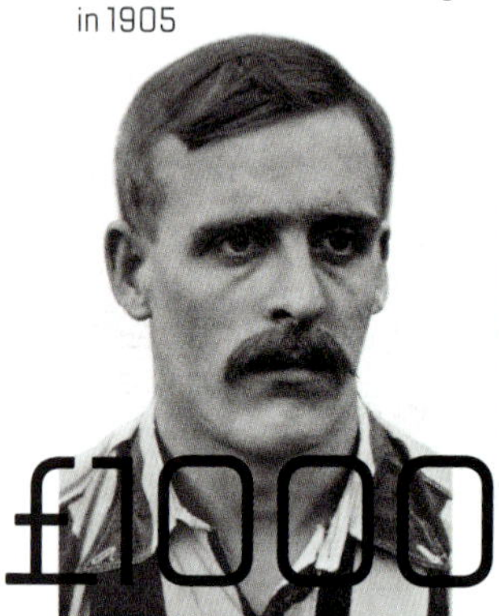

1901

- Maximum wage rule formalized
- Southern League Tottenham Hotspur become first professional club to take FA Cup south
- Argentina beat Uruguay 3-2 in first international between South American countries

1902

- Ibrox Park disaster: 25 killed when stand collapses (above)
- Real Madrid formed
- The Mexican League Championship, the first in Central and North America, is founded
- Austria beat Hungary 5-0 in the first international between teams outside the home countries

1904

- FIFA formed in Paris with seven members: Belgium, Denmark, France, Holland, Spain, Sweden and Switzerland
- Galt FC from Canada beat Christian Brothers College from the USA 2-0 in an Olympic medal game

1905

- England join FIFA
- Argentina and Uruguay meet in Buenos Aires in the first official international in South America

1906-7

1906 The laws of the game are substantially rewritten for the first time

1907 FIFA admits Bohemia to membership - then excludes it because it is only a region within the Austro-Hungarian empire

- Charles W. Alcock (above), inventor of the FA Cup and winner of one cap for England, dies

INFAMOUS HISTORY
ACROSS THE LINES

During the First World War, on Christmas Day, 1915, a truce was observed between German and British forces. At Laventie in northern France, soldiers of both sides ventured out of their trenches to exchange seasonal greetings. The last survivor of those Royal Welsh Fusiliers, Bertie Felstead, recalled: "When we met them, someone suggested football. It wasn't a game as such, more of a kick around and a free-for-all. There could have been 50 on each side for all I know. I played because I really liked football. I don't know how long it lasted, probably half an hour. No one was keeping score." The football truce ended with the order "to kill the Hun, not make friends with him". Felstead died in July 2001, aged 106.

It was under Woolfall's leadership that the British agreed to admit foreign representation to the law-making International Board. It was also under his leadership that FIFA became a truly world federation rather than a European one: in 1910 South Africa was admitted to membership and, in 1912, so was Argentina.

The notion of competitive international football took shape once FIFA had formalized the notion of the nation state as a football entity. The British home championship was the forerunner followed by the Olympics.

The sport entered the Games in a one-match exhibition form in Athens in 1896 and further unofficial competitions followed in 1900 and 1904. In London in 1908, Great Britain had the honour of becoming first official Olympic champions by defeating Denmark 2-0. Great Britain would win again in 1912.

Meanwhile, the South Americans, cut off from the Eurocentric Olympic movement by travel restrictions, organized their own regional championship, the future Copa America, in 1916.

By then football in Europe had been halted by war. That had not only international but personal implications. English coaching missionaries such as Jimmy Hogan and Steve Bloomer - the former an England inside-right - were both interned in Germany where they had been working.

HOW IT BEGAN
PRESIDENTS OF FIFA

1904–06
Robert Guerin (France)

1906–18
D.B. Woolfall (England)

1921–54
Jules Rimet (France)

1954–5
Rodolphe Seeldrayers (Belgium)

1955–61
Arthur Drewry (England)

1961–74
Sir Stanley Rous (England)

1974–98
João Havelange (Brazil)

1998–2015
Joseph "Sepp" Blatter (Switzerland)

2016–
Gianni Infantino (Switzerland)

Brazil's first team colours were white with blue collars, which they wore until home defeat in the 1950 World Cup

Boots had changed very little – they remained high-sided with thick leather and long laces

1908

- Transfer limit of £350 introduced in January, withdrawn in April
- Great Britain beat Denmark to win the first official Olympic football title at Shepherds Bush (above)
- In June, England play their first internationals abroad, beating Austria twice, including an 11-1 victory in Vienna

1910

- Argentina win the first unofficial South American Championship
- A national championship is launched in the Philippines, the first in Asia

1913-14

1913 China and the Philippines meet in the first international in Asia

1914 Brazil make their international debut, against Argentina

1915

1915 In what becomes known as the "Khaki Cup Final", Sheffield United beat Chelsea in front of a crowd mostly dressed in army uniform (above, injured soldiers in the crowd)

1916-19

1916 CONMEBOL, in South America, is created as the first regional confederation

1919 The Football League is extended to 44 clubs as league football in England is resumed after the war

1920–1939

The First World War proved disastrous for Europe and FIFA suffered from the fall-out. The British home nations quit in 1920 in a row over international contact with wartime antagonists Austria, Hungary and Germany.

This British absence lasted four years and then the home FAs quit again in 1928 in a row over broken-time payments for amateurs. The home countries continued to play against their former partners in FIFA but only in friendly matches. Hence they missed out where it really mattered, at the launch of the World Cup in 1930.

In the 1920s, Austrian pioneer Hugo Meisl launched two other international competitions, the Dr Gero Cup was the first for European national teams outside the United Kingdom, while the Mitropa Cup - a contraction of the German Mittel Europa (Central Europe) - proved a successful forerunner of today's European club tournaments.

The free scoring that helped popularize these competitions had been encouraged by the most significant change of all in the laws of the game.

In 1873, offside had been introduced with a law demanding that three opponents should be between attacker and goal when the ball was played forward. But the wiles of Newcastle United's Irish fullback, Billy McCracken, changed history.

In the early 1920s, he perfected the ruse of

THE WHITE HORSE FINAL

BOLTON WANDERERS 2–0 WEST HAM UNITED

FA Cup Final, Wembley Stadium London, April 28, 1923

King George V was there, and somehow a match was laid on for him, which, through good fortune and the crowd's good sense, was not the tragedy it might have been. Thanks to the self-discipline of the fans in a less impatient age, and to the police - led by Constable George Scorey on his legendary white horse, Billy - the Cup final took place, starting almost an hour late. Capacity was officially 125,000, but the combination of a fine spring day, the new arena and the appearance of a London club in the final led to an estimated 250,000 trying to gain admittance - with most succeeding. The first goal came as an opponent was trying to climb back out of the crowd. The second was a rebound, either off a post… or spectators standing alongside the goal.

➔ The International Football Association Board (IFAB) decrees that international goalkeepers should wear yellow, to distinguish them from other players

➔ 1927: English fans hear a first radio commentary (Arsenal v Sheffield United)

1920-1

1920 The four home FAs withdraw from FIFA when other members reject their demand not to play matches against First World War enemies
1921 Jules Rimet becomes president of FIFA (above)

1922-4

1923 Football pools introduced
1924 First Wembley international: England 1, Scotland 1
▮ Goal can be scored direct from corner kick
▮ The four home FAs rejoin FIFA
▮ Uruguay become the first non-European nation to win the Olympics

1925-6

1925 Offside rule change: a player needs two, not three, players between him and goal to stay onside
▮ German becomes, after French and English, the third official FIFA language
1926 Huddersfield complete first hat-trick of championships

1927-8

1927 The Mitropa Cup, predecessor of the European club cups, is launched in Europe
1928 Bill "Dixie" Dean (above) scores 60 First Division goals, still a record
▮ Uruguay win the Olympic title a second time to prompt FIFA into formulating a World Cup

1929

▮ FIFA's Barcelona congress awards hosting rights of the first World Cup to Uruguay in 1930
▮ Goalkeepers ordered to stay on goal-line until penalty is kicked
▮ England lose to foreign opposition for the first time, by 4-3 to Spain
▮ Unified Italian league championship set up

stepping forward just in time to catch forwards offside. The furore prompted the International Board into a change in wording and numbers: instead of "three" it would now be "two".

Goal-scoring rates rocketed. In the season before the law change, the 462 matches of the English first division produced 1,192 goals at a match average of 2.58. The next season, 1925-26, the 462 games generated 1,703 goals at an average of 3.68.

Arsenal manager Herbert Chapman and his Scottish forward Charlie Buchan worked out a counter: pulling the traditional attacking centre-half back between the fullbacks. By the end of the 1930s, the new WM formation had caught on across most of Europe.

In time, the nations of South America would find a different tactical route, as they demonstrated at the first World Cup in Uruguay in 1930. Uruguay, celebrating a centenary of independence, offered to foot the travel bill for European entries and build a giant new venue named the Centenario.

THE FIRST WORLD CHAMPIONS

URUGUAY 4–2 ARGENTINA

World Cup Final, Centenary Stadium, Montevideo, July 30, 1930

Few papers outside South America and Central Europe bothered to report the match. Yet the game went into history simply because it could not be repeated. The first World Cup was over and international football now had a standard to emulate. Hosts Uruguay just managed to get a stadium built in time and fittingly reached the final against neighbours Argentina. The Uruguayans took the lead, fell behind, then went ahead again at 3-2 before Stabile, top scorer in the competition with eight goals, hit their bar. Castro, who had lost part of an arm in childhood, then headed the goal that clinched Uruguay's victory, to be greeted by a national holiday in his country.

Only four European nations sent teams to the tournament, which was won by the hosts: Uruguay beat neighbours Argentina 4-2 in the final in Montevideo. The "Celeste" were the outstanding national team of their era, having won both the 1924 and 1928 Olympic titles.

Italian dictator Benito Mussolini saw the 1934 World Cup as an ideal vehicle to promote the fascist "wonders" of Italy, while Adolf Hitler's will to use the 1936 Berlin Olympics as a showcase for "Aryan supremacy" has remained a grim focus for sports politics historians throughout the years.

In 1934, Italy, managed by Vittorio Pozzo, beat Czechoslovakia 2–1 in the final in Rome. Four years later, Eastern Europe took another beating as Hungary lost 4–2 to the Italians in Paris.

Pozzo and Italy had tactically moved with the times. In 1934, they had won by using an "old-fashioned" attacking centre-half in the Argentinian Luisito Monti; victory in 1938 was accomplished by the effective use of a new "stopper" central defender in the Uruguayan, Michele Andreolo.

Only two players survived from the 1934 winners to the 1938 team: inside-forwards Giuseppe Meazza and Gianni Ferrari. Skipper Meazza gave the fascist salute before hoisting the World Cup trophy high in the Stade Colombes. It was the last the world saw of the gold statuette for 12 war-enshrouded years.

GERMANY 3
ENGLAND 6
Berlin, May 14, 1938
The England team were ordered to join the Germans in giving the Nazi salute as the German national anthem was played. The players reluctantly got on with it, then showed their feelings by beating a very good German team out of sight. Don Welsh, one of two men making their England debut, was to say later: "Only when the heat got to us in the second half did we have to slow down a bit. I honestly thought we could have scored ten."

1934: Sudden death of Arsenal manager Herbert Chapman on January 6. Chapman was one of the game's great modernisers, championing innovations like floodlights and shirt numbers

1937: The official weight of the ball is increased from 13/15 oz to 14/16 oz

1938: FA secretary and future president Stanley Rous rewrites the laws of the game

1930-1

1930 Austria's "Wunderteam" beat Scotland 5-0, Germany 6-0 and lose only 4-3 to England
1931 Argentina is the first South American country to accept professionalism
▮ Athletic Bilbao win the Spanish league and Cup double for the second successive season

1932-3

1932 Substitutions are permitted for the first time in non-competitive matches when agreed
1933 Numbered shirts, 1-22, worn in the FA Cup final for first time
▮ Uruguay decide to ignore the second World Cup because so many European nations stayed at home in 1930

1934-5

1934 Hosts Italy win the first World Cup to be staged in Europe
▮ Bologna of Italy win the Mitropa Cup for the second time in three years
1935 Juventus win a fifth successive Italian league title
▮ Sparta Prague win the Mitropa Cup for the second time

1936-7

1936 Italy add Olympic gold to their World Cup
▮ Civil war brings Spanish league football to a halt for three years
1937 A world attendance record of 149,547 watch Scotland v England at Hampden Park, Glasgow
▮ Germany's legendary "Breslau-Elf" thrash Denmark 8-0

1938-9

1938 Arsenal set a world transfer record by paying £14,000 for Wolves' forward Bryn Jones
1939 England refuse to play in the World Cup after the withdrawal of Austria following the Anschluss with Germany
▮ Italy become the first double winners of the World Cup, in France

➔ ENGLAND 3
HUNGARY 6
Wembley Stadium, London, November 25, 1953
"This will be easy," said one England player, "they've all got carpet slippers on." Hungary's footwear did look like slippers compared with England's boots, but they could smack the ball pretty hard. The defeat was England's first by a continental invader and the manner and margin forced a furious tactical rethink in succeeding seasons.

1940–1959

The 1940s were confused years for football. Official competition had been suspended in the United Kingdom on the outbreak of the Second World War but was maintained through the early years of fighting in both Italy and Germany.

When FIFA reconvened in 1946, it had 57 members and no money. So Stanley Rous, secretary of the FA, negotiated the re-entry of the four home countries. In return, Rous offered FIFA gate receipts from a Hampden Park friendly between the four home countries and the Rest of the World.

Shrewdly, he also negotiated a guarantee of the individual status of the four home nations within FIFA. The final piece of his jigsaw was their admission to the World Cup in 1950.

Disasters accompanied the game's journey back to health. In 1946, some 33 fans died when a wall collapsed at Bolton before an FA Cup tie against Stanley Matthews's Stoke City; three years later, Torino's magnificent Italian champions were wiped out in an air crash on returning from a game in Lisbon.

The World Cup in Brazil at the start of the 1950s saw football's first modern steps towards becoming the planet's dominant sport.

Brazil and England started as joint favourites. Holders Italy, robbed of their playing nucleus by the Torino air crash, went out in the first round. So did England, losing humiliatingly 1-0 to the United States. Brazil went all the way to the final before losing 2-1 to tiny old enemy Uruguay in front of 200,000 home fans at the Maracanã.

By now a new force was rising in Europe. Hungary's Magical Magyars underlined their status by winning Olympic gold in 1952 in Helsinki and then, the following year, by thrashing England 6-3 at Wembley. It was the first time England had lost at home to continental opposition.

An even bigger shock than Brazil's 1950 defeat was in store at the 1954 finals in Switzerland. Hungary, an amalgam of players dragooned into their two top clubs by the communist regime and unbeaten in four years, lost the one match which mattered most: the World Cup Final.

West Germany, remarkably, hit back from 2-0 down and against all the odds to win 3-2. What made victory even more of a shock was the fact that skipper Ferenc Puskás and his Hungarians

➔ THE GREAT STADIUMS
Estadio Santiago Bernabéu Madrid, Spain. Capacity 81,044 Hosts: Spain, Real Madrid

£20,000

1940-1

1940 Central American championship launched
▮ Representative football is revived in England (Eddie Hapgood for an FA XI and Stan Cullis of The Army shake hands, above)
▮ Rapid Vienna defeat favourites Schalke 4-3 in controversial German league championship play-off final

1942-3

1942 Italy beat Croatia and Spain both 4-0 in April in their last matches before war halts the Azzurri's international activity
1943 Santiago Bernabéu, new president of Real Madrid, launches an investment scheme to build the stadium, later named after him (above)

1944-5

1944 Dresdner SC defeat LSV Hamburg 4-0 in the last wartime championship play-off in Germany
▮ Malmö win the Swedish championship for the first time in one of the few European leagues uninterrupted by war
1945 Moscow Dynamo make a sensational tour of Britain

1946-7

1946 British Associations rejoin FIFA
▮ 33 killed and 500 injured as wall collapses at Bolton v Stoke FA Cup tie
▮ FIFA expels Germany from membership at its Luxembourg congress
1947 First £20,000 transfer: Tommy Lawton (above), from Chelsea to Notts County

1948-9

1948 Separate federation set up for East Germany
▮ Sweden surprisingly win London Olympic Games
1949 Entire Torino team killed when aircraft taking Italian champions home crashes near Turin (above)
▮ Argentine league players undertake the first players' strike for better pay and terms

BRAZIL FAIL AT THE FINISH

BRAZIL 1–2 URUGUAY

World Cup final pool, Maracanã, Rio de Janeiro, July 11, 1950

Figures for attendance vary, but this was certainly the highest at any match since Wembley 1923. The first post-war World Cup, played without a knockout final stage, provided what was in effect a final and established the tournament as the leading worldwide competition. Brazil, huge favourites, won their first two games, scoring 13 goals to 2. Uruguay trailed both Spain and Sweden 2-1, but drew the first game and won the second. So they had to beat Brazil at the newly built Maracanã, while Brazil needed only to draw. Coach Flavio Costa's warnings about previous encounters in which Uruguay had disturbed Brazil went unheeded. Even after Friaca hit their 22nd goal in six games (as seen in the picture below), Brazil kept pressing forward: Costa later protested that he had ordered men back, but his words had gone unheeded. Uruguay, calm amid the crescendo, equalized through Juan Schiaffino. Then Alcides Ghiggia slipped through on the right and shot between Barbosa and his near post. All Brazil went into mourning.

had beaten the Germans 8-3 in the first round.

Simultaneously, Europe's associations, concerned at a loss of power within expanding FIFA, created their own federation: UEFA. Within a year it was handed the goose to lay its golden eggs. French newspaper L'Équipe had created a European Champions Cup but lacked the resources to run it. UEFA took over with results that would revolutionise the game.

European fans were thrilled by the glamour and style of Spain's Real Madrid. They were inspired by their great Argentinian centre-forward Alfredo Di Stéfano to win the first five cups from 1956 until a legendary 7-3 triumph over Eintracht Frankfurt at Hampden Park in 1960.

But the thrills were accompanied by disaster. In February 1958, eight Manchester United players died after their plane crashed at Munich while returning from a European Cup tie.

The deaths of Roger Byrne, Duncan Edwards and Tommy Taylor undermined England's prospects at the 1958 World Cup. They managed a goalless first round draw with ultimate winners Brazil, but failed to reach the quarter-finals.

Brazil reacted to the England draw by producing the explosive genius of Pelé and Garrincha. They also opened up a new tactical front. Instead of the old WM formation, Brazil strung four players across their defence, pulled one inside-forward back into midfield and attacked with four men instead of five. Suddenly everyone woke up to 4-2-4.

➔ 1953: After Brazil's defeat in the 1950 World Cup, a kit-design competition results in the sacred yellow, green and blue colours

➔ 1951: White ball comes into use for first time

➔ 1954: Adidas claim to have invented the screw-in stud for the German team to combat the slippery conditions of the World Cup final. Puma, however, claim to have been supplying studs to leading players as early as 1952

£91k

1950-1

1950 England humbled 1-0 by US in World Cup ▌Scotland first beaten at home by foreign team (Austria, 1-0) ▌West Germany is readmitted to FIFA **1951** Milan win Italy's Serie A for the first time ▌Argentina play England for the first time, losing 2-1 at Wembley

1952-3

1952 Ferenc Puskás's Hungary win Olympic gold in Helsinki **1953** Stanley Matthews inspires Blackpool to beat Bolton 4-3 in the FA Cup final ▌Hungary beat England 6-3 at Wembley and then 7-1 the next year in Budapest

1954-5

1954 European federation UEFA is founded ▌Real Madrid, inspired by Alfredo Di Stéfano, win their first Spanish league title since 1933 **1955** The European Champions Club Cup is launched on the initiative of the French sports newspaper, *L'Équipe*

1956-7

1956 Real Madrid, from an entry of 16 teams, win first European Cup ▌South Korea defeat Israel to win first Asian Cup **1957** First African Nations Cup Final: Egypt 4-1 Ethiopia ▌Juventus pay a world record £91,000 for Omar Sívori (above) from River Plate

1958-9

1958 Munich air disaster kills 19, including eight Manchester United players ▌Barcelona beat a London Select team to win first Inter City Fairs Cup ▌Pelé, at 17, becomes youngest World Cup-winner with Brazil **1959** Real Madrid win their fourth European Champions Cup

1960–1979

The 1960s and 1970s saw football's last romantic era washed away by a wave of pragmatism. The tactics of success underlined the nature of the change. Brazil had introduced 4-2-4 to the world in 1958 but retreated to 4-3-3 while claiming a 3-1 victory over Czechoslovakia in 1962.

Tactical caution continued in 1966 when hosts England won the World Cup with a 4-2 extra-time victory over West Germany. Manager Alf Ramsey scrapped wingers in favour of a four-man midfield; the effort and energy of Nobby Stiles and Alan Ball balanced Martin Peters' perceptiveness and Bobby Charlton's brilliance. Geoff Hurst scored the only World Cup final hat-trick.

In 1960, Real Madrid had reached a glorious pinnacle of European Champions Cup perfection with their 7–3 victory over Eintracht Frankfurt. Not content with their fifth European crown they then collected the first FIFA Club World Cup. The proud champions of Europe and the world were then almost instantly eliminated from the next European Cup by domestic arch rivals Barcelona, who then lost the 1961 final to Benfica. They were deposed in turn by Milan, who were subsequently succeeded by neighbours, Internazionale.

Coached by a catenaccio perfectionist in Helenio Herrera, Inter ground out two Champions Cup victories before falling prey to a marauding masterpiece in 1967 when Scotland's Celtic became the first British winners.

One year later, Manchester United followed in their footsteps: Bobby Charlton, scored in the 4–1 defeat of Benfica at Wembley under manager Matt Busby. English clubs went on to dominate the 1970s through Liverpool and then Brian Clough's Nottingham Forest.

However, officialdom failed to provide the supporter safety that the game's popularity needed. More than 600 fans died in stadium

GLASGOW SEES THE GREATEST

REAL MADRID 7–3 EINTRACHT FRANKFURT

European Cup Final, Hampden Park, Glasgow, May 18, 1960

Real Madrid's fifth successive European Cup was achieved by their greatest performance in front of yet another great crowd. In their seven matches they scored 31 goals and were watched by 524,097 people - an average of nearly 75,000 per game. In the semi-final Real beat Barcelona 3-1 home and away, after Barça had crushed Wolves, the English champions, 9-2 on aggregate. In the other semi-final, Eintracht performed the barely credible feat of twice scoring six goals against Rangers, but in the final they conceded hat-tricks to both Di Stéfano and Puskás in a wonderful performance watched by a crowd so big that only one larger attendance has been recorded in Britain since. Hardly any left early, even though the Germans were a beaten team well before the end. The fans stayed to bay a seemingly never-ending roar of tribute to one of the finest displays ever put on by any team, anywhere. The Scots were quick to appreciate their good fortune.

£100,000

➔ Nobby Stiles, Bobby Moore, Geoff Hurst and Martin Peters celebrate England's World Cup triumph in 1966

➔ Adidas Diamant: worn by Geoff Hurst and Bobby Moore. 75% of the 1966 World Cup players used the Adidas boots

1960–1

1960 European champions Real Madrid win first World Club Championship
▮ Soviet Union win the first European Championship
▮ Peñarol of Uruguay win first Copa Libertadores
1961 First £100,000 British transfer: Denis Law (above) from Manchester City to Torino

1962–3

1962 Brazil win second successive World Cup
▮ Pelé's club, Santos, win the Copa Libertadores for the first time (above)
1963 Tottenham beat Atlético Madrid 5-1 in Cup-winners' Cup Final to become first British club to win European trophy

1964–5

1964 318 die and 500 injured in riot over disallowed goal during Peru v Argentina in Lima
▮ Oryx Douala of Cameroon defeat Stade Malien of Mali 2-1 to win first African Champions Club Cup
1965 Substitutes allowed for injured players in English league matches

1966–7

1966 Hosts England win World Cup, beating West Germany 4-2 after extra time at Wembley (above)
▮ Real Madrid win a record-extending sixth European Champions Cup
1967 Jock Stein's Celtic beat Internazionale 2-1 to become first British winners of European Cup

1968–9

1968 74 die at Nunez, Buenos Aires, when panic breaks out during River Plate v Boca Juniors match
▮ Manchester United become first English winners of European Cup
1969 200 die in the so-called "football war" between El Salvador and Honduras after a World Cup qualifier

accidents in the 1960s, some 318 in Lima, Peru, at an Olympic qualifier against Argentina. In 1971, some 66 fans died and 150 were injured on a stairway at a Glasgow Old Firm derby at Ibrox Park between Rangers and Celtic.

Players also died due to the increase in air travel: Green Cross of Chile and The Strongest of Bolivia both lost entire first-team squads in 1961 and 1969, respectively. Worse still, football even prompted a border war after El Salvador beat Honduras in a 1969 World Cup qualifying play-off.

On and off the pitch, the 1970s belonged to Brazil. The national team became the first three-time World Cup winners and, in 1974, a Brazilian sat at the head of FIFA, the first and only non-european to ever hold the position.

In the 1970 World Cup, Brazil had more and better skilled individuals than anyone else. They beat holders England 1-0 in the first round and crushed Italy 4-1 in a glorious demonstration of their beautiful game or *jogo bonito* in the final in Mexico City. Pelé scored one superb goal to crown a watershed event, the first to be broadcast worldwide for colour television viewing.

Four years later, Brazil were winning again, but this time off the pitch. João Havelange, now president of the Brazilian confederation, ousted England's Sir Stanley Rous at FIFA. No incumbent president had ever faced an election challenge before but Havelange made history by promising to expand the World Cup to accommodate Third-World ambitions.

As Brazil's political mettle rose so its football hegemony faded. They finished fourth at a 1974 World Cup made memorable by the "total football" played by Holland, even though Johan Cruyff's Oranje lost 2–1 in the final to Franz Beckenbauer's West German hosts.

Four years later, in Argentina, Brazil finished "only" third and had to watch their neighbours win the World Cup for the first time. Again, luckless Holland were beaten in the final, this time by 3–1 after extra time.

Liverpool's Phil Neal, Emlyn Hughes and Jimmy Case share European Cup-winning delight.

Stylo Matchmaker: designed in collaboration with George Best this was the start of "branding" the player and his kit. His autograph was stamped in gold on each boot

Shirts get tighter, shorts shorter and sleeves longer. Leeds United change to white overall (right) and are the first team to have sponsored kit

Puma King: worn by Pelé, Johan Cruyff and Maradona. Pelé led Brazil to World Cup victory in 1970 wearing the German-made Puma boots

£1m

1970-1

1970 Brazil beat Italy 4-1 to capture World Cup for the third time and win the Jules Rimet trophy outright
1971 66 fans trampled to death and 100 injured in second Ibrox disaster
▮ Ajax Amsterdam win the first of three successive Champions Cups

1972-3

1972 Fairs Cup becomes UEFA Cup and is won by Tottenham
▮ West Germany beat the Soviet Union 3-0 to win European Championship
1972 Barcelona pay record £922,000 to buy Johan Cruyff (above)
▮ Russia expelled from the World Cup after refusing to play Chile

1974-5

1974 Magdeburg become first and last East German winners in Europe, beating Milan in Cup-winners' Cup final
1975 English hooliganism makes its first mark on the Champions Cup Final after Leeds United lose to Bayern Munich at the Parc des Princes in Paris

1976-7

1976 Czechoslovakia become the first European champions courtesy of a penalty shootout
▮ East Germany win Olympic gold in Montreal
▮ Bayern Munich win their third European Champions Cup in a row
1977 Liverpool win League Championship and European Cup

1978-9

1978 Ban on foreign players in English football lifted.
▮ Argentina, as hosts, win the World Cup; Holland are again runners-up
▮ First £1m British transfer: Trevor Francis (above), from Birmingham City to Nottingham Forest

1980–1989

Diego Maradona and Michel Platini were the dominant players of the 1980s; Liverpool, Juventus, Milan, Peñarol and America Cali were the leading clubs; Italy and Argentina won the decade's two World Cup Finals. But the 1980s will be remembered, most of all, for the negligence of associations, officials and clubs which led to unnecessary death and destruction on the terraces.

This was the decade in which football had to fight for its soul against the threat of hooliganism. Almost every year brought a terrace disaster somewhere in the world, starting in Colombia in 1981 when 18 fans died after a wall collapsed in Ibague. A little later, again in Colombia, 22 died in a supporter stampede in Cali. The same year more than 300 Soviet fans died on the icy terracing of Moscow's Lenin Stadium at a UEFA Cup tie between Spartak and Holland's Haarlem.

By now, the curse of hooliganism had eaten its way deep into the heart of the English game. In 1985 English football drew the horrible consequences of inadequate stadia and inadequate security.

First, 56 fans died and more than 200 were injured when fire swept through Bradford City's old wooden stand before half-time in the last match of the season. From Bradford to Brussels:

ROSSI'S TIMELY RETURN

ITALY 3–2 BRAZIL

World Cup Group C, Sarria Stadium, Barcelona, July 5, 1982

On the morning of April 29, 1982, Paolo Rossi returned from suspension, having been banned for three years - later reduced to two - for allegedly accepting a bribe and helping "fix" a match in the Italian league. Eleven weeks later Rossi was the hero of all Italy. He scored three goals in this vital group qualifying match and one in the final, when Italy beat West Germany 3-1. His six goals made him the tournament's leading marksman and completed a remarkable comeback for one of the most effective strikers of his generation. He always protested his innocence - and his demonic efforts to regain match fitness, plus his finishing, took Italy to a merited success. Brazil needed a draw to reach the semi-finals, but their two brilliant goals encouraged them to keep on attacking and their over-stretched defence made errors against a forward in such inspired mood as Rossi.

Queens Park Rangers, managed by Terry Venables, lay the first artificial pitch in English football in 1981

1981: Tottenham win 100th FA Cup Final

20-0

1984: Britain's biggest score of twentieth century: Stirling Albion beat Selkirk 20–0 in Scottish Cup

1980

- West Germany win European title for second time in Italy
- All four semi-finalists in the UEFA Cup are West German clubs: Eintracht Frankfurt then beat Borussia Mönchengladbach in the final

1981

- Liverpool win European Cup, becoming first British side to hold it three times
- Three points for a win introduced in Football League
- Record British transfer: Bryan Robson, from West Bromwich Albion to Manchester United for £1.5m

1982

- 340 fans crushed to death during Spartak Moscow v Haarlem UEFA Cup tie at Lenin Stadium
- Aston Villa become sixth consecutive English winners of European Cup (above)
- Italy defeat West Germany 3-1 in Madrid to complete third World Cup triumph

1983

- England's Football League sponsored by Canon for three years
- Hamburg break the six-year English monopoly of the European Champions Cup
- Bob Paisley (above) retires after leading Liverpool to 20 honours in nine seasons

1984

- Aberdeen win Scottish Cup for third straight season and win championship
- Northern Ireland win last British Home Championship
- France win their first honour - the European Championship

just 17 days later the world's television viewers watched more tragedy.

The stage was the European Cup final between holders Liverpool and Juventus in the ageing Heysel stadium in Brussels. English hooligans undertook a terrace charge which pushed Italian fans back against a maintenance wall. It collapsed under the pressure and 39 fans died.

In the immediate aftermath, the Football Association withdrew English clubs from European competitions. Later UEFA formalized the separation with a blanket ban which lasted for five years.

This was indeed football's "Killing Fields" era. In 1988 more than 30 fans died in Libya and another 100 in Kathmandu, Nepal. More was to come in April 1989 when 95 Liverpool supporters were crushed to death before an FA Cup semi-final against Nottingham Forest at Sheffield Wednesday's Hillsborough.

Subsequent inquiries and investigations laid bare a string of basic security, crowd control and emergency services errors whose true nature was emasculated by a police cover-up which was not unearthed entirely for more than 25 years. The disaster prompted the Taylor Report which forced the introduction of all-seater stadiums, a concept picked up internationally by FIFA and UEFA.

Amid the gloom, Maradona and Platini played some of the best football for years. Their shadows had first touched at the 1978 World Cup. Maradona was named in host Argentina's initial squad of 25 but was then among one of the three players omitted because manager César Luis Menotti doubted he could withstand the pressure. Menotti had a point: four years later Maradona was sent off at the 1982 World Cup for sticking a boot into a Brazilian's groin.

Platini, five years older, had played for France at the 1978 finals, then took a starring role when they reached the 1982 and 1986 semi-finals. Each time France lost to West Germany who finished runners-up, first to Italy then to Argentina.

In between these World Cup runs, Platini scored a tournament record nine goals as hosts France won the European Championship for the first time in 1984. That was also the year in which Barcelona sold Maradona to Napoli for a world record £3 million. Two years later he led Napoli to the Serie A crown and captained Argentina to World Cup glory.

Maradona led by example. He scored wondrous solo goals against England and Belgium before providing the winner for Jorge Burruchaga against West Germany in the final.

⬆ THE GREAT STADIUMS
Camp Nou, Barcelona
Capacity 99,354
Hosts: Barcelona.
Built between 1954 and 1957, Europe's largest football stadium creates an atmosphere like no other, as tens of thousands of fervent Catalans cheer on the team they are certain is the world's greatest. Camp Nou means "new ground" in Catalan, the old ground being Camp de Les Corts, which even with a capacity of 60,000 was considered too small for the ambitions of FC Barcelona. By 2012, the Camp Nou will have been redeveloped into a stadium for 105,000 at a cost of nearly £500 million.

⬇ Real Madrid are the first La Liga team to be sponsored as shirt sponsorship takes over the major European leagues

⬇ Wreaths of flowers turn the Kop into a memorial to the Hillsborough victims in 1989

1985

- Bradford City fire disaster kills 56
- Kevin Moran (Manchester United) is first player sent off in Cup final
- Heysel disaster: 39 die as a result of rioting at Liverpool v Juventus European Cup final in Brussels. UEFA bans English clubs indefinitely from European football

1986

- Sir Stanley Rous dies, aged 91
- Wales FA move HQ from Wrexham to Cardiff after 110 years
- Diego Maradona's Argentina win the World Cup (above) for the second time on its second hosting in Mexico

1987

- Play-offs introduced for last promotion place; re-election abolished; automatic promotion for winners of Conference
- The 18-strong squad plus youth players and officials of Alianza Lima die in plane crash

1988

- Wimbledon (above) beat Liverpool in FA Cup Final
- Holland win the European Championship, beating the Soviet Union 2-0 in Munich

1989

- Hillsborough disaster: 96 fans died at Liverpool v Nottingham Forest FA Cup semi-final
- Milan win their first European Champions Cup of the Berlusconi era, beating Steaua Bucharest 4-0 in the final in Barcelona

1990–1999

This decade proved one of the most energizing decades in football history both on and off the pitch. Yet they were launched to an inauspicious start by a World Cup in Italy in which both the quality of football and the standards of refereeing fell far below expectations.

The Italian public made some amends by providing a great carnival atmosphere but their semi-final defeat by Argentina left the tournament to end in anti-climax. Argentina produced angry football which reached a nadir in the final in Rome when they had two players sent off, the first World Cup Final dismissals in history. West Germany won 1-0.

Off the pitch, European club football was entering a new, enriched phase of development. In England, in 1992, the top division clubs broke away from the Football League and created the Premier League under the auspices of the Football Association.

The Premier League proved a highly effective rebranding, underpinned by hitherto undreamed-of monies generated by satellite television in general and Rupert Murdoch's Sky in particular.

Internationally, the club elite took command as well, when UEFA was carried down the road of the Champions League. This was the old European Cup repackaged. A mini-league format headed off a threatened breakaway by the big clubs and was financed by the sale of rights to exclusive

UNFORTUNATE END TO A CLASSIC

WEST GERMANY 1–1 ENGLAND

World Cup semi-final, Stadio delle Alpi, Turin, July 4, 1990

Two of football's oldest rivals served up a magnificent match, sadly decided by FIFA's only solution to draws after 120 minutes: the penalty shootout. England went so very, very close to reaching the final for only the second time but their post-1966 record of failing to win a competitive match against Germany continued. Despite the trials and tribulations besetting their manager, Bobby Robson, and despite the lack of class players – in the English game at large, let alone the squad – there was only the merest fraction between the teams. The splendid spirit in which the match was contested was another bownus.

So, on a more personal level, was the flood of tears released by the enigma, Paul Gascoigne, which made him a media and public darling overnight and earned him a wallet of gold to go with his later-revealed feet of clay. Germany ground their way through 4-2 on penalties.

10 seconds

1990: Giuseppe Lorenzo of Bologna sets a world record by being sent off after 10 seconds for striking Parma opponent

➋ 1994: The Predator, designed by Craig Johnson, revolutionises modern football boots. With distinctive "teeth" moulded on to the front, the boots allowed more power and swerve on ball-striking

1990

- International Board amends offside law (player level no longer offside); FIFA makes professional foul a sending-off offence
- English clubs restored to European competition
- West Germany avenge their 1986 defeat by beating Argentina 1-0 in the World Cup final

1991

- Manchester United climax first season English clubs allowed back in Europe after Heysel Stadium disaster by winning Cup-winners' Cup (above)
- End of artificial pitches in Division One (Oldham and Luton)

1992

- Premier League of 22 clubs launched (above)
- Yugoslavia expelled from European Championship finals on security grounds
- 15 killed and 1,300 injured when temporary stand collapses at Bastia
- Late entrants Denmark, replacing Yugoslavia, score shock victory in European finals in Sweden

1993

- Marseille are the first French team to win European Cup, but cannot defend their trophy following bribery scandal
- Bernard Tapie (above), president of Marseille, accused of involvement in match-fixing scandal, which saw his team relegated and stripped of its French league title

1994

- Manchester United win "double"
- Colombia defender Escobar shot dead after returning home following World Cup own goal in game against hosts United States
- Brazil become first country to win the World Cup on penalties

groups of broadcasters and sponsors. The pursuit of Champions League riches raised an even more sinister issue: match fixing. A worst-case scenario was provided after Marseille won the 1993 European Cup with a 1-0 win over Milan. It later emerged that they had fixed the result of the previous weekend's French league match. Marseille were kicked out of the Champions League and relegated; their president Bernard Tapie went to jail.

Milan bounced back to regain the Champions League in 1994. The Rossoneri had been virtually bankrupt when media magnate Silvio Berlusconi took over in the mid-1980s and turned their finances around. Milan won three European Cups in the years which saw European football plunder media millions.

Football's progress knew no bounds. In 1994 even the United States was conquered with its staging of the World Cup: Brazil beat Italy in the final after winning the first Cup-deciding penalty shootout.

But governing bodies' confidence about the status quo was about to be shattered for ever. In December 1995 the European Court of Justice threw the game into confusion by ruling in favour of a restraint-of-trade claim from a minor Belgian footballer named Jean-Marc Bosman. His contract with second divison Liege had expired but their refusal to sanction a transfer to Dunkerque in France prompted him to go to court.

Bosman not only won his case but the court outlawed end-of-contract restraints as well as all restrictions on the number of European Union players clubs could employ and select. Within months, leagues across the EU had scrapped restrictions on the cross-border movement of EU citizen players.

Western European clubs - and not only the giants - threw a tidal wave of Champions League income into the international transfer market. Soon the big Italian, Spanish and English clubs had more foreign players in their starting line-ups than home-grown talent. Juventus, Real Madrid, Manchester United and Barcelona firmed up the club elite's command of the Champions League.

FIFA president João Havelange and his general secretary Sepp Blatter railed in powerless impotence against the impending threat to the old order. An increasingly embattled Havelange retired, appropriately on the eve of Brazil's defeat by hosts France in the 1998 World Cup Final. Blatter outmanoeuvred UEFA president Lennart Johansson to win a presidential election thst would set FIFA on course for disaster.

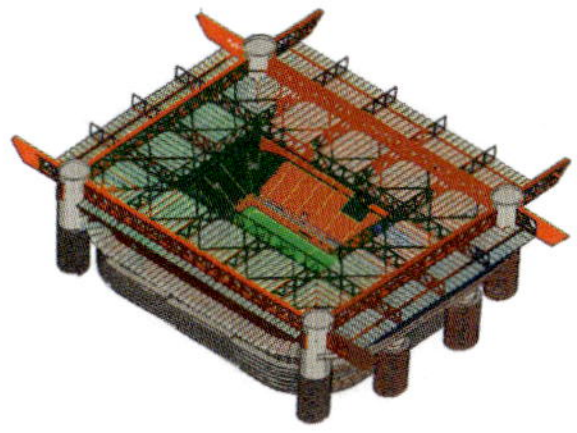

➊ THE GREAT STADIUMS
San Siro, Milan, Italy.
Capacity 80,018
Hosts: Italy, AC Milan, Internazionale.
Of all the ground shares in Europe, none involves two such fierce local rivals as AC Milan and Inter. The San Siro, named after the Milan district in which it stands, is, officially, the Stadio Giuseppe Meazza. Tyre magnate Piero Pirelli bankrolled the stadium – his "gift" to the city – in 1926. AC Milan played there first, joined by Inter in 1947. The San Siro has been extensively redeveloped three times, the last in 1990, when its 11 futuristic cylindrical towers were added.

6
MONTHS

➋ Players names appear on shirts for the first time, as does an excess of pattern, colour and detailing – as in the Borussia Dortmund kit for the Champions League final in 1997

1995

- Jean-Marc Bosman wins landmark European Court judgment against European Union player transfer restrictions
- Manchester United's Eric Cantona is suspended for six months by the FA for a kung-fu assault on a Crystal Palace supporter

1996

- Manchester United become first club to win English "double" twice
- Germany beat the Czech Republic to win the first European Championship hosted in England

1997

- Ronaldo becomes the first Brazilian to be voted European Footballer of the Year after a change in the rules
- Eric Cantona announces his sudden retirement from football

1998

- Arsenal unbeaten in the league for last five months to win "double-double"
- Real Madrid beat Juventus to win first European Champions Cup in 32 years
- Former general secretary Sepp Blatter elected new president of FIFA (above)
- France defeat Brazil 3-0 to win the World Cup

1999

- Manchester United, managed by Alex Ferguson (above), win historic treble of Premiership, FA Cup, and European Cup
- Lazio win the last ever European Cup-winners' Cup at Villa Park, England

➊ Real Madrid's Galacticos were a force to be reckoned with. Four of the best, from left, Luís Figo, Ronaldo, Zinedine Zidane and David Beckham.

2000–2009

FIFA president Sepp Blatter said, at the start of the new millennium, that "in the twenty-first century the face of football will be feminine". What he meant, presumably, was that men's football had taken over as the planet's leading sport in the previous century and now the changing nature of society would bring the women's game on in its wake.

In fact, the early signs of the twenty-first century were anything but encouraging for his vision. The 2003 Women's World Cup had to be switched from China to the United States because of the SARS epidemic in the Far East; then, on the eve of the finals, the women's football league in the United States collapsed for lack of sponsors.

By the end of the decade, however, the picture was very different. The Women's World Cup had established itself in the international calendar, the women's tournament at the Olympic Games drew attendances to rival those of the men's matches and professionalism was taking root.

For all that, the men's game still dominated the headlines, broadcasting channels and the increasingly strident voices of social media networks. Indeed, apart from the United States where progress remained steady rather than spectacular, association football worldwide had achieved a position of virtual sports dictatorship.

That status had been enhanced by FIFA's decision to take the World Cup out beyond its traditional homes of Europe and the Americas. In 2002 South Korea and Japan introduced co-hosting to the first World Cup to be held in Asia.

Co-hosting was an expensive indulgence born of political compromise. Japan had been lobbying for years to host the World Cup but then South Korea rushed in with a late campaign to share the spoils. Co-hosting for the Japanese was a defeat, for the Koreans, a victory.

➋ Arsenal become the first English club since Preston's "Invincibles" in 1888-89 to complete a season unbeaten and become champions of the Premiership in 2005.

In the event – and after initial problems stemming from a legacy of historical enmity – the finals were organized extremely well. Brazil made up for their final failure at France '98 to regain the trophy with a climactic win over Germany. Centre-forward Ronaldo emerged from four injury-plagued years to score both goals in the final.

Ronaldo then returned to Europe to generate controversy by transferring to join Real Madrid's so-called Galacticos. French playmaker Zinedine Zidane, Portugal winger Luís Figo, Spain striker Raul and, later, England midfielder David Beckham would be his partners in glamour. However, Madrid, if anything, had too much ego and not enough energy.

The year 2002 saw not only repeat – if temporary – success for Brazil and Madrid, but turmoil within FIFA. President Sepp Blatter faced opposition at the presidential election from Cameroon's Issa Hayatou, president of the African confederation. Blatter was vulnerable after the corporate suicide of Swiss sports marketing company International Sport and Leisure, the collapse of the Kirch media empire and the cancellation – in the wake of the 9/11 terror attack – of Axa's World Cup insurance.

At the FIFA Congress in Seoul, Blatter managed to hold on to his presidency before purging the organization of any elements who were not demonstrably in his corner. He set the world federation on a new course which would encourage both corporate and personal greed.

Danny Jordaan, leader of South Africa's bids to host the World Cup in 2006 and then 2010, summed it up by saying: "Everything that has happened over the last few years has changed FIFA's emphasis. It's not so much a sports association now as a business empire."

The South African bid for 2006 had fallen short

PLUCKY BASQUES GO DOWN FIGHTING

LIVERPOOL 5–4 ALAVÉS

UEFA Cup Final, Westfalenstadion, Dortmund, May 16, 2001

Former Liverpool player Alan Hansen called this "the best final ever". Liverpool had conquered Roma, Porto and Barcelona on their way to a 10th European final – the first since the post-Heysel ban was lifted in 1991. Alavés had put nine goals past Kaiserslautern to reach their first European final. Liverpool were soon 2-0 up with goals from Marcus Babble and Steven Gerrard. Alavés pulled one back through Ivan Alonso, but a Gary McAllister penalty took liverpool into the break at 3-1. Alavés hit back with two scores from Javi Moreno. Substitute Robbie Fowler edged Liverpool in front, only for Jordi Cruyff, son of Johan, to head in at the death and take the game to extra time. A disallowed goal apiece and two red cards for Alavés followed, but still the brave Basques hung on. Then, cruelly, a Gary McAllister free kick found the head of left back Delfi Geli, and his own goal became the "golden goal" that sank gutsy Alavés.

➔ Cameroon played sleeveless in the 2002 World Cup – a short-lived fashion

➔ Nike, the world's biggest sportswear company, made its entry into the world of football boots with the Mercurial. In 2002, the Brazilian forward Ronaldo wore Mercurials as he helped himself to eight goals at the World Cup

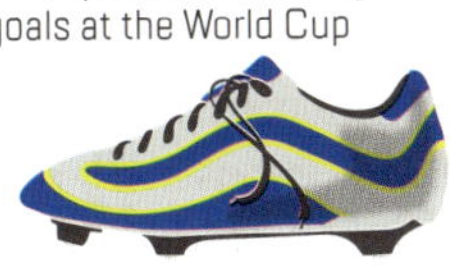

£200m

2000

- First all-Spanish European Champions' final ends in 3-0 win for Real Madrid against Valencia
- Real Madrid sign Barcelona's Luís Figo (above) for new world record transfer fee of €60 million

2001

- FIFA is rocked by the financial collapse of the marketing group ISL, the TV rights agency Kirch and Axa's cancellation of its World Cup insurance
- Australia break the record for largest win in an international, defeating American Samoa 31-0; Archie Thompson scored 13 goals

2002

- Real Madrid mark their centenary by winning a record ninth UEFA Champions League, beating Bayer Leverkusen 2-1
- First World Cup in Asia is the first to be co-hosted – by South Korea and Japan
- Brazil win a record fifth World Cup; fit-again Ronaldo wins Golden Boot

2003

- Milan wins sixth UEFA Champions League, beating Juventus on penalties in the final
- Boca Juniors win their fifth Copa Libertadores
- Russian billionaire Roman Abramovich (above) invests over £200 million in Chelsea, wiping out the club's debt and buying a host of superstars

2004

- Greece score a shock success in the European Championship (above).
- FIFA decides that the first World Cup to be staged in Africa will be held in South Africa in 2010
- The International Board scraps golden and silver goal solutions to drawn matches

by one vote after the Oceania president, Charles Dempsey, quit the FIFA executive meeting ahead of the decisive vote, muttering darkly about death threats. Germany, their bid spearheaded by Franz Beckenbauer, won the day instead.

The 2006 Finals provided a memorable party atmosphere, with host nation Germany surprising and delighting with not only the expected efficiency of the organisation but the friendly unity of fans and tourists across nationality and ethnicity.

German fans had put their faith in the managerial leadership of old goal-scoring hero Jürgen Klinsmann but they fell just short after losing a superb semi-final to Italy after extra time. The final in Berlin was set up for a grand finale from France and their inspiration, Zinedine Zidane.

In the event, Zidane created the wrong type of headlines, being sent off in the closing stages of extra time for head-butting Italian defender Marco Materazzi. Zidane had said before the game that he would retire whenever France were eliminated so the last sight of him as a player was being red-carded in disgrace. Italy provided extra punishment by winning the penalty shootout.

For all the short-term colour of the World Cup, the early years of FIFA's second century bore no resemblances to its first. National team football was coming under increasing pressure from the richest clubs. The creation of the G-14 group of Europe's most powerful clubs was an example of growing unrest over the game's governance.

One of G-14's major complaints was the absence of compensation payments from national associations for players summoned for internationals. A non-G-14 club, Charleroi, sued FIFA in the Belgian and then European courts over a serious injury to Moroccan midfielder Abdelmajid Oulmers while on national duty.

In 2006, FIFA created an insurance and compensation system for clubs whose players went to the major finals. As part of the deal, G-14 folded into the new European Club Association.

The clubs had survival concerns of their own. In 2004, UEFA introduced a licensing system which compelled clubs to produce stable accounts if they wished to compete in Europe. As if to underline the need for greater control and transparency, some of Europe's greatest clubs tottered to the brink of financial collapse.

In England, Leeds United spent extravagantly to try to secure Champions League permanence before crashing to relegation when the gamble dismally failed to pay off.

In Italy, Fiorentina, one-time winners of the Cup Winners' Cup, did indeed go bankrupt; the new club that was then created from the financial ashes had to start all over again in the fourth division. Roma, Lazio, Parma and Napoli all teetered over

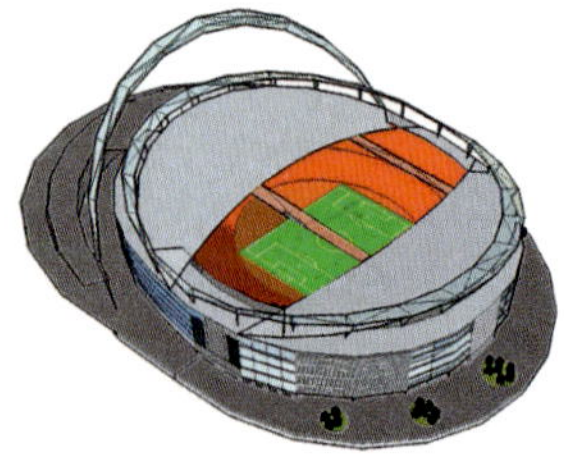

THE GREAT STADIUMS
Wembley, London, UK.
Capacity 90,000
Hosts: England.
A sense of international sadness filled the air when the revered "twin towers" of the original Wembley Stadium were pulled down in 2002. They have been replaced, though, by just as potent a London and world football landmark in the Wembley arch, which at 315m is the world's longest single-span roof structure. The old Wembley opened its doors in 1923 for the FA Cup final and closed them after a 1-0 defeat for England against Germany in 2000. The new Wembley kicked off in March 2007 in style with an exciting 3-3 draw between the Italy and England under-21s.

2005

- Liverpool come back from being 3-0 down at half-time against AC Milan to win the Champions League Final
- German referee Robert Hoyzer admits to accepting bribes from gambling syndicate to fix matches
- Ronaldinho (above) voted the FIFA World Player of the Year

2006

- Drawing 1-1 after extra time, Italy defeat France 5-3 on penalties to win the World Cup for the fourth time
- Juventus win the Serie A, starting a wide-ranging match-fixing scandal
- Lyon enjoy their fifth consecutive Ligue 1 title win

2007

- Juventus, the only Serie A club to be relegated in the match-fixing scandal, win the Serie B championship
- Milan avenge their 2005 Champions League Final loss by beating Liverpool 2-1 in Athens
- David Beckham signs a five-year deal with MLS team Los Angeles Galaxy

2008

- Spain end a 44-year title drought by defeating Germany 1-0 to win Euro 2008 (above)
- Manchester United win the Club World Cup, Champions League and English Premier League

2009

- Pep Guardiola guides Barcelona to a treble of Champions League plus Spanish league and cup
- José Mourinho (above) wins, with Inter in Italy, a third league in a different country
- Shakhtar Donetsk win the UEFA Cup, the first European cup for a club from independent Ukraine

the abyss but somehow survived; in France, Monaco were threatened by the French league with relegation over accounting problems – yet revived effectively enough to reach the Champions League final 15 months later; Kaiserslautern – home club of 1954 World Cup-winning hero Fritz Walter – sold a share of centre-forward Miroslav Klose to the local authority to buy financial time; in Spain, Real Madrid pulled every available political string so their Sports City land could be reclassified for development to purge a £100m-plus debt.

The battle for control of the club game intensified after the multi-million investment in Chelsea launched in 2003 by the Russian oligarch, Roman Abramovich. Not that money was everything. Chelsea won three Premier League titles in six seasons but could not match Arsenal's achievement in becoming the first club to complete a league season unbeaten since Preston's "Invincibles" in 1889.

Liverpool, Milan, Manchester United and even old enemy Real Madrid were outclassed by Barcelona in the Champions League. The Catalan side became the latest claimants to the label of "greatest club team of all time", owing their acclaimed superiority to their mesmeric tiki-taka short-passing style and Lionel Messi's record-breaking marksmanship.

Messi thus established himself as yet another Argentinian enabled, through superstar talent and personality, to rise beyond the confines of the mere footballing arena, after the manner of Diego Maradona in the 1980s.

LIVERPOOL BACK FROM THE BRINK

LIVERPOOL 3–3 MILAN

(3-2 on penalties after extra time)

UEFA Champions League Final, Atatürk Stadium, Istanbul, May 25, 2005

Liverpool won their fifth European club crown in the most dramatic of circumstances. They were 3-0 down at half-time, then recovered with three goals in seven second-half minutes, and after extra time finally triumphed in a penalty shootout. The first half was an Italian walkover. Milan went ahead in the opening minutes through skipper Paolo Maldini and added two further goals through Argentinian striker Hernan Crespo before the interval. The Milan players denied later that they had begun noisy celebrations at half-time but they relaxed fatally and Liverpool hit back with rapid-fire goals from the inspirational midfielder Steven Gerrard, Vladimir Smicer and Xabi Alonso. The comeback effort left Liverpool dangerously wearied in extra time but they held out for a shootout in which Polish keeper Jerzy Dudek starred with saves from Andrea Pirlo and, finally, Andriy Shevchenko.

➔ The formidable treble winning Barcelona team of the noughties. (Front row L-R) Lionel Messi, Thierry Henry, Daniel Alves, Andrés Iniesta, Xavi. (Back row L-R) Eric Abidal, Yaya Toure, Rafael Marquez, Gerard Pique, Samuel Eto'o and Victor Valdes.

2010–2017

The second decade of the twenty-first century began with no hint of the turmoil ahead. An increasing global focus on the Premier League in England brought worldwide acclaim for Chelsea in achieving a league and FA Cup double under Carlo Ancelotti; Chelsea's old boss, José Mourinho, guided Italy's Internazionale to victory over Bayern Munich in the Champions League.

A unique World Cup then took centre stage as South Africa became the first African nation to play host. All manner of gloomy headlines about delayed and inadequate preparations had preceded the tournament but these were soon forgotten once the finals had begun.

South Africa achieved the disappointing record of becoming the first hosts not to qualify for the knockout stages; France's players went on strike briefly in a row over selection and tactics; the European champions, Spain, eventually emerged as winners. La Roja, managed by Vicente Del Bosque, owed victory over a physical Dutch team to a late extra-time goal from Andrés Iniesta.

Another significant moment came in a second-round tie in Bloemfontein between Germany and England. A long-range shot from Frank Lampard hit the underside of the bar, crashed down behind the goal-line then ricocheted back out. Uruguayan referee Jorge Larrionda waved play on and Germany ultimately won 4-1.

THE BELO HORIZONTE MUGGING

BRAZIL 1–7 GERMANY

Word Cup semi-final, Estádio Mineirão, Belo Horizonte, July 8, 2014

This was not meant to be. It was Brazil's World Cup. Even without injured star Neymar, passions and expectations for the home team were running sky high. No one underestimates Germany, but what unfolded was a Brazilian nightmare – the heaviest defeat for a host nation in World Cup history. The match began evenly enough until, in the 11th minute, Thomas Müller scored from Germany's first corner. Then, in the space of a bewildering 6 minutes of football madness, Miroslav Klose, Toni Kroos (twice) and Sami Khedira put four past a dazed Júlio César. And so, the half ended 5-0, with zero shots on target from Brazil, many of whose stunned supporters were now in tears. The home team improved after the break but still let in a brace from André Shürrle. Although Oscar scored a consolation goal in the final minute, humiliation was complete.

2010: The lightweight, superfast Adidas F50 Adizero attracts the top footballers around the world, such as Lionel Messi, Luis Suárez and Gareth Bale

Alex Ferguson retires from Manchester United after 26 years and 38 trophies

2010

- José Mourinho leads Inter Milan to Champions League triumph before departing for Real Madrid
- The first World Cup to be held on African soil takes place
- Spain win their first World Cup, defeating Holland 1-0 in extra time as Andrés Iniesta scores

2011

- Lionel "Leo" Messi is crowned FIFA World Player for a second successive year
- Manchester United win a record 19th English league title
- Barcelona win a fourth UEFA Champions League (above) by overwhelming Manchester United 3-1

2012

- Zambia win the African Nations Cup
- Chelsea win the Champions League for the first time (above)
- Leo Messi sets a world record 91 goals in the calendar year
- Spain become the first country to retain the European Championship

2013

- Losing-2012 finalists Bayern Munich go one better to win the Champions League; holders Chelsea crash out in the group stages before winning the Europa League as consolation
- Gareth Bale (right) moves to Real Madrid for a record €100 million

2014

- Germany beat Argentina with a goal from Mario Götze in extra time to win the World Cup in Brazil
- Real Madrid win their 10th Champions League, but Atlético Madrid break the Real and Barcelona chokehold on the Spanish league to win their 10th title

THE GREAT STADIUMS
Allianz Arena, Munich, Germany. Capacity 75,000 Hosts: Germany, Bayern Munich, TSV 1860 Munich. The two major Munich football clubs have now shared three stadiums. They moved from the Olympiastadion, built for the 1972 Olympics, to the newly constructed Allianz Arena, on the northern outskirts of the city, in 2005, with TSV having the honour of playing the first match. The stadium's most distinctive feature is the exterior cladding, made up of 2,874 inflated panels that illuminate at night in the colours of the home team.

The next day FIFA president, Sepp Blatter, a lifelong opponent of technological assistance, returned from Bloemfontein to announce a change of mind. By the start of the 2014 finals in Brazil goal-line technology had been tested by the International Board and approved for use in domestic and international football.

The hosts had high hopes of winning the World Cup for a record-extending sixth time. Instead they suffered their most spectacular defeat since the 2–1 upset at the hands of Uruguay in the 1950 final. This time the margin was even more humiliating as Brazil collapsed unthinkably by 7–1 to Germany in the semi-finals.

Germany, like Spain in 2010, won the final with a last-minute extra-time goal. In their case it was a magnificent strike from substitute Mario Götze which downed Leo Messi's Argentina.

With the World Cup done and dusted, the clubs took command once more. Real Madrid, inspired by the record-breaking goals of Cristiano Ronaldo, regained the Champions League crown for a 10th time in 2014. French superstar-turned-coach Zinedine Zidane then guided them to a hat-trick of titles between 2016 and 2018 and to a record-extending 13 in all.

Madrid triumphed in Europe despite the domestic dominance of Messi's Barcelona in Spain, Bayern Munich in Germany and high-spending Paris Saint-Germain in France. PSG obliterated all previous world transfer records by splashing €222m on Brazilian superstar Neymar in 2017. However England's Premier League remained world football's financial champion. A broadcasting deal with television channels Sky and British Telecom for 2015 to 2019 generated £5.136bn for 168 live matches.

All was not so well elsewhere, however. In December 2010 FIFA's executive committee had prompted howls of disbelief in awarding the 2018 and 2022 World Cups to massive Russia and minnow Qatar, respectively.

Accusations of corruption swirling through Zürich were vindicated in May 2015 when seven senior football bosses were hauled from their hotel beds by police on the eve of the FIFA Congress in Zürich. All were indicted on charges brought by the United States Department of Justice over a $200m corruption investigation into bribes and kickbacks siphoned off from TV and marketing deals in the Americas.

The "House of Blatter" came tumbling down. He and UEFA's French president, Michel Platini, were handed long bans over misuse of funds. Subsequently, UEFA's Swiss general secretary, Gianni Infantino, was voted in as new FIFA president with a daunting mandate to clean up the mess. This included a future World Cup expansion to 48 teams and the introduction of video assistant referees at the 2018 finals, where France beat Croatia 4-2 to claim a second title.

€100m

2015

- FIFA investigated by the FBI for corruption, leading to multiple arrests and the suspension of Sepp Blatter
- Barcelona completes an historic Treble with victory over Juventus in the Champions League final

2016

- Gianni Infantino becomes FIFA president
- Brazilian club Chapecoense are wiped out in a tragic plane crash
- Leicester City become long-shot Premier League champions (above)
- Cristiano Ronaldo inspires Portugal to Euro 2016 victory over France

2017

- Cameroon win their 5th Africa Cup of Nations championship (above), beating Egypt 2–1 in the final
- Graham Taylor, an unsuccessful England boss but inspiring and highly respected club manager of Aston Villa and Watford, among others, dies

2018

- Real Madrid win a third successive European Champions crown, for a record-extending 13th time.
- Russia hosts the first FIFA World Cup in Eastern Europe. France beat Croatia 4-2 in the final to win their second tournament

2

MAJOR INTERNATIONAL COMPETITIONS

Football has always had a competitive spirit, which has led to many entrancing international competitions. While many regions have their own tournaments, there can be no doubt that for pure drama and entertainment the pinnacle of the footballing calendar is the World Cup.

The World Cup

The driving force behind the World Cup was FIFA's French president, Jules Rimet. Italy, Holland, Spain and Sweden all applied to play host but withdrew after Uruguay, celebrating 100 years of independence, promised to build a new stadium and pay all the teams' travel costs.

1930

URUGUAY

Final: Centenario, Montevideo (93,000)

URUGUAY 4–2 ARGENTINA

Dorado, Cea, Iriarte, Castro • Peucelle, Stabile

Dorado shot Uruguay into a 12th-minute lead but Peucelle equalized and Argentina forged ahead in the 35th minute with a disputed goal by Stabile - who the Urugayans claimed was offside! Excitement grew when Pedro Cea made it 2-2 just after the break. for Uruguay, who underlined their victory with a fourth goal by Castro in the closing seconds.

Ball: *T-Model*

TOP SCORER
8 *Stabile (Argentina)*

Only thirteen nations took part in the first finals, including just four from Europe. On Sunday, July 13, France opened the tournament with a 4-1 win over Mexico. Lucien Laurent scored the historic first goal. Argentina topped Group 1, while Group 2 saw Yugoslavia qualify with victories over Brazil and Bolivia. From Group 4, the US reached the semi-finals without conceding a goal. They were then no match for Argentina, who cruised into the final by 6-1. Hosts Uruguay dispatched Yugoslavia by the same score to set up a repeat of the 1928 Olympic final. Uruguay won again, by 4-2, after trailing 2-1 at half-time.

1934

ITALY

Final: Flaminio, Rome (55,000)

ITALY 2-1 CZECHOSLOVAKIA

(after extra time; 1-1 full time)

Orsi, Schiavio • Puc

Puc shot the Czechs into a deserved 70th-minute lead, then Svoboda rattled a post as the Czechs impressed with their short-passing game. With eight minutes left, Italy's left-winger Orsi left defenders in his wake as he equalized. Veteran spearhead Angelo Schiavio grabbed Italy's winner seven minutes into extra time.

Ball: *Federale 102*

TOP SCORER
4 *Nejedlý (Czechoslovakia)*

Uruguay did not defend their title. Upset by European reluctance to participate in 1930 and plagued by players' strikes, they decided to stay at home. The knockout format saw Brazil and Argentina both travelling 8,000 miles to play one solitary, losing game. Of the 16 finalists, Italy and Hugo Meisl's Austrian "Wunderteam" were the clear favourites. Italy, urged on by dictator Benito Mussolini, beat Austria 1-0 in the semi-finals, but Czechoslovakia prevented an "axis final" by defeating Germany 3-1. They took the lead late in the final but lost 2-1 after extra time.

Pelé breaks down in tears on the shoulders of goalkeeper Gilmar after Brazil's 1958 triumph in Stockholm.

1938

FRANCE

Final: Stade Colombes, Paris (55,000)

ITALY 4-2 HUNGARY

Colaussi (2), Piola (2) • Titkos, Sarosi

Colaussi shot ahead in the 6th minute after a scintillating run, but within a minute Titkos equalized from close range. Then, with inside-forwards Meazza and Ferrari in dazzling form, Piola scored in the 15th minute, and Colaussi made it 3-1 in the 35th. In the 65th, minute Sarosi forced the ball over the Italian line, but a magnificent back-heeled pass from Biavati set up Piola to smash in the decisive goal.

Ball: *Allen*

TOP SCORER
8 *Leônidas (Brazil)*

Europe was in political turmoil as Cuba, Poland and Dutch East Indies made their finals debuts. The first round saw champions Italy saved from a shock defeat against Norway by goalkeeper Aldo Olivieri. Brazil beat Poland 6-5 in a mud-drenched Strasbourg with rival centre forwards Leônidas and Ernst Willimowski both scoring four times. But Brazil lost in the semi-finals to Italy, for whom captain Giuseppe Meazza converted the winning penalty. The other semi-final saw Hungary beat Sweden 5-1 but they were outplayed by Italy in the final, losing 4-2.

1950

BRAZIL

Final: Maracanã, Rio (199,854)

BRAZIL 1–2 URUGUAY

Friaca • Schiaffino, Ghiggia

The hosts, Brazil, were favourites as they faced Uruguay in the last pool game (the final by any other name), a point ahead. It proved to be a real thriller. Brazil's inside-forward trio of Zizinho, Ademir and Jair found keeper Máspoli playing the game of his life. Friaca found a way through in the 47th minute, but Schiaffino equalized in the 65th. The fizz went out of Brazil and Ghiggia scored the winner on 75 minutes.

Ball: *Super Duplo T*

TOP SCORER
9 *Ademir (Brazil)*

Brazil hosted the first post-war finals with England making their World Cup debut. The finals were played in mini-leagues. Brazil won Pool 1 despite a 2-2 draw with Switzerland, and Uruguay topped two-team Pool 4 by thrashing Bolivia 8-0. Shocks in Pools 2 and 3 saw holders Italy lose 3-2 to Sweden and England crash 1-0, humiliatingly, to the USA. Brazil, Uruguay, Sweden and Spain reached the final round. Brazil and Uruguay played out the decisive match in the Maracanã, where the 200,000-strong home crowd was stunned into silence when Uruguay won 2-1 through Alcides Ghiggia.

1954

SWITZERLAND

Final: Wankdorf, Berne (60,000)

W. GERMANY 3–2 HUNGARY

Morlock, Rahn (2) • Puskás, Czibor

The Hungarians came into the final still recovering from a gruelling 120-minute semi-final with Uruguay. The injured Puskás scored the opening goal for Hungary in the 6th minute, followed two minutes later by a second from Czibor. Germany retaliated almost immediately through Morlock, and then Rahn struck two fine goals - the last seven minutes from time - to win the cup.

Ball: *Swiss World Champion*

TOP SCORER
11 *Kocsis (Hungary)*

Hungary were the hottest World Cup favourites. The magic of Ferenc Puskás and company had won Olympic gold in 1952 and also ended England's unbeaten home record against foreign opposition. Their cruise to the final included wins by 8-3 over West Germany and 4-2 over both Brazil and Uruguay. Puskás, hurt against the Germans, returned barely fit for the final against the same opposition. The gamble failed. He scored the opening goal but the Germans battled back to win 3-2. Thus Hungary lost, for the first time in four years, in the match that mattered the most.

1958

SWEDEN

Final: Rasunda, Stockholm (49,737)

BRAZIL 5–2 SWEDEN

Vavá (2), Pelé (2), Zagallo • Liedholm, Simonsson

Sweden took a shock lead through Liedholm in the 4th minute, with Vara, fed by Garrincha, equalising and putting Brazil into the lead. In the 55th minute, the 17-year-old Pelé added a touch of magic, bringing the ball down on his thigh, hooking it over his head and volleying thunderously home. He then added another. Brazil were now the best in the world.

Ball: *Top Star*

TOP SCORER
13 *Fontaine (France)*

Brazil enthralled the world with the individual brilliance of Didi, Garrincha and the teenage Pelé, plus the tactical revolution of 4-2-4. France performed with style, courtesy of 13-goal marksman, Just Fontaine, and playmaker Raymond Kopa. These were the only finals for which the British quartet qualified. Only Wales and Northern Ireland reached the quarter-finals, before losing to Brazil and France, respectively. France went on to finish third, while Brazil became the first South Americans to win in Europe by thrashing the hosts 5-2 in the final.

CHILE

Final: Nacional, Santiago (68,679)

BRAZIL 3-1 CZECHOSLOVAKIA

Amarildo, Zito, Vavá • Masopust

The two teams had already met in the group stage, sharing a tame 0-0 draw. Come the final, the Czechs threatened to upset the odds when star midfielder Masopust gave them the lead in the 16th minute. But order was restored when Amarildo, Pelé's replacement for the match, equalized two minutes later. It then took until the 69th minute for Zito to head Brazil into the lead. Vavá made it 3-1 when Czech goalkeeper Schrojf fumbled a lob.

Ball: *Crack*

TOP SCORERS

4 *Garrincha, Vavá (Brazil), Ivanov V. (USSR), Albert (Hungary), Sánchez L. (Chile), Jerković (Yugoslavia)*

Brazil retained the World Cup with outside right Garrincha taking centre stage and employing a tactical shift to 4-3-3. But the finals were marred by a violent clash between hosts Chile and Italy, full of spitting, fighting and two-footed tackles. It was remarkable that English referee Ken Aston sent off only two players. Brazil continued to thrill, even without Pelé, who was injured in a group match against Mexico. Garrincha mesmerized England to defeat, then took hosts Chile apart in the semi-final before being sent off. Happily he escaped suspension from the final against Czechoslovakia, the surprise package of the tournament, helping his team to a 3-1 triumph.

ENGLAND

Final: Wembley, London (96,924)

ENGLAND 4-2 W. GERMANY

Hurst (3), Peters • Haller, Weber

Germany struck first through Haller. Hurst equalized, and his West Ham colleague Martin Peters gave England the lead. But a late scrambled goal from Weber forced the game into extra time. Hurst's second goal, where the ball ricocheted back into play from behind the goal line, was a moment of controversy, rendered irrelevant by his fierce strike at the death.

⬆ England's glory: skipper Bobby Moore is hoisted high by his teammates at Wembley after the 4–2 defeat of West Germany.

Ball: *4-Star*

TOP SCORER

9 *Eusébio (Portugal)*

For the first time in 32 years, the hosts, England, won the title after finals that saw a memorable upset when North Korea felled Italy. The event saw a slow start, with England held 0-0 by Uruguay, while holders Brazil disappointed. They exited in the first round after defeats by Hungary and Portugal, whose nine-goal-striker Eusébio proved a tournament hero, especially helping to claw back a 3-0 deficit against North Korea in the quarter-final. Eusébio was a semi-final loser, however, against England, who duly met West Germany at Wembley in the final. There they triumphed 4-2 after extra time and Geoff Hurst's amazing three goals - the only hat-trick ever scored in a World Cup final.

1970

MEXICO

Final: Azteca, Mexico City (107,000)

BRAZIL 4-1 ITALY

Pelé, Gerson, Jairzinho, Carlos • Boninsegna

The final proved to be a marvellous affirmation for attacking football. Pelé opened the scoring, but Boninsegna made it 1-1, capitalizing on a dreadful error by midfielder Clodoaldo. After the break, Gerson drove in a powerful cross-shot, and the match was sewn up with goals from Jairzinho and Carlos Alberto, the latter finishing off one of the greatest World Cup moves, involving eight outfield players.

Ball: *Top Star*

TOP SCORER
10 *Müller (Germany)*

Football triumphed in Mexico where the colourful free-flowing Brazilians delighted. They overcame the heat, the altitude and - in a final full of drama - Italy, the acknowledged masters of defensive caution. Brazil beat holders, England, 1-0 in the finest group game, which included a legendary save from Pelé by goalkeeper Gordon Banks. England lost their crown after extra time in the quarter-finals against West Germany who then lost 4-3 after the extra halfhour themselves to Italy in a dramatic semi-final. Italy, drained, duly collapsed 4-1 to Brazil in the Final. Jairzinho scored in every round while Pelé, scoring one of the triple champions' goals in the final, went out in glory.

1974

WEST GERMANY

Final: Olympiastadion, Munich (77,833)

W. GERMANY 2-1 HOLLAND

Breitner (pen), Müller • Neeskens (pen)

The final began dramatically, with Cruyff brought down close to goal and Johan Neeskens converting the penalty - all in two minutes. West Germany were outplayed for the first quarter but managed to fight back. On a rare break, Bernd Hölzenbein was tripped by Wim Jansen, and Paul Breitner rammed in the resultant penalty to make it 1-1. A 43rd-minute goal from Gerd Müller then sealed the World Cup for the hosts.

Ball: *Top Star*

TOP SCORER
7 *Lato (Poland)*

Europe dominated finals that saw West Germany regain the World Cup after 20 years. A team led by the magisterial Franz Beckenbauer and starring five other Bayern Munich players conceded the final's first-ever penalty before recovering to win 2-1 in their home stadium. Gerd Müller's sixty-eighth, last and most important goal for his country won the day. However, the Dutch were the most stylish of the finalists with their "total football", built around the peripatetic talents of Johan Cruyff and Johan Neeskens. Poland finished third thanks to the seven goals of Grzegorz Lato. East Germany made only appearance in the finals, defeating West Germany 1-0 in Hamburg in the group stage.

1978

ARGENTINA

Final: Monumental, Buenos Aires (77,260)

ARGENTINA 3-1 HOLLAND

Kempes (2), Bertoni • Nanninga

The final proved to be a bad-tempered clash. The Dutch accused the Argentinians of delays, while the plaster cast on René van de Kerkhof's wrist was viewed with suspicion. Nanninga cancelled out Kempes' first goal to take the game into extra time, when further strikes from Kempes and Bertoni ended Dutch hopes.

Ball: *Top Star*

TOP SCORER
6 *Kempes (Argentina)*

Euphoria greeted Argentina's first triumph as hosts. Holland, missing the retired Johan Cruyff, again finished runners-up. The finals were shrouded in controversy concerning the country's military dictatorship. Six-goal Mario Kempes, the only foreign-based star selected by coach César Luis Menotti, was top scorer. Argentina opened with wins over Hungary and France but lost to Italy. That dropped them into a tough second-round group with Brazil, Peru and Poland. In the last game, Argentina needed to beat Peru by four goals. Contentiously, they beat them by six to reach the final, where they overcame the Dutch 3-1 in extra time. For neutrals, the failure of Holland, as in 1974, to claim their rightful crown as the best team in the world left a void. For Argentinians, the feeling was total ecstacy.

The home fans had to wait until after extra time for the party to begin, a perfect end for the hosts of a colourful tournament.

SPAIN

Final: Bernabeu, Madrid (90,000)

ITALY 3-1 W. GERMANY

Rossi, Tardelli, Altobelli • Breitner

The final did not quite live up to its billing. There was not one shot on target in the opening 45 minutes, and that includes the penalty effort from Italy's Antonio Cabrini. In the second half the Germans paid, in fatigue, the price of their extra-time victory over France. Breitner scored late, but goals from Rossi, Marco Tardelli and Alessandro Altobelli sealed Italy's 3-1 win.

Ball: *Tango España*

TOP SCORER
6 *Rossi (Italy)*

Italy burst through after a slow start in which they drew all three of their group games. West Germany, who were to finish runners-up, were on the wrong end of a shock 2-1 defeat in their opening tie against Algeria but, like Italy, improved as the tournament progressed. England made a dream start with victory over France after a 27th-second goal from Bryan Robson but faded out in the second round. Northern Ireland fielded the World Cup's youngest-ever player in the barely 17-year-old Norman Whiteside. The outstanding tie saw Italy defeat favourites Brazil with a hat-trick from Paolo Rossi, back after a two-year suspension. In the semi-finals Rossi scored twice to beat an impressive Poland, while West Germany and France, revived after the initial setback against England, staged a pulsating thriller.

Marco Tardelli races off on his unstoppable celebratory dash after shooting Italy's second goal against West Germany in Madrid.

The French led 3-1 but ultimately lost in the finals' first penalty shootout. Italy were deserved winners of the final and their third World Cup.

MEXICO

Final: Azteca, Mexico City (114,590)

ARGENTINA 3-2 W. GERMANY

Brown, Valdano, Burruchaga • Rummenigge, Völler

Germany appeared to sleepwalk into the final, as Argentina led 2-0 after 56 minutes through goals from Jorge Brown and Jorge Valdano. Almost too late, West Germany awoke to launch a remarkable comeback and draw level through Karl-Heinz Rummenigge and Rudi Völler. It was all in vain. With five minutes left, Maradona sent Jorge Burruchaga away to snatch Argentina's winner and their second World Cup win.

Ball: *Azteca*

TOP SCORER
6 *Lineker (England)*

Mexico became the first country to host the finals twice when Colombia pulled out at short notice. Argentina's captain Diego Maradona proved the outstanding individual, creating and scoring crucial goals. Other memorable moments included Gary Lineker's hat-trick for England against Poland, Emilio Butragueño's four-goal feat against Denmark and a quarter-final in which France beat Brazil on penalties when three of the world's greatest players - Zico, Socrates and Michel Platini - all missed spot kicks. Argentina topped their first-round group ahead of Italy then beat Uruguay in the second round to set up a high-tension quarter-final with England. The legacy of the Falklands War hung over the match in Mexico City, which Argentina won 2-1. The first goal was Maradona's infamous "Hand of God", their second came from his superb slalom from the halfway line. Maradona scored a similar goal against Belgium in the semis before serving up Jorge Burruchaga's winner against West Germany in the final.

Diego Maradona's "Hand of God" raises the World Cup in Mexico City.

1990

ITALY

Final: Stadio Olimpico, Rome (70,603)

W. GERMANY 1-0 ARGENTINA

Brehme (pen)

Ball: *Etrusco*

TOP SCORER
6 *Schillaci (Italy)*

Bad memories of 1986 and an ugly mood pervaded the entire final. The Germans were the deserved winners on their overall contribution though their goal was controversial. Argentina accused Rudi Völler of diving for the 85th-minute penalty. Skipper Lothar Matthäus handed responsibility for taking it to Andy Brehme and Goycochea was beaten from the spot.

The 14th finals did not live up to Italy's passionate setting, offering a miserly shortage of goals. A dramatic start saw Cameroon beat Maradona's Argentinian cup-holders, who still recovered to reach the final. Cameroon fell in extra time against England in the quarter-finals. England then lost a dramatic semi-final on penalties against a West German side managed by former World Cup-winning captain Franz Beckenbauer. Hosts Italy put their faith in Juventus striker "Toto" Schillaci. He became an overnight hero after scoring goals against Austria and Czechoslovakia as the Azzurri topped Group A. Ultimately, Italy finished third, beating England in the third-fourth play-off after falling on penalties to Argentina in the semi-finals. The final was one of the worst in World Cup history. West Germany won 1-0 with a late penalty from Andreas Brehme, while Argentina made history of the wrong sort when Pedro Monzón and Gustavo Dezotti became the first players sent off in a World Cup final.

1994

Joy and disaster: Brazil celebrate Roberto Baggio's penalty miss.

UNITED STATES

Final: Rose Bowl, Pasadena (94,000)

BRAZIL 0-0 ITALY

(Brazil 3-2 on penalties)

Ball: *Questra*

TOP SCORER
6 *Salenko (Russia), Stoichkov (Bulgaria)*

The final was a game of few chances, most of which fell to Brazil. With no goals after extra time, the game went to penalties. There were hits and misses on both sides. Then, at 3-2, Baggio needed to score with Italy's last kick of five to keep his country alive. He scooped the ball over the bar. Brazil were back on top.

History was made twice over in the United States when Brazil secured a fourth title. To do so they had to win the first-ever penalty shootout at the end of extra time in a goalless final. FIFA introduced radical measures in an attempt to improve the quality of the action with three points for a win and a crackdown on violent conduct. The changes added up to 15 sendings-off and a record 235 bookings but an improved match average on 1990 of 2.71 goals per game. Argentina's campaign ended in the second round after Maradona was banned for failing a first-round dope test. South American pride was thus carried forward by Brazil. Their main strength was the striking partnership of Romario and Bebeto. Romario either scored or had a creative hand in 10 of Brazil's 11 goals. Italy reached their fourth final and risked the fragile fitness of superstar striker Baggio and veteran sweeper Franco Baresi. The gambles backfired. Both men missed spot kicks in the shootout, which Brazil won 3-2.

FRANCE

Final: Stade de France, Paris (75,000)

Ball: *Tricolore*

TOP SCORER
6 *Rossi (Italy)*

FRANCE 3–0 BRAZIL

Zidane (2), Petit

Brazil looked out of spirits from the start. France, by contrast, were simply magnificent. Two headed goals from the inspirational Zidane, both from corners, put them in control, and Emmanuel Petit rounded off the 3-0 win after dashing the full length of the pitch in the closing minutes. The scale of the victory equalled the largest winning margin in a final.

France, the nation that invented the World Cup, finally won it in 1998 with a spectacular 3-0 victory over Brazil on home soil. An expanded line-up of 32 teams included four nations making their debuts, one of these being a spectacular Croatia who finished third. Holders Brazil launched the party by defeating Scotland's Tartan Army 2-1 in Group A thanks to an own goal from Tommy Boyd. When the samba stars went on to crush Morocco 3-0, they became the first team to qualify for round two. In Group C, France defied fears that they would struggle for goals by beating South Africa 3-0, Saudi Arabia 4-0 (despite having playmaker Zinedine Zidane sent off) and runners-up, Denmark, 2-1. Group F saw the most memorable match of the first round in a politically sensitive clash won 2-1 by Iran in an exemplary dual with the United States. In the second round the most dramatic tie ended with Argentina defeating England on penalties in Saint-Étienne after David Beckham had been sent off for a petulant kick at Diego Simeone. Argentina then lost in the quarter-finals to Holland, who subsequently went down to Brazil in the semis. In the final, the French, improving all the time, were surprisingly decisive 3-0 winners against a Brazil side confused in the dressing room before kickoff by the late inclusion at centre forward of Ronaldo, who had been taken ill shortly before the game.

⬇ Zinedine Zidane heads France into the lead against Brazil in the 1998 Final in the Stade de France.

2002

JAPAN & SOUTH KOREA

Final: Yokohama, Japan (69,029)

BRAZIL 2-0 GERMANY

Ronaldo 2

Ball: *Fevernova*

TOP SCORER
8 *Ronaldo (Brazil)*

The reflexes of keeper Oliver Kahn kept Germany on terms for 66 minutes. He then spilled a drive from Rivaldo and Ronaldo shot Brazil ahead. Germany had to open up, and Ronaldo punished them a second time to finish as the finals' eight-goal top scorer.

Brazil seized the World Cup for a record fifth time as Ronaldo put his 1998 demons to rest when scoring the goals to beat Germany 2-0 at the climax of the first co-hosted finals. In Group A, newcomers Senegal provided a sensational start by undermining holders France 1-0 in the opening match. Group C was dominated by Brazil, who scored 11 goals in their three victories. South Korea escaped the first round for the first time in taking Group D by athletically irresistible storm under Dutch coach Guus Hiddink. In Group E, Germany opened in explosive style by crushing Saudi Arabia 8-0 thanks to a headed hat-trick from Miroslav Klose. It was the biggest finals victory in 16 years. Group F turned on Argentina's 1-0 defeat by England indoors in Sapporo. Skipper David Beckham, settling a score from 1998, converted a penalty. Bizarre scheduling denied players a chance to catch their breath between the group stage and the knockout round. South Korea defeated an angry Italy 2-1 with a golden goal, then upset Spain on penalties before losing 1-0 in the semis to Germany. Ultimately they finished fourth after losing the third-place play-off to an impressive Turkey, including Hakan Şükür, who scored the fastest goal in World Cup finals history at 10.8 seconds. Ronaldo stole the show in the final, scoring both superbly taken goals, as Germany could find no answer to the Brazilian star and capitulated to a 2-0 defeat.

A double from Ronaldo, the tournament's top finisher, sent Brazil cruising home in the first Asian World Cup final.

2006

GERMANY

Final: Olympiastadion, Berlin (69,000)

ITALY 1-1 FRANCE

(Italy 5-3 on penalties)

Materazzi • Zidane (pen)

Ball: *Teamgeist*

TOP SCORER
5 *Klose (Germany)*

Zidane put France ahead in only the seventh minute. Materazzi then headed in an equaliser 12 minutes later. Zidane's dismissal in extra time and the substitution of Thierry Henry lost France their best two penalty takers. All nine players in the shootout hit the target - with the exception of French striker David Trezeguet. Fabio Grosso-rasped home Italy's fifth penalty.

Italy carried off the World Cup for a European-record fourth time, but the final in Berlin also went down as the night on which Zinedine Zidane's career ended in disaster. He was sent off in extra time for head-butting Marco Materazzi before the Azzurri beat France in a shootout after a 1-1 draw. A dour final had contrasted with the positivity of the "summer fairytale" that surprised even hosts Germany. World Cup-winning player turned manager Jurgen Klinsmann guided his team, despite low expectations, from an opening 4-2 win over Costa Rica to third place after a play-off victory over Luis Figo's Portugal. The finest team performance was Argentina's 6-0 group thrashing of Serbia before, with brilliant young Leo Messi kept on the bench, they lost on penalties to Germany in the quarter-finals. Elsewhere, England, seriously hampered by the absence of Michael Owen due to ligament injury, lost on penalties to Portugal, after striker Wayne Rooney was sent off, while disappointing holders Brazil were fortunate to lose only 1-0 against France, for whom Thierry Henry volleyed a superb winner. Italy had it easy. They cruised to a 3-0 win over Ukraine and were thus fresher and fitter for the semi-final against Germany, in which they dismissed their hosts with late extra-time strikes from Fabio Grosso and Alessandro Del Piero. A tired Portugal lost the other semi-final to France. Zidane scored the winner from a penalty, just as he would open the scoring in the final, before the rush of blood that ruined his, and France's, World Cup.

2010

SOUTH AFRICA

Final: Soccer City, Johannesburg (84,490)

SPAIN 1-0 HOLLAND

Iniesta

Spain's first World Cup win came courtesy of a 116th-minute strike from Andrés Iniesta, one of a core of Barcelona players in the team. The goal was scored after the over-aggressive Dutch had been reduced to 10 men following the expulsion of defender John Heitinga by English referee Howard Webb.

Ball: *Jabulani*

TOP SCORER
5 *Villa (Spain), Müller (Germany), Forlán (Uruguay), Sneijder (Holland)*

South Africa's hosting of the 2010 World Cup finals was hailed as a remarkable success and outstanding reward for FIFA's vision in taking its elite event to the African continent for the first time. But the football was of a modest quality. Justice was done when Spain triumphed for the first time, yet they were the lowest-scoring winners, having mustered a meagre eight goals in their seven games.

The fringe honours saw Germany claim a record fourth win in the third-place play-off, while losers Uruguay had the consolation of seeing forward Diego Forlan hailed as best player. German pride in their young team was boosted by 20-year-old Thomas Muller, from Bayern Munich, collecting the awards for young player and top scorer; his points total from five goals and three assists edged out Forlan, Holland's Wesley Sneijder and Spain's David Villa.

South Africa had campaigned initially to win host rights in 2006 but had been outmanoeuvred by Germany. FIFA then introduced a rotation system which skewed the 2010 designation in favour of Nelson Mandela and his Rainbow Nation. The only home disappointment was the failure of their own team. Bafana Bafana - The Boys - were the first host nation ever to fail to reach the knockout stage.

One notable incident occurred in England's second round defeat by Germany. A shot from Frank Lampard struck the bar, bounced down behind the goal-line and back into play. The referee waved play on. FIFA subsequently scrapped its opposition to goal-line technology.

↑ After 116 minutes of often fractious and spiteful football, Andrés Iniesta (6) shoots past Holland goalkeeper Maarten Stekelenburg to give Spain the World Cup.

2014

BRAZIL

Final: Maracanã, Rio (74,738)

GERMANY 1-0 ARGENTINA

Gotze

A fabulous goal from Götze, six minutes from the end of extra time, won the final for Germany. Götze ran clear through the inside left slot as fellow substitute André Schürrle raced down the wing. He controlled the cross on his chest before volleying home left-footed.

Ball: *Brazuca*

TOP SCORER
6 *Rodríguez (Colombia)*

Germany's fourth World Cup also brought history as the first European nation to win football's greatest prize in the Americas. In the final, Germany and Argentina battled to a near standstill before Mario Götze's late winner. The only consolation for Argentinian captain Lionel Messi was an award as the finals' best player.

Brazil, playing host for the second time, suffered a disaster similar to that in 1950. Then their fans saw them reach the final match before losing narrowly to Uruguay. This time they endured a nightmare of historic proportions in collapsing 7-1 to Germany in Belo Horizonte in the semi-finals.

The run-up to the 2014 finals had been marred by street protests against the expenditure on 'white elephant' stadia but the eventual staging in 12 venues across the length and breadth of a vast country was comparatively trouble-free. Goal-line technology was employed for the first time in a World Cup.

Brazil were not the only members of the established order to be embarrassed. Italy and defending champions Spain failed to progress beyond the group stage. The Azzurri succumbed 1-0 to Uruguay, whose Luis Suarez was later banned for nine games for biting Italy defender Giorgio Chiellini.

↓ Mario Götze, the first substitute to score in a World Cup final, celebrates his strike late in extra time at the Maracanã in 2014.

An unfortunate own goal from Mario Mandzukic (the first ever in a World Cup final) gives France the lead against Croatia.

RUSSIA

Final: Luzhniki Stadium, Moscow (78,011)

FRANCE 4-2 CROATIA
Mandzukic (OG), Griezmann, Pogba, Mbappé • Perisic, Mandzukic

The highest-scoring 90 minutes of a World Cup Final in 60 years saw France triumph for the second time with a 4-2 defeat of Croatia in Moscow's Luzhniki Stadium. Didier Deschamps became only the third man to have won the World Cup as both player and manager, after Brazil's Mario Zagallo and Germany's Franz Beckenbauer.

Ball: *Telstar 18*

TOP SCORER
6 *Kane (England)*

History was also made with the use of a video assistant referee for the first time, The innovation was acclaimed for helping correct refereeing decisions, in particular with penalties, offside and pushing in the penalty box. Belgium finished a best-ever third after defeating England 2-0 in the losers' play-off.

The first World Cup staged in eastern Europe was one of the most entertaining for years, with dramatic matches and a wealth of upsets. Hosts Russia surprised themselves by reaching the quarter-finals before losing to Croatia on penalties. There were some unpleasant surprises, too, for some of football's traditional powers.

Defending cup-holders Germany were knocked out in the first round for the first time since 1938. Coach Joachim Löw's team failed to recover effectively from an opening 2-0 defeat by Mexico, who went on to reach the knockout stage for the seventh successive finals.

Argentina, beaten finalists in 2014, were unable to capitalise on the talent of their captain Lionel Messi, and scraped through narrowly to the second round where they were beaten 4-3 by France in the game of the tournament. The 19-year-old Paris Saint-Germain forward Kylian Mbappé struck twice to become the first teenage scorer in the knockout rounds since Brazil's Pele in 1958.

A second round defeat was also the fate of 2010 champions Spain after a penalty shootout against Russia. Spain struggled in a tournament they began in the worst possible way by sacking coach Julen Lopetegui three days before the start, after it emerged he was planning to quit and take over Real Madrid after the finals.

The second round saw England end a 28-year penalties jinx with a shootout victory over Colombia. Manager Gareth Southgate's team delighted fans by reaching the semi-finals before losing to Croatia in extra-time. The other semi-final brought a narrow 1-0 win for France over Belgium, who had earlier knocked Brazil, along with their superstar forward Neymar.

In the final, France went ahead with an own goal by Croatia striker Mario Mandzukic. The first-time finalists struck back through Ivan Perisic but fell behind again when referee Nestor Pitana awarded France a penalty for handball after checking his video monitor. That proved crucial. Paul Pogba and Mbappé scored further French goals before Croatia claimed a late second through Mandzukic after a blunder by keeper Hugo Lloris. It was too late for a dramatic recovery.

Croatia captain Luka Modric was named Best Player and Mbappé the Best Young Player as France collected the cup in an end-of-match thunderstorm.

European Championship

The European Championship was the last of the continental tournaments set under way and, like the World Cup and the European Champions Cup, was another French innovation. Kick off was in 1958 with the inaugural final in 1960.

EUROPEAN CHAMPIONSHIP

1960	Soviet Union 2-1 Yugoslavia
1964	Spain 2-1 USSR
1968	Italy 2-0 Yugoslavia *(replay)*
1972	West Germany 3-0 USSR
1976	Czechoslovakia 2-2 West Germany *(aet)* *(Czechoslovakia 5–3 on penalties)*
1980	West Germany 2-1 Belgium
1984	France 2-0 Spain
1988	Holland 2-0 USSR
1992	Denmark 2–0 Germany

1960-1992 The inaugural European Nations Cup saw 17 countries enter a knock-out competition followed by semi-finals, third-place play-off and final in France. England, West Germany and Italy did not enter for fear of fixture congestion. Thus the Soviet Union, inspired by legendary goalkeeper Lev Yashin, recovered from a goal down to beat Yugoslavia 2-1 in the final in the old Parc des Princes.

England entered for the first time in 1964, but new manager Alf Ramsey suffered an embarrassing debut with a 6-3 aggregate defeat by France. The semi-finals in Spain saw the Soviet Union defeat Denmark 3-0 while the hosts scrambled past Hungary 2-1 in extra time. Spain conceded an early goal in the final in Madrid but recovered to beat the holders through strikes by Jesus Pereda and Zaragoza's Marcelino.

The competition was renamed the European Championship for 1968 in Italy. England reached the finals with largely the same squad as the 1966 World Cup, but hopes of more glory ended in a 1-0 semi-final defeat by Yugoslavia. Italy beat the Soviet Union in the other semi-final on the competition's first and last coin toss. Luck was with them. A late goal rescued a 1-1 draw against Yugoslavia in the final and the Italians then rolled over their tired rivals 2-0 in a replay.

West Germany served up superb football in claiming a first triumph in 1972 in Belgium. Manager Helmut Schon built a team around 1970 World Cup heroes Franz Beckenbauer and Gerd Muller, plus new stars in attacking leftback Paul Breitner and playmaker Gunter Netzer. They swept aside the Soviet Union 3-0 in the final with Muller scoring twice.

The 1976 tournament, in Yugoslavia, was the last in which the hosts were chosen after the qualifiers. In the semi-finals, Czechoslovakia stunned Johan Cruyff's Dutch "total footballers" while West Germany hit back from 2-0 down to beat their Yugoslav hosts 4-2. They also recovered from two goals down in the final but a 2-2 draw with the Czechs sent the duel to extra time. Antonín Panenka's delicate penalty chip decided the shootout in the Czechs' favour.

In 1980, UEFA expanded the tournament in Italy with two groups of four with the winners progressing to the Rome final. West Germany again emerged triumphant with two goals from giant centre forward Horst Hrubesch.

The 1984 finals in France were dominated by Les Bleus' inspirational Michel Platini. He scored a finals-record nine goals in five games while captaining the hosts to their first major trophy. Platini, on his way to winning the European Footballer of the Year, struck the lone winner against Denmark in the opening match, and hat-tricks against Belgium and Yugoslavia, a goal against Portugal in the semis and France's first in a 2-0 win over Spain in the final.

In 1988, in West Germany, Holland finally landed their first major prize thanks to the goals of Marco Van Basten, with a hat-trick against England, followed up with a semi-final winner against hosts West Germany before executing a magisterial volley in the Dutchmen's 2-0 dismissal of the Soviet Union in the final.

However, Van Basten was out of luck in 1992 in Sweden. In the semi-final, he missed a penalty in a shootout defeat by outsiders Denmark. The Danes provided one more giant-killing as goals from John Jensen and Kim Vilfort upset over-confident Germany 2-0 in Gothenburg.

➜ Czech players claim offside in vain after Oliver Bierhoff's golden goal winner for Germany in 1996.

1996

ENGLAND

Final: Wembley, London (73,611)

GERMANY 2-1 CZECH REPUBLIC

Bierhoff (2) • Berger

The final was a much more even contest than many had predicted, and the Czechs took a surprise lead through a Patrick Berger penalty. German manager, Jupp Derwall, responded by sending on substitute Oliver Bierhoff. First he equalized and then, five minutes into extra time, wrote himself into the record books with the first-ever golden goal in a major tournament.

Ball: *Questra Europa*

TOP SCORER
5 *Shearer (England)*

The number of finalists doubled to sixteen in 1996, for the first major tournament in England since the 1966 World Cup. The successful staging re-established England's position on the footballing map after the failure to qualify for the previous World Cup and a decade of disaster.

A superb goal from Paul Gascoigne against Scotland set the tournament alight, and England followed this up by sweeping Holland aside 4–1. In the semi-finals, however, Germany broke the spell by holding their nerve in a shootout to progress to a final at Wembley against an underrated Czech Republic, who had edged France, also on penalties.

Germany were the favourites, the underdog Czech Republic were playing in only their first European Championship. The Germans struggled to break down the counter-attacking Czechs, and it took extra time to decide who would emerge victorious. In the end the form book prevailed, and Germany lifted the European national trophy for the third time.

2000

HOLLAND & BELGIUM

Final: Feijenoord Stadion, Rotterdam (48,200)

FRANCE 2-1 ITALY

Wiltord, Trezeguet • Delvecchio

France had two substitutes to thank for their defeat of the Azzurri. Sylvain Wiltord scored a dramatic equalizer in the final seconds of the 90 minutes, after Marco Delvecchio had broken the early deadlock after 55 minutes. Then, step forward David Trezeguet, who settled it with a sweetly struck golden goal in extra time.

Ball: *Terrestra Silverstream*

TOP SCORER
5 *Milosevic (FR Yugoslavia), Kluivert (Holland)*

Euro 2000, played in Holland and Belgium, was the first co-hosted tournament. World champions, France, were favourites and lived up to expectations. They beat both Portugal in the semi-finals and Italy in the final on a golden goal, only just snatching the trophy out of Italian hands. France thus became the first nation to add the European crown to the World Cup.

Portugal had set the group stage alight with victories over England, Romania and, most impressively, Germany, with Sérgio Conceição scoring a hat-trick. The Dutch were equally impressive, recording three victories, including a 6–1 thrashing of Yugoslavia, in a display worthy of their 1970s predecessors, and a memorable 3–2 beating of France. It proved, however, to be a frustrating tournament for the Dutch, who lost their nerve in the semis. Not only did they miss two penalties in normal time against Italy but even lost the shootout.

England fell back after the heights of Euro 1996: Kevin Keegan's team failed to progress beyond the group stage, sunk by a late penalty in their final game against Romania. Germany also had a rare fall from grace. They came bottom of their group, with a paltry single point.

➔ French captain Didier Deschamps holds aloft the European Championship trophy in 2000.

2004

PORTUGAL

Final: Estadio da Luz, Lisbon (62,865)

GREECE 1-0 PORTUGAL
Charisteas

Defying 150-1 tournament odds, Greece surprisingly ruined the party for Portugal. The final was a dour affair, with the Greeks nullifying the attacking flair of their hosts. Victory came courtesy of an opportunist effort by Angelos Charisteas from Greece's first corner, on 57 minutes. Portugal could find no way back.

Ball: *Roteiro*

TOP SCORER
5 *Baros (Czech Republic)*

The 2004 finals produced an upset barely anyone had predicted. Greece, who had qualified previously for only one World Cup (1994) and one European Championship (1980), shocked hosts Portugal 1-0 in a dramatic final after having beaten them in the opening game. On their way, the Greeks, who had begun as 150-1 outsiders, also eliminated holders France as well the Czech Republic with a silver goal, a rule which replaced the previous golden goal in 2003 before being abolished soon itself.

Greece's victory stunned Europe. However, it was not the only surprise after Germany, Italy and Spain had all been knocked out in the group stage. Greece owed their success not only to the manner in which their players rose to the occasion but to the disciplined tactics instilled by their veteran German coach, Otto Rehhagel.

The proudest moment in Greek football, as the celebrations begin after one of the biggest shocks in international footballing history.

2008

AUSTRIA & SWITZERLAND

Final: Ernst Happel Stadion, Vienna (51,428)

SPAIN 1-0 GERMANY
Torres

Spain came into the final undefeated and, despite the meagre scoreline, this was a dominant performance from the Iberians. Victory came courtesy of a coolly taken 33rd-minute goal from Fernando Torres, who also headed an effort against a post.

Ball: *Europass*

TOP SCORER
4 *Villa (Spain)*

Spain regained title form after 44 years by defeating Germany 1-0 in Vienna, their first appearance in a final since 1984. David Villa carried off the top scorer award with four goals. Both co-hosts Austria and Switzerland were eliminated in the first round, which featured a spectacular Group C where Italy fought back in gritty fashion after collapsing 3-0 against Holland. France were a disappointment: they were held goalless by Romania, thrashed 4-1 by Holland and then fell 2-0 to Italy.

The knockout stages brought more drama: Portugal went down 3-2 to quick-out-of-the-blocks Germany, while Holland surprisingly lost 3-1 to Russia in extra time. Shootouts decided the other two ties. Spain overcame jinx rivals Italy after a goalless draw, while Turkey beat Croatia after a 1-1 stalemate. Turkey's luck then ran out against Germany when they lost 3-2. Spain used an easy 3-0 win over Russia as a springboard to ultimate victory and a long-awaited championship crown.

2012

POLAND & UKRAINE

Final: Olympic Stadium, Kiev (63,170)

SPAIN 4-0 ITALY

Silva, Alba, Torres, Mata

Italy huffed and puffed in the final, but they were passed into submission by the magisterial Spanish, who were on the very top of their technically brilliant game. Goals from David Silva and Jordi Alba in the first half were followed by two late strikes from substitutes Fernando Torres and Juan Mata in the second.

Ball: *Tango 12*

TOP SCORER
3 *Torres (Spain), Balotelli (Italy), Dzagoev (Russia), Mandžukić (Croatia), Ronaldo (Portugal)*

Superb Spain fashioned football history after demolishing Italy 4-0 at the Euro 2012 final. The 2008 winners and 2010 world champions thus became the only European nation to raise three major trophies in a row and the only one ever to retain the European title. Ironically, Italy had applied to host the tournament, the last to feature 16 qualified teams, and lost out to Poland and Ukraine. Now they had finished second-best again.

Italy and Spain had already drawn 1-1 in Gdansk in the group stage, which, as in 2008, saw the twin hosts both fail to progress to the knockout stage. In the semi-finals, the superb Andrea Pirlo inspired Italy's 2-1 win over Germany, both goals scored by an on-fire Mario Balotelli, while Spain edged past Portugal only through a penalty shootout. Spain's triumph in the final also offered father-figure manager Vicente Del Bosque a personal footnote in history: he was the first coach to win World Cup, European Championship and Champions League titles.

↑ The sight of the Spanish team triumphant after a major international was becoming commonplace by the time they thrashed Italy in 2012.

2016

FRANCE

Final:Stade de France, Paris (75,868)

PORTUGAL 1-0 FRANCE

Eder

The abiding image of the 2016 final is that of the injured but fired-up Cristiano Ronaldo screaming encouragement to his teammates. The hero, though, was Eder, who calmly slotted home Portugal's winner in extra time.

Ball: *Beau Jeu*

TOP SCORER
6 *Griezmann (France)*

Portugal scored a shock 1-0 win over hosts France in extra time to win Euro 2016 with a goal from substitute striker Eder. The Portuguese claimed their first major trophy despite losing captain and superstar Cristiano Ronaldo to injury in the first half. Minor consolation for France was that striker Antoine Griezmann ended as six-goal tournament top scorer.

Expanding the finals from 16 to 24 teams had increased UEFA's revenues by 34 per cent compared with 2012 but at a cost to the quality of the football. Euro 2016 provided some memorable goals but few memorable matches, and anyone looking at the early results would never have put money on Portugal winning the tournament. The Portuguese scraped through their group as one of the top third-placed teams, following three draws, and needed extra time to defeat Crotia and then Poland in the last round of 16 and the quarter-final.

The main headlines were written by the David and Goliath giant-killing exploits of middle-class nations in rising beyond their status. The greatest achievement was that of Gareth Bales's Wales in beating the highly fancied Belgians 3-1 in the quarter-finals before falling to Ronaldo and company in the semis. Close behind were fellow newcomers Iceland, representatives of a population smaller than that of Cardiff, who reached the quarter-finals with a historic 2-1 win over dismal England in the second round.

← Portugal had to win the final the hard way, without their talisman and their best player of the tournament Cristiano Ronaldo.

Copa América

The South American Championship is the oldest running international competition in the world. Run by the South American confederation, CONMEBOL, it pre-dates its European equivalent by half a century.

The initial championship was staged in Argentina in 1910, but over the next 40 years a number of the tournaments staged were not considered "official". Hence the first formal South American champions were Uruguay, whose team sailed back across the River Plate in triumph in 1916 after spoiling host Argentina's celebrations of a century of independence.

The next tournament, in 1919, is considered a watershed in the history of Brazilian football. Fluminense had built a 20,000-capacity stadium for a sport which had been viewed, until then, as a pastime for the upper classes in their private clubs. Suddenly, football became the people's game. Brazil's first superstar, Arthur Friedenreich, was also their first title-winning hero. Brazil beat Argentina 1-0 in a replayed final. The teams agreed to play on beyond the end of a goalless extra time before Friedenreich's decisive strike.

Between 1916 and 1959, the Copa America was held every two years. Uruguay won six of the first 11 tournaments. Argentina then gained the upper hand, winning 11 of the 18 tournaments between the 1920s and the 1950s.

Argentina's greatest era began in 1955 in Chile. They lost their crown to old rivals Uruguay in 1956 then regained it in Peru in 1957. This remained for years a high point in Argentinian history thanks to a team featuring one of the great inside-forward trios in South American history: Humberto Maschio, Antonio Valentín Angelillo and Omar Sívori.

The manner of victory made Argentina South America's favourites to win the World Cup the following year. Instead, it was Brazil who grabbed the glory after Argentina flopped in Sweden. The reason was simple: by then Maschio, Angelillo and Sívori had all been lured away to Italy. Ever afterwards they were known bitterly, after the popular film of the day, as the "Angels with Dirty Faces".

Brazil have enjoyed comparatively little success in the Copa America. The first four of their eight titles, in 1919, 1922, 1949 and 1989, were all on home soil, but at their peak in the 1960s only two tournaments were staged there.

After an experiment with a two-leg knockout format, the competition returned to a finals system in 1987 in Argentina - with old rivals Uruguay winning. Brazil played host in 1989 and won their first title in 40 years.

In 1993, in Ecuador, another face-lift saw Mexico and the United States invited to join the party as guests. Mexico almost spoiled it by reaching the final, where

Chile triumphed on penalties once again to go down in history as the "Centenario" champions.

they lost 2-1 to Argentina. In Uruguay, 1995, it was US's turn to dismiss the South Americans, reaching the semi-finals before losing 1-0 to Brazil, who then lost to Uruguay after a penalty shootout.

Brazil made up for lost time by claiming the Cup in 1997 and 1999 before Colombia won at home in 2001 with a 1-0 final victory over Mexico. The Brazilians hit back by taking the 2004 title on a penalty shootout against Argentina. They also won in 2007, with Colombia squeezing in a lone success in 2001.

The South American confederation had now decided to fix the event on a four-year calendar basis in the year after a World Cup. The Brazilians were duly dethroned in 2011 by a Uruguayan side still powered by the momentum gained from their fourth-place finish at the World Cup in South Africa a year earlier.

Chile then not only carried off the title for the first time in 2015, after 99 years of trying, but followed up with a repeat victory in a centenary tournament the next year in the US. Both times, the Chileans defeated Argentina on penalties after a goalless final.

One of the greats, Ronaldo, celebrates scoring Brazil's third against Uruguay in 1999.

43	MOST APPEARANCES IN THE CHAMPIONSHIP	**URUGUAY**
28	MOST APPEARANCES IN A FINAL	**ARGENTINA**
120	MOST WINS	**ARGENTINA**
82	MOST LOSSES	**CHILE**
455	MOST GOALS SCORED	**ARGENTINA**
311	MOST GOALS CONCEDED	**ECUADOR**

• Up to and including 2015–16 season

COPA AMERICA FINALS

1910	BUENOS AIRES 1st Argentina, 2nd Uruguay*
1916	BUENOS AIRES 1st Uruguay, 2nd Argentina*
1917	MONTEVIDEO 1st Uruguay, 2nd Argentina
1919	RIO DE JANEIRO (play-off) Brazil 1, Uruguay 0
1920	VINA DEL MAR 1st Uruguay, 2nd Argentina
1921	BUENOS AIRES 1st Argentina, 2nd Brazil
1922	Rio de Janeiro (play-off) Brazil 3, Paraguay 1
1923	Montevideo 1st Uruguay, 2nd Argentina
1924	MONTEVIDEO 1st Uruguay, 2nd Argentina
1925	BUENOS AIRES 1st Argentina, 2nd Brazil
1926	SANTIAGO 1st Uruguay, 2nd Argentina
1927	LIMA 1st Argentina, 2nd Uruguay
1929	BUENOS AIRES 1st Argentina, 2nd Paraguay
1935	LIMA 1st Uruguay, 2nd Argentina*
1937	BUENOS AIRES (play-off) Argentina 2, Brazil 0
1939	LIMA 1st Peru, 2nd Uruguay
1941	SANTIAGO 1st Argentina, 2nd Uruguay*
1942	MONTEVIDEO 1st Uruguay, 2nd Argentina
1945	SANTIAGO 1st Argentina, 2nd Brazil*
1946	BUENOS AIRES 1st Argentina, 2nd Brazil*
1947	GUAYAQUIL 1st Argentina, 2nd Paraguay
1949	RIO DE JANEIRO (play-off) Brazil 7, Paraguay 0
1953	LIMA (play-off) Paraguay 3, Brazil 2
1955	SANTIAGO 1st Argentina, 2nd Chile
1956	MONTEVIDEO 1st Uruguay, 2nd Chile*
1957	LIMA 1st Argentina, 2nd Brazil
1959	BUENOS AIRES 1st Argentina, 2nd Brazil*
1959	GUAYAQUIL 1st Uruguay, 2nd Argentina
1963	BOLIVIA 1st Bolivia, 2nd Paraguay
1967	MONTEVIDEO 1st Uruguay, 2nd Argentina
1975	BOGOTA (1st leg) Colombia 1–0 Peru LIMA (2nd leg) Peru 2–0 Colombia CARACAS (play-off) Peru 1–0 Colombia
1979	ASUNCIÓN (1st leg) Paraguay 3–0 Chile SANTIAGO (2nd leg) Chile 1–0 Paraguay BUENOS AIRES (play-off) Paraguay 0–0 Chile *(Paraguay won on goal difference)*
1983	MONTEVIDEO (1st leg) Uruguay 2–0 Brazil SALVADOR (2nd leg) Brazil 1–1 Uruguay
1987	BUENOS AIRES Uruguay 1–0 Chile
1989	BRAZIL 1st Brazil, 2nd Uruguay
1991	CHILE 1st Argentina, 2nd Brazil
1993	GUAYAQUIL Argentina 2, Mexico 1
1995	MONTEVIDEO Uruguay 1–1 Brazil *(aet)* *(Uruguay 5–3 on penalties)*
1997	LA PAZ Brazil 3–1 Bolivia
1999	ASUNCIÓN Brazil 3–0 Uruguay
2001	BOGOTA Colombia 1–0 Mexico
2004	LIMA Brazil 2–2 Argentina *(aet)* *(Brazil 4–2 on penalties)*
2007	MARACAIBO Brazil 3–0 Argentina
2011	BUENOS AIRES Uruguay 3–0 Paraguay
2015	SANTIAGO Chile 0–0 Argentina *(aet)* *(Chile 4–1 on penalties)*
2016	EAST RUTHERFORD Chile 0–0 Argentina *(aet)* *(Chile 4–2 on penalties)*†

Notes: Details of finals or championship play-offs are given where applicable. All other tournaments, played on a league basis, only first and second are listed.
** unofficial "extraordinarios" tournaments.*
† Copa América Centenario

Africa Cup of Nations

The Africa Cup of Nations is the blue riband event of African football, and the tournament is as old as the Confederation of African Football (CAF) itself. Held every two years, it has grown from humble beginnings to embrace the continent.

The first finals took place in Khartoum in 1957 and involved only Sudan, Egypt and Ethiopia. South Africa were initially due to take part, but would only send either an all-black team or an all-white team. The CAF insisted on a multi-racial team, South Africa refused and withdrew, and, until readmitted to the CAF in 1992, took no further part in African or international football.

Egypt won the first tournament and the same three nations took part in the second in 1959. Ethiopia hosted the third tournament in 1962, where Tunisia and Uganda took part for the first time. Ghana and Nigeria joined for the 1963 tournament, held in Ghana, with two groups of three producing the finalists - Ghana and Sudan. The hosts won 3-0 going on to become the dominant early force in African football.

The tournament had by now grown to eighteen entrants, and a qualifying tournament was introduced to produce eight finalists, with the hosts and holders automatically entered into the final round. Success was shared around subsequently between Congo, Zaíre (Democratic Republic of Congo), Morocco and then Ghana once again. The two-overseas-players rule, which had become impractical with so many earning a living in Europe, was then abolished, with Cameroon emerging for their first victory in the 1984 finals.

After South Africa's readmittance into the international football family in 1992, Bafana Bafana, also known as The Boys, failed to qualify for the finals in 1994 but were awarded host rights in 1996 and triumphed 2-0 over Tunisia in the final.

South Africa were again finalists in 1998 when Ajax forward Benni McCarthy was star player and joint top-scorer with seven goals. But he failed to score in the final and South Africa lost 2-0 to Egypt.

That was the first of the Egyptian Pharaohs' four victories in a 12-year spell which included a hat-trick in 2006, 2008 and 2010. But they failed surprisingly to even reach the 2012 finals. Zambia were popular and poignant winners, 19 years after 18 members of their national team squad had been killed in an air crash.

To illustrate the rapid growth in the competition's popularity, some 51 vied for the 15 qualification spots at the last finals in 2017 alongside already-seeded hosts, Gabon.

Egypt's Pharaohs have won a record seven titles and been runners-up twice, including 2017 when they lost 2-1 to Cameroon on goals from substitutes Nicolas Nkoulou and Vincent Aboubakar.

Cameroon celebrate winning their fifth Africa Cup of Nations title in 2017. A late goal from Vincent Aboubakar gave them a 2–1 victory over Egypt.

ALL-TIME TOP SCORER
SAMUEL ETO'O
CAMEROON
18

AFRICA CUP OF NATIONS

1957	Egypt 4-0 Ethiopia
1959	1st Egypt, 2nd Sudan
1962	Ethiopia 4–2 Egypt *(aet)*
1963	Ghana 3–0 Sudan
1965	Ghana 3–2 Tunisia *(aet)*
1968	Zaíre (DRC) 1–0 Ghana
1970	Sudan 1–0 Ghana
1972	Congo 3–2 Mali
1974	Zaíre (DRC) 2–2 Zambia *(aet)* *Zaíre 2–0 Zambia (replay)*
1976	1st Morocco, 2nd Guinea
1978	Ghana 2–0 Uganda
1980	Nigeria 3–0 Algeria
1982	Ghana 1–1 Libya *(aet)* *(Ghana 7–6 on penalties)*
1984	Cameroon 3–0 Nigeria
1986	Egypt 0–0 Cameroon *(aet)* *(Egypt 5–4 on penalties)*
1988	Cameroon 1–0 Nigeria
1990	Algeria 1–0 Nigeria
1992	Ivory Coast 0–0 Ghana *(aet)* *(Ivory Coast 11–10 on penalties)*
1994	Nigeria 2–1 Zambia
1996	South Africa 2–0 Tunisia
1998	Egypt 2–0 South Africa
2000	Cameroon 2–2 Nigeria *(aet)* *(Cameroon 4–3 on penalties)*
2002	Cameroon 0–0 Senegal *(aet)* *(Cameroon 3–2 on penalties)*
2004	Tunisia 2–1 Morocco
2006	Egypt 0–0 Ivory coast *(aet)* *(Egypt 4-2 on penalties)*
2008	Egypt 1–0 Cameroon
2010	Egypt 1–0 Ghana
2012	Zambia 0-0 Ivory Coast *(aet)* *(Zambia 8-7 on penalties)*
2013	Nigeria 1–0 Burkina Faso
2015	Ivory Coast 0-0 Ghana *(aet)* *(Ivory Coast 9-8 on penalties)*
2017	Cameroon 2-1 Egypt

Asian Cup & Asian Games

Asian Cup

The Asian Cup for national teams started in 1956 and, until the 1980 tournament, was dominated by South Korea and Iran. The South Koreans were the first winners of what was initially a mini-league tournament. From 1972 the Asian confederation switched to the traditional format of group stage and knockout phase. Since then Kuwait and Saudi Arabia have enjoyed success but Japan, with four victories in all, have dominated in the twenty-first century. Australia, amid some controversy, abandoned Oceania to join the Asian confederation in 2007. Eight years later the Socceroos were awarded hosting rights to the Asian Cup and won top prize for the first time by defeating South Korea 2-1 after extra-time in Sydney. Juventus midfielder John Troisi scored the winner. The other goalscorer, Massimo Luongo, was named the tournament's most valuable player.

Asian Games

The first Asian Games were staged by India in 1951 with six countries entering the football competition. Originally open only to amateur players, the Games are staged every four years between an Olympiad, expanding in importance when Arab nations joined in the early 1970s. Host India defeated Iran in the first final which was played over 80 minutes rather than 90, as this was considered more appropriate for amateur players. Political problems erupted in the 1970s when the Gulf states boycotted the 1974 Games in Tehran because of Israel's states boycotted the 1974 Games in Tehran because of Israel's presence. A year later the Asian Football Confederation (AFC) expelled Israel and welcomed in mainland China. They made their debut in 1978 in Bangkok and took the bronze medal. A further significant rebalancing of power occurred in the 1990s after the collapse of the Soviet Union. Seven new states joined the AFC, these included Uzbekistan, who marked their Games "arrival" by defeating China 4-2 in the 1994 final.

The recent Asian entrants, Australia, won their first trophy in 2015 after James Troisi's extra time winner.

	ASIAN CUP
1956	RR: winners South Korea
1960	RR: winners South Korea
1964	RR: winners Israel
1968	RR: winners Iran
1972	Iran 2–1 South Korea *(aet)*
1976	Iran 1–0 Kuwait
1980	Kuwait 3–0 South Korea
1984	Saudi Arabia 2–0 China
1988	Saudi Arabia 0–0 South Korea *(aet)* *(Saudia Arabia 4–3 on penalties)*
1992	Japan 1–0 Saudi Arabia
1996	Saudi Arabia 0–0 UAE *(aet)* *(Saudi Arabia 4–2 on penalties)*
2000	Japan 1–0 Saudi Arabia
2004	Japan 3–1 China
2007	Iraq 1–0 Saudi Arabia
2011	Japan 1-0 Australia *(aet)*
2015	Australia 2-1 South Korea *(aet)*

	ASIAN GAMES FINALS
1951	India 1–0 Iran
1954	Taiwan 5–2 South Korea
1958	Taiwan 3–2 South Korea
1962	India 2–1 South Korea
1966	Myanmar 1–0 Iran
1970	Myanmar 0–0 South Korea
1974	Iran 1–0 Israel
1978	North Korea 0–0 South Korea
1982	Iraq 1–0 Kuwait
1986	South Korea 2–0 Saudi Arabia
1990	Iran 0–0 North Korea *(Iran 4–1 on penalties)*
1994	Uzbekistan 4–2 China
1998	Iran 2–0 Kuwait
2002	Iran 2–1 Japan
2006	Qatar 1–0 Iraq
2010	Japan 1-0 UAE
2014	South Korea 1-0 North Korea *(aet)*

Notes: The trophy was shared in 1970 and 1978

Olympic Games

The origins of Olympic football are hidden in the mists of time. The first FIFA-recognised tournament was in London in 1908. England won easily and again in 1912, inspired by Vivian Woodward, one of the greatest early heroes of English football. Also in 1912 Germany's Gottfried Fuchs scored a remarkable 10 goals in a 16-0 thrashing of Tsarist Russia.

After the First World War the balance of Olympic power changed. Uruguay won in both 1924 and 1928 with the nucleus of their 1930 World Cup-winning team. Los Angeles did not want football in 1932, but Germany expected to win at home in Berlin in 1936. Shockingly, they lost in the first round to tiny Norway, leaving Italy to win in a golden era with their Games victory sandwiched between World Cup wins in 1934 and 1938.

Sweden won in London in 1948 with a team starring the Gre-No-Li trio - Gunnar Gren, Gunnar Nordahl and Nils Liedhom - who were soon enhancing their legend status with Milan. But that was the last time a western European nation took gold until France in 1984. In between, the so-called "state amateurs" of eastern Europe took all the honours, led by Ferenc Puskas's Magical Magyars from Hungary in 1952.

Barcelona in 1992 saw the restriction to players aged under 23 in a bargain which saw women's football introduced in Atlanta in 1996. That was the year Nigeria secured Africa's first Olympics football gold against Argentina. The Argentinians made amends in 2004 and 2008, the latter team starring Leo Messi and Angel Di Maria.

Latin America's command was extended by Mexico at London 2012 and by hosts, Brazil, in Rio de Janeiro in 2016. Brazil claimed their first football gold with a last-kick penalty from superstar captain, Neymar, against Germany at the Maracanã.

OLYMPIC GAMES FINALS

1908	LONDON England 2-0 Denmark
1912	STOCKHOLM England 4-2 Denmark
1920	ANTWERP Belgium 2-0 Czechoslovakia
1924	PARIS Uruguay 3-0 Switzerland
1928	AMSTERDAM Uruguay 1-1 Argentina *Uruguay 2-1 Argentina (replay)*
1936	BERLIN Italy 2-1 Austria
1948	LONDON Sweden 3-1 Yugoslavia
1952	HELSINKI Hungary 2–0 Yugoslavia
1956	MELBOURNE Soviet Union 1–0 Yugoslavia
1960	ROME Yugoslavia 3–1 Denmark
1964	TOKYO Hungary 2–1 Czechoslovakia
1968	MEXICO CITY Hungary 4–1 Bulgaria
1972	MUNICH Poland 2–1 Hungary
1976	MONTREAL East Germany 3–1 Poland
1980	MOSCOW Czechoslovakia 1–0 East Germany
1984	LOS ANGELES France 2–0 Brazil
1988	SEOUL Soviet Union 2–1 Brazil
1992	BARCELONA Spain 3–2 Poland
1996	ATHENS, USA Nigeria 3–2 Argentina
2000	SYDNEY Cameroon 2–2 Spain *(aet)* *(Cameroon 5–3 on penalties)*
2004	ATHENS, GREECE Argentina 1–0 Paraguay
2008	BEIJING Argentina 1–0 Nigeria
2012	LONDON Mexico 2–1 Brazil
2016	RIO DE JANEIRO Brazil 1–1 Germany *(aet)* *(Brazil 5–4 on penalties)*

Brazil captain Neymar is surrounded by German players at the 2016 Olympic Games. Brazil won the gold medal on home soil.

OFC Nations Cup

A championship was launched in 1973 before the region had been recognised as a confederation by FIFA. Regional giants Australia stayed away so hosts New Zealand were first champions, defeating Tahiti 2-0. Seven years passed before a second tournament was organised. New Caledonia played host and this time it was Australia who beat Tahiti, by 4-2. Oceania subsequently gained FIFA recognition in 1996 and revived the championship. Australia were again winners and Tahiti runners-up. The event's status was upgraded from 2001 when the winners were admitted to the FIFA Confederations Cup. Australia quit Oceania for the Asia confederation in 2006 but New Zealand did not have the event all their own way. Tahiti claimed a surprise win in 2012 and thus progressed to the Confederations Cup in Brazil and an appearance at Rio de Janeiro's Maracanã stadium.

5.2 NUMBER OF **GOALS SCORED** PER GAME BY AUSTRALIA

OFC NATIONS CUP FINALS

1973	New Zealand 2–0 Tahiti
1980	Australia 4–2 Tahiti
1996	RR: winners Australia
1998	New Zealand 1–0 Australia
2000	Australia 2–0 New Zealand
2002	New Zealand 1–0 Australia
2004	RR: winners Australia
2008	RR: winners New Zealand
2012	Tahiti 1–0 New Caledonia
2016	New Zealand 0–0 Papua New Guinea *(aet)* *(New Zealand 4–2 on penalties)*

RR: Round-robin tournament

Pan American Games

The Pan Am Games is the major multi-sport event in the Americas, organised by the Pan American Sports Organization (PASO). Football has featured ever since the inaugural event in 1951 and a women's competition since 1999. The men's competition is now reserved for under-21 players. Argentina won the first gold medal in 1951 and have claimed a record six overall, followed by Mexico and Brazil (four each), Uruguay (two) then Ecuador and United States (one each). Surprisingly, considering their dominance at senior level, the US have won only one of the five women's tournaments. Brazil claim three gold medals and Canada, one. The great Marta inspired their successive victories in 2003 and 2007. In 2007, she scored four times in a 10-0 win over Ecuador, five in a 7-0 defeat of Canada and two in the 5-0 gold-medal win over the US.

PAN AMERICAN GAMES FINALS

1951	RR: winners Argentina
1955	RR: winners Argentina
1959	RR: winners Argentina
1963	RR: winners Brazil
1967	Mexico 4–0 Bermuda *(aet)*
1971	RR: winners Argentina
1975	Mexico 1–1 Brazil *(aet-title shared)*
1979	Brazil 3–0 Cuba
1983	RR: winners Uruguay
1987	Brazil 2–0 Chile
1991	USA 2–1 Mexico *(aet)*
1995	Argentina 0–0 Mexico *(aet)* *(Argentina 5–4 on penalties)*
1999	Mexico 3–1 Honduras
2003	Argentina 1–0 Brazil
2007	Ecuador 2–1 Jamaica
2011	Mexico 1–0 Argentina
2015	Uruguay 1-0 Mexico

RR: Round-robin tournament

A young Uruguayan team after defeating Mexico in the Pan American Games final in Canada in 2015.

CONCACAF Gold Cup

Two regions of the Confederation of North, Central American and Caribbean Association Football had been staging their national team championships since the 1940s. Subsequently, the Central and Caribbean tournament merged with its North American counterpart after the creation of CONCACAF in 1961. The initial CONCACAF event was staged in 1963 in El Salvador, with Costa Rica the winners of a mini-league series. Four times the championship doubled up as the regional qualifying competition for the World Cup. In 1991, the competition was relaunched as the Gold Cup, contested every two years. Since then the US has always played host, alone or jointly, and has won on six occasions, including a 2-1 final victory over Jamaica in Santa Clara, California, in 2017. Jozy Altidore and Jordan Morris scored the goals. It was the second successive time Jamaica had finished runners-up.

18

GOLD CUP ALL-TIME TOP SCORER
LANDON DONOVAN
USA

➋ The Canadians perform an intricately acrobatic celebration routine after winning the 2000 final.

CONCACAF GOLD CUP WINNERS

1941	RR: Costa Rica winners
1943	RR: El Salvador winners
1946	RR: Costa Rica winners
1948	RR: Costa Rica winners
1951	RR: Panama winners
1953	RR: Costa Rica winners
1955	RR: Costa Rica winners
1957	RR: Haiti winners
1960	Costa Rica 4–1 Dutch Antilles*
1961	RR: Costa Rica winners
1963	RR: Costa Rica winners
1965	RR: Mexico winners
1967	RR: Guatemala winners
1969	RR: Costa Rica winners
1971	RR: Mexico winners
1973	RR: Haiti winners
1977	RR: Mexico winners
1981	RR: Honduras winners
1985	RR: Canada winners
1989	RR: Costa Rica winners
1991	USA 0–0 Honduras *(aet)* *(USA 4–3 on penalties)*
1993	Mexico 4–0 USA
1996	Mexico 2–0 Brazil
1998	Mexico 1–0 USA
2000	Canada 2–0 Colombia
2002	USA 2–0 Costa Rica
2003	Mexico 1–0 Brazil *(aet/sudden death)*
2005	USA 0–0 Panama *(aet)* *(USA 3–1 on penalties)*
2007	USA 2–1 Mexico
2009	Mexico 5–0 USA
2011	Mexico 4–2 USA
2013	USA 1–0 Panama
2015	Mexico 3–1 Jamaica
2017	USA 2–1 Jamaica

RR: Round-robin tournament
** Round robin play-off*

Confederations Cup

Germany are jubilant after defeating Chile in the 2017 Confederations Cup final, winning yet another trophy to add to their cabinet.

Confederations Cup

The Confederations Cup, which brings together the champions of the six world regions plus the world champions and host nation, began life as the King Fahd Cup in Saudi Arabia in 1995 and 1997. Argentina and Denmark were the first two winners.

From 1997, FIFA took over the organisation of the tournament to help satisfy sponsor pressure to squeeze full value out of the four-year contracts with the world football federation. Since 2001 the Cup has served as a valuable warm-up event for the next year's World Cup hosts.

The tournament was played every two years until after tragedy struck in 2003 in France: Cameroon captain Marc-Vivien Foe collapsed and died during a semi-final against Colombia. Subsequently, the competition has been played only every four years.

Brazil won all three tournaments from 2005 to 2013, scoring decisive victories in the finals over Argentina, the United States and Spain respectively. In the 2013 final at the Maracanã, Rio de Janeiro, goals from Fred (two) and Neymar meant Brazil ended Spain's record of 29 games without a defeat. Spain's Sergio Ramos missed a penalty. In the third-place playoff Italy beat Uruguay 3-2 on penalties after a 2-2 draw.

Brazil missed the 2017 tournament which saw a first success for Germany. They defeated Chile 1-0 in the final in St Petersburg with a goal from Lars Stindl. Captain Julian Draxler was player of the tournament.

Copa Centroamericana

A Central American and Caribbean championship was created in 1941 and staged regularly for the next two decades. Costa Rica won seven times with El Salvador, Panama and Haiti winning once each. Competition was discontinued after the creation of CONCACAF in 1961. However, in 1991, the Central American nations (excluding Mexico) decided to revive their own regional tournament, officially the Copa de Naciones de UNCAF (the Union Centroamericana de Futbol). Costa Rica have the most outstanding record with seven victories between 1991 and 2017, followed by Honduras (four), and Guatemala and Panama (who both have only accrued one a piece).

In 2014, Costa Rica beat Guatemala 2-1 in the final, two months after reaching the quarter-finals of the World Cup in Brazil. In 2017, the Copa reverted to the original mini-league system after six years with a playoff final.

FIFA CONFEDERATIONS CUP WINNERS

1992	Argentina 3–1 Saudi Arabia
1995	Denmark 2–0 Argentina
1997	Brazil 6–0 Australia
1999	Mexico 4–3 Brazil
2001	France 1–0 Japan
2003	France 1–0 Cameroon (*aet*)
2005	Brazil 4–1 Argentina
2009	Brazil 3–2 USA
2013	Brazil 3–0 Spain
2017	Germany 1–0 Chile

Note: The first two tournaments were in fact the now-defunct King Fahd Cup. FIFA later recognized them retrospectively as the Confederrations Cup

COPA CENTROAMERICANO WINNERS

1991	RR: winners Costa Rica
1993	RR: winners Honduras
1995	Honduras 3–0 Guatemala
1997	RR: winners Costa Rica
1999	RR: winners Costa Rica
2001	RR: winners Guatemala
2003	RR: winners Costa Rica
2005	Costa Rica 1–1 Honduras (*aet*) (*Costa Rica 7–6 on penalties*)
2009	Panama 0–0 Costa Rica (*aet*) (*Panama 5–3 on penalties*)
2011	Honduras 2–1 Costa Rica
2013	Costa Rica 1–0 Honduras
2014	Costa Rica 2–1 Guatemala
2017	RR: winners Honduras

RR: Round-robin tournament

COUPE

3

MAJOR CLUB COMPETITIONS

Club football has always been the heart of the sport. Since the Second World War, with the vast influx of TV and sponsorship revenue, the continental club competitions have grown to equal national team football in importance.

The Champions League

The UEFA Champions League, originally the European Champions Club Cup, is not only the most lucrative club event in the world, but it has also become the most prized trophy in world club football.

Reputations have been made and broken over the five decades since the competition began, and it has always had an aura of romance and glamour about it, some say even more so than national-team competitions.

The idea came, typically, from the French. Gabriel Hanot, a former international and then editor of the French daily sports newspaper *L'Équipe*, was up in arms in regard to English newspaper claims that Wolverhampton Wanderers were the champions of Europe because they had beaten Honved and Moscow Spartak in friendlies.

Hanot decided to launch a competition to find the real champions of Europe and, in 1955, invited representatives of 20 leading clubs to discuss the idea in Paris. The meeting was attended by 15 clubs and it was agreed that the competition should begin in the 1955–56 season. Administration was subsequently taken over by the new European federation, UEFA.

Eligibility was restricted to the champions of each country plus the holders after the first series, to play home and away matches on a knockout basis, and the result would be decided by the aggregate score – except in the final, which was a one-off match played at a neutral venue. Drawn ties used a play-off to produce a winner until 1967, when a new method was introduced, whereby the team scoring most away goals progressed. In the event of a draw, even after away goals were counted, a toss of a coin decided the winner; that being the case until 1971, when penalty kicks were introduced.

By a happy coincidence, just as the competition was launched, Real Madrid were blossoming into one of the greatest club sides the world had seen. In the final, fittingly played in Paris, Real faced a Reims side containing the legendary

Real Madrid's Juan Santisteban (left) foils Reims's Roger Piantoni in Stuttgart in 1959.

REAL MADRID 13
1956 1957 1958 1959 1960 1966 1998 2000 2002 2014 2016 2017 2018

MILAN 7
1963 1969 1989 1990 1994 2003 2007

BAYERN MUNICH 5
1974 1975 1976 2001 2013

BARCELONA 5
1992 2006 2009 2011 2015

LIVERPOOL 5
1977 1978 1981 1984 2005

CHAMPIONS CUP FINALS 1956–1986

1956	Real Madrid 4–3 Stade de Reims	PARIS
1957	Real Madrid 2–0 Fiorentina	MADRID
1958	Real Madrid 3–2 Milan	BRUSSELS
1959	Real Madrid 2–0 Stade de Reims	STUTTGART
1960	Real Madrid 7–3 Eintracht Frankfurt	GLASGOW
1961	Benfica 3–2 Barcelona	BERN
1962	Benfica 5–3 Real Madrid	AMSTERDAM
1963	Milan 2–1 Benfica	LONDON
1964	Internazionale 3–1 Real Madrid	VIENNA
1965	Internazionale 1–0 Benfica	MILAN
1966	Real Madrid 2–1 Partizan Belgrade	BRUSSELS
1967	Celtic 2–1 Internazionale	LISBON
1968	Manchester United 4–1 Benfica	LONDON
1969	Milan 4–1 Ajax	MADRID
1970	Feyenoord 2–1 Celtic	MILAN
1971	Ajax 2–0 Panathinaikos	LONDON
1972	Ajax 2–0 Internazionale	ROTTERDAM
1973	Ajax 1–0 Juventus	BELGRADE
1974	Bayern Munich 1–1 Atlético Madrid *(replay)* Bayern Munich 4–0 Atlético Madrid	BRUSSELS
1975	Bayern Munich 2–0 Leeds United	PARIS
1976	Bayern Munich 1–0 Saint-Étienne	GLASGOW
1977	Liverpool 3–1 Borussia Mönchengladbach	ROME
1978	Liverpool 1–0 Club Brugge	LONDON
1979	Nottingham Forest 1–0 Malmö	MUNICH
1980	Nottingham Forest 1–0 Hamburg	MADRID
1981	Liverpool 1–0 Real Madrid	PARIS
1982	Aston Villa 1–0 Bayern Munich	ROTTERDAM
1983	Hamburg 1–0 Juventus	ATHENS
1984	Liverpool 1–1 AS Roma *(aet Liverpool 4–2 on penalties)*	ROME
1985	Juventus 1–0 Liverpool	BRUSSELS
1986	Steaua Bucharest 0–0 Barcelona *(aet Steaua 2–0 on penalties)*	SEVILLE

Lisbon's Estadio Nacional rises to Celtic's Billy McNeill after the historic comeback victory over Internazionale.

Raymond Kopa, who joined Real the next season. Despite leading twice, Reims could not cope with Real's deadly Alfredo Di Stéfano, Hector Rial and Francisco "Paco" Gento, and lost 4-3.

Real went on to win the Cup for the next four years, a feat which is unlikely to be matched in the modern game. Fiorentina (1957), Milan (1958), Reims again (1959) and Eintracht Frankfurt (1960) were all beaten in successive Finals, with the match against Frankfurt being arguably the best final ever. In front of 135,000 fans at Hampden Park in Glasgow, Real thrashed the West German champions 7-3, with Ferenc Puskás, the "galloping major" of the

➔ Trevor Francis of Nottingham Forest heads the winning goal past Malmö keeper Jan Moller in Forest's 1–0 victory over the Swedish club at the Munich Olympiastadion in 1979. Forest made it back-to-back wins in 1980 by beating Hamburg 1–0 in Madrid.

➔ Manchester United celebrate in Moscow's Luzhniki Stadium after winning their second Champions League in 2008 following a tense penalty shootout against Chelsea.

great Hungarian team of the 1950s, scoring four goals and Di Stéfano, a hat-trick.

Real's run came to an end the next season in the second round, beaten by a Barcelona side inspired by great Hungarians of their own in Ladislav Kubala and Sandor Kocsis. Their dream of glory was shattered, however, when they lost the 1961 final 3–2 to Portuguese outsiders Benfica.

The Eagles of Lisbon contained the bulk of the Portuguese national side and would go on to play in five finals during the 1960s, and win two of them. Their star was Mozambique-born striker Eusébio who struck twice with Benfica, who won a second cup in 1962, beating Real Madrid 5–3 despite Puskás scoring another hat-trick. In 1963, the Lisbon Eagles appeared in their third consecutive final, but lost 2–1 to Italy's Milan.

Milan's victory was the first of three for the city of Milan in the mid-1960s, as their city rivals Internazionale emerged to win the trophy in 1964 and 1965. Coached by the legendary Helenio Herrera, Inter fielded a host of international stars including Italy's Giuliano Sarti, Tarcisio Burgnich, Giacinto Facchetti and Sandro Mazzola, Jair from Brazil plus the Spaniard Luis Suarez. Their victims in these finals were Real Madrid and Benfica.

Real's sixth triumph, in 1966, marked the end of an era in the European Cup. For the first 11 years of its existence, the Cup had only been won by clubs from Latin countries. Now the power-base of European club football shifted to northern Europe – Britain, Holland and Germany, to be precise.

The 1967 final paired Inter with Scotland's Celtic. The Scots, under the guiding hand of the great Jock Stein, won everything open to them that season, rounding off with a fine 2–1 win over the Italians in Lisbon. Manchester United followed up by becoming England's first winners the following season. Benfica were the unfortunate losers again in the final, at Wembley, where Matt Busby's side won 4–1 after

CHAMPIONS CUP FINALS 1987–2017

1987	Porto 2–1 Bayern Munich	VIENNA
1988	PSV Eindhoven 0–0 Benfica *(aet PSV 6–5 on penalties)*	STUTTGART
1989	Milan 4–0 Steaua Bucharest	BARCELONA
1990	Milan 1–0 Benfica	VIENNA
1991	Red Star Belgrade 0–0 Marseille *(aet Red Star 5–3 on penalties)*	BARI
1992	Barcelona 1–0 Sampdoria	LONDON
1993	Marseille 1–0 Milan	MUNICH
1994	Milan 4–0 Barcelona	ATHENS
1995	Ajax 1–0 Milan	VIENNA
1996	Juventus 1–1 Ajax *(aet Juventus 4–2 on penalties)*	ROME
1997	Borussia Dortmund 3–1 Juventus	MUNICH
1998	Real Madrid 1–0 Juventus	AMSTERDAM
1999	Manchester United 2–1 Bayern Munich	BARCELONA
2000	Real Madrid 3–0 Valencia	PARIS
2001	Bayern Munich 1–1 Valencia *(aet Bayern 5–4 on penalties)*	MILAN
2002	Real Madrid 2–1 Bayer Leverkusen	GLASGOW
2003	Milan 0–0 Juventus *(aet Milan 3–2 on penalties)*	MANCHESTER
2004	Porto 3–0 Monaco	GELSENKIRCHEN
2005	Liverpool 3–3 Milan *(aet Liverpool 3–2 on penalties)*	ISTANBUL
2006	Barcelona 2–1 Arsenal	SAINT-DENIS
2007	Milan 2–1 Liverpool	ATHENS
2008	Manchester United 1–1 Chelsea *(aet Manchester United 6–5 on penalties)*	MOSCOW
2009	Barcelona 2–0 Manchester United	ROME
2010	Internazionale 2–0 Bayern Munich	MADRID
2011	Barcelona 3–1 Manchester United	LONDON
2012	Chelsea 1–1 Bayern Munich *(aet Chelsea 4–3 on penalties)*	MUNICH
2013	Bayern Munich 2–1 Borussia Dortmund	LONDON
2014	Real Madrid 4–1 Atlético Madrid	LISBON
2015	Barcelona 3–1 Juventus	BERLIN
2016	Real Madrid 1–1 Atlético Madrid *(aet Real Madrid 5–3 on penalties)*	MILAN
2017	Real Madrid 4–1 Juventus	CARDIFF
2018	Real Madrid 3–1 Liverpool	KIEV

↑ Barcelona's Lionel Messi celebrates by kissing the Champions League trophy after the Catalans had defeated Manchester United 3–1 at Wembley Stadium. Messi scored the second goal in what was his third Champions League win as a Barcelona player.

extra time with goals by Bobby Charlton, George Best and a young Brian Kidd.

Milan regained the trophy in 1969, with a 4-1 demolition of Ajax in Madrid, but it was the last Latin success in the Cup for 17 years as Holland, Germany and then England dominated during the 1970s and early 1980s.

Feyenoord of Rotterdam were the first Dutch winners, in 1970, before great rivals Ajax won three times in a row, introducing the game to the "total football" style inspired by the great Johan Cruyff. His departure in 1973 saw Ajax cede European command to Bayern Munich. Franz Beckenbauer, Gerd Müller and Co won three cups in a row and were crucial to West Germany's victory over Cruyff's Holland in the 1974 World Cup final.

Now it was England's turn. In 1977, Liverpool clinched the first of six consecutive English victories with a 3-1 win over Germany's Borussia Mönchengladbach. Nottingham Forest and Aston Villa helping extend a monopoly which ended in tragedy in 1985 when 39 Italian fans died in the tragic, hooligan-scarred 1985 final which Liverpool lost 1-0 to Michel Platini's Juventus at the Heysel Stadium in Brussels. Subsequently English clubs were banned from Europe for five years.

In the meantime shootout success paid off twice in three years - for Steaua Bucharest against Terry Venables's Barcelona and for PSV Eindhoven against Benfica - before Milan reclaimed the trophy. Two years in a row they rewarded

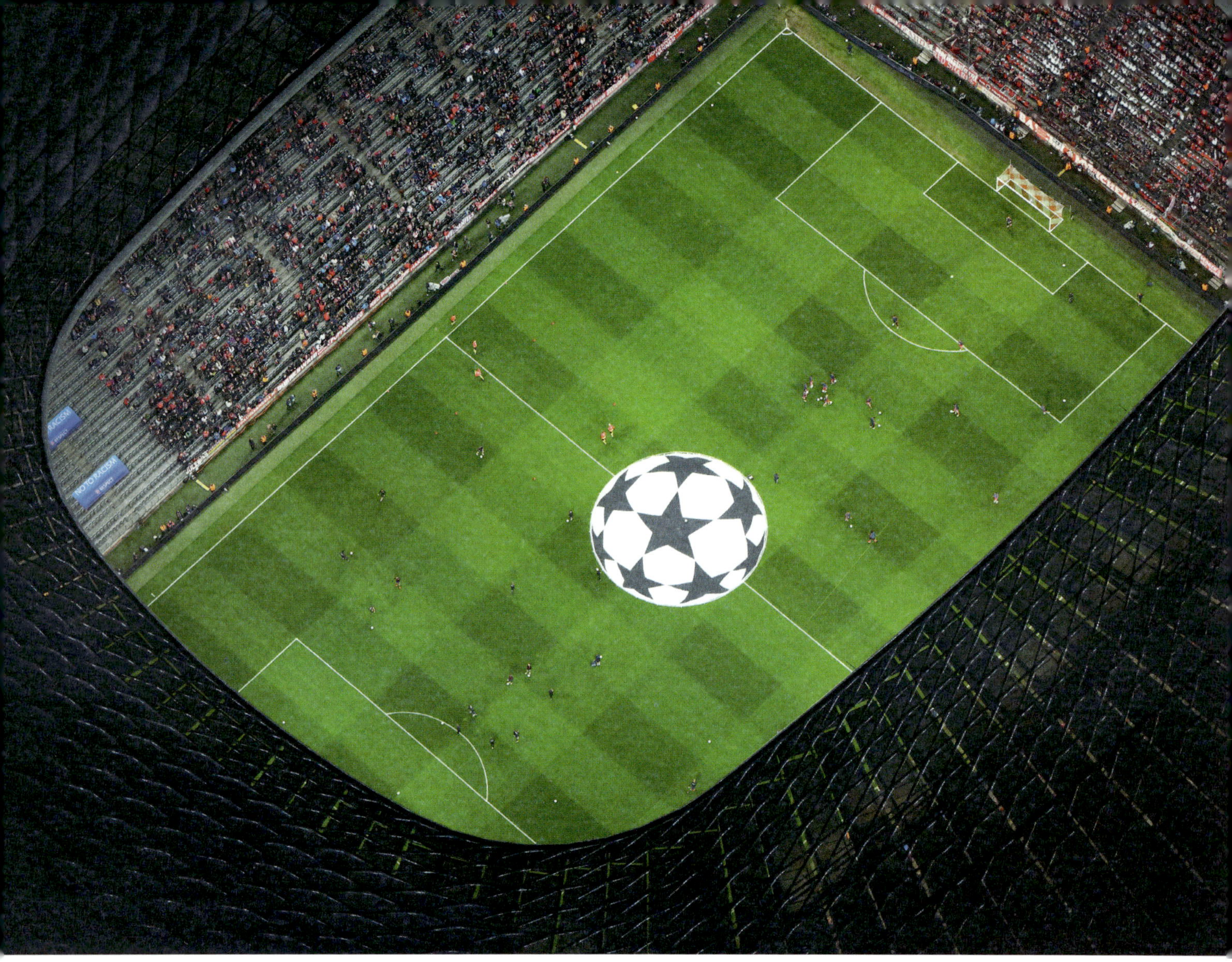

↑ Barcelona were a class apart in 2011 and deserving winners of their fourth Champions League title.

ALL-TIME TOP SCORERS*
LIONEL MESSI & CRISTIANO RONALDO

100 121

* up to and including season 2017/18

media magnate Silvio Berlusconi's investment in the Dutch triumvirate of Ruud Gullit, Marco Van Basten and Frank Rijkaard.

Berlusconi and other directors of the big clubs were instrumental in sparking the evolution toward the present Champions League. They threatened a breakaway super league if UEFA did not provide them with the guarantee of mini-league income. They achieved their aim before Barcelona put a gloss on the saga by winning the cup for the first time. An extra-time rocket from Ronald Koeman edged out Sampdoria at Wembley.

The evolution of the competition to include a group stage was in full flow by the time Manchester United achieved a historic tour de force in 1999. Two goals in injury time from substitutes Teddy Sheringham and Ole-Gunnar Solskjær turned what looked like a sure 1-0 defeat by Bayern Munich into a win. United thus became the first English club to achieve the treble of European Cup, domestic league and FA Cup in the same season.

Spain remained a dominant force, however, with history repeating itself to uncanny effect in 2002. Real Madrid returned to Hampden Park, scene of their most glorious triumph in 1960, to claim a record-extending ninth crown after a 2-1 win over German opposition in the shape of Bayer Leverkusen. Zinedine Zidane volleyed a winning goal as spectacular as anything Di Stéfano or Puskás had produced in their day.

England's glory was aroused in spectacular shootout victories for Liverpool – hitting back from 3-0 to beat Milan in 2005 – and Chelsea, who defeated Bayern against all the odds in Munich.

But command was exerted mostly by the Spanish giants. Barcelona looked to their own superstar, Lionel Messi, in a flowing stream of glorious attacking football which brought four further

400 000 000

ESTIMATED GLOBAL REACH OF TV VIEWERS FOR 2018 FINAL – IN MORE THAN 200 COUNTRIES

PRIZE MONEY 2017-2018

FIRST QUALIFYING ROUND:	€280,000
SECOND QUALIFYING ROUND:	€380,000
THIRD QUALIFYING ROUND:	€480,000
PLAY-OFFS ELIMINATED:	€5,000,000
BASE FEE FOR GROUP STAGE:	€15,250,000
GROUP WIN BONUS:	€2,700,000
GROUP DRAW BONUS:	€900,000
ROUND OF 16:	€9,500,000
QUARTER-FINALS:	€10,500,000
SEMI-FINALS:	€12,000,000
LOSING FINALIST:	€15,000,000
WINNING THE FINAL:	€19,000,000

60%
REAL MADRID
Champions League games won

59%
BARCELONA
Champions League games won

57%
BAYERN MUNICH
Champions League games won

TOP WINNERS BY NATION

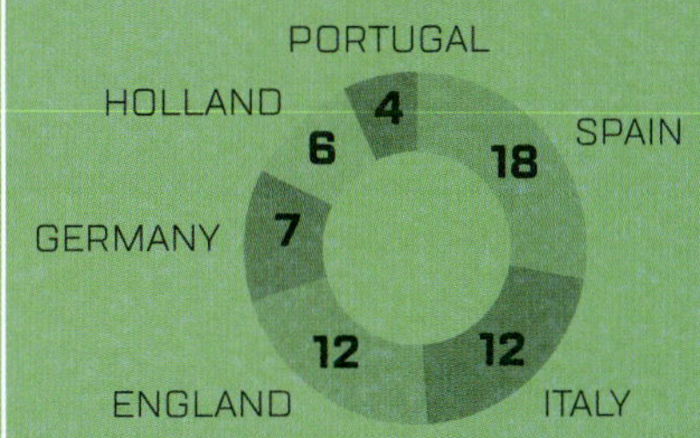

MANAGERS WITH MOST GAMES

190 SIR ALEX FERGUSON

172 ARSÈNE WENGER

144 CARLO ANCELOTTI

135 JOSÉ MOURINHO

triumphs between 2006 and 2015.

Old rivals Real Madrid responded by winning Europe's elite club trophy four times in five seasons between 2014 and 2018. They were the first club to win three in a row since Bayern Munich in the 1970s, and the first to defend the crown in the Champions League era. Cristiano Ronaldo struck decisively in victories over Atlético Madrid (twice) and Juventus, while Wales's Gareth Bale converted one of the greatest goals in the competition's history in the 2018 defeat of Liverpool.

Ronaldo's contest with Messi, both in European and Spanish competitions, was the defining individual duel of the era in world football. For veterans it was all eerily reminiscent of the early days of the Champions Cup when Di Stéfano and Kubala ruled the club game.

➔ Real Madrid's Sergio Ramos lifts the Champions League trophy after the 2018 final between Real Madrid and Liverpool when a pulsating match finished 3–1.

Europa League

Just as UEFA was coming to life in 1954, FIFA vice-president Ernst Thommen devised a European competition to test teams from cities known for their international trade or industrial fairs. The original title was the cumbersome International Inter-Cities Fairs Cup and the first edition was an equally clumsy affair. Taking four years, between 1955 and 1958, Barcelona drew 2–2 with, then finally crushed, a London Select XI 6–0 in the final.

Barcelona repeated the trick in the 1958-60 tournament. A team built around Hungarian émigrés Ladislav Kubala, Sandor Kocsis and Zoltan Czibor retained the trophy undefeated.

Their opponents were again English, this time Birmingham City, the first British club with the honour of having reached a European final. A 0-0 draw at St Andrew's set up Barcelona for the 4-1 return win, with goals by Eulogio Martinez, Czibor (two) and Luis Coll.

Barcelona had been playing simultaneously in the European Champions Cup but the pressure, and Roma, overtook them in 1961. Valencia (twice) and Zaragoza reclaimed Spanish command before a European trophy headed east for the first time. Hungary's Ferencváros defeated Juventus in a one-off final in Turin with a late goal from left-winger Matos Fenyvesi.

Barcelona won a third trophy in 1966 against fellow Spaniards Zaragoza but only to presage an era of English dominance. Leeds reached the 1967 final, where they lost to Dinamo Zagreb, but made amends the next season by beating Ferencváros 1-0 overall. This was the first of six consecutive English victories in the late 1960s and early 1970s.

UEFA claimed full administrative command of the cup to herald a largely northern European era with victories by Tottenham (over Wolverhampton Wanderers), Liverpool (twice), Ipswich, Holland's Feyenoord and PSV Eindhoven as well as Germany's Borussia Mönchengladbach (twice) and Eintracht Frankfurt. Juventus were brief Latin interlopers in 1977, beating a Bilbao side featuring future Spanish federation president and FIFA vice-president Angel Maria Villar.

IFK Gothenburg, Anderlecht, Tottenham and Real Madrid all celebrated in turn with Madrid looking

FAIRS CUP* FINALS

1958	London XI 2–2 Barcelona Barcelona 6–0 London XI
1960	Birmingham City 0–0 Barcelona Barcelona 4–1 Birmingham City
1961	Birmingham City 2–2 Roma Roma 2–0 Birmingham City
1962	Valencia 6–2 Barcelona Barcelona 1–1 Valencia
1963	Dinamo Zagreb 1–2 Valencia Valencia 2–0 Dinamo Zagreb
1964	Real Zaragoza 2–1 Valencia
1965	Juventus 0–1 Ferencváros
1966	Barcelona 0–1 Real Zaragoza Real Zaragoza 2–4 Barcelona
1967	Dinamo Zagreb 2–0 Leeds Utd Leeds Utd 0–0 Dinamo Zagreb
1968	Leeds Utd 1–0 Ferencváros Ferencváros 0–0 Leeds Utd
1969	Newcastle Utd 3–0 Újpest Dózsa Újpest Dózsa 2–3 Newcastle
1970	Anderlecht 3–1 Arsenal Arsenal 3–0 Anderlecht
1971	Juventus 2–2 Leeds Utd Leeds utd 1–1 Juventus *(Leeds won on away goals)*

**In 1972, the Fairs Cup became known as the UEFA Cup. Except for 1964 and 1965, the final was played over two legs, with away goals counting double in the event of a tie.*

Fernando Llorente and Coke of Sevilla celebrate winning a third straight Europa League in 2016.

UEFA CUP MOST APPEARANCES
GIUSEPPE BERGOMI
all for
INTERNAZIONALE

96

twice to the bright new generation of the Quinta del Buitre, starring striker Emilio Butragueño.

For the rest of the 20th century, the UEFA Cup was dominated by Italian clubs, with 14 out of 22 finalists coming from Serie A. Most notable success was that of Napoli in 1989, led by Diego Maradona, his only European club success. Other Italian winners were Juventus, Fiorentina, Internazionale and Parma, propelled to a brief flirtation with the giants by the support of sponsor Parmalat.

The system of entry into the UEFA Cup, based on past record, ensured that countries such as Italy, Germany, Spain and England enjoyed the bias of four entrants each. Hence, UEFA, trying to increase the competition's status and sense of event, introduced a single-match final in 1998 when Inter beat Italian "cousins" Lazio 3-0 in Paris. One year later the UEFA Cup became Europe's only formal second-tier competition after Lazio defeated Mallorca in the last final of the Cup-winners Cup.

In 2000, Galatasaray made history by becoming the first Turkish club not only to reach a European final but to win one, with a shootout victory over Arsenal in Copenhagen. Then, in 2001, Liverpool defeated outsiders Alavés 5-4 in one of the most memorable of all finals in Dortmund. Gerard Houllier's side thus completed a unique English treble in carrying off the two domestic cups plus a European trophy.

More of Europe's classic great "golden oldies" teams, such as Feyenoord, Valencia and Porto (on a one-off "silver goal" against Celtic) followed their example before UEFA tinkered again with the format to mirror the group system of the Champions League.

Spanish clubs dominated the opening decade of the reorganised Europa League, just as they had lorded it over the original Fairs Cup in the 1950s and 1960s. Sevilla landed three in a row to add to two earlier victories, while Atlético Madrid also triumphed three times, most recently by outclassing French home favourites Marseille in Lyon.

UEFA CUP* FINALS

1972 Wolverhampton Wanderers 1–2 Tottenham Hotspur
Tottenham Hotspur 1–1 Wolverhampton Wanderers

1973 Liverpool 3–0 Borussia Mönchengladbach
Borussia Mönchengladbach 2–0 Liverpool

1974 Tottenham Hotspur 2–2 Feyenoord
Feyenoord 2–0 Tottenham Hotspur

1975 Borussia Mönchengladbach 0–0 Twente
Twente 1–5 Borussia Mönchengladbach

1976 Liverpool 3–2 Club Brugge
Club Brugge 1–1 Liverpool

1977 Juventus 1–0 Athletic Bilbao
Athletic Bilbao 2–1 Juventus
(Juventus won on away goals)

1978 Bastia 0–0 PSV Eindhoven
PSV Eindhoven 3–0 Bastia

1979 Red Star Belgrade 1–1 Borussia Mönchengladbach
Borussia Mönchengladbach 1–0 Red Star Belgrade

1980 Borussia Monchengladbach 3–2 Eintracht Frankfurt
Eintracht Frankfurt 1–0 Borussia Mönchengladbach

1981 Ipswich 3–0 AZ Alkmaar
AZ Alkmaar 4–2 Ipswich

1982 IFK Gothenburg 1–0 Hamburg
Hamburg 0–3 IFK Gothenburg

1983 Anderlecht 1–0 Benfica
Benfica 1–1 Anderlecht

1984 Anderlecht 1–1 Tottenham Hotspur
Tottenham Hotspur 1–1 Anderlecht
(aet Tottenham 4–3 on penalties)

1985 Videoton 0–3 Real Madrid
Real Madrid 0–1 Videoton

1986 Real Madrid 5–1 Koln
Koln 2–0 Real Madrid

1987 IFK Gothenburg 1–0 Dundee United
Dundee United 1–1 IFK Gothenburg

1988 Espanyol 3–0 Bayer Leverkusen
Bayer Leverkusen 3–0 Espanyol
(aet Leverkusen 3–2 on penalties)

1989 Napoli 2–1 Stuttgart
Stuttgart 3–3 Napoli

1990 Juventus 3–1 Fiorentina
Fiorentina 0–0 Juventus

1991 Internazionale 2–0 Roma
Roma 1–0 Internazionale

1992 Torino 2–2 Ajax
Ajax 0–0 Torino
(Ajax won on away goals)

1993 Borussia Dortmund 1–3 Juventus
Juventus 3–0 Borussia Dortmund

1994 Salzburg 0–1 Internazionale
Internazionale 1–0 Salzburg

1995 Parma 1–0 Juventus
Juventus 1–1 Parma

1996 Bayern Munich 2–0 Bordeaux
Bordeaux 1–3 Bayern Munich

1997 Schalke 04 1–0 Internazionale
Internazionale 1–0 Schalke 04
(aet Schalke 4–1 on penalties)

1998 Internazionale 3–0 Lazio

1999 Parma 3–0 Marseille

2000 Galatasaray 0–0 Arsenal
(aet Galatasaray 4–1 on penalties)

2001 Liverpool 5–4 Alavés
(Liverpool won on golden goal)

2002 Feyenoord 3–2 Borussia Dortmund

2003 Porto 3–2 Celtic
(Porto won on silver goal)

2004 Valencia 2–0 Marseille 0

2005 CSKA Moscow 3–1 Sporting Lisbon

2006 Sevilla 4–0 Middlesbrough

2007 Sevilla 2–2 Espanyol
(aet Sevilla 3–1 on penalties)

2008 Zenit St Petersburg 2–0 Rangers

2009 Shakhtar Donetsk 2–1 Werder Bremen

EUROPA LEAGUE* FINALS

2010 Atlético Madrid 2-1 Fulham

2011 Porto 1–0 Braga

2012 Atlético Madrid 3–0 Athletic Bilbao

2013 Chelsea 2–1 Benfica

2014 Sevilla 0–0 Benfica
(aet Sevilla 4–2 on penalties)

2015 Sevilla 3–2 Dnipro Dnipropetrovsk

2016 Sevilla 3–1 Liverpool

2017 Manchester United 2–0 Ajax

2018 Atlético Madrid 2–0 Marseille

**The UEFA Cup was played over two legs, with extra time and penalties in the event of a draw. In 1998 the final became a single match with either golden (2001) or silver (2003) goal extra time, although this was later dropped. In 2010 the UEFA Cup became known as the Europa League.*

FIFA Club World Cup

Club football's original world championship was merely a challenge between the champions of Europe and South America. Subsequently, the tournament was opened up to the champion clubs from all of FIFA's six regional confederations.

Henri Delaunay, the general secretary of UEFA, first suggested the idea of a challenge match between the champions of Europe and South America in a letter in 1958 to CONMEBOL, the South American Confederation. CONMEBOL duly launched the Copa Libertadores to create its own champion club.

Up until 1980, matches in the original Intercontinental Club Cup were played on a two-leg, home-and-away basis. A flying start was made in 1960, when Real Madrid met Peñarol of Uruguay. Real, having just won a fifth European Cup, grabbed a goalless draw in Montevideo before Alfredo Di Stéfano and two-goal Ferenc Puskás pounded the Uruguayans 5-1 in Madrid.

In 1961, it was Peñarol's turn to chalk up five goals, this time against Portugal's Benfica. The Eagles of Lisbon had no more luck in 1962 when they were crushed by Brazil's Santos and their young star, Pelé.

However, after this bright start, the cup ran into severe problems in the late 1960s and early 1970s as clashes of continental styles descended into violence. The 1967 series between Argentina's Racing Club and Scotland's Celtic reached the nadir in a play-off in Montevideo. Six players were sent off before Racing won 1-0.

Next up for South America, for three years running, were Estudiantes de La Plata of Argentina. In 1968, they battered out a victory over Manchester United, who had Nobby Stiles sent off and Bobby Charlton taken off with a shin injury.

Worse was to follow. Milan won in 1969 despite striker Nestor Combin having his nose broken and Pierino Prati being kicked in the back while receiving treatment. A year later, Feyenoord survived similar treatment, prompting Ajax, in 1971, to refuse to play Uruguay's Nacional.

Further European withdrawals prompted a revamp in the 1980s with the two-legged tie being replaced by a single game in Japan at the behest of local officials and sponsors targeting a bid to host the World Cup.

A 3-0 victory in 1981 for Flamengo, starring Zico and Junior, over Liverpool, was the one memorable display of football in a series undermined by cool temperatures and hard pitches in Tokyo and then Yokohama. European clubs won 13 times against 12 successes for South America in the years before FIFA stepped in.

The world governing body, envious at the sums being raised by UEFA through club football, launched its own Club World Championship in 1999. The first such event, won by Corinthians of São Paulo in Brazil, proved a false start because of cash issues. However, in 2005, FIFA then took over the December slot and Japanese venue for an expanded tournament.

INTERCONTINENTAL CUP* FINALS

1960	Peñarol 0–0 Real Madrid Real Madrid 5–1 Peñarol *Real Madrid won on points*
1961	Benfica 1–0 Peñarol Peñarol 5–0 Benfica *Peñarol 2–1 Benfica (play-off)*
1962	Santos 3–2 Benfica Benfica 2–5 Santos *Santos won on points*
1963	Milan 4–2 Santos Santos 4–2 Milan *Santos 1–0 Milan (play-off)*
1964	Independiente 1–0 Internazionale Internazionale 2–0 Independiente *Internazionale 1–0 Independiente (play-off)*
1965	Internazionale 3-0 Independiente Independiente 0–0 Internazionale *Internazionale won on points*
1966	Peñarol 2–0 Real Madrid Real Madrid 0–2 Peñarol *Peñarol won on points*
1967	Celtic 1–0 Racing Club Racing Club 2–1 Celtic *Racing Club 1–0 Celtic (play-off)*
1968	Estudiantes 1–0 Manchester Utd Manchester Utd 1–1 Estudiantes *Estudiantes won on points*
1969	Milan 3–0 Estudiantes Estudiantes 2–1 Milan *Milan 4–2 on aggregate*
1970	Estudiantes 2–2 Feyenoord Feyenoord 1–0 Estudiantes *Feyenoord 3–2 on aggregate*
1971	Panathinaikos 1–1 Nacional Nacional 2–1 Panathinaikos *Nacional 3–2 on aggregate*
1972	Independiente 1–1 Ajax Ajax 3-0 Independiente *Ajax 4–1 on aggregate*
1973	Independiente 1–0 Juventus
1974	Independiente 1–0 Atlético Madrid Atlético Madrid 2–0 Independiente *Atlético Madrid 2–1 on aggregate*
1975	not played
1976	Bayern Munich 2–0 Cruzeiro Cruzeiro 0–0 Bayern Munich *Bayern Munich 2–0 on aggregate*
1977	Boca Juniors 2–2 Borussia Mönchengladbach Borussia Mönchengladbach 0–3 Boca Juniors *Boca Juniors 5–2 on aggregate*
1978	not played
1979	Malmö 0–1 Olimpia Olimpia 2–1 Malmö *Olimpia 3–1 on aggregate*
1980	Nacional 1–0 Nottingham Forest
1981	Flamengo 3–0 Liverpool
1982	Peñarol 2–0 Aston Villa
1983	Grêmio 2–1 Hamburg
1984	Independiente 1–0 Liverpool
1985	Juventus 2–2 Argentinos Juniors *(aet Juventus 4–2 on penalties)*
1986	River Plate 1–0 Steaua Bucharest
1987	Porto 2–1 Peñarol
1988	Nacional 2–2 PSV Eindhoven *(aet Nacional 7–6 on penalties)*
1989	Milan 1–0 Nacional
1990	Milan 3–0 Olimpia
1991	Red Star Belgrade 3–0 Colo-Colo
1992	São Paulo 2–1 Barcelona
1993	São Paulo 3–2 Milan
1994	Vélez Sarsfield 2–0 Milan
1995	Ajax 0–0 Gremio *(aet Ajax 4–3 on penalties)*
1996	Juventus 1–0 River Plate
1997	Borussia Dortmund 2–0 Cruzeiro
1998	Real Madrid 2–1 Vasco da Gama
1999	Manchester United 1–0 Palmeiras
2000	Boca Juniors 2–1 Real Madrid
2001	Bayern Munich 1–0 Boca Juniors
2002	Real Madrid 2–0 Olimpia
2003	Boca Juniors 1–1 Milan *(aet Boca 3–1 on penalties)*
2004	Porto 0–0 Once Caldas *(aet Porto 8–7 on penalties)*

FIFA CLUB WORLD CUP FINALS

2000	Corinthians 0–0 Vasco Da Gama *(aet Corinthians 4–3 on penalties)*
2005	São Paulo 1–0 Liverpool
2006	Internacional 1–0 Barcelona
2007	Milan 4–2 Boca Juniors
2008	Manchester United 1–0 LDU Quito
2009	Barcelona 2-1 Estudiantes
2010	Internazionale 3–0 TP Mazembe
2011	Barcelona 4–0 Santos
2012	Corinthians 1–0 Chelsea
2013	Bayern Munich 2–0 Raja Casablanca
2014	Real Madrid 2–0 San Lorenzo
2015	Barcelona 3–0 River Plate
2016	Real Madrid 4–2 Kashima Antlers
2017	Real Madrid 1–0 Gremio

**From 1960 to 1968, the Intercontinental Cup was decided over two legs on points, with a play-off if the points were level. From 1969 to 1979, the final was decided on the aggregate scores over two legs. From 1980 onwards it was a one-off match held in Japan.*

Opening it up meant nothing, however, in term of competitive balance. The subsequent years brought 10 wins for Europe and only a mere three even for South America. Only three times did outsiders even reach the final, in the shape of TP Mazembe from DR Congo (2010), Raja Casablanca (2013) and Kashima Antlers (2016). The trio duly lost to Internazionale, Bayern Munich and Real Madrid respectively.

Real Madrid players show off the FIFA World Club Cup and their winners' medals after defeating the Argentine club San Lorenzo 2–0 in the 2014 final, held in Morocco.

The Bayern Munich team celebrates winning the FIFA Wolrd Club Cup for the first time after its 2–0 victory over Raja Casablanca in 2013.

CAF Champions League

Africa's senior club competition was launched in 1964 as the African Champions Cup at the behest of ambitious clubs in Francophone countries eager to copy the European model. Soon the event attracted entries from across all of Africa though financial and transport problems have proved an ongoing headache for organisers.

First winners were Cameroon's side Oryx Douala, who beat Stade Malien of Mali 2–1 in a one-off final. No competition was organised in 1965 but action resumed in 1966, when the first two-leg final ended in Stade d'Abidjan of the Ivory Coast defeating another Malian club, Real Bamako, 5-4 on aggregate. Between 1971 and 1980, clubs from Cameroon and Guinea dominated with Canon Yaoundé and Hafia Conakry both claiming a hat-trick of titles.

Since then, Northern African clubs have taken over, led by Egyptian rivals Al Ahly (eight wins) and Zamalek (five). Al Ahly were also runners-up three times including in 2017 against Wydad of Morocco. The 2010 champions TP Mazembe went on to become the first African side to reach the FIFA Club World Cup final.

CONCACAF Champions League

The premier club competition for the Central American and Caribbean regions has been contested since 1962, albeit on a confused basis because it does not end within the "proper" calendar year. The winners qualify for the FIFA Club World Cup.

Mexican sides have dominated with 34 triumphs overall. America FC are the most successful club with seven victories, followed by fellow Mexicans Cruz Azul with six. They are two of the only four teams to have defended the league title successfully. The others are Pachuca and Monterrey. The second most successful country is Costa Rica with six titles in total.

AFC Champions League

Asia's club championship is the most challenging in all FIFA's six regional confederations because of the size and breadth of the continent. A first Champions Cup was contested in 1967 when Hapoel Tel-Aviv were winners before Israel was expelled from the confederation.

The tournament was then abandoned until a revival in 1985 as the Asian Club Championship. This was followed by conversion into the AFC Champions League in 2002. The top club of the modern era are South Korea's Pohang Steelers with three titles. The 2016 winners, Korea's Jeonbuk Hyundai Motors, were barred from a title defence because of a domestic bribery scandal. Urawa Red Diamonds subsequently became Japan's first winners in nine years.

Club América midfielder Osvaldo Martinez leaps onto teammate Dario Benedetto to celebrate the striker's third goal in the second leg of the CONCACAF Champions League final against Montreal Impact in 2015.

CAF CHAMPIONS LEAGUE FINALS

1965	Oryx Douala (Cameroon)
1966	Stade d'Abidjan (Ivory Coast)
1967	TP Englebert (DR Congo)
1968	TP Englebert (DR Congo)
1969	Ismaily (Egypt)
1970	Asante Kotoko (Ghana)
1971	Canon Yaoundé (Cameroon)
1972	Hafia (Guinea)
1973	AS Vita Club (Zaïre)
1974	CARA Brazzaville (Congo)
1975	Hafia (Guinea)
1976	MC Alger (Algeria)
1977	Hafia (Guinea)
1978	Canon Yaoundé (Cameroon)
1979	Union Douala (Cameroon)
1980	Canon Yaoundé (Cameroon)
1981	JE Tizi-Ouzou (Algeria)
1982	Al Ahly (Egypt)
1983	Asante Kotoko (Ghana)
1984	Zamalek (Egypt)
1985	FAR Rabat (Morocco)
1986	Zamalek (Egypt)
1987	Al Ahly (Egypt)
1988	ES Sétif (Algeria)
1989	Raja Casablanca (Morocco)
1990	JS Kabylie (Algeria)
1991	Club Africain (Tunisia)
1992	Wydad Casablanca (Morocco)
1993	Zamalek (Egypt)
1994	Espérance de Tunis (Tunisia)
1995	Orlando Pirates (S Africa)
1996	Zamalek (Egypt)
1997	Raja Casablanca (Morocco)
1998	ASEC Mimosas (Ivory Coast)
1999	Raja Casablanca (Morocco)
2000	Hearts of Oak (Ghana)
2001	Al Ahly (Egypt)
2002	Zamalek (Egypt)
2003	Enyimba (Nigeria)
2004	Enyimba (Nigeria)
2005	Al Ahly (Egypt)
2006	Al Ahly (Egypt)
2007	Etoile du Sahel (Tunisia)
2008	Al Ahly (Egypt)
2009	TP Mazembe (DR Congo)
2010	TP Mazembe (DR Congo)
2011	Espérance de Tunis (Tunisia)
2012	Al Ahly (Egypt)
2013	Al Ahly (Egypt)
2014	ES Sétif (Algeria)
2015	TP Mazembe (DR Congo)
2016	Mamelodi Sundowns (S Africa)
2017	Wydad Casablanca (Morocco)

CONCACAF CHAMPIONS LEAGUE FINALS

1962	CD Guadalajara (Mexico)
1963	Racing Club (Haiti)
1967	Alianza (El Salvador)
1968	Toluca (Mexico)
1969	Cruz Azul (Mexico)
1970	Cruz Azul (Mexico)
1971	Cruz Azul (Mexico)
1972	Olimpia (Honduras)
1973	Transvaal (Surinam)
1974	Municipal (Guatemala)
1975	Atlético Español (Mexico)
1976	Aguila (El Salvador)
1977	Club América (Mexico)
1978	Universidad de Guadalajara (Mexico) Comunicaciones (Guatalmala) Defence Force (Trinidad & Tobago)
1979	FAS (El Salvador)
1980	UNAM (Mexico)
1981	Transvaal (Surinam)
1982	UNAM (Mexico)
1983	Atlante (Mexico)
1984	Violette (Haiti)
1985	Defence Force (Trinidad & Tobago)
1986	Alajuelense (Costa Rica)
1987	Club América (Mexico)
1988	Olimpia (Honduras)
1989	UNAM (Mexico)
1990	Club América (Mexico)
1991	Puebla (Mexico)
1992	Club América (Mexico)
1993	Deportivo Saprissa (Costa Rica)
1994	Cartaginés (Costa Rica)
1995	Deportivo Saprissa (Costa Rica)
1996	Cruz Azul (Mexico)
1997	Cruz Azul (Mexico)
1998	DC United (USA)
1999	Necaxa (Mexico)
2000	LA Galaxy (USA)
2002	Pachuca (Mexico)
2003	Toluca (Mexico)
2004	Alajuelense (Costa Rica)
2005	Deportivo Saprissa (Costa Rica)
2006	Club América (Mexico)
2007	Pachuca (Mexico)
2008	Pachuca (Mexico)
2009	Atlante (Mexico)
2010	Pachuca (Mexico)
2011	Monterrey (Mexico)
2012	Monterrey (Mexico)
2013	Monterrey (Mexico)
2014	Cruz Azul (Mexico)
2015	Club América (Mexico)
2016	Club América (Mexico)
2017	Pachuca (Mexico)
2018	Guadalajara (Mexico)

1964–66, 2001 not completed or contested.

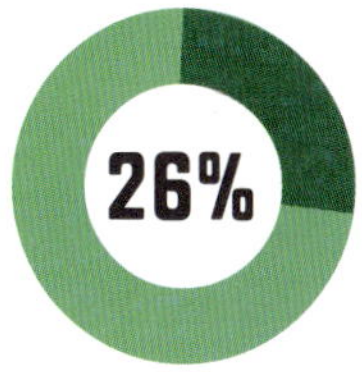

RECORD NUMBER OF CAF CHAMPIONS LEAGUE WINNERS FROM **EGYPT** – 26% OF ALL WINS

RECORD NUMBER OF AFC CHAMPIONS LEAGUE WINNERS FROM **SOUTH KOREA** – 31% OF ALL WINS

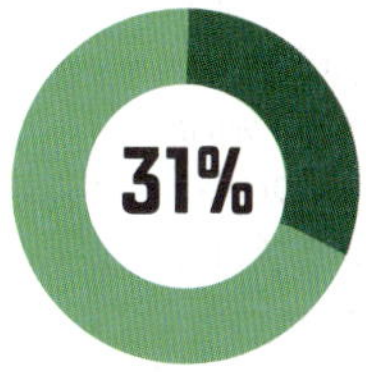

AFC CHAMPIONS LEAGUE FINALS

1967	Hapoel Tel-Aviv (Israel)
1969	Maccabi Tel-Aviv (Israel)
1970	Taj Tehran (Iran)
1971	Maccabi Tel-Aviv (Israel)
1985	Daewoo Royals (S Korea)
1986	Furukawa Electric (Japan)
1987	Yomiuri (Japan)
1989	Al Saad (Qatar)
1990	Liaoning (China)
1991	Esteghlal (Iran)
1991	Al Hilal (Saudi Arabia)
1993	PAS Tehran (Iran)
1994	Thai Farmers Bank (Thailand)
1995	Thai Farmers Bank (Thailand)
1995	Ilhwa Chunma (S Korea)
1997	Pohang Steelers (S Korea)
1998	Pohang Steelers (S Korea)
1999	Jubilo Iwata (Japan)
2000	Al Hilal (Saudi Arabia)
2001	Suwon Bluewings (S Korea)
2002	Suwon Bluewings (S Korea)
2003	Al Ain (UAE)
2004	Al Ittihad (Saudi Arabia)
2005	Al Ittihad (Saudi Arabia)
2006	Jeonbuk Hyundai Motors (S Korea)
2007	Urawa Red Diamonds (Japan)
2008	Gamba Osaka (Japan)
2009	Pohang Steelers (S Korea)
2010	Seongnam Ilhwa Chunma (S Korea)
2011	Al Sadd (Qatar)
2012	Ulsan Hyundai (S Korea)
2013	Guangzhou Evergrande (China)
2014	Western Sydney Wanderers (Aus)
2015	Guangzhou Evergrande (China)
2016	Jeonbuk Hyundai Motors (S Korea)
2017	Urawa Red Diamonds (Japan)

1968, 1972–84, 1988, 1992, 1996 not contested. Two finals contested in 1991 and 1995.

Copa Libertadores

⬆ Rever (left) from Atlético Mineiro of Brazil tussles with Eduardo Aranda from Olimpia of Paraguay, during the second leg of their Libertadores Cup final in Belo Horizonte, Brazil, on 24 July 2013.

	COPA LIBERTADORES*
1960	Peñarol (Uruguay)
1961	Peñarol (Uruguay)
1962	Santos (Brazil)
1963	Santos (Brazil)
1964	Independiente (Argentina)
1965	Independiente (Argentina)
1966	Peñarol (Uruguay)
1967	Racing Club (Argentina)
1968	Estudiantes (Argentina)
1969	Estudiantes (Argentina)
1970	Estudiantes (Argentina)
1971	Nacional (Uruguay)
1972	Independiente (Argentina)
1973	Independiente (Argentina)
1974	Independiente (Argentina)
1975	Independiente (Argentina)
1976	Cruzeiro (Brazil)
1977	Boca Juniors (Argentina)
1978	Boca Juniors (Argentina)
1979	Olimpia (Paraguay)
1980	Nacional (Uruguay)
1981	Flamengo (Brazil)

South America's premier club event has had a long history of problems both on and off the pitch.

A one-off South American Champion Clubs Cup had been organized by Chile's Colo Colo in 1948 but the competition, won by Brazil's Vasco da Gama, had been a financial disaster. In 1960, the Copa Libertadores was launched in response to UEFA's proposition that South America's best should face Europe's champions for a world title.

The first two competitions were won by Uruguay's Peñarol with prolific Alberto Pedro Spencer scoring in both final victories over Olimpia of Paraguay and Brazil's Palmeiras. He remains overall top scorer with 54 goals.

Next year, 1962, the initial knockout event was replaced by a group system which has remained the format ever since. Peñarol's final clash with Pelé's Santos resulted in the first of many unsavoury incidents to scar the Copa. The Montevideo leg ended in a 2–1 win for Santos but the second leg took three and a half hours because of suspensions after both referee and a linesman were knocked unconscious by missiles thrown from the crowd. In the end, Santos won a play-off 3-0.

Argentina boasts the most victories (24) followed by Brazil (18) and Uruguay (eight). Independiente's seven triumphs has established them as the most successful club in the Copa's history, followed by Boca Juniors (six) and Peñarol (five).

TOP SCORER
ALBERTO SPENCER
PEÑAROL

54

1982	Peñarol (Uruguay)
1983	Grêmio (Brazil)
1984	Independiente (Argentina)
1985	Argentinos Juniors (Argentina)
1986	River Plate (Argentina)
1987	Peñarol (Uruguay)
1988	Nacional (Uruguay)
1989	Atlético Nacional (Colombia)
1990	Olimpia (Paraguay)
1991	Colo-Colo (Chile)
1992	São Paulo (Brazil)
1993	São Paulo (Brazil)
1994	Vélez Sarsfield (Argentina)
1995	Grêmio (Brazil)
1996	River Plate (Argentina)
1997	Cruzeiro (Brazil)
1998	Vasco da Gama (Brazil)
1999	Palmeiras (Brazil)
2000	Boca Juniors (Argentina)
2001	Boca Juniors (Argentina)
2002	Olimpia (Paraguay)
2003	Boca Juniors (Argentina)
2004	Once Caldas (Colombia)
2005	São Paulo (Brazil)
2006	Internacional (Brazil)
2007	Boca Juniors (Argentina)
2008	LDU Quito (Ecuador)
2009	Estudiantes (Argentina)
2010	Internacional (Brazil)
2011	Santos (Brazil)
2012	Corinthians (Brazil)
2013	Atlético Mineiro (Brazil)
2014	San Lorenzo (Argentina)
2015	River Plate (Argentina)
2016	Atlético Nacional (Colombia)
2017	Grêmio (Brazil)

**The first series was held in 1960, with home and away matches on a knock-out basis. The final is played over two legs, with games won, not goal difference, deciding.*

Copa Sudamericana

South America's secondary club competition was launched in 2002 after dissatisfaction with various short-lived tournaments created to generate revenue for clubs missing out on the Copa Libertadores. First winners were Argentina's San Lorenzo who, invited as winners of the scrapped Copa Mercosur, thrashed Colombia's Atlético Nacional 4-0 on aggregate in the final.

In 2016, the competition drew worldwide headlines for the tragically wrong reasons when a plane carrying Brazil's Chapecoense crashed on the approach to Medellin in Colombia where they were due to play Atlético Nacional in the first leg of the final. The death toll was 71, including 19 of the 22 players, 25 officials and 21 journalists. The final was cancelled and Chapecoense were awarded the cup at the Colombians' suggestion.

COPA SUDAMERICANA* FINALS

2002	San Lorenzo (Argentina)
2003	Cienciano (Peru)
2004	Boca Juniors (Argentina)
2005	Boca Juniors (Argentina)
2006	Pachuca (Mexico)
2007	Arsenal de Sarandi (Argentina)
2008	Internacional (Brazil)
2009	LDU Quito (Ecuador)
2010	Independiente (Argentina)
2011	Universidad de Chile (Chile)
2012	São Paulo (Brazil)
2013	Lanus (Argentina)
2014	River Plate (Argentina)
2015	Santa Fe (Colombia)
2016	Chapecoense (Brazil)
2017	Independiente (Argentina)

**The final is played over two legs, home and away, with the result decided on points. In 2016, the title was awarded to Chapecoense after the plane carrying the team to the first leg crashed, killing most of the first team and coaching staff.*

Fans of the Argentinian club Estudiantes cheer their team on to victory in the 2009 Copa Libertadores final, first leg, against Cruzeiro of Brazil.

UEFA Cup Winners' Cup

⬆ Tottenham become the first English club to win a European trophy.

When Lazio held aloft the Cup Winners' Cup after beating Mallorca at Villa Park, Birmingham, in May 1999, they were also celebrating the end of an era: UEFA was scrapping the tournament to enable expansion of the Champions League and the UEFA Cup.

Launched in 1960-61, one of the initial purposes of the Cup Winners' Cup was to raise the focus on domestic cup competitions that stirred little interest in many European countries. Fiorentina were the first winners, beating Scotland's Rangers in the only two-leg final. Subsequently all the finals were single-match events staged at neutral venues.

Fiorentina lost their grip on the cup the next year in a replayed final against Atlético Madrid. Atlético were back the following year, 1963, but found Tottenham Hotspur invincible in Rotterdam. Spurs wrote their name into history as England's first European winners with a 5-1 victory on goals from Jimmy Greaves and Terry Dyson (two each) and John White.

In 1969, the original draw was abandoned after Soviet troops entered Czechoslovakia, and a new draw, keeping East and West apart, was made. Most Eastern countries, with the exception of Czechoslovakia, withdrew in protest but its own Slovan Bratislava, ironically, lifted the trophy.

In 1974, Magdeburg beat Milan to become the only East German winners of a European trophy before Ukraine's Kiev Dynamo (twice) and Georgia's Dynamo Tbilisi proved impressively skilful winners for the Soviet Union. Along the way, Anderlecht enjoyed a commanding three years in which they carried off the trophy twice and were

CUP WINNERS' CUP FINALS

1961	Rangers 0–2 Fiorentina Fiorentina 2–1 Rangers *Fiorentina won 4–1 on aggregate*
1962	Atlético Madrid 1–1 Fiorentina Atlético Madrid 3–0 Fiorentina *(replay)*
1963	Tottenham Hotspur 5–1 Atlético Madrid
1964	Sporting Lisbon 3–3 MTK Budapest Sporting Lisbon 1–0 MTK Budapest *(replay)*
1965	West Ham United 2–0 TSV 1860 Munich 1860
1966	Borussia Dortmund 2–1 Liverpool
1967	Bayern Munich 1–0 Rangers
1968	Milan 2–0 Hamburg
1969	Slovan Bratislava 3–2 Barcelona
1970	Manchester City 2–1 Gornik Zabrze
1971	Chelsea 1–1 Real Madrid Chelsea 2–1 Real Madrid *(replay)*
1972	Rangers 3–2 Dynamo Moscow
1973	Milan 1–0 Leeds United
1974	FC Magdeburg 2–0 Milan
1975	Dynamo Kiev 3–0 Ferencváros
1976	Anderlecht 4–2 West Ham Utd
1977	Hamburg 2–0 Anderlecht
1978	Anderlecht 4–0 Austria Vienna
1979	Barcelona 4–3 Fortuna Dusseldorf
1980	Valencia 0–0 Arsenal *(aet Valencia 5–4 on penalties)*
1981	Dynamo Tbilisi 2–1 Carl Zeiss Jena
1982	Barcelona 2–1 Standard Liege
1983	Aberdeen 2–1 Real Madrid
1984	Juventus 2–1 Porto
1985	Everton 3–1 Rapid Vienna
1986	Dynamo Kiev 3–0 Atlético Madrid
1987	Ajax 1–0 Lokomotive Leipzig
1988	Mechelen 1–0 Ajax
1989	Barcelona 2–0 Sampdoria
1990	Sampdoria 2–0 Anderlecht
1991	Manchester Utd 2–1 Barcelona
1992	Werder Bremen 2–0 Monaco
1993	Parma 3–1 Royal Antwerp
1994	Arsenal 1–0 Parma
1995	Real Zaragoza 2–1 Arsenal
1996	Paris Saint-Germain 1–0 Rapid Vienna
1997	Barcelona 1–0 Paris Saint-Germain
1998	Chelsea 1–0 Stuttgart
1999	Lazio 2–1 Mallorca

➔ Goalkeeper Manuel Neuer of Bayern Munich celebrates after keeping out the decisive penalty from Romelu Lukaku of Chelsea to win the UEFA Super Cup final in 2013.

runners-up once to Hamburg.

The 1979 tournament produced the highest-scoring final as Barcelona beat Fortuna Dusseldorf 4–3 in Basel while Everton, in 1985, were the last English winners before the five-year ban prompted by the Heysel Stadium tragedy. Manchester United celebrated England's return in 1991 by defeating Barcelona 2–1.

All in all, 16 clubs from 11 countries won the Cup Winners' Cup: Barcelona (four), Anderlecht, Milan, Chelsea and Kiev Dynamo (two each) being the only multiple winners.

European Super Cup

The European Super Cup was brought to life in 1972. European champions Ajax refused to play the World Club Cup after violence visited upon Milan and Feyenoord in previous years. So they arranged a two-leg clash with Scotland's Rangers, holders of the Cup Winners' Cup, instead.

After the creation of the Champions League group system, UEFA threatened to squeeze the Super Cup out of existence and rescheduled it as a European competitions' curtain-raiser. Initially, it was staged in Monaco at the end of August but then UEFA decided to spread it around cities and countries that were unlikely to ever stage one of the major finals.

OFC Champions League

The Oceania confederation had launched a regional club championship in 1987 when the original Qantas Pacific Champions' Cup was staged as a single-venue competition in Adelaide. Hosts Adelaide City beat New Zealand's Mount Wellington 4–1 on penalties after a 1–1 draw in the final. Only four other intermittent tournaments were staged before the event was converted into the annual OFC Champions League in 2007.

By then Australia had left Oceania for Asia, so New Zealand dominated the subsequent decade with Auckland City winning seven years in a row until 2017. The only Kiwi slip-up saw Waitakere United beaten 4-2 on aggregate in 2009-10 by outsiders Hekari United from Papua New Guinea. By now the Oceania champions had the extra lure of entry into the FIFA Club World Cup.

UEFA SUPER CUP

1972	Ajax
1973	Ajax
1974	*Not contested*
1975	Dynamo Kiev
1976	Anderlecht
1977	Liverpool
1978	Anderlecht
1979	Nottingham Forest
1980	Valencia
1982	Aston Villa
1983	Aberdeen
1984	Juventus
1986	Steaua Bucharest
1987	Porto
1988	Mechelen
1989	Milan
1990	Milan
1991	Manchester United
1992	Barcelona
1993	Parma
1994	Milan
1995	Ajax
1996	Juventus
1997	Barcelona
1998	Chelsea
1999	Lazio
2000	Galatasaray
2001	Liverpool
2002	Real Madrid
2003	Milan
2004	Valencia
2005	Liverpool
2006	Sevilla
2007	Milan
2008	Zenit St Petersburg
2009	Barcelona
2010	Atlético Madrid
2011	Barcelona
2012	Atlético Madrid
2013	Bayern Munich
2014	Real Madrid
2015	Barcelona
2016	Real Madrid
2017	Real Madrid

OFC CHAMPIONS LEAGUE

1987	Adelaide City (Australia)
1999	South Melbourne (Australia)
2001	Wollongong Wolves (Australia)
2005	Sydney FC (Australia)
2006	Auckland City (New Zealand)
2007	Waitakere United (New Zealand)
2008	Waitakere United (New Zealand)
2009	Auckland City (New Zealand)
2010	Hekari United (Papua New Guinea)
2011	Auckland City (New Zealand)
2012	Auckland City (New Zealand)
2013	Auckland City (New Zealand)
2014	Auckland City (New Zealand)
2015	Auckland City (New Zealand)
2016	Auckland City (New Zealand)
2017	Auckland City (New Zealand)
2018	Team Wellington (New Zealand)

1988–98, 2002–04 not contested.

1916-2016

4

FOOTBALL NATIONS

Football developed internationally just as the world was adjusting to the concept of the nation state, and FIFA was created out of the need to offer nations an international sporting platform within the football family. However, political interference is frowned upon, while a sense of fraternal community is encouraged.

AFRICA

Africa has supplied a steady stream of outstanding players to the game for years but it is only in the past two decades that its strength and potential have been recognized. The reason for this lies partly in the fact that for many years outstanding soccer players were either unable to gain access to the international stage or were lured away to play for European nations. France 'adopted' the Moroccan-born stars Just Fontaine and Larbi Ben Barek while Portugal capitalized on Mozambique for the likes of Eusebio.

The African confederation was created in Lisbon in 1956 during the FIFA Congress. Egypt, Ethiopia, South Africa and Sudan were the founding members of the Confédération Africaine de Football (CAF) and the African Nations Cup.

FIFA TEAM RANKINGS (as of June 2018)

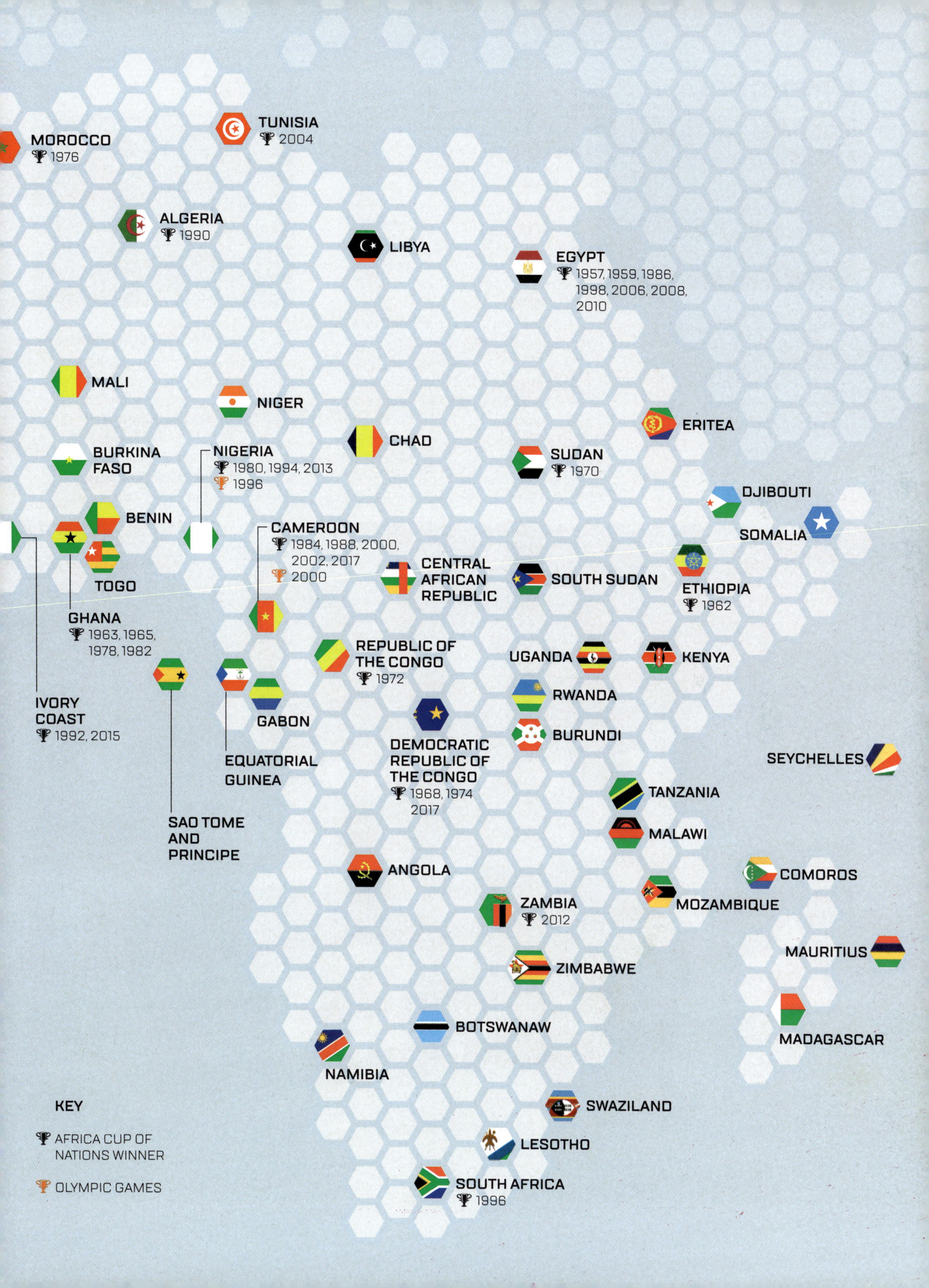

MOROCCO
1976
TUNISIA
2004
ALGERIA
1990
LIBYA
EGYPT
1957, 1959, 1986, 1998, 2006, 2008, 2010
MALI
NIGER
CHAD
ERITEA
BURKINA FASO
NIGERIA
1980, 1994, 2013
1996
SUDAN
1970
DJIBOUTI
SOMALIA
BENIN
CAMEROON
1984, 1988, 2000, 2002, 2017
2000
CENTRAL AFRICAN REPUBLIC
SOUTH SUDAN
ETHIOPIA
1962
TOGO
GHANA
1963, 1965, 1978, 1982
REPUBLIC OF THE CONGO
1972
UGANDA
KENYA
RWANDA
IVORY COAST
1992, 2015
GABON
BURUNDI
DEMOCRATIC REPUBLIC OF THE CONGO
1968, 1974 2017
EQUATORIAL GUINEA
SEYCHELLES
TANZANIA
MALAWI
SAO TOME AND PRINCIPE
ANGOLA
COMOROS
ZAMBIA
2012
MOZAMBIQUE
MAURITIUS
ZIMBABWE
BOTSWANAW
MADAGASCAR
NAMIBIA
SWAZILAND
LESOTHO
SOUTH AFRICA
1996
KEY
AFRICA CUP OF NATIONS WINNER
OLYMPIC GAMES

Cameroon

Cameroon Football Federation founded 1959	
FIFA affiliated 1962	Cup of Nations 1984 1988 2000 2002 2017

Cameroon have made by far the biggest impact of all the African nations to have reached the World Cup finals. Making their debut at the finals in Spain in 1982, they drew their three first round games, one against eventual winners Italy, but were eliminated. They qualified again in 1990, beating reigning champions Argentina in the opening match before reaching the quarterfinals where they lost in extra time to England. However, in 1994, the "Indomitable Lions" were disappointing, torn apart by internal strife. Administrative, managerial and financial problems also contributed to their inability to progress beyond the first round of the finals in 1996, 2002, 2010 and 2014.

Cameroon can take pride, in between, in becoming only the second African nation to win the Olympic title. They secured a historic Games gold in 2000 in Sydney by defeating Spain in a penalty shootout after a 2-2 draw. Cameroon have also won the African Cup of Nations five times, most recently in February 2017 when they came from behind to beat Egypt 2-1 in the final in Libreville, Gabon.

Egypt

Egypt FA founded: 1921	
FIFA affiliated 1923	Cup of Nations 1957 1959 1986 1998 2006 2008 2010

Egypt, in 1923, was the first north African nation to join FIFA. Given this 20-year start on most of their neighbours, it is no surprise that Egypt became one of the great African powers, winning the first two Nations Cups in 1957 and 1959. They finished fourth in the 1928 Olympics and became the first African national team to enter the World Cup in 1934.

Cameroon players mob Joy Nkoulou after he scored his team's first goal in the 2–1 victory over Egypt in the 2017 Africa Cup of Nations in Gabon.

Unquestionably Egypt's brightest star, forward Mohamed Salah helped fire the national team to the 2018 World Cup. He was also named African Footballer of the Year for 2017 after a stellar season playing for Liverpool.

After a dip in success, a revival in the 1970s saw them finish third in the African Nations Cup in 1970 and 1974, fourth in 1976 and reach the Olympic quarter-finals in 1984. They have won the Africa Cup of Nations a record seven times and finished runners-up twice - most recently in February 2017 when they lost 2-1 to Cameroon in the final in Gabon.

Allied to their success at national level, Egyptian clubs are among the most powerful in Africa. Well organised, wealthy and well supported, Egypt's clubs, led by Cairo rivals Al Ahly and Zamalek, have won the African club cups repeatedly.

Ghana

Ghana FA founded	
1957	
FIFA affiliated	**Cup of Nations**
1958	1963 1965 1978 1982

Ghana achieved independence in 1957 and the Black Stars quickly established themselves as a powerful force in African football. They won the Nations Cup at first attempt in 1963, retained the trophy two years later and were runners-up in the following two events. In 1982, Ghana became the first nation to win the Cup four times but it was not until 2006 that they reached the World Cup finals for the first time. They reached the second round both then and in 2010 in South Africa. They faced Uruguay as only the third African team ever to have reached the World Cup quarterfinals. However, star striker Gyan Asamoah missed a penalty against the South Americans with the last kick of extra time and Ghana lost the subsequent penalty shootout.

Ghana have triumphed four times in the Africa Cup of Nations and finished runners-up on five occasions, most recently in 2015.

Nigeria

Nigeria Football Federation founded	
1945	
FIFA affiliated	**Cup of Nations**
1960	1980 1994 2013

Nigeria emerged in the 1990s as one of the most powerful footballing nations in Africa. Earlier their youth teams had led the international way for years. In 1985 they won the World Under-17 Championship - the first African side to win a FIFA world tournament.

In the 1994 World Cup, Nigeria topped their first-round group and almost eliminated eventual finalists Italy in the second round. Two years later they became the first African nation to win the Olympic tournament, beating Argentina in the final.

Not surprisingly, there was plenty of expectation for the 1998 World Cup finals, where they again reached the second round, but lost 4-1 to Denmark. Fallow years followed, finishing bottom of their group in 2002 and missing the 2006 finals before exiting at the group stage once more in 2010. They did reach the second round in 2014 but fell in the first round four years later.

Nigeria have triumphed in the Africa Cup of Nations three times and have been runners-up four times.

Algeria

Algeria Football Federation founded	
1962	
FIFA affiliated	Cup of Nations
1964	1990

The French brought football to Algeria in the late 1880s when major clubs were founded, including future African champions Mouloudia Challia. At the World Cup finals, Algeria made a controversial debut in 1982 when they were squeezed out of a place in the second round by Germany and Austria. They reached the second round for the first time in Brazil in 2014, where they became the first African team to score four times in a single game at the finals in defeating South Korea 4-2 before losing narrowly in the second round to eventual world champions Germany. Surprisingly, Algeria have won the African Cup of Nations only once, as hosts in 1990.

DR Congo

DR Congo Football Federation founded	
1919	
FIFA affiliated	Cup of Nations
1964	1968 1974

DR Congo, then known as Zaíre, won the Africa Cup of Nations twice in six years in 1968 and 1974. This latter occasion was also the year in which they also became the first sub-Saharan African side to qualify for the World Cup finals. Nerves got the better of them in West Germany, however, where they lost 2-0 to Scotland, a humiliating 9-0 to Yugoslavia and 3-0 to Brazil. In the African Cup of Nations the Congolese have failed to emulate their early successes despite promising performances. They finished third in 2015 and were beaten quarter-finalists in 2017.

➋ Didier Drogba of the Ivory Coast embarks on a characteristic driving run between Colombia players during a World Cup group match in 2014.

Ivory Coast

Ivory Coast Football Federation founded	
1960	
FIFA affiliated	Cup of Nations
1964	1992 2015

The Ivory Coast are one of Africa's great football enigmas. The nation has a well-organized league and yet success at international level eluded them until 1992 when "The Elephants" won the African Nations Cup, defeating Ghana on penalties in the final, a feat they repeated in 2015 against the same opposition. Greater European experience among their players helped the Ivorians develop an outstanding national team in the 2000s, and they finished runners-up in the African Cup of Nations in both 2006 and 2012. They also considered themselves unlucky not to progress beyond the first round in both the 2006 and 2010 World Cup finals.

Mali

Mali Football Federation founded
1960

FIFA
1964

Mali have never yet quite fulfilled their potential. They reached the African Cup of Nations final back in 1972, only to fall 3-2 to Congo. Then they did not qualify again until 1994 when they reached the semi-finals. In 2002, Mali finished runners-up as hosts and they reached the semi-finals again in 2004 and 2012. In the meantime, in 2010, they made headlines by hitting back from four goals down to force a 4-4 draw with Angola. Mali are one of several African countries to take advantage of player eligibility rule changes, selecting Frederic Kanoute despite an appearance for France U-21.

Senegal

Senegal Football Federation founded
1960

FIFA affiliated
1964

In international terms, Senegal came from nowhere in sensational style at the 2002 World Cup. A team led by El Hadji Diouf and Khalil Fadiga beat holders France 1-0 in the opening match in Seoul, South Korea, and went on to reach the quarterfinals before losing on a golden goal to Turkey. That good work went to waste, however, as they have not qualified since, and have yet to win the African Cup of Nations, having finished runners-up once, to Cameroon in 2002. Senegal lost 3-2 to Cameroon in a penalty shootout after a goalless extra-time draw in Bamako, Mali.

Tunisia

Tunisia Football Federation founded
1957

FIFA affiliated
1960

Cup of Nations
2004

Tunisia have appeared five times in the World Cup finals including three times in a row: in 1998, 2002 and 2006. Scoring goals proved a problem on all three occasions however as they managed a total of only four goals and twice finished bottom of their group. However, French manager Roger Lemerre gave fans plenty to celebrate by guiding them to victory as hosts in the 2004 African Nations Cup, beating neighbours Morocco 2-1 in the final. Their hero was four-goal striker Francileudo Santos who had been born in Brazil, had played in France and was granted citizenship only weeks before the tournament began.

Morocco

Morocco Football Federation founded
1955

FIFA affiliated
1960

Cup of Nations
1976

Morocco first qualified for the World Cup finals in 1970 when they gave West Germany a fright before losing 2-1 in the second round. They qualified again in 1986 and won their group before losing to the Germans again. At the 1998 World Cup they were possibly the unluckiest side. They thought they had qualified for the second stage after a 3-0 victory over Scotland, but Norway beat Brazil to steal second spot in the group. Morocco have won the African Cup of Nations once, in 1976. In 2015, they were favourites to win as hosts but, weeks before the kick off, the government withdrew as host for fear of visiting fans spreading the Zika virus.

South Africa

South Africa FA founded
1991

FIFA affiliated
1992

Cup of Nations
1996

South Africa made history as first African hosts of the World Cup finals in 2010. A courageous decision by FIFA was rewarded with a fanatically supported and controversy-free event. The only local disappointment was that South Africa's own national team made unwanted history as the first host side not to progress beyond the first round. At least international projection of the finals taught the rest of the world about the country's passion for football which had been most popularly evidenced for years locally by the fierce rivalry of Soweto's Kaizer Chiefs and Orlando Pirates.

Zambia

Zambia FA founded
1929

FIFA affiliated
1964

Cup of Nations
2012

Zambia's national side have been semi-finalists in the African Cup of Nations four times but went further only in 2012 when they secured success by defeating Ivory Coast 8-7 on penalties. Along the way, Zambia marked their steady progress by pulling off a brilliant victory over Italy in the 1988 Olympic Games. Sadly, Zambia will always be remembered for the 1993 plane crash that killed the entire national squad - bar the five overseas-based professionals who were not travelling with them. Astonishingly, the Zambians rebuilt their squad around their five exports, and went on to reach the 1994 African Cup of Nations final.

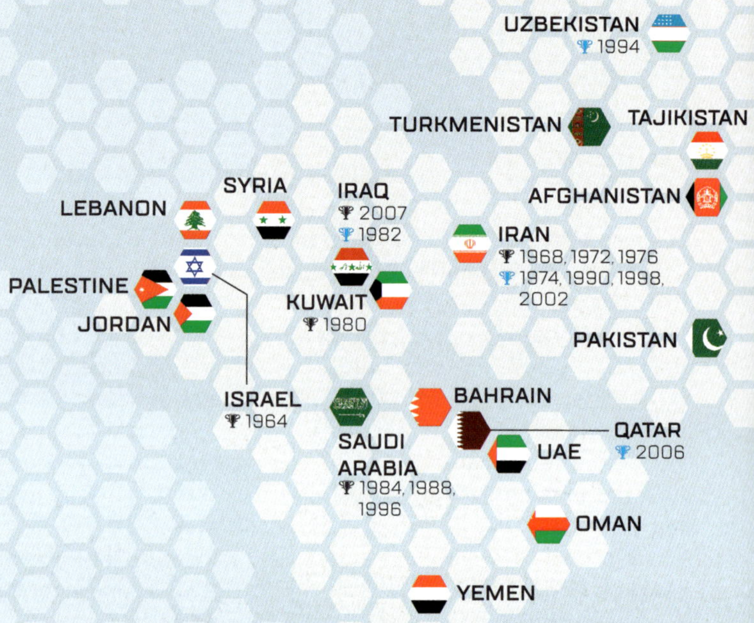

ASIA

Asian football's regional confederation was founded in the same year as Europe's UEFA, in 1954. Originally it had nine members: Hong Kong, India, Indonesia, Japan, Malaysia, Philippines, Singapore, South Korea and South Vietnam. Israel joined in 1956 followed by other eastern and southern Asian nations and then the Middle Eastern and Gulf states. The more members who signed up, however, meant more political problems, largely concerning Israel, which was eventually forced out. Asia's status within world football took a major leap forward with the staging of the World Cup finals in Japan and South Korea in 2002.

FIFA TEAM RANKINGS (as of June 2018)

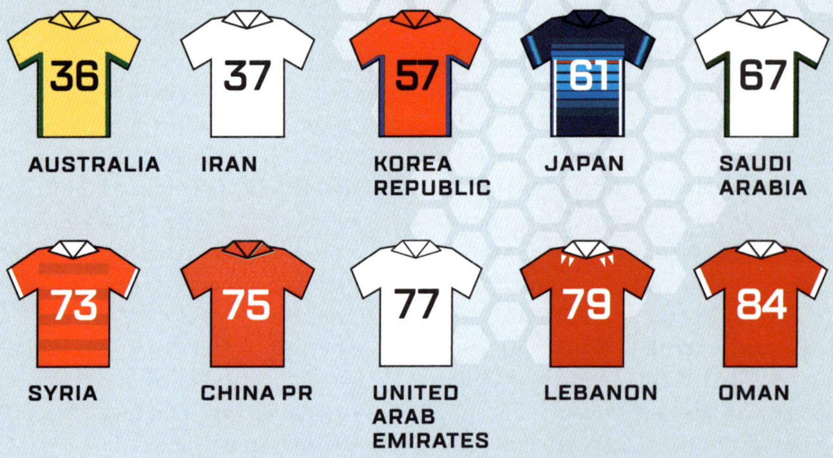

MONGOLIA
KYRGYZSTAN
NORTH KOREA
1978
CHINA
JAPAN
1992, 2000, 2004, 2011
2010
SOUTH KOREA
1956, 1960
1970, 1978, 1986, 2014
NEPAL
BHUTAN
TAIWAN
1954, 1958
MYANAMAR
1966, 1970
HONG KONG
INDIA
1951, 1962
BANGLADESH
MACAU
LAOS
VETNAM
GUAM
THAILAND
PHILIPPINES
CAMBODIA
MALAYSIA
SRI LANKA
BRUNEI
SINGAPORE
INDONESIA
MALDIVES
TIMOR-LESTE
AUSTRALIA
2015
KEY
ASIAN CUP
ASIAN GAMES

Australia

Australia Football Federation founded 1961	
FIFA affiliated 1963	AFC Asian Cup 2015

Football has struggled to gain a foothold down under, with Aussie rules and both codes of rugby being the football sports of choice. Hence the game is known locally as soccer, the 19th century English alternative title is taken up for similar reasons as in the United States.

"The Socceroos" hold the remarkable record of having been the only national team to have won two different conferedations' championships. Australia won the Oceania Nations Cup four times between 1980 and 2004, but then transferred to the Asian Football Confederation in search of a higher standard of competition. The move did not meet with the approval of all the Asian nations but they were happy enough to benefit from Australian hospitality at the Asian Cup finals there in 2015. The Socceroos capitalised on home advantage to defeat South Korea 2-1 after extra time in the final in Sydney.

The national association had been founded in 1911 as the Commonwealth Football Association, which evolved via various titles into the Australia Soccer Football Association then Soccer Australia in 1995. In 2004, after political concerns over the organisation of the game, millionaire businessman Frank Lowy took charge of what became Football Federation Australia. Lowy's ambition brought a reorganisation of senior league football as well as a bid to host the 2022 World Cup, which, embarrassingly, gathered only one vote in the decisive ballot by the executive committee of world federation FIFA in December 2010.

The Socceroos, however, made steady progress. They first competed at the World Cup finals in 1974 but missed out, one step short, in the intercontinental play-offs for 1994, 1998 and 2002. Dutch coach Guus Hiddink then guided them not only to Germany in 2006 but through the group stage and in to the second round. This remains their best performance. They fell in the group stage three times in succession in 2010, 2014 and then again in 2018.

31–0

AUSTRALIA — AMERICAN SAMOA

2001 WORLD CUP OCEANIA QUALIFIER – BIGGEST VICTORY IN AN INTERNATIONAL MATCH

13 GOALS SCORED BY ARCHIE THOMPSON – A WORLD INTERNATIONAL RECORD

1 SHOT ON TARGET FROM AMERICAN SAMOA

↑ Australian talisman Tim Cahill wins a header against Chile at the 2014 World Cup. Cahill scored five goals across three World Cup tournaments, and retired in 2018 as the country's leading scorer.

Japan

Japan FA founded 1921	
FIFA affiliated 1921	AFC Asian Cup 1992 2000 2004 2011

Football had always taken a back seat in Japan's sporting hierarchy until the federation decided, in the early 1990s, to launch its ambitious bid to be the first Asian hosts of the World Cup. They signalled their arrival among the powers of the Asian game for their impressive co-hosting of the 2002 World Cup finals alongside South Korea. The organisation was almost perfect and the national team, coached by Philippe Troussier, reached the second round for the first time in their history before losing only 1-0 to Turkey. With a sound professional foundation in the J.League, the Japanese national team went from strength to strength. The country demonstrated its increasing power in both 2010 and 2018 when they reached the second round on foreign soil, falling on penalties to Paraguay and then 3–2, dramatically, to Belgium.

South Korea

Korea FA founded 1928	
FIFA affiliated 1948	AFC Asian Cup 1956 1960

South Korea made history for Asian football by reaching the semi-finals of the 2002 World Cup, which they co-hosted with Japan. They initially made their mark on the international stage by winning the first two Asian Championships in 1956 and 1960 before development stalled. The creation of a professional league though was rewarded with appearances at nine successive World Cups finals between 1986 and 2018.

A decisive step forward came in 1996 when the Korean federation persuaded FIFA to award Korea co-hosting rights to the 2002 finals. The Koreans owed their success to positive memories of the 1988 Olympics in Seoul, their World Cup pedigree and an aggressive campaign carried out in the corridors of power. Dutch coach Guus Hiddink was appointed national coach at the start of 2001 and worked a minor miracle. Fired up by passionate supporters, Korea defeated Poland 2-0, played out a 1-1 draw with the United States then beat Portugal 1-0 to progress beyond the group stage. Victories over Italy and Spain earned a place in history as the only Asian nation to reach the World Cup semi-finals.

Japan were a surprise package at the 2018 World Cup, but a dramatic last-minute goal saw them lose 3–2 against Belgium in the second round.

China

China FA founded 1924	
FIFA affiliated 1931	

China is one of the sleeping giants of world football, the country's poor performances at international level belying its potential strength considering its population. Only once has the national team reached the World Cup finals and that was in 2002 under veteran World Cup coaching specialist Bora Milutinović. Disappointingly, China lost all three games, conceding nine goals overall against Costa Rica, Brazil and Turkey.

Yet, back in 1913, China had led the way by contesting the first international match on Asian soil when they met the Philippines in Manila in the Far Eastern Games. International success subsequently eluded them however and their best honours achievement to date remains the runners-up spot at the 1984 Asian Cup.

A side containing only Hong Kong players took part in the 1954 Asian Games, calling themselves China. The Chinese FA protested that it was the legitimate ruling body and subsequently withdrew from FIFA in 1958. It was not until Brazilian João Havelange took over as FIFA president in 1974 that negotiations were launched to bring about China's readmission to the world governing body.

In a belated sign of a reawakening of the game's value, commercial property giant Wanda became a FIFA World Cup sponsor in time for the 2018 finals.

Chinese Super League

The Chinese Super League has made itself felt far beyond eastern Asia with the remarkable transfer spending of its leading clubs over recent years. However, for years, Chinese football and its league competition drew attention only for a lack of competitive credibility earnt after a string of match-fixing scandals. Eventually, dozens of officials, players and referees were banished from the game and a new era began with significant commercial investment in facilities and players.

Among the initial star imports were veteran Chelsea forwards Nicolas Anelka and Didier Drogba at Shanghai Shenhua. Star coaches included Italian World Cup-winner Marcello Lippi to head the national team as well as Jean Tigana and Gabriel Batistuta at Shanghai and former Brazil boss Luiz Felipe Scolari at Guangzhou Evergrande. Scolari had been in China only a matter of months when he led Guanzhou to their sixth successive Super League title as well as success in the Asian Champions League.

The popularity of Brazil and the Brazilian game was underlined in December 2016 when local rivals SIPG Shangai paid a Chinese record £60m for Chelsea playmaker, Oscar. Within weeks the Sports Ministry imposed tighter restrictions on the signing of foreign players.

↑ Brazilian midfielder Oscar smashed the Asian transfer record with a reported £60 million deal that took him from Chelsea to Shanghai SIPG.

CHINESE SUPER LEAGUE by the numbers

16 NUMBER OF TEAMS	**2004** CHINESE SUPER LEAGUE FOUNDED	**5** FORIEGN PLAYERS ALLOWED
7 MOST TITLE WINS: **GUANGZHOU EVERGRANDE**	**7** FASTEST GOAL (SECONDS): **JI XIANG** FOR JIANGSU SAINTY AGAINST GUANGZHOU EVERGRANDE IN 2012	**28** MOST GOALS IN ONE SEASON (2014): **ELKESON** GUANGZHOU EVERGRANDE

TOP **3** TEAMS QUALIFY FOR AFC CHAMPIONS LEAGUE (2 IN PLAY-OFFS)
BOTTOM **2** TEAMS ARE RELEGATED TO CHINA LEAGUE ONE

Iran

Iran Football Federation founded	AFC Asian Cup
1920	1968 1972 1976
FIFA affiliated 1948	

Iran emerged as a major Asian power in the 1960s and were the continent's most successful side in the 1970s. They claimed a hat trick of Asian titles in 1968, 1972 and 1976 - winning every game they played in the tournament over an eight-year period. They also won gold at the 1974 Asian Games and made a World Cup debut in 1978. They set what was then a World Cup record by beating the Maldives 17-0 in a qualifying tie in 1997 on their way to the finals in France, where a 2-1 win in a politically sensitive match against the United States was a tournament highlight. Iran disappointed in the first round in 2006 but impressed in 2014 and 2018, although they still failed to reach the knockout stage. An issue for the international sports community remains the ban on women fans from attending men's matches inside Iran.

Saudi Arabia

Saudi Arabia Football Federation founded	AFC Asian Cup
1956	1984 1988 1996
FIFA affiliated 1956	

Saudi Arabia is one of the most powerful nations within the Asian region and, with untold oil-based wealth on tap, could dominate at both national team and club level if a wider exchange of coaching and playing talent were possible.

First honours came with two Asian championship wins in the 1980s and construction of the notable King Fahd Stadium in Riyadh to host the inaugural FIFA Confederations Cup in 1993. That commitment to the game was rewarded with four successive appearances at the World Cup finals of 1994, 1998, 2002 and 2006, reaching the knockout stages in 1994. Outstanding midfielder Saeed Al-Owairan scored the goal of the tournament after a 70-yard dash against Belgium. But there was no revival in 2018 after they crashed 5-0 to hosts Russia in the opening match.

Saudi Arabia have won the Asian Cup three times but only back in the 1980s and 1990s; their record in the Arab Nations Cup includes two wins, in 1998 and 2002.

500 000
LA LIGA
LIONEL MESSI / BARCELONA
£500,000 PER WEEK* [AFTER TAX]

500 000
PREMIER LEAGUE
ALEXIS SANCHEZ / MANCHESTER UNITED
£500,000 PER WEEK* [AFTER TAX]

400 000
CHINESE SUPER LEAGUE
OSCAR / SHANGHAI SIPG
£400,000 PER WEEK*

*2017–2018

Passionate Iranian fans cheer on their national team before the start of a group match against Portugal at the 2006 World Cup in Germany.

Iraq

Iraq FA founded 1948

FIFA affiliated 1950

AFC Asian Cup 2007

The 1970s witnessed a shift in the balance of power in Asian football towards the Arab states: Iraq were at the forefront of this movement. They won gold at the Asian Games in 1982 and four years later qualified for the World Cup finals in Mexico. Iraq were thrown out of FIFA and suspended from international football in 1991 because of the invasion of Kuwait, but were soon readmitted to the international fold. The second Gulf War meant Iraq's football administration had to be rebuilt once again. The national team not only quickly resumed international duty but secured a shock victory in the 2007 Asian Cup, beating Saudi Arabia 1-0 in the final.

North Korea

DPR Korea FA founded 1945

FIFA affiliated 1958

North Korea's national side has consistently lived in the shadow of its much more successful Southern neighbours but, in 1966, the North made headlines around the world by beating Italy 1-0 in the first round of the World Cup. Following that, during an incredible quarterfinal against Portugal, the North Koreans went 3-0 ahead after 22 minutes. But the dream faded almost as dramatically, as Portugal won 5-3.

Some 44 years later, the North Koreans returned to the finals, in South Africa, but with a far-less-dramatic effect. A hard-working team lost only 2-1 to Brazil in their opening game but crashed 7-0 to Portugal and 3-0 to the Ivory Coast.

Qatar

Qatar FA founded 1960

FIFA affiliated 1972

The enormous wealth of the tiny Gulf state was put to work on behalf of sport in general and football in particular in the early 2000s and was crowned by a shock success in winning host rights to the 2022 World Cup. This will be the first major finals hosted in the Middle East. World federation FIFA has remained firmly in support of Qatar despite negative publicity over the working conditions of foreign construction workers. Concern is also rife over whether the national team will be up to the challenge. They have won the Gulf Cup three times and the Asian Games football title once but have never qualified for the World Cup.

➜ The Doha Port stadium is pictured in this artist's impression, which was part of the Qatar 2022 World Cup bid, unveiled on September 16, 2010, in the captial, Doha. The stadium architecture references its waterside location by creating a shape reminiscent of a marine creature.
➜ Barcelona football legend Xavi Hernandez, who signed with Qatar's Al Sadd football club, celebrates with teammates after scoring during a Qatar Stars League match.

Syria

Syria Football Federation founded
1936

FIFA affiliated
1937

Syria's footballers drew attention to themselves in December 2012 when, despite the war-torn state of their nation, they won the West Asia Cup in the WAFF Championship, their first major trophy, overcoming Iraq 1-0 in the final in Kuwait. Ahmad Al Salih, from the Chinese Super League club Henan Jianye, scored the late winning goal. Syria have never qualified for the World Cup finals although they were one of the first Asian nations to enter the qualifying tournament ahead of the 1950 finals in Brazil. The furthest they have progressed was in the 1986 qualifying competition when they reached the final preliminary round before losing to Iraq.

UAE

UAE FA founded
1971

FIFA affiliated
1974

With a population of nine million the sporting potential of the UAE is limited, but the financial resources have created excellent facilities, as endorsed by FIFA when it staged the 2003 Under-17 World Youth Cup there. Local ambitions were emphasised in 1977 when the UAE Football Association hired then England manager, Don Revie. In 1990 the UAE qualified for the only time for the World Cup finals in Italy. They lost all three games, against Colombia, champions West Germany and Yugoslavia. Their best year in the Asian Cup came as hosts in 1996 when they reached the final only to lose 4-2 on penalties against Saudi Arabia after a 0-0 draw.

Uzbekistan

Uzbekistan Football Federation founded
1946

FIFA affiliated
1994

Uzbekistan gained its independence after the collapse of the Soviet Union at the start of the 1990s; the national team played its first recognised international in 1992 against Tajikistan. Two years later, they made their debut in the Asian Games in Japan, where they took the football gold medal after a surprise 4-2 win over China in the final in Hiroshima. They have never qualified for the World Cup finals, but have been represented there by top match official Ravshan Irmatov, who refereed the opening match of the 2010 World Cup finals. In the Asian Cup, Uzbekistan reached the quarter-finals in 2004, 2007 and 2015. They finished fourth in 2011.

EUROPE

Europe generates more than 85pct of football's estimated wealth, a ratio sparking concerns over financial imbalance in the world game. European federation UEFA came to life in 1954, half a century after the debut of world governing body FIFA and national team football on the continent. The first international was staged between Austria and Hungary in 1902; central Europe saw the launch of the Mitropa Cup, forerunner of today's popular European club competitions in 1927.

UEFA, with 55 members having built on an initial membership of 33, is based near Geneva in Switzerland. The current president is Aleksander Ceferin, a lawyer from Slovenia, who succeeded the former France star Michel Platini in September 2016.

ICELAND

FIFA TEAM RANKINGS (as of June 2018)

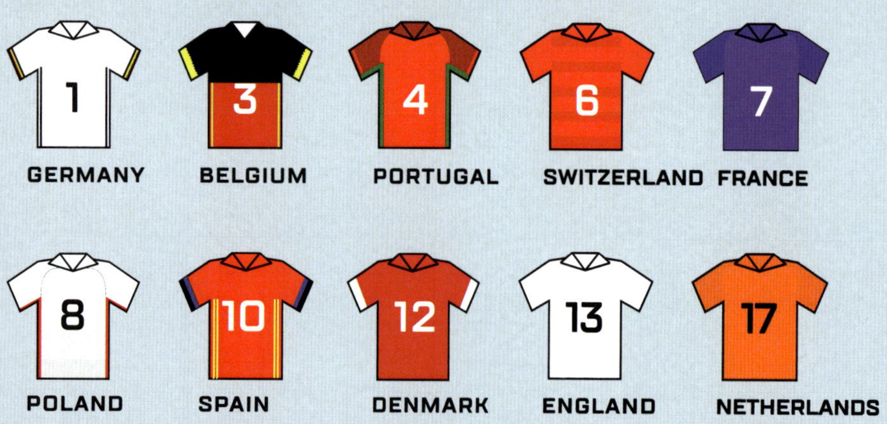

FINLAND
FAROE ISLANDS
NORWAY
HOLLAND
1988
SWEDEN
1948
NORTHERN IRELAND
RUSSIA
1956, 1988
1960
ESTONIA
DENMARK
1992
1995
SCOTLAND
LATVIA
ENGLAND
1966
1908, 1912
GERMANY
1954, 1974, 1990, 2014
1976
1972, 1980, 1996
2017
LITHUANIA
WALES
BELARUS
SLOVAKIA
BELGUIM
1920
AUSTRIA
POLAND
1972
UKRAINE
KAZAKHSTAN
IRELAND
LUXEMBOURG
CZECH REPUBLIC
1980
1976
ROMANIA
FRANCE
1998, 2018
1984
1984, 2000
2001, 2003
SLOVENIA
HUNGARY
1952, 1964, 1968
MOLDOVA
SERBIA
CROATIA
KOSOVO
BULGARIA
LIECHTENSTEIN
SWITZERLAND
BOSNIA
MACEDONIA
SAN MARINO
MONTENEGRO
ANDORRA
PORTUGAL
2016
ITALY
1934, 1938, 1982, 2006
1936
1968
GEORGIA
ALBANIA
SPAIN
2010
1992
1964, 2008, 2012
TURKEY
GREECE
2004
ARMENIA
GIBRALTAR
AZERBAIJAN
MALTA
CYPRUS
ISRAEL
KEY
WORLD CUP
OLYMPIC GAMES
EUROS
CONFEDERATIONS CUP

LONGEST CAREER
STANLEY MATTHEWS
22 YEARS
228 DAYS

WIN PERCENTAGE
57

GOALS SCORED PER MATCH
2.2

TOP SCORER
WAYNE ROONEY
53

MOST CAPPED
PETER SHILTON
125

England

England gave codified modern football to the world but the national team has struggled in the attempt to maintain such pre-eminence.

The FA Cup was introduced in 1871, the first tournament in the world, and was fundamental to the development of the game. A year later, the very first international match was played between England and Scotland in Glasgow. Later, in 1888, the Football League was formed in order to organize what was, by then, a largely professional game based mostly in the industrial north.

By the new century, the British Championship - played between England, Scotland, Wales and Ireland - was the zenith of world football. Until the First World War, England and Scotland were the best in the world and, as Great Britain, won Olympic gold in 1908 and 1912.

The interwar period, however, was a time of increasing isolation. Although the FA had joined FIFA in 1905, it took a disdainful attitude towards the organisation and withdrew in 1920 and, after a brief return, again in 1928.

Even after the Second World War, England's superiority complex was intact. An ignominious 1-0 defeat by the United States in the 1950 World Cup could be dismissed but the 1953 6-3 loss to Hungary's "Magical Magyars" at Wembley finally hurt the English arrogance. Further defeats at the 1954, 1958 and 1962 World Cup finals confirmed that England were no longer the game's leaders.

England FA founded
1863

FIFA affiliated
1905–1920
1924–1928
1946–

World Cup
1966

Hundreds of balloons take to the air at Wembley Stadium during the opening ceremony of Euro 1996, held in England. One of England's most memorable moments – the 5–1 defeat of Germany in their own back yard in 2001.

The challenges presented by the new order were spectacularly answered in 1966, when England's "The Wingless Wonders" won the World Cup on home soil.

Sir Alf Ramsey moulded his side around the outstanding talents of goalkeeper Gordon Banks, captain Bobby Moore, and the Charlton brothers Bobby and Jack. With the innovaitve new system in place, he also instilled a team spirit and an understanding that proved difficult to match.

The 1966 success was the springboard from which English club sides launched an unprecedented assault on the three European competitions, winning trophy after trophy between 1964 and 1985. Conversely, as the clubs prospered the national side suffered.

Failure to qualify for the 1974 and 1978 finals confirmed England's slide. From then on, English teams at successive World Cups and European Championships have been consistent only in underachievement, albeit laced with ill fortune: England went out of the 1986 World Cup finals after Diego Maradona's infamous "Hand of God" goal, and lost to Germany on penalties too often.

Similar bad luck struck again at the 1998 World Cup in France when England reached the second round but lost on penalties to old foes, Argentina.

The experiment with a first foreign manager saw England, under Sweden's Sven-Goran Eriksson, reach the quarter-finals of the 2002 and 2006 World Cups and Euro 2014. However successors Steve McClaren, Fabio Capello and Roy Hodgson failed to match his status despite fielding talent such as David Beckham, Steven Gerrard and Wayne Rooney.

Only in the 2018 World Cup in Russia did England regain lost pride. Manager Gareth Southgate built a new team around young players he knew from his work with the under-21s. In the knockout stage England ended their 28-year-old shootout jinx against Colombia, then beat Sweden to reach the semi-finals for only the third time. An extra-time defeat by Croatia was followed by a loss to Belgium in the third place play-off.

Deutschland
England
1 : 5
Olympiastadion
München

English Premier League

History was made on September 8, 1888. That was the day the very first league football match was played. Not only in England. Anywhere. This was the original kickoff of the oldest such competition in world football – a day whose five simple matches would evolve, ultimately, into the English Premier League, the Bundesliga, La Liga and Serie A, to name just the most famous.

This league system has formed the bedrock of English football ever since. Two previous crucial dates had preceded this one. On October 26, 1863, the Football Association was founded and on July 20, 1885, professionalism was legalised.

Regular fixtures were needed to pay the wages and it was William McGregor of Aston Villa who decided something had to be done. On March 2, 1888, he sent a proposal to the committees of his own club, Blackburn Rovers, Bolton Wanderers, Preston North End, Stoke and West Bromwich Albion. He proposed the forming of a league competition which would provide a number of guaranteed fixtures each season.

The 12 interested clubs met at Anderton's Hotel in London on March 23, 1888, on the eve of the FA Cup final. Less than a month later, on April 17, the Football League was founded at the Royal Hotel in Manchester.

McGregor had proposed the name of Association Football Union but the meeting considered this too similar to the Rugby Football Union. The title of Football League was proposed by Major William Sudell from Preston North End.

All the clubs came from the Midlands or the north of England: Accrington Stanley, Aston Villa, Blackburn Rovers, Bolton Wanderers, Burnley, Derby County, Everton, Notts County, Preston North End, Stoke (renamed Stoke City in 1926), West Bromwich Albion and Wolverhampton Wanderers. The geography was no coincidence. It was northern clubs - led by Sudell with Preston - which had led the way in paying players to move south from Scotland.

When the Football League kicked off it had been decided that whichever club won the most games would be declared champions. A few weeks into the season this was superseded by a system of two points for a win and one for a draw.

PREMIER LEAGUE by the numbers

20 NUMBER OF TEAMS

1992 PREMIER LEAGUE FOUNDED

13 MOST TITLE WINS: **MANCHESTER UNITED**

10 FASTEST GOAL (IN SECONDS): **LEDLEY KING** TOTTENHAM HOTSPURS

260 MOST GOALS EVER: **ALAN SHEARER** BLACKBURN ROVERS & NEWCASTLE UNITED

106 MOST GOALS IN ONE SEASON: **MANCHESTER CITY** (2017–18)

18 MOST CONSECUTIVE WINS: **MANCHESTER CITY** (26 AUG–27 DEC 2017)

32 MOST WINS IN A SEASON: **MANCHESTER CITY** (2017–18)

1 FEWEST WINS IN A SEASON: **DERBY COUNTY** (2007–08)

TOP **4** TEAMS QUALIFY FOR CHAMPIONS LEAGUE
BOTTOM **3** TEAMS ARE RELEGATED TO EFL CHAMPIONSHIP

Roy Keane, captain of Manchester United, holds aloft the 2003 Premier League trophy.

In 1981 the Football League would lead the world in switching to three points for a win.

Preston went on to win the first league title without losing a game, a feat not matched until Arsenal in 2003-04.

In time, three further lower divisions were added with the development of a promotion and relegation system. Initially the third division was split into north and south sections. This was abandoned in favour of a national fourth division in 1958. Later, a promotion/relegation system with the so-called "non-league" system was agreed. Title sponsorship arrived in 1983 with the involvement of the Japanese multi-national, Canon.

Power in the Football League remained vested in the north-west of England. Sunderland, Aston Villa, Liverpool, Manchester United and Newcastle enjoyed periods of dominance before the First World War. The mid-1920s saw a hat-trick of league titles seize by Huddersfield Town, whose

manager, Herbert Chapman, then moved to London and built the foundations of Arsenal.

In the 1930s, Chapman and, after his death, successor George Allison, led the Gunners to five league titles in eight seasons. Everton were the last winners before the Second World War and Merseyside rivals Liverpool the first winners after

↑ Alan Shearer celebrates scoring for Newcastle United against Fulham in 2003 – one of the 260 goals he netted in the Premier League.

653

GARETH BARRY OF ASTON VILLA, MANCHESTER CITY, EVERTON AND WEST BROMWICH ALBION HOLDS THE RECORD FOR THE MOST PREMIER LEAGUE APPEARANCES OF ALL TIME

the restoration of peace.

The 1950s brought glory for Tottenham's push-and-run team, Stan Cullis's long-ball physicality at Wolverhampton Wanderers and Matt Busby's brilliant young "Busby Babes" at Manchester United. The latter's potential was cut tragically short by the 1958 Munich air disaster. North-west rivals Liverpool were the dominant club of the next three decades, winning 13 league titles, five FA Cups, four Leagues Cups and seven European club prizes between 1964 and 1992.

Meanwhile, clubs grew increasingly impatient to harvest what they considered their full financial due. Hence in 1992 the "Big Five" (Arsenal, Everton, Liverpool, Manchester United and Spurs) decided the only route to survival was to break away from the four-division Football League.

The Football Association, led by its then general secretary Graham Kelly, supported the move. Relations between the FA and the Football League had always been bad. Hence the creation

➋ Premier League champions in 2016, Leicester City were 5000-1 outsiders when the season began.

of what was initially named the FA Premier League.

Timing was everything. The 1989 Hillsborough disaster had prompted the introduction of redeveloped all-seater stadia that were filled by the attraction of star foreign players, a wave of imports having been legalised by a 1995 European Court of Justice decision.

English clubs' ability to outspend almost all their foreign rivals was fuelled by the commercial explosion generated from the satellite television revolution plus the financial investment of a plethora of foreign owners from the United States, China, Russia and the Middle East.

Media mogul Rupert Murdoch's newly created BSkyB paid what was considered a staggering £304m payment for an initial five-year deal. Subsequently, this escalated to the 2015 figure of £5.136bn over three years.

The Premier League's first season, 1992-93, ended up with a top five of Manchester United, Aston Villa, Norwich, Blackburn Rovers and Queens Park Rangers. The latter four are all now in the lower divisions while United have gone from strength to strength, winning the Premier League a record 13 times under manager Sir Alex Ferguson.

William McGregor and Major Sudell could never have dreamed of it.

The FA Cup

The Football Association Challenge Cup was the FA's first formal competitive creation. The FA was founded in 1863 and launched the FA Cup eight years later during the 1871–72 season. Thus it "owns" a historic role in the history of the game as the oldest of competitions.

The promotional and commercial focus on European and domestic league football in recent years has done little to harm the dreams generated by a competition with an attractive tradition for unpredictability and giant-killings. Lincoln City maintained that romance in 2016-17 on becoming the first non-league side to reach the quarter-finals since 1914.

Administratively little has changed. Non-league clubs are joined in the first round proper by outfits from League One and Two. The giants of the Premier League and Championship (second tier) enter the fray in the third round in early January. Winning the Cup is rewarded with not only the latest, fifth version of the historic trophy but entry into the following season'sw Europa League.

Arsenal are record 13-time winners, closely followed by Manchester United on 12. Chelsea drew level with Tottenham on eight after beating United in the 2018 final. Still high in the record books are the now-defunct Wanderers club, who won the first FA Cup in 1872 and then on four

FA CUP by the numbers

1871-72
INAUGURAL FA CUP

13
MOST WINS: **ARSENAL**

9
GOALS IN SINGLE GAME: **TED MacDOUGALL** 1971

737
TEAMS COMPETED IN 2017–18 SEASON

4
SECONDS: FASTEST GOAL **GARETH MORRIS** ASHFORD UTD 2001

660
MINUTES: LONGEST TIE – OVER 6 GAMES **OXFORD CITY vs ALVECHURCH** 1971

2.20
MINUTES/SECONDS: FASTEST HAT-TRICK **ANDY LOCKE** NANTWICH TOWN 1995

Wembley Stadium, the "home of football", has hosted the FA Cup final almost unbroken since 1923, when Bolton Wanderers beat West Ham United 2–0. The old stadium saw its last final in 2000, before the new Wembley took over in 2007. From 2001 to 2006, the final took place at the Millennium Stadium in Cardiff.

(bottom) Arsenal celebrate their 13th FA Cup title, beating Chelsea 2–1 in 2017 to win their third trophy in four years.

more occasions in the ensuing six years.

Wanderers were a London club whose members and players were drawn largely from public schools and included Charles Alcock and Lord Kinnaird, two of the founding fathers of the modern game. They remain one of only two clubs to have won the FA Cup three years in succession.

Their achievement in 1876-88 was emulated only by Blackburn Rovers in 1883-85 as the advent of professionalism and the creation of the Football League swung the power in English competitive football away from the south-east of England to the north-west.

Hence, Preston North End became the first club to win the coveted League and FA Cup double in 1889, followed by Aston Villa in 1897. In the 20th century the double appeared to be an achievement too far for even the finest club sides until Tottenham Hotspur made history in 1961. Since then, four more clubs have doubled up - Arsenal in 1971, 1998 and 2002, Liverpool in 1986, Manchester United in 1994, 1996 and 1999 and Chelsea in 2010.

Former England left-back Ashley Cole was the most successful individual to date, winning the Cup three times with Arsenal and on four occasions with Chelsea.

Germany

German football is among the most respected in the world, not only for the achievement of its national team, whatever the political circumstances, but its organisational powers.

"Die Mannschaft" have won the World Cup four times, most recently in 2014, plus the European Championship on three occasions, while seven German clubs have won 15 European prizes.

Germany took to football at the start of the 20th century despite opposition from among the gymnastic sports community. Third place at the 1934 World Cup was the peak of the national team's interwar achievements.

The restoration of peace saw Germany divided, meaning East Germany, under Soviet Union influence, created its own association, national side and league in 1948. Not until the early 1960s did West Germany set up a single Bundesliga and abandon its historic regional leagues system.

East Germany, with a state-sponsored emphasis on individual rather than team sports, never matched the success of their countrymen. East Germany managed only two successes of note: Olympic gold in Montreal in 1976 and a 1-0 victory over West Germany at the 1974 World Cup, the only time the two sides ever met.

While the East floundered, the West flourished. Banished from FIFA in 1946, they were readmitted in 1950 as West Germany and won the World Cup four years later. A victory, led by coach Sepp Herberger, was made more special because their opponents were Hungary's "Golden Team", whose 3-2 defeat was only their second loss in five years. Later, Germany were semi-finalists in 1958, quarter-finalists in 1962 and runners-up in 1966.

1970s Europe belonged to Bayern Munich and West Germany. Bayern won a hat-trick of European Cups in 1974, 1975 and 1976, and then provided the nucleus of the national side that won the World Cup again in 1974 plus the European Championship in both 1972 and 1980.

Germany FA founded
1900

FIFA affiliated
1904

World Cup
1954*
1974*
1990
2014

European Championship
1972*
1980*
1996

Olympics Gold
1976+

*As West Germany
+As East Germany

National team captain Franz Beckenbauer revolutionised the sweeper's role while Bayern club-mate Gerd Müller proved one of international football's most remarkable goal machines. In 62 internationals, he scored 68 goals including the winner against Holland in the 1974 World Cup final at Bayern's then home ground, the Munich Olympic Stadium.

Almost seamlessly, each and every successful national side managed to replace one generation of stars with another. Thus, the heroes of the 1970s were replaced in the 1980s and 1990s by the likes of Lothar Matthäus, Karl-Heinz Rummenigge, Rudi Völler and Jurgen Klinsmann.

Following both World Cup success and German reunification in 1990, Germany capitalised on their new-found resources by securing victory in the 1996 European Championship in England with a 2-1 defeat of the Czech Republic thanks to a golden goal scored in extra time by Oliver Bierhoff.

Comparative failures at the quarter-finals of the 1998 World Cup and the group stage of Euro 2000 prompted a major reappraisal of youth coaching structures. The rewards were semi-final finishes at both the 2010 World Cup and 2012 European Championship then victory at the 2014 World Cup.

Manager Joachim Low's men did not enjoy their pre-eminence for long. They fell in the semi-finals of Euro 2016, then lost their world crown in Russia in 2018. After an opening defeat by Mexico, Germany failed to progress beyond the first round for the first time since 1938.

BIGGEST WIN
16–0
GERMANY vs RUSSIAN EMPIRE (1 JULY 1912)

WIN PERCENTAGE
59

GOALS SCORED PER MATCH
2.24

TOP SCORER
MIROSLAV KLOSE
71

← West Germany line up against East Germany for the one and only time – in the 1974 World Cup. East beat West 1–0.
↑ Pierre Littbarski and captain Lothar Matthaus share World Cup delirium after the final in 1990.

→ German players go on a victory dash after Jonas Hector scores the winning penalty in the shootout against Italy in the Euro 2016 quarter-final.

Bundesliga

The German Bundesliga has registered the highest average attendances in European football in recent years, testimony to the popularity of the game, the enduring appeal of a nucleus of traditional clubs, comparatively low ticket prices, solid sponsor and television support and a strategy of supporter outreach.

40

BAYERN MUNICH LEGEND **GERD MULLER** HOLDS THE RECORD FOR THE MOST BUNDESLIGA GOALS IN ONE SEASON

After the English Premier League, the Bundesliga has outperformed every other major European league in commercial and revenue terms. The top division has shown a 56pct increase in revenue over the past five years and commercial revenues are double that of the Spanish league.

But such popularity was not always the case. The first attempts to launch a German federation ended in failure, and success was only achieved with the founding of the Deutscher Fussband-Bund (DFB) in 1900.

A national championship was launched a mere two years later but organisation was a challenge. Germany, back then, stretched far to the east including much of what is now Poland and Belarus. So, rather than try to imitate the English model of a single league, the DFB organised regional championships with an end-of-season play-off tournament.

The 11 championships held before the First World War were divided variously between clubs from Berlin, Freiburg, Furth, Karlsruhe, Kiel and Leipzig. The interwar years were dominated by first Nurnberg and then Schalke, from the heart of the industrial Ruhr.

Nurnberg, known familiarly as "Der Club", won six championships between the wars; Schalke also won six titles before domestic competition was abandoned in 1942. It could have been seven but the club was dramatically beaten 4-3 by Rapid Vienna in the 1941 play-off - Austria having been swallowed up into Greater Germany in the Anschluss of 1938.

German football took several years to reclaim stability after the chaos and confusion following the end of the Second World War. Nurnberg won the first post-war championship in 1948, followed by Mannheim, Stuttgart and then a Kaiserslautern team led by national captain Fritz Walter. "The Lauterers" won the title twice in three seasons and provided the nucleus of the national side that achieved a shock victory at the 1954 World Cup in neighbouring Switzerland.

At this point, German club football was essentially part-time, which meant star players were being lured away regularly by the riches on offer in Italy. This weakened the national team, and was one of the factors which prompted the DFB to launch a unified professional Bundesliga "Federal League" in 1963-64.

No single club dominated the early years but then came Bayern Munich. To their one German championship in the 1930s they added a record 27 Bundesliga crowns, including six in succession between 2013 and 2018.

Their riches and star status have earned Bayern the nickname of "FC Hollywood", though debate reigns about whether a one-club dominance is good for the Bundesliga in the long term. The Bavarian club's power grew so vast that, even when Borussia Dortmund were their closest challengers, it was still possible for Bayern to

BUNDESLIGA by the numbers

18 NUMBER OF TEAMS	**1963** BUNDESLIGA FOUNDED	**27** MOST TITLE WINS: **BAYERN MUNICH**
602 MOST APPEARANCES: **KARL-HEINZ KÖRBEL** ALL FOR EINTRACHT FRANKFURT 1972–91	**0** NUMBER OF CLUBS FROM **BERLIN** THAT HAVE WON THE BUNDESLIGA	**101** MOST GOALS IN ONE SEASON: **BAYERN MUNICH** (1971–72)
442 MOST CONSECUTIVE GAMES: **SEPP MAIER** ALL WITH BAYERN MUNICH (1966–79)	**832** GAMES MANAGED BY **OTTO REHHAGEL** INCLUDING 14 YEARS AT WERDER BREMEN (1981–95)	**26** GOALS SCORED BY KEEPER **HANS-JÖRG BUTT** FOR HAMBURG AND BAYER LEVERKEUSEN

TOP **4** TEAMS QUALIFY FOR CHAMPIONS LEAGUE
BOTTOM **2** TEAMS ARE RELEGATED TO 2. BUNDESLIGA

Philipp Lahm lifts the Bundesliga trophy in 2015, surrounded by his joyous teammates, after a 2–0 victory over Mainz 05.

persist in signing the Ruhr club's finest players every year. These have included 2014 World Cup winners Mario Gotze and Mats Hummel, plus top-scoring Polish centre-forward Robert Lewandowski.

Bayern have also won the German cup more times (18) than any other club, followed in the far distance by Werder Bremen (six) then Schalke and Eintracht Frankfurt (five each).

Borussia Dortmund were one of the first German clubs to make a mark in European competition, along with Hamburg and Eintracht Frankfurt. Borussia were the first German club to win a European prize, the now-defunct Cup-winners Cup in 1966; Frankfurt were the first German side to reach a final when they lost a historic Champions Cup duel 7-3 to Real Madrid in 1960; and Hamburg became the first German winners of the Champions Cup when they defeated Juventus 1-0 in Athens in 1983.

However, German clubs have been held back from mounting significant challenges for international prizes by domestic regulation which bars influential foreign investment.

Clubs were run by their members until 1998 when they were permitted to convert into public or private limited companies. However, the so-called "50+1 rule" means a club must retain at least 51pc of the football company. Exceptions are permitted only when an individual or company has provided major financial support for at least 20 years, such as the Bayer pharmaceuticals corporation with Leverkusen and Volkswagen with VfL Wolfsburg.

35

GAMES UNBEATEN WORLD RECORD (SHARED WITH BRAZIL) 2007–09

WIN PERCENTAGE

58

GOALS SCORED PER MATCH

1.97

59

TOP SCORER **DAVID VILLA**

Spain

Spain set a new benchmark at national team level with their historic hat-trick of World Cup and European Championship crowns between 2008 and 2012. That balanced the history books because, until then, Spanish football's high reputation had been based largely on the exploits of its clubs, notably Real Madrid and Barcelona.

Spain Football Federation founded **1913**

FIFA affiliated **1904**

World Cup **2010**

European Championship **1964 2008 2012**

Olympics Gold **1992**

The national team's success in winning the European Championship in 2008 was long overdue, since Spain had gone 44 years without anything to celebrate. However, this proved merely a launch pad towards even grander achievements with a World Cup triumph in 2010 and then a European title repeat in Poland and Ukraine in 2012.

Football gained a foothold in the Basque country of northern Spain through migrant British workers in the 1890s. The regional organisations were brought together in 1913 when the Real Federación Española de Fútbol was formed.

In 1920, the national side made their debut, with a 1-0 win over Denmark; until the Spanish Civil War Spain's record was good. They reached the quarter-finals of the 1928 Olympics and the 1934 World Cup, losing to Italy both times. Their hero was goalkeeper Ricardo Zamora.

The Civil War and Second World War halted national team competition for almost a decade. But the domestic rivalry between Real Madrid and Barcelona intensified in the 1950s as both began importing foreign talent.

Madrid, inspired by Argentina's Alfredo Di Stéfano, won the six European Champions Cups (1956-60 and 1966) while Barcelona won the Fairs Cup, now the Europa League, in 1959, 1960 and 1966; Valencia won it in 1962 and 1963, Zaragoza in 1964. Atlético Madrid won the Cup-winners' Cup in 1962.

The national side also saw success with a European Championship victory in 1964. A side containing Luis Suárez, among the greatest Spanish playmakers of all time and one of comparatively few Spaniards to play in Italy (with Internazionale), beat the Soviet Union 2-1 in Madrid to clinch Spain's first major trophy.

A subsequent ban on foreign imports, intended to enhance the national team, backfired. Over the next 30 years, the best Spain achieved was in finishing runners-up in the 1984 European Championship and in reaching the World Cup quarter-finals in 1986. An easing of import restrictions saw the arrival of stars such as Johan Cruyff of Holland and Diego Maradona of Argentina at Barcelona, and West Germany's Gunter Netzer and Paul Breitner at Real Madrid. Even so, the clubs struggled to reclaim their domination of the international scene.

Madrid won the UEFA Cup twice in succession in the 1980s, while Barcelona twice picked the Cup-winners' Cup and then laid their Champions Cup jinx to rest in 1992, with Cruyff as coach.

That same year Spain also won Olympic gold in Barcelona but national team success remained elusive even while Real Madrid regained old glories by winning three Champions League crowns around the turn of the millennium.

A dramatic change of fortune was on the way, however, courtesy of a core of outstanding home-grown players players from Barcelona such as Xavi, Andrés Iniesta and Carles Puyol. These, along with other clubmates and Madrid stars such as goalkeeper-captain Iker Casillas and defender Sergio Ramos provided the nucleus of a national team which set new standards of both success and style.

Spain secured an unprecedented hat-trick of success with World Cup triumph in 2010 coming in between European Championship glory in 2008 and 2012. However the retirement of playmaker Xavi Hernandez heralded the fading of the old guard amid disappointing World Cup campaigns in both 2014 in Brazil and 2018 in Russia.

➔ Iker Casillas (left) and Xavi (right) hold the Euro 2012 trophy after Spain's emphatic 4–0 victory over Italy in the final. Casillas won 167 caps for his country, a Spanish record, while Xavi was not not far behind on 133.

➔ Fernando Torres slots the ball past Italian goalkeepr Gianluigi Buffon in the Euro 2012 final to seal Spain's historic hat-trick of world and European titles.

La Liga

Confrontation has always been a central feature of Spanish domestic football, right back to the creation of the Liga Professional del Fútbol Español in 1929.

An association had been founded in 1905, three years after the first clubs had started contesting a cup competition. Not until 1929, after professionalism arrived, could a league come to life. There was much contention over which clubs would be allowed to enter the inaugural competition and it seemed that FIFA, or even King Alfonso XIII, might be asked to mediate.

In the end, a 10-club league was established featuring the last six to have won the cup, three runners-up and the winners of a play-off tournament (Racing de Santander). The decision was taken in November 1928 but competition did not start until February 1929. In the end it all came down to a duel between Real Madrid and Barcelona, setting the pattern for the next 90 years. Barcelona were crowned the first Spanish champions with a two-point advantage over their all-time rivals.

Only seven more seasons followed before the league was shut down by the civil war. In that time, Madrid, having strengthened their defence by signing legendary goalkeeper Ricardo Zamora, were crowned champions twice. Betis of Seville were surprise champions once but the dominant force were Athletic Bilbao. The Basque club won the league on four occasions.

Spanish football had to pick up the wreckage, literally, after the end of the civil war in 1939. Several football grounds had been used as prison camps and there was little money available to start again. In the circumstances it was probably no surprise that the first post-war champions, in 1939–40, were Atlético Aviación, an air force club built around the former Atlético Madrid.

Atlético triumphed again in 1941 and then twice more, restored as Atlético Madrid, in 1950 and 1951. Barcelona regained the title in 1952, since when they and Real Madrid have won all but 15 of the subsequent 66 championships.

The rivalry has been reflected in every aspect of the game. Real Madrid opened their new Chamartin stadium in 1957, Barcelona moved from the old Las Corts into the vast Camp Nou in 1957; for all the star foreigners Madrid signed - Alfredo Di Stéfano and Hector Rial (Argentina), José Santamaria (Uruguay), Ferenc Puskás (Hungary) etc. - Barcelona matched them with Ladislav Kubala, Sandor Kocsis and Zoltan Czibor (all Hungary) and the likes of Evaristo (Brazil).

Simultaneously, the clasico rivalry extended into the international arena. Madrid won the initial five European Champions Cup while Barcelona won the first two Fairs Cups. When they clashed in the Champions Cup, Madrid won their semi-final in 1960 and Barcelona triumphed in the second round the next season.

Madrid won the league eight times in the 1960s and five times in the 1970s, during which decade Barcelona's world-record acquisition of Dutch superstar Johan Cruyff "earned" them just one title. Madrid claimed five more in the 1980s with the emergence of the home-grown Quinta del Buitre (starring Emilio Butragueno). Basque rivals Bilbao and Real Sociedad from San Sebastian even got in on the act, with two titles each.Barcelona's high-price gamble on Diego Maradona in the early 1980s proved a failure but

300

BARCELONA LEGEND **LIONEL MESSI** WAS THE FIRST TO SCORE 300 LA LIGA GOALS. IT TOOK JUST 334 GAMES, FASTER THAN ANYONE IN THE TOP 5 EUROPEAN LEAGUES.

LA LIGA by the numbers

20
NUMBER OF TEAMS

1929
LA LIGA FOUNDED

32
MOST TITLE WINS: **REAL MADRID**

121
MOST TEAM GOALS IN ONE SEASON: **REAL MADRID** (2011–12)

622
MOST APPEARANCES: **ANDONI ZUBIZARRETA** (1981–98)

757
GAMES MANAGED BY **LUIS ARAGONES** (1974–2004)

50
MOST PLAYER GOALS IN ONE SEASON: **LIONEL MESSI** (2011–12)

3
CLUBS THAT HAVE PLAYED EVERY SEASON: **REAL MADRID, BARCELONA, ATHLETIC BILBAO**

93%
BEST PENALTY KICK CONVERSION RATE: **RONALDO**

TOP **4** TEAMS QUALIFY FOR CHAMPIONS LEAGUE
BOTTOM **3** TEAMS ARE RELEGATED TO SEGUNDA DIVISON

↑ The Camp Nou has been home to Barcelona since 1957. With a capacity of just under 100,000, it is Europe's largest stadium.

↓ Real Madrid's victory in 2016 gave the Spanish team a record eleventh Champions League win. They also stand tall in La Liga with 33 titles, seven more than their fiercest rivals, Barcelona.

they turned the tables in the 1990s, landing six titles to Madrid's two. Cruyff had returned to Camp Nou as coach and created a "Dream Team" around the attacking talents of Brazil's Romario, Denmark's Michel Laudrup and Bulgarian Hristo Stoichkov. To anchor the midfield, Cruyff put his trust in fellow Dutchman Ronald Koeman and a young local product named Pep Guardiola.

Under Cruyff, Barcelona beat their European champions jinx with an extra-time victory over Sampdoria in 1992, and carried off four consecutive league titles between 1991 and 1994.

Madrid, led by home-town favourite Raul Gonzalez, reclaimed domestic command around the start of the 21st century and added three more Champions Leagues to the roll of honour. Guardiola then re-emerged at Barcelona as a coach with the Midas touch.

He benefited from the emergence of a brilliant new generation featuring the creative brilliance of Xavi and Andres Iniesta in support of the world-class talent of Argentinian youngster Lionel Messi. Later, they were joined by Uruguay's Luis Suárez and Brazil's Neymar.

The year-by-year duel between Barcelona and Madrid was personalised in the record-breaking goal-scoring achievements of Messi on the one hand and Cristiano Ronaldo on the other. Currently, the tally stands with Real Madrid boasting a record 33 titles, followed by Barcelona on 25.

10-0
BIGGEST WIN
vs AZERBAIJAN
SEPTEMBER 1995

WIN PERCENTAGE
49

GOALS SCORED PER MATCH
1.76

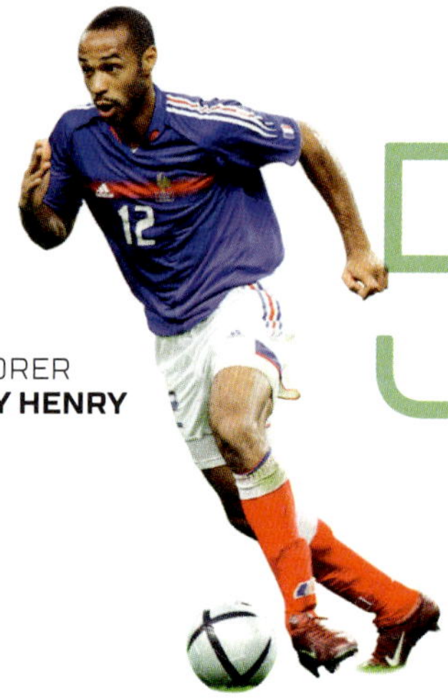

TOP SCORER
THIERRY HENRY
51

France

France played a key role in creating governing bodies FIFA and UEFA, and competitions like the World Cup and European Championship. Their rewards have included World Cup success in both 1998 and 2018.

Success on the pitch was long in coming, however. Not until the 1950s, when Reims twice reached the European Cup final, did French football gain new respect. Raymond Kopa, the first great French footballer, was their star when they lost to Real Madrid in the 1956 final. He then transferred to Madrid and helped them beat Reims, and his successor Just Fontaine, in the 1959 final.

Kopa and Fontaine had thus never played together in club football when they teamed up the following month for France at the 1958 World Cup in Sweden. They struck up a perfect partnership: Kopa was behind most of Fontaine's record 13 goals in the finals; France finished third.

International club success proved elusive until 1993, when Marseille beat Milan 1-0 to win the Champions Cup. France went wild, but only briefly. Within a month, Marseille had been engulfed by a match-fixing scandal that prevented them defending the Cup, prompted their relegation and brought suspensions and legal action against players and officials. Marseille president Bernard Tapie, a millionaire businessman and sometime MP, incurred a two-year jail sentence.

On the international front, Michel Platini arrived in the 1970s and transformed France into one of Europe's most attractive sides. Platini, an attacking midfielder with immense skill, vision and grace, inspired France to reach the final stages of three World Cups (1978, 1982 and 1986) and win the 1984 European Championship. Key team mates in this era included midfielders Alain Giresse and Jean Tigana, defenders Patrick Battiston and Maxime Bossis, plus goalkeeper Fabien Barthez.

In the 1984 European finals, French captain Platini ended up as nine-goal top scorer. In due course, he would progress to become national team manager, joint organising head of the 1998 World Cup finals and then president of European federation UEFA from 2007 until 2016.

Prior to that, the greatest day in Les Bleus' history saw the historic World Cup triumph over Brazil as hosts in 1998, with two goals from playmaker Zinedine Zidane. Two years later, France achieved the double by winning the European Championship title on a golden goal against Italy. Italy took revenge with a shootout win over France in the 2006 World Cup final; Zidane was sent off sensationally in extra time in the 1-1 draw after headbutting Italian defender Marco Materazzi.

Hopes of a revival in 2010 in South Africa were rudely shattered by internal divisions, which sparked a row between coach Raymond Domenech and striker Nicolas Anelka prior to a players' training-ground strike. Domenech was succeeded by Didier Deschamps, who had captained France to the World and European triumphs in 1998 and 2000.

Under Deschamps, a new French team reached the quarter-finals of the 2014 World Cup and were favourites to win the European Championship in 2016 when the country played host to the finals. France reached the final but, despite dominating possession against Portugal, lost 1-0 in extra-time.

Two years later, France reclaimed the World Cup, topping their group and beating Argentina, Uruguay and Belgium on their way to a 4-2 victory over Croatia in Moscow. Antoine Griezmann and Kylian Mbappé were among the leading scorers.

France Football Federation founded
1919

FIFA affiliated
1904

World Cup
1998

European Championship
1984
2000

Confederations Cup
2001
2003

DIDIER DESCHAMPS
CAPTAINED THE FRENCH TEAM THAT WON BOTH THE 1998 WORLD CUP AND EURO 2000 AND IS CURRENTLY HEAD COACH OF THE NATIONAL SIDE, WINNING THE WORLD CUP AS MANAGER IN 2018.

↑ Olivier Giroud attempts an overhead kick in the 2018 World Cup final. Giroud failed to score, but it didn't prevent France from beating Croatia 4–2 to win their second title.

← Michel Platini shoots France 1–0 ahead from a free kick in the 1984 European Championship final against Spain. It was one of nine goals that Platini, the captain, scored in the tournament.

French Ligue 1

French football is unusual in that the power of the club game is commanded by the regional game and not the capital.

League football also has a chequered history. A first championship was set up in the late 1890s by the Union des Sociétés Françaises de Sports Athlétiques, a second in 1905 by the Fédération Gymnastique et Sportive des Patronages de France, a third in 1906 by the Fédération Cycliste et Athlétique France and a fourth, in 1911, by breakaway clubs under the banner of Ligue de Football Association.

Finally, the leagues all merged under the Comité Français Interfédéral which evolved in 1918 into the Fédération Francaise de Football (FFF), headed by future FIFA president Jules Rimet.

For a further decade, the Coupe de France remained the premier competition, while squabbles continued between amateur and professionals clubs. In 1932, the FFF sanctioned professionalism and launched a regionally split championship whose play-off was won by Lille. Séte won the first unified league the next year.

Sochaux (twice), Racing Club de Paris, Olympique Marseille and Séte again won subsequent championships until competition ceased in 1940.

LIGUE 1 by the numbers

20 NUMBER OF TEAMS

1932 LIGUE 1 FOUNDED

10 MOST TITLE WINS: **SAINT-ÉTIENNE**

299 MOST GOALS: **DELIO ONNIS** (1971–1986)

618 MOST APPEARANCES: **MICKAEL LANDREAU** (1997–2014)

1 THE ONE CLUB FROM OUTSIDE FRANCE TO PLAY IN LIGUE 1: **MONACO**

TOP **3** TEAMS QUALIFY FOR CHAMPIONS LEAGUE
BOTTOM **2** TEAMS ARE RELEGATED TO LIGUE 2

Peace-time saw Stade de Reims and OGC Nice emerge as new powers in the league. Nice won four titles in the 1950s, while Reims secured six between 1949 and 1962. The Champagne club also finished runners-up twice in the European Champions Cup and provided the backbone of the national team who finished third at the 1958 World Cup.

The early 1960s proved financially challenging. A number of famous old clubs collapsed into bankruptcy or were forced into mergers to survive. The vacuum was filled, briefly, by the Breton club Nantes and then, commandingly, by Saint-Étienne. Les Verts won the championship seven times in ten seasons in the late 1960s and 1970s, while also restoring French pride in Europe. However it was Marseille, crowning their own dominant era in the 1980s and early 1990s, who became first French winners of the Champions Cup.

Marseille were eclipsed by Paris Saint-Germain after the latter's purchase by Qatar Sports Investments. PSG spent heavily on new players, including a world record €222m purchase of Brazil superstar Neymar from Barcelona. Their reward was to win five Ligue titles in six years.

Dimitri Payet goes on the attack for Marseille, his fourth Ligue 1 team.

Italian Serie A

The San Siro stadium in Milan hosts two great Serie A teams – Internazionale and Milan. Just over 80,000 fans fill the three giant tiers.

Italian businessman Edoardo Bisio is the man often credited with introducing modern football to Italy, in 1887, in particular in Turin. Appropriately, local giants Juventus are record champions with 32 Serie A titles (and two revoked after a matchfixing scandal).

Regional leagues were the original order of the day until Serie A was launched in 1929-30 with 18 clubs. Ambrosiana Inter were the inaugural champions thanks largely to the 31 goals of young striker Giuseppe "Peppino" Meazza. But their success was the prelude to the long reign of Juventus, empowered by financial support from the Agnelli family's FIAT motor company.

Juventus were duly overtaken by Bologna (four times), Ambrosiana-Inter (twice) and Roma before Torino won the last title in 1943, before war forced a shutdown. Torino, inspired by captain and inside left Valentino Mazzola, picked up where they left off after the war, winning four leagues in a row between 1946 and 1949 before the club was tragically wiped out in the Superga air disaster.

The financial strength of the big clubs prompted the wholesale importation of foreign players. Milan led the way with their Swedish trio of Gunnar Gren, Gunnar Nordahl and Nils Liedholm. Smaller clubs responded by developing the stultifying catenaccio defensive system. Even so, Milan and Inter enjoyed success in the European club competitions, as did Juventus in the 1980s through the inspiration of Michel Platini.

A subsequent Milan revival, financed by millionaire businessman and politician Silvio Berlusconi, brought further European successes for a side starring Dutchmen Ruud Gullit, Marco Van Basten and Frank Rijkaard. Milan and Juventus dominated Serie A with occasional interruptions from the likes of Diego Maradona's Napoli, Sampdoria (Genoa), Lazio and Roma.

In 2006, Italy were apparently flying high after a fourth World Cup success. However, simultaneously, information emerged about the Calciopoli matchfixing scandal, which undermined the credibility of the domestic game. Juventus were punished with relegation for the first time in their history but bounced back to win seven Serie A titles in a row between 2012 and 2018.

THE GREAT DEFENDER **PAOLO MALDINI** SPENT ALL 25 OF HIS SERIE A SEASONS PLAYING FOR MILAN AND DID NOT RETIRE UNTIL THE AGE OF 41 IN 2009. HE WON SEVEN SERIE A TITLES.

SERIE A by the numbers

20
NUMBER OF TEAMS

1929
SERIE A FOUNDED

34
MOST TITLE WINS: **JUVENTUS**

2
TITLES STRIPPED FROM **JUVENTUS** FOR INVOLVEMENT IN MATCH RIGGING (2004–05, 2005–06)

647
MOST APPEARANCES: **PAOLO MALDINI** ALL FOR MILAN (1985–2009)

274
MOST GOALS: **SILVIO PIOLA** (1929–54) PRO VERCELLI, LAZIO, TORINO, JUVENTUS, NOVARA

TOP **3** TEAMS QUALIFY FOR CHAMPIONS LEAGUE
BOTTOM **3** TEAMS ARE RELEGATED TO SERIE B

Italy

Italian football possesses an aura and style beyond every other nation in Europe, whether the national team and its clubs are riding high with success or down in the doldrums. Italy have won the World Cup four times and the European Championship once, while clubs such as Juventus, AC Milan and Internazionale boast reputations and fans far beyond Turin and Milan.

Yet the early years of Italian football were chaotic and complicated as a rival mixture of regional leagues competed for power. The Italian association finally settled in Rome in 1929 and a national league was formed in 1930, providing the launchpad for international success in the 1930s.

Under legendary coach Vittorio Pozzo, Italy lost only seven games during the decade, winning the World Cup in 1934 and 1938 and the 1936 Olympic title in between. The 1930s also saw Italian clubs start to import foreign talent: outstanding figures in this era included Argentinian Luisito Monti and Italy's own double World Cup-winner Giuseppe Meazza.

After the war, Torino were immediately dominant, winning four consecutive titles, and providing virtually all of the national team. But in 1949, returning from a friendly in Lisbon, Torino's plane crashed into Superga Hill outside Turin, killing all on board, including 10 internationals.

Many blamed the national team's subsequent failures on the plethora of foreign imports. The borders were shut in 1964, which may have hampered Italian clubs in European competition, but allowed a new generation of home-grown players to emerge and win the 1968 European Championship.

Even so, Milan and Inter still won the European Champions Cup four times between them in the 1960s and the national side finished runners-up to brilliant Brazil in the 1970 World Cup. The heroics primarily focused around Milan's Gianni Rivera and Inter's Sandro Mazzola plus Cagliari's free-scoring Luigi Riva.

Club pressure wrought a progressive lifting of the imports ban without, this time, any apparent detrimental effect on the national team. Italy finished fourth at the 1978 World Cup then triumphed four years later, in Spain. A team spurred on by the goals of Paolo Rossi and captained by 40-year-old goalkeeper Dino Zoff grafted out a third World Cup victory by a 3-1 scoreline over West Germany in Madrid.

Rossi stepped out at those finals having only just completed a three-year ban arising from a betting-and-bribes scandal. This was just one of a string of matchfixing upsets to have dogged the domestic game since the early 1930s.

Italy finished third as World Cup hosts in 1990, before losing agonisingly on penalties to Brazil in the 1994 final after shootout misses from Franco Baresi and Roberto Baggio.

The unfortunate manner of the Azzurri's exits from major tournaments continued when they lost on a golden goal to France in the final of Euro 2000, but they turned the tables on the French in the 2006 World Cup final.

Yet even this fourth World Cup triumph was accompanied by the simultaneous revelations of matchfixing back home which led to the enforced relegation of Juventus. The "Old Lady" of Italian football recovered but the domestic game's failure to move with the commercial times saw Italian football fall financially behind its main European rivals.

Italy Football Federation founded
1898

FIFA affiliated
1905

World Cup
1934
1938
1982
2006

European Championship
1968

Olympics Gold
1936

OLDEST PLAYER
DINO ZOFF
41
YEARS 89 DAYS

35

TOP SCORER
LUIGI RIVA

GOALS SCORED PER MATCH
1.73

WIN PERCENTAGE
53

Paolo Rossi ends up in the goal – alongside the ball – after heading home to open the scoring against West Germany in the 1982 World Cup final in Madrid.

Italy's captain Fabio Cannavaro leads the World Cup-winning party in Berlin in 2006.

Holland

The Netherlands may be a small nation in terms of size but is a giant when it comes to international football and providing many star players to all Europe's major leagues.

The Dutch were early devotees of football and were among the leading amateur sides in the early 1900s. Indeed, they reached the semi-finals of four consecutive Olympic Games from 1908 to 1924, albeit losing every time.

The 1920s marked a move away from amateurism in other countries and Dutch football entered a decline that lasted until the 1960s. Up until that decade, internationals were mostly played against European neighbours, especially Belgium, and first-round defeats in the 1934 and 1938 World Cups did little to encourage them to venture further afield.

The lowest point came just after the Second World War, when a dismal sequence of results, with only one victory in more than five years, prompted a modernisation of the domestic game. In 1957, a national league was created and professionalism was introduced in an attempt to staunch the flow of Dutch players abroad.

The main beneficiaries of the reorganisation in both domestic and international competition were the "big three" clubs: Ajax of Amsterdam, Feyenoord of Rotterdam and PSV Eindhoven. Ajax coach Rinus Michels oversaw the "total football" revolution, starring Johan Cruyff, which saw the national team finish World Cup runners-up in both 1974 and 1978.

A further generation emerged in the 1980s, generating European club competition successes, while Ruud Gullit, Marco Van Basten and Frank Rijkaard became key components of the national team's 1988 European Championship triumph.

That remains Holland's only trophy. They were semi-finalists in the 1998 World Cup and Euro 2000 (which they co-hosted with Belgium), then lost a third World Cup final 1–0 to a late extra-time goal against Spain in South Africa in 2010. Four years later, in Brazil, the Dutch finished third.

Holland FA founded
1889

FIFA affiliated
1904

European Championship
1988

50 TOP SCORER **ROBIN VAN PERSIE**

1905 YEAR OF FIRST GAME HOLLAND 4–1 BELGIUM

WIN PERCENTAGE 50

GOALS SCORED PER MATCH 2.04

Eredivisie

Football was brought to Holland in the mid-1860s and the Nederlandsche Voetbal-bond (later the KNVB) was the second oldest FA outside the British Isles, founded in 1889. However development of clubs and players was held back because domestic competition remained officially amateur until the mid-1950s.

Once professionalism had arrived progress was achieved at high speed. Ajax in Amsterdam and Feyenoord in Rotterdam were quickest to capitalise. In the late 1950s and 1960 Ajax won five league titles and Feyenoord four. The outstanding player of the era was Feyenoord left-winger Coen Moulijn, following in the footsteps of Puck Van Heel in the 1920s and 1930s then Faas Wilkes in the 1940s and early 1950s.

Feyenoord led the international breakthrough in 1970 when they became the first Dutch club to win the European Champions Cup. This launched a golden era for Dutch football in which Ajax won a hat-trick of European Champion Cups (1971, 1972, 1973), while Feyenoord and PSV Eindhoven both won the UEFA Cup.

This trio have carried off the league title every season since 1965, with the exceptions of two interruptions by AZ Alkmaar in 1981 and 2009, as well as by FC Twente under English manager Steve McClaren in 2010.

The restricted domestic market in terms of revenue sources from television and sponsors meant the clubs had more and more difficulties holding on to their most talented players. PSV did win the European Champions Cup in 1986, while Ajax won the Cup-winners' Cup in 1987, the UEFA Cup in 1992 and then the Champions Cup again in 1995. However, Feyenoord's UEFA Cup win in 2002 remains the last Dutch success in Europe.

Ajax are record domestic champions with 33 titles followed by PSV (24). Feyenoord ended a prolonged slump after their UEFA Cup peak in 2002 by regaining the league title for the 15th title in 2017.

A playoff system is used to resolve issues of relegation and promotion from the Eerste Divisie. The bottom club are relegated automatically while the next two lowest-placed clubs enter two playoff groups against three second division teams.

EREDIVISIE by the numbers

18
NUMBER OF TEAMS

1956
EREDIVISIE FOUNDED

33
MOST TITLE WINS: **AJAX**

62
MOST SEASONS IN TOP FLIGHT: **AJAX, PSV EINDHOVEN, FEYENOORD**

311
MOST GOALS: **WILLY VAN DER KUIJLEN** PSV EINDHOVEN, MVV MAASTRICHT (1964–82)

687
MOST APPEARANCES: **PIM DOESBURG** (1962–87)

TOP **2** TEAMS QUALIFY FOR CHAMPIONS LEAGUE
BOTTOM TEAM IS RELEGATED TO ERSTE DIVISIE
(16TH AND 17TH TEAMS GO INTO RELEGATION PLAY-OFFS)

Holland line up for the 1978 World Cup final against Argentina. The Dutch hold the record for playing the most World Cup finals without ever winning the tournament. They finished second in the 1974, 1978 and 2010 World Cups.

The Amsterdam Arena, home to Ajax, is the largest stadium in Holland. It was opened in 1996 and has a capacity of 53,738 seats for football matches.

GOALS (41) PER GAME (64) **EUSÉBIO**
0.64
(0.51 FOR RONALDO)

WIN PERCENTAGE
46

GOALS SCORED PER MATCH
1.59

TOP SCORER **CRISTIANO RONALDO**
*May 2017
71

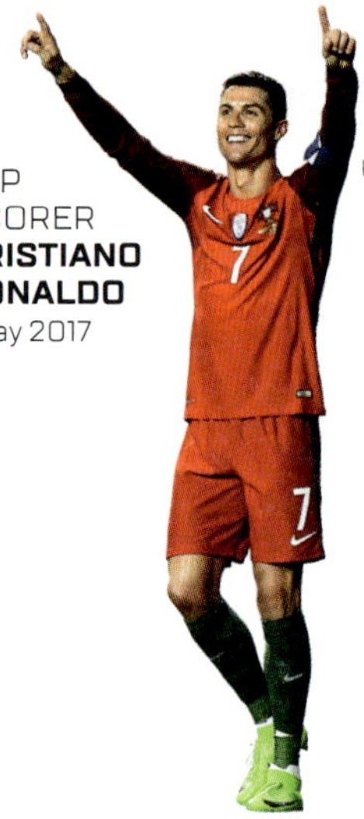

Portugal

Portugal celebrated their greatest day after winning the 2016 European Championship by defeating hosts France 1-0 after extra time. Victory was long-overdue reward for Portugal's contribution to the world game.

Portugal Football Federation founded
1914

FIFA affiliated
1923

European Championship
2016

The Federação Portuguesa de Futebol was founded in 1914 by a merger of the associations of Lisbon and Oporto. But Portugal had to wait 50 years to shine on the international stage, when Benfica won the European Champions Cup twice (1961 and 1962) and reached three more finals. Benfica also provided the bulk of the national team who finished third at the 1966 World Cup in England. Their hero was Mozambique-born striker Eusébio, who was the tournament's nine-goal leading scorer.

Playmaker Mario Coluna, also from Mozambique, was another "adopted" player from the then-Portuguese colonies in an impressive side which included Benfica wingers José Augusto and António Simões and centre-forward José Torres.

After a "lost decade" in the 1970s, Portugal revived in the 1980s. Porto won the Champions Cup and Benfica reached the finals of both the Champions Cup and UEFA Cup. A "golden generation" won the World Youth Cups of 1989 and 1991 and star graduate Luís Figo would later be crowned World Player of the Year.

Porto, under José Mourinho, won the UEFA Cup and Champions League in 2003 and 2004 to spark a renewal of confidence in the national team, who duly finished runners-up as hosts at Euro 2004 and then took fourth place at the 2006 World Cup.

New starlet Cristiano Ronaldo grew up into a modern superstar. At Euro 2016 he inspired Portugal's first major success, despite injury early in the final. Unfortunately his four goals, including a hat-trick against Spain, could not inspire a repeat at the 2018 World Cup.

Portugal's players celebrate after winning the Euro 2016 quarter-final match against Poland.

Portuguese Primeira Liga

FC Porto won the first Portuguese national championship in 1922, but that was a false start. The event was organised on a knockout basis and is now considered a predecessor of the cup rather than the league, which was finally launched in 1934–35.

PRIMEIRA LIGA by the numbers

18	1934	36
NUMBER OF TEAMS	PRIMEIRA LIGA FOUNDED	MOST TITLE WINS: **BENFICA**
29	**331**	**0**
CONSECUTIVE WINS EUROPEAN RECORD: **BENFICA** (1971–73)	MOST GOALS: **FERNANDO PEYROTEO** SPORTING LISBON (1937–49)	NUMBER OF WINNERS OUTSIDE OF LISBON AND PORTO

TOP **3** TEAMS QUALIFY FOR CHAMPIONS LEAGUE
BOTTOM **2** TEAMS ARE RELEGATED TO LIGAPRO

Porto were again the winners of a competition whose immediate success led to the creation of a regionalised second division in 1938 and third division in 1947. Benfica, Lisbon rivals Sporting Clube and Porto have monopolised the competition with Benfica winning 36 titles, Porto 28 and Sporting 18. The only two clubs to challenge this dictatorship have been Belenenses in 1946 and Porto's neighbours Boavista in 2001.

The command of "Os Tres Grandes" has been almost total. None of the trio have ever been relegated; the closest any of the three came to relegation was in 1970 when Porto finished a modest ninth. This dominance has been underlined by several championships having been won without defeat.

Benfica's most outstanding season was 1972–73 when they won 28 games and drew two, setting a record for the most consecutive victories (23). They also finished 18 points ahead of second-placed Belenenses, which was remarkable when only two points, rather than three, rewarded a victory. Benfica won the title unbeaten again in 1978 as did FC Porto in 2011 and 2013.

↑ Porto players revel in the club's second UEFA Europa League triumph, in Dublin in 2011.

The most dominant era was established by Porto who won five successive league titles between 1995 and 1999. A run of four consecutive crowns was achieved by Sporting between 1951 and 1954, by Porto again between 2006-09 and then Benfica from 2014-17.

Only four coaches have managed all three clubs: Brazilian Otto Glória, Chilean Fernando Riera and Portuguese trainers Fernando Santos and Jesualdo Ferreira. Fernando Santos achieved a permanent place in any Portuguese sport hall of fame by guiding the national team to their victory at Euro 2016.

➔ A Russian postage stamp from 2016 shows an artist's impression of the Cosmos Arena, in Samara, one of the new stadiums being built in Russia for the 2018 World Cup.

Russia

Russia's modern football history is inextricably entwined with that of the former Soviet Union. But a major step towards establishing an independent sporting identity was taken by Russia's successful staging of the 2018 FIFA World Cup.

Football had been introduced by British engineers at the start of the 20th century, and leagues were soon formed in most of the cities of the old Russian empire, most notably in the then-capital of St Petersburg. In 1912, an all-Russian federation was created, a national championship introduced and a representative team competed - and immediately crashed out to Finland - in the Stockholm Olympics.

The national team vanished from sight in the interwar years after the Russian Revolution that brought the communist party to power. Not until the early 1950s did the Soviet Union begin to venture abroad. They won the football gold medal at the 1956 Olympic Games in Melbourne and reached the quarter-finals of the 1958 World Cup on their debut.

This side contained some of Soviet football's greatest names, including captain and left-half Igor Netto, inside forwards Valentin Ivanov and Nikita Simonyan and the great goalkeeper Lev Yashin. In 1960, they won the inaugural European Championship (then termed the Nations Cup) but this remains the only major triumph of either the Soviet Union or Russia.

Russia Football Union founded
1912

FIFA affiliated
1912

European Championship*
1960

Olympics Gold*
1956
1988

*as Soviet Union

In subsequent years, the USSR came close to more success but never close enough. They were runners-up in the European Championship in 1964 and 1972 and reached the semi-finals in 1968. In the World Cup, they reached the quarter-finals in 1962 and the semi-finals in 1966.

In the 1970s, Dynamo Kiev winger Oleg Blokhin emerged as the Soviet Union's greatest-ever forward but the national side continued to decline, before reviving to reached the European Championship final again in 1988. This Soviet side was the best since the 1960s. Now the USSR relied mainly on Ukrainian players from Dynamo Kiev, who won the European Cup-winners' Cup twice, in 1975 and 1986. Dynamo Tbilisi, from Georgia, won the same tournament in 1981.

Ten years later the Soviet Union disintegrated into 15 separate states. Russia took up the USSR's football mantel but the national team struggled to match the achievements of their Soviet predecessors. In 2018, however, Russia staged a highly-successful FIFA World Cup at which the host team surprised even their own fans and media by reaching the quarter-finals before losing only in a penalty shootout to Croatia.

MOST CAPS
SERGEI IGNASHEVICH
120

WIN PERCENTAGE
49

GOALS SCORED PER MATCH
1.64

TOP SCORER
ALEKSANDR KERZHAKOV
30

Russian Premier League

League football started up in St Petersburg at the end of the 19th century and in Moscow at the start of the 20th.

RUSSIAN PREMIER LEAGUE by the numbers

16 NUMBER OF TEAMS

1992 PREMIER LEAGUE* FOUNDED *Known as The Highest League until 2001

10 MOST TITLE WINS: **SPARTAK MOSCOW**

6 TITLES IN A ROW WON BY **SPARTAK MOSCOW** (1996–2001)

143 MOST GOALS EVER: **OLEG VERETENNIKOV** (1992–2008)

28 MOST GOALS IN ONE SEASON: **SEYDOU DOUMBIA** CSKA MOSCOW 2011–12

TOP **2** TEAMS QUALIFY FOR CHAMPIONS LEAGUE
BOTTOM **2** TEAMS ARE RELEGATED TO RUSSIAN FOOTBALL NATIONAL LEAGUE (13TH AND 14TH TEAMS GO INTO RELEGATION PLAY-OFFS).

The size of the country prevented organisation of a national championship until the mid-1930s. Moscow was the central power thanks to its five new, great workers' clubs: Dynamo (electrical trades), Spartak (producers co-operatives), Torpedo (car manufacturers), Lokomotiv (railways) and CSKA (the army).

The first season, 1936, saw leagues run in both spring and autumn which were won respectively by Dynamo and Spartak. The star player was Dynamo's Mikhail Yakushin, who coached the team on its legendary tour of Britain and Sweden in the winter of 1945.

Expansion of the Soviet league led to its ultimate domination by the more skilled approach of the Ukrainian clubs, notably Dynamo Kiev. In the two decades from 1971 to the end of the Soviet era, the title went to Moscow only six times.

All that changed after the reversion to a Russian championship in 1992. Now a football revolution was under way. Russian players could transfer freely to western Europe and the newly-enriched oligarchs filled the gaps by investing in a flurry of foreign players from all around the world.

Brazil's Roberto Carlos, Cameroon's Samuel Eto'o and Ivory Coast's Yaya Toure were among the most notable imports. Many, for all the high wages, struggled to adjust to the climate, distances and outbursts of racist abuse.

Now, at least, Moscow clubs regained their pre-eminence. After 26 years of strictly national competition, Spartak established themselves as record champions with 10 titles, followed by CSKA (six) and Lokomotiv (three). The major out-of-town challenge has come from Zenit St Petersburg with four triumphs and Rubin Kazan (two).

Andrei Arshavin of Zenit St Peterburg scores as Andrei Stepanov of Torpedo Moscow makes a challenge during a 2005 Russian Premier League match in Moscow.

Belgium

ENZO SCIFO
BELGIUM'S "LITTLE PELÉ" SCORED 19 GOALS IN 89 APPEARANCES FOR BELGIUM. HE IS ONE OF A SELECT BAND OF PLAYERS WHO HAVE PARTICIPATED IN FOUR WORLD CUPS, INCLUDING FELLOW BELGIAN GREATS FRANKY VAN DER ELST AND MARC WILMOTS.

Belgium FA founded 1895	
FIFA affiliated 1904	Olympics Gold 1920

1

BELGIUM HIGHEST FIFA RANKING NOVEMBER 2015–MARCH 2016

Belgium's long wait to prove themselves among the most competitive of nations ended at the 2018 World Cup finals in Russia when they finished a best-ever third. The Red Devils' campaign was long overdue reward for a so-called 'golden generation' featuring English Premier League stars Eden Hazard, striker Romelu Lukaku, playmaker Kevin de Bruyne, central defender Vincent Kompany and goalkeeper Thibaut Courtois. Coach Roberto Martinez's men won all three group matches then knocked out Japan and Brazil before losing to eventual champions France and beating England in the third place play-off.

That prompted the greatest celebrations in the history of a national association formed in 1895. Belgium had been one of the driving forces behind the formation of FIFA and one of only four European sides to go to Uruguay for the first World Cup in 1930. But the strictly amateur nature of the domestic game hindered progress. The national team only began to progress in 1980 when they were European Championship runners-up to West Germany. Six years later a team starring goalkeeper Jean-Marie Pfaff and forward Jan Ceulemans reached the World Cup semi- finals for the first time. Other great players down the years included forwards Raymond Braine in the 1930s then Paul Van Himst in the 1960s. Belgium's leading club are Anderlecht from Brussels who have won the league a record 34 times, the cup on nine occasions and five European club titles in now-defunct Cup-winners Cup, UEFA Cup and UEFA Super Cup.

Eden Hazard and Kevin de Bruyne were two of the star-studded, but ultimately under-achieving, Belgium team at the European Championship 2016.

Luka Modric battles against France's Antoine Griezmann in the 2018 World Cup final. Croatia lost, but Modric received the Golden Ball as best player.

Austria

Austria FA founded
1904

FIFA affiliated
1905

Austrian capital Vienna was the centre of continental football in the first half of the last century. Britons in Vienna provided football's early impetus and, in 1902, Austria beat Hungary 5–0 in the world's second oldest international fixture, after England v Scotland. The interwar period was Austria's most successful era when, from 1931 to 1934, the "Wunderteam" - led by Matthias Sindelar - scored 101 goals in 30 matches. They were favourites for the 1934 World Cup, but lost in the semi-finals to hosts Italy. A new side came together in the 1950s, led by halfbacks Ernst Ocwirk and Gerhard Hanappi. In 1954 they reached the semi-finals again before losing to West Germany. Austria's two greatest clubs are the only ones to have reached European finals. Both lost in the Cup-winners Cup - FK Austria in 1978 and Rapid Vienna in 1985. Modern stars have included Herbert Prohaska, Hans Krankl and David Alaba.

Croatia

Croatia Football Federation founded
1912

FIFA affiliated
1992

Croatia stunned the international game at the 2018 World Cup in Russia when they reached the final. Not only had Croatia been independent for only 27 years but, with a population of just over four million people, were the second-smallest nation ever to reach this stage (after Uruguay). A team inspired by playmaker and captain Luka Modric lost 4-2 to France, but had still surpassed the achievements of their predecessors who had finished third in the finals in 1998 - and who had, coincidentally, lost to hosts France in the semi-finals.

Croatia emerged as an independent nation after the fragmentation of Yugoslavia at the start of the 1990s. Quickly they made an impact by reaching the quarter-finals of Euro 96, beating Italy along the way, before finishing third at the 1998 World Cup. Stars then included midfielders Zvonimir Boban and Robert Prosinecki, plus centre-forward Davor Suker (all World Youth Cup-winners with Yugoslavia in 1987). Suker, who went on to become federation president, is Croatia's all-time leading scorer with 45 goals ahead of one of the country's heroes in the 2018 World Cup, Mario Mandzukic (33).

Greece

Greece Football Federation founded 1926

FIFA affiliated 1927

European Championship 2004

Greek football's development was hampered initially by the unstable political climate in the Balkans. These factors, linked to the "Olympian" adherence to the amateur spirit of the game, meant that a national league was not formed until 1960, and full professionalism arrived as late as 1979. Consequently, success for Greek sides at national and club level has been rare. However the national team sprang a major surprise in 2004 when a team managed by veteran German coach Otto Rehhagel won the European Championship. Greece defeated hosts Portugal in the final in Lisbon on a goal from Angelos Charisteas. Only one Greek club has ever reached a European final. That was in 1971, when Panathinaikos from Athens were runners-up to Ajax Amsterdam in the European Champions Cup final at Wembley.

The club game has been marred down the years by fan violence, incurring several government-ordered halts to competition, and a long-running matchfixing scandal. Record domestic champions are Olympiakos from Piraeus.

Hungary

Hungary Football Federation founded 1901

FIFA affiliated 1907

Olympics Gold 1952 1964 1968

Hungary will always be renowned for the "Magical Magyars" side of the 1950s. The so-called "Golden Team" lost only one international in five years before failing in the 1954 World Cup final. The forward line of Laszlo Budai, Sandor Kocsis, Nandor Hidegkuti, Zoltan Czibor and Ferenc Puskás – the greatest player of his era – terrorized opposition defences and scored 173 goals between them. In 1953, they became the first non-British side to beat England at home. Yet this was not the first outstanding side Hungary had produced. In 1938 a national team containing stars of the era such as Gyorgy Sarosi and Gyula Zsengeller were World Cup runners-up to Italy. The Hungarian uprising of 1958 broke up the "Golden Team" but by the 1960s another emerged, starring were Florian Albert and Ferenc Bene, who led Hungary to the 1962 and 1966 World Cup quarter-finals and Olympic gold in 1964 and 1968. The Hungarian game then entered a long decline before new investment after 2010 was rewarded with Hungary returning to the international stage at Euro 2016 in France.

Northern Ireland

Northern Ireland FA founded 1880

FIFA affiliated 1911

The story of Irish football runs parallel to that of mainland Britain, with the founding of the Irish Football Association in November 1880 and launch of the Irish Cup. In 1905, Shelbourne became the first Dublin side to win the trophy, but in 1911-12 a split in the IFA presaged political schism. The Football Association of Ireland was founded in 1921 while the IFA continued to run the game in Ulster. At international level one of Northern Ireland's most memorable years came in 1957 when the international team beat England 3-2 at Wembley for the first time. They also qualified, once more for the first time, for the World Cup in Sweden, managing to successfully reach the quarter-finals. They also achieved World Cup qualification in 1982 and 1986 under Billy Bingham. In 1982, World Cup, Northern Ireland created a sensation by defeating hosts Spain 1-0. In the 1986 finals, in Mexico, goalkeeper Pat Jennings played a then-world record 119th international on his 41st birthday. Unfortunately, they lost 3-0 to Brazil and were eliminated after managing only a single point in a 1-1 draw with Algeria.

← History in the making: Ferenc Puskás (left) and his Hungarians prepare to demolish England at Wembley in 1953.
→ George Best, playing here against England in Belfast in 1971, won 37 caps and scored 9 goals for Northern Ireland. Sadly for fans, he was destined to be one of the greatest footballers never to grace a World Cup.

Poland

Poland FA founded 1919	
FIFA affiliated 1923	Olympics Gold 1972

The Polish state was created in 1921 and Poland made their debut the same year against Hungary. Despite reaching the 1938 World Cup finals, the pre-war record was poor. The post-war communist takeover brought great change; old clubs became attached to government bodies while new ones were formed - notably, Gornik Zabrze, who reached the European Cup-winners' Cup final in 1969. In 1972, Poland won the gold medal at the Munich Olympics with a side containing striker Wlodzimierz Lubanski and playmaker Kazimierz Deyna and left-winger Robert Gadocha. For the 1974 World Cup finals, this trio was joined by striker Grzegorz Lato. Poland finished third and reached the World Cup finals again in 1978. In 1982, with new star Zbigniew Boniek, they reached the semi-finals. The collapse of communism led to the collapse of state subsidies. Clubs were forced to sell star players abroad, to the detriment of the national team. There were first-round failures at the World Cups of 2002, 2006 and 2018, as well as Euro 2012 despite the advantage of being co-hosts.

PAT JENNINGS
IN AN INTERNATIONAL CAREER THAT LASTED FROM 1964 TO 1986, JENNINGS PLAYED IN A RECORD 119 GAMES FOR NORTHERN IRELAND AS GOALKEEPER. HE AND GEORGE BEST MADE THEIR INTERNATIONAL DEBUTS IN THE SAME GAME.

FERENC PUSKÁS
A PROLIFIC FORWARD, PUSKÁS SCORED 84 GOALS IN 85 MATCHES FOR HUNGARY. HE ALSO WON FOUR CAPS FOR SPAIN, AFTER TAKING SPANISH CITIZENSHIP IN 1962, THOUGH HIS GOALSCORING KNACK DESERTED HIM IN THOSE GAMES.

3.59

ROBERT LEWANDOWSKI
3 MINUTES 59 SECONDS IS ALL THE TIME IT TOOK THE POLISH STRIKER TO SCORE A HAT-TRICK AGAINST GEORGIA IN JUNE 2015. EVEN MORE REMARKABLY, THE FIRST GOAL ONLY WENT IN ON 89 MINUTES, FOLLOWED BY TWO IN ADDED TIME.

Republic of Ireland

Republic of Ireland FA founded
1921

FIFA affiliated
1923

The Irish Republic developed as an independent football nation after the creation of the Irish Free State in the early 1920s. They competed in the World Cup qualifiers of 1934 and 1938, while clubs founded before partition lived on and gained new strength. Many old links survived. Several players appeared for both Irelands, and the first foreign nation to beat England in England was the Irish Republic, 2-0 in September 1949. However, it was not until an English manager, Jack Charlton, took advantage of the parental qualification loophole that the Republic gained international prestige. In 1988, he led them to their first appearance in the European Championship finals, where they beat England 1-0 in their opening game. Two years later the Irish reached the World Cup quarter-finals before losing to hosts Italy. In 1994, they beat Italy on the way to the second round but the 2002 campaign was marred by a clash between manager Mick McCarthy and skipper Roy Keane. After a blank decade the Irish returned to finals football at Euro 2012 and 2016.

Scotland

Scotland FA founded
1873

FIFA affiliated
1910

Scotland has a proud football heritage on and off the pitch. The Scottish FA was founded in 1873, and still retains a permanent seat on the law-making international board. Scotland was also the venue for the world's first international match on November 30, 1872, when Scotland and England drew 0–0. The rivalry has continued ever since,

➊ Scotland's Graeme Souness and Kenny Dalglish watch as teammate Archie Gemmill looks up to pick his spot before bending in his team's third goal, one of the best seen in a World Cup finals, against Holland in 1978 in Argentina.
➋ A great goalscorer and a scorer of great goals, Zlatan Ibrahimović celebrates his four goals that stunned England in 2012.

90

ZLATAN IBRAHIMOVIĆ
IS ONE OF ONLY TWO FOOTBALLERS TO SCORE A GOAL IN EVERY MINUTE OF THE GAME. THE OTHER IS RONALDO OF REAL MADRID.

KENNY DALGLISH
IS SCOTLAND'S MOST CAPPED PLAYER, WITH 102 APPEARANCES, AND JOINT-LEADING GOAL SCORER, WITH 30 GOALS. DENIS LAW ALSO NETTED 30 – IN ONLY 55 GAMES.

sharpened by the fact that many of England's most successful club sides have contained or been managed by Scots such as Bill Shankly (Liverpool) and Sir Matt Busby and Sir Alex Ferguson (both Manchester United). Star players have included Alex James, Denis Law, Jimmy Johnstone and Kenny Dalglish. Scottish club football was at its peak in the 1960s, with Celtic winning the European Champions Cup in 1967 - the first British winners - and reaching the final again in 1970. Rangers won the Cup-winners' Cup in 1972, but the Old Firm rivalry with Celtic was later wrecked by their collapse into financial chaos. Scotland have never progressed beyond the finals first round of either World Cup or European Championship.

Serbia

Serbia FA founded 1919	
FIFA affiliated 1923	

Serbia emerged from the fragmentation of the former Yugoslavia. In 2003, the country became Serbia and Montenegro and then, in 2006, Serbia alone. Yugoslavia had been nicknamed the "Argentina of Europe" for its apparent production line of talented players who were exported all over Europe, starting with Ivan Bek, who starred in the Yugoslav team that reached the semi-finals of the inaugural World Cup in 1930. Later, Yugoslavia were Olympic winners as European Championship runners-up in 1960 then World Cup semi-finalists two years later. Powerful clubs such as Red Star and army club Partizan from Belgrade achieved notable success in the European Champions Cup: Partizan were runners-up in 1966 and Red Star the first (and last) Yugoslav champions of Europe in 1991. The outbreak of civil strife saw Yugoslavia barred from competing in the 1992 European finals but, as Serbia, they returned to reach the last eight in 2000. Disappointing first-round failures followed, however, in both World Cup finals tournaments of 2010 and 2018.

Sweden

Sweden FA founded 1904	
FIFA affiliated 1904	Olympics Gold 1948

Sweden are Scandinavia's leading nation, as they proved in the 2018 World Cup. The Blagult pipped Netherlands in their qualifying group then beat Italy in the play-offs. In Russia, Sweden finished ahead of champions Germany in the groups on their way to the quarter-finals. The FA had been founded in 1904 and the national team first made their mark in the late 1940s when they boasted one of their most famous forward lines. Gunnar Gren, Gunnar Nordahl and Nils Liedholm sparked Sweden to Olympic gold in 1948 and were signed by Milan. A decade later, Gren and Liedholm came home to lead hosts Sweden to the World Cup final, where they lost to Brazil. Other fine finishes include third place at the 1994 World Cup and semi-finalists as hosts of Euro 1992. At club level Malmö reached the Champions Cup final in 1979 and IFK Gothenburg twice won the UEFA Cup (forerunner of the Europa League). In the 21st century, a new superstar emerged in Zlatan Ibrahimović, scorer of a record 62 goals in 116 internationals.

Switzerland

Switzerland FA founded
1895

FIFA affiliated
1904

The Swiss, as host to both FIFA and UEFA, have always had a role at the forefront of world football. Early British influence remains clear in the club names such as Grasshopper (Zürich) and Young Boys (Bern). The national side was a power in the interwar years. They were runners-up at the 1924 Olympics and World Cup quarter-finalists in both 1934 and 1938. Stars were the Abegglen brothers, Max and André, who scored more than 60 goals between them. The man responsible for this success was coach Karl Rappan. He devised the "Swiss Bolt" system, which involved using a "free" central defender. Under Rappan, the Swiss also reached the finals of four of the first five World Cups played after the war. Later they were revitalised by Englishman Roy Hodgson and reached the second round in 2006, then again in 2014 and 2018. They made unwanted history in 2006 when a penalties defeat by Ukraine meant the Swiss were the first country ever eliminated without having conceded a goal.

Wales

Wales FA founded
1876

FIFA affiliated
1910

The FA of Wales was formed in 1876, though it was not until 31 years later, in 1907, that they won the British Championship for the first time. Wales qualified first for the World Cup finals in 1958 through a "lucky losers" play-off and surprised even themselves by reaching the quarter-finals with a fine team led by "Gentle Giant" John Charles. Other key players included goalkeeper Jack Kelsey and winger Cliff Jones. That was first and last time the Welsh reached a major finals until Gareth Bale inspired their progress to the last four at Euro 2016 in France. The major Welsh clubs play competitively in the English league system, albeit without top-level success. However, Cardiff City did become the only non-English club ever to win the FA Cup when they beat Arsenal in the 1927 final. Against the odds, as a second-tier club, they returned to the final in 2008 but lost to Portsmouth. The FAW remains a member of the law-making International Football Association Board.

↓ Regarded as one of, if not the, finest footballer Wales has ever produced, John Charles represented his country at its only World Cup in 1958. He remains one of the most successful British players abroad, winning three Italian league titles with Juventus.
→ Bosnia and Herzegovina's Edin Džeko (right) and Wales' Joe Ledley battlei it out in a Euro 2016 qualifier match at the Cardiff City stadium.

SWITZERLAND
BECAME, IN 2006, THE FIRST TEAM IN A WORLD CUP FINALS TO BE ELIMINATED WITHOUT HAVING CONCEDED A GOAL.

GARETH BALE
IS THE RECORD GOALSCORER FOR WALES WITH 29 GOALS FROM 2006 ONWARD. BALE HAS ALSO NETTED 148 GOALS TO DATE AT CLUB LEVEL, DURING SPELLS AT SOUTHAMPTON, TOTTENHAM HOTSPUR AND REAL MADRID.

Albania

Albania FA founded 1930

FIFA affiliated 1932

Football's inroads in Albania were obstructed, initially by the ruling Turks, and then Mussolini's annexation in 1939. The communist takeover in 1944, under Enver Hoxha, promised a new dawn, but not for long. Albania remained in isolation throughout the 1950s. Between 1954 and 1963, they played only one international, against fellow international outcasts East Germany. In the 1960s, Albania finally entered both the World Cup and the European Championship but the isolationist legacy saw its football prospects remain as poor as its economy. After the collapse of the communist regime, the domestic game was also weakened by the flight of Albania's best players to more affluent nations in central Europe.

Belarus

Belarus Football Federation founded 1989

FIFA affiliated 1992

Belarus gained independence after the Soviet Union's collapse. Their football boasts a permanent reminder of those years through the club Minsk Dynamo, who were Soviet champions in 1982. Local players who starred for the USSR included midfielder Sergei Aleinikov and defenders Sergei Borovsky, Sergei Gotsmanov and Andrei Zygmantovich. Forward Eduard Malofeyev was a star of the Soviet national side who finished fourth at the 1966 World Cup. Initially, Dynamo dominated Belarus domestic competition, winning the league title for the first five years of independence. They were dethroned by BATE Borisov, who have won the league title every year for the past decade. Belarus have never qualified for a major finals.

Bosnia and Herzegovina

Bosnia and Herzegovina FA founded 1992

FIFA affiliated 1996

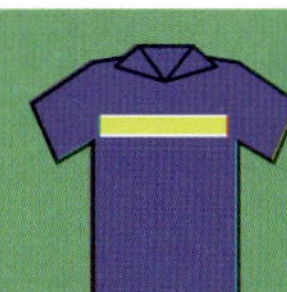

Bosnia made history as UEFA's 50th member nation. However, that was not until 1998, six years after the state's independence, owing to the political and civil strife following the collapse of Yugoslavia. Cities such as Sarajevo and Mostar boast long football traditions stretching back to the early 1900s. Bosnia produced fine footballers in the Yugoslav era, including the likes of goalkeeper Enver Marić, defender Josip Katalinski, playmaker Ivica Osim and forwards Vahid Halilhodźić, Safet Sušić and Dusan Bajević. In the modern era, new heroes, including goalkeeper Asmir Begović, midfielder Miralem Pjanić and striker Edin Džeko took them to the World Cup finals for the first time in 2014 in Brazil, where they picked up a win over Iran.

Bulgaria

Bulgaria Football Union founded: 1923

FIFA affiliated 1924

Bulgarian football has fallen from grace since they finished fourth in the 1994 World Cup in the United States, knocking out holders Germany along the way. Occasional appearances followed in World Cup and European finals, while the domestic game struggled to cope with an increasing wave of hooligan violence and matchfixing scandals. Like many Eastern Bloc countries, Bulgaria made little impact in international football until after the communist takeover and reorganisation in 1944. Outstanding players included Ivan Kolev in the 1950s, followed by Georgi Asparuhov, who scored 19 goals in 50 games before his death in a 1971 car crash. Hristo Stoichkov later won the Champions Cup with Barcelona. Dometically, rivals CSKA and Lexski from Sofia lead the way.

Czech Republic

Czech Republic FA founded 1901

FIFA affiliated 1907

Ever since Czechoslovakia came into being in 1918, the Czechs have been at the forefront of European football. They were runners-up in the 1920 and 1964 Olympics, as well as at the 1934 World Cup, with a side containing star forward Oldřich Nejedlý and goalkeeper František Plánicka. Sparta and Slavia Prague were among Europe's leading clubs before the war, with army team Dukla Prague rising to prominence after it. Dukla provided the basis of the team that finished runners-up at the 1962 World Cup. The star now was playmaker Josef Masopust. New heroes emerged in 1976 when Czechoslovakia beat West Germany on penalties to win the European title. After the political split with Slovakia, the Czech Republic were Euro runners-up in 1996.

Denmark

Denmark FA founded 1889

FIFA affiliated 1904

European Championship 1992

Denmark was one of the first countries in continental Europe to take up football, and has some of the oldest clubs in the world. For many years their proudest moments were achieved at the Olympics. Winners in 1906 and runners-up in 1908 and 1912, the Danes produced some outstanding players, including Nils Middelboe, who played for Chelsea. The 1970s saw progress with an outstanding generation of players, led by forward Allan Simonsen and Michael Laudrup. In the late 1980s, a new generation of players – including Michael Laudrup's brother, Brian – emerged to propel Denmark to a surprise European Champions title in 1992. That has proved impossible to emulate though they have reached the major finals on a further eight occasions.

13 GOALS

PETER SCHMEICHEL
UNUSUALLY FOR A GOALKEEPER, SCHMEICHEL SCORED 13 GOALS DURING HIS CAREER, INCLUDING ONE FOR THE NATIONAL TEAM. HE IS ALSO THE MOST CAPPED PLAYER FOR THE DENMARK NATIONAL TEAM, WITH 129 GAMES BETWEEN 1987 AND 2001.

Bulgaria's Yordan Letchkov topples World Cup-holders Germany in New Jersey in 1994.

Michael Laudrup lays claim to being Denmark's greatest-ever player.

Iceland

Iceland FA founded	FIFA affiliated
1947	1947

Iceland belied their long-time status as one of Europe's minnow nations by not only qualifying for the finals of the the 2016 European Championship but reaching the quarter-finals. Along the way Iceland, appearing in their first major finals, drew 3-3 with eventual champions Portugal in the group stage and then eliminated England 2-1 in the second round. Iceland made their international debut "only" in 1946 and subsequently produced various fine player exports, including Ásgeir Sirgurvinsson, Pétur Pétursson, Eidur Guðjohnsen and Gylfi Sigurðsson. Iceland made history in 1996 when a father and son, Arnor and Eiður-Smari Guðjohnsen, both played in a friendly against Estonia, with Eiður-Smari coming on as a substitute for his father.

Israel

Israel FA founded	FIFA affiliated
1928	1929

Israel have had to tread a difficult path in international football because of the region's political turbulence. In the 1958 World Cup qualifying competition, Israel's scheduled Asian opponents all refused to play them, forcing FIFA to order a playoff against Wales, which they lost. Similar issues disrupted the Asian Cup, which Israel hosted and won in 1964, their only major international honour. In 1976, Israel were expelled from the Asian Confederation on political grounds. They then led a nomadic existence as associate members of Oceania, until being formally accepted into the European fold by UEFA in 1991. Israel have reached major finals only once, failing to progress beyond the group stage at the 1970 World Cup.

Montenegro

Montenegro FA founded	FIFA affiliated
1931	2007

Montenegro is one of Europe's youngest football nations, having joined the international federation only in 2007. That was a year after the nation split away from Serbia, with which it had remained united for more than a decade following the fragmentation of the former Yugoslavia in the early 1990s. Thus far, Montenegro have not qualified for the finals of the World Cup or European Championship, and leading clubs such as Buducnost Pogorica and Rudar Pljevlja have yet to make a mark in continental club competition. Old heroes during the Yugoslavia years included playmaker Dejan Savićević, who later became Montenegro federation president. New stars have included forwards Stevan Jovetić and Mirko Vučinić.

10.8
SECONDS

HAKAN ŞÜKÜR
OF TURKEY SCORED THE FASTEST-EVER WORLD CUP GOAL IN 2002 WHEN HE SLOTTED HOME AFTER 10.8 SECONDS IN THE THIRD-PLACE PLAY-OFF AGAINST SOUTH KOREA.

← Ole Gunnar Solskjær scored 23 goals in 67 games for Norway. He formed a formidable striking partnership with Tore André Flo.
↘ Turkey overcome shock outsiders Senegal to reach the 2002 World Cup semi-finals.

Norway

Norway FA founded 1902

FIFA affiliated 1908

Norway, once a European minnow, upset the form book in the 1994 World Cup qualifiers, easily winning their group ahead of Holland, England and Poland. Subsequently, the Norwegians beat Brazil 2-1 in a group-stage match in France in the 1998 World Cup, before losing to Italy in the second round. It was a remarkable rise up the national rankings for the Scandinavian side, thanks largely to the fact that most of their senior players are based abroad. Many have enjoyed outstanding careers in England, including Chelsea's Tore André Flo, Manchester United's Ole Gunnar Solskjaer and Henning Berg and Tottenham's Steffen Iversen. Norway last appeared in a finals at Euro 2000, when they failed to get past the group stage.

Romania

Romania Football Federation founded 1909

FIFA affiliated 1923

Romania embraced football before most of its Balkan neighbours. King Carol was determined Romania should enter the inaugural World Cup, where they were beaten by Uruguay in the first round. They also entered the 1934 and 1938 tournaments but could not progress beyond the first round, despite the presence of Iuliu Bodola, for years their top scorer. Post-Second World War, two new Bucharest clubs, army team Steaua and police outfit Dinamo, dominated for 30 years. In 1986, Steaua became the first team from behind the Iron Curtain to win the European Champions Cup when they defeated Barcelona on penalties in Seville. Simultaneously, Romania reached three World Cups in a row and qualified five times for the Euro finals.

Slovakia

Slovakia FA founded 1938

FIFA affiliated 1994

Slovakia were always poor relations in the former Czechoslovakia. After the political split in the mid-1990s, it took them 17 years to find their international football feet. Then, they not only reached the finals of the World Cup in 2010 for the first time, but eliminated holders Italy on their way to reaching the second round. Three-goal Róbert Vittek was briefly the tournament's joint top scorer. Slovakia's only other appearance at major finals came in the 2016 European Championship in France. They reached the second round before losing 3-0 to Germany. The most notable achievement by a Slovak club was Slovan Bratislava's victory in the European Cup-winners' Cup in 1969, more than two decades before the split from Czechoslovakia.

Slovenia

Slovenia FA founded
1920

FIFA affiiiated
1992

Slovenia were the first newly independent country to emerge from the fragmentation of the former Yugoslavia at the start of the 1990s. For a small new nation their international progress was remarkable. They first joined the elite at the finals of Euro 2000 then reached the subsequent World Cup, only to lose their nerve when an initial 3-1 defeat by Spain prompted a row between coach Srečko Katanec and star forward Zlatko Zahović. They returned to the finals in South Africa in 2010 and were in sight of reaching the second round for the first time until narrowly losing their last group game by 1-0 to England. In 2016 senior Slovene football official Aleksander Čeferin was elected president of European federation UEFA.

Turkey

Turkey Football Federation founded:
1923

FIFA affiliated
1923

Turkey's third place finish at the 2002 World Cup underlined their rise up Europe's football ladder. Until then they had managed only one lone finals appearance, in 1954. Decisive progress was sparked by the TV and commercial revolution of the mid-1990s. The big three Istanbul clubs – Galatasaray, Beşiktaş and Fenerbahçe – began buying foreign players and coaches, who in turn helped inspire domestic stars to raise their game. Hakan Şükür scored the fastest-ever World Cup finals goal in 2002 when he scored after 10.8 seconds. The national team also reached the semi-finals of the European Championship in 2008, Weeks earlier, Galatasaray became the first Turkish club to land a European trophy in the UEFA Cup.

Ukraine

Ukraine Football Federation founded:
1991

FIFA affiliated
1992

Leading club Dynamo Kyiv had been a power within the Soviet system before the collapse of the communist system, winning the league 13 times and the European Cup-winners' Cup twice. They then dominated independent Ukrainian football, along with main rivals Shakhtar Donetsk. The national team have reached the finals of the World Cup only once, reaching the quarter-finals in 2006 before losing on penalties to Switzerland. Ukraine were group stage losers in the European Championship in both 2012 and 2016. The 2012 exit was especially painful since Ukraine were co-hosts. and claimed the match officials wrongly denied them what could have been a decisive goal in their last group game against England.

NORTH & CENTRAL AMERICA

CONCACAF, the Caribbean, Central and North American confederation, covers a huge geographical space but its overall international successes have been few and far between. Even so, Mexico has long been a power in the Latin American game and has hosted the World Cup twice. The development of the game at grass roots level in the United States has also been remarkable since it hosted the 1994 World Cup.

Many Central American nations may appear little more than a statistical dot in the world game's atlas but have begun to benefit from CONCACAF's commercial expertise with income poured into coaching schemes and administrative improvements. Costa Rica proved the point by reaching the quarterfinals of the 2014 World Cup in Brazil. The entire region's football will receive a major fillip in the run-up to the co-hosting of the 2026 World Cup between the United States, Canada and Mexico.

USA
1991
1991, 2002, 2005, 2007, 2013

MEXICO
2012
1967, 1975, 1999, 2011
1965, 1971, 1977, 1993, 1996, 1998, 2003, 2009, 2011, 2015
1999

FIFA TEAM RANKINGS (as of June 2018)

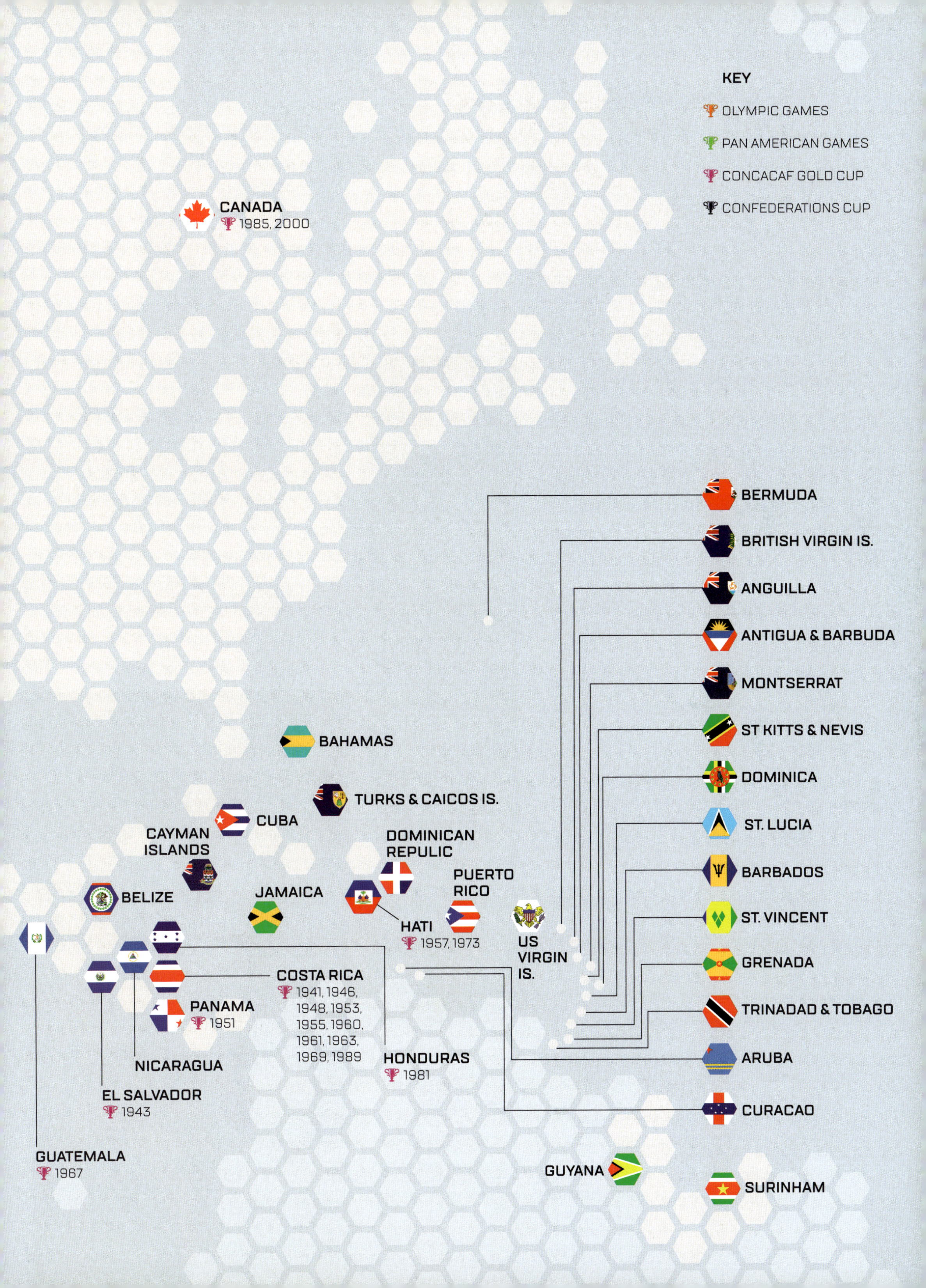
KEY
OLYMPIC GAMES
PAN AMERICAN GAMES
CONCACAF GOLD CUP
CONFEDERATIONS CUP
CANADA
1985, 2000
BERMUDA
BRITISH VIRGIN IS.
ANGUILLA
ANTIGUA & BARBUDA
MONTSERRAT
ST KITTS & NEVIS
DOMINICA
ST. LUCIA
BARBADOS
ST. VINCENT
GRENADA
TRINADAD & TOBAGO
ARUBA
CURACAO
BAHAMAS
TURKS & CAICOS IS.
CUBA
CAYMAN ISLANDS
DOMINICAN REPULIC
PUERTO RICO
BELIZE
JAMAICA
HATI
1957, 1973
US VIRGIN IS.
COSTA RICA
1941, 1946, 1948, 1953, 1955, 1960, 1961, 1963, 1969, 1989
PANAMA
1951
NICARAGUA
HONDURAS
1981
EL SALVADOR
1943
GUATEMALA
1967
GUYANA
SURINHAM

MOST CAPS WON
COBI JONES
164

WIN PERCENTAGE
42

GOALS SCORED PER MATCH
1.44

TOP SCORER
LANDON DONOVAN (right) AND **CLINT DEMPSEY**
57

United States

The respectable displays given by the United States' national team in 21st century World Cups, where they reached the quarterfinals in 2002 then the 2010 second round after finishing ahead of England in their group, ended perceptions of the US as a non-footballing nation.

Indeed, the organised game's history in the US reaches back almost as far as that of England. In 1869, two leading colleges - Rutgers and Princeton - played each other on Rutgers' New Jersey campus, basing the game on the new FA rules. Rutgers took the game 6-4, but were trounced 8-0 in the return at Princeton. The university authorities banned a third and deciding game and, by 1877, football had vanished from college fields.

Like cricket and rugby, football was considered "un-American" although it did not disappear thanks to the efforts of European immigrants - mostly British, German and Irish. A national side entered the 1924 and 1928 Olympics and then reached the semi-finals of the inaugural World Cup in Uruguay.

Nothing much changed in the immediate inter-war years although football was no longer limited to the north-east, but was now played all over the US with St Louis emerging as the sport's new capital. But the Second World War brought waves of new European immigrants whose passion for the game injected a new dynamism.

Air travel made it easier for foreign teams to tour the US. In 1948, England's Liverpool played Djurgårdens of Sweden at the Brooklyn Dodgers' baseball stadium. It was billed as the first meeting of foreign teams on American soil and more than 18,000 fans turned out.

Two years later a US team including a carpenter, a teacher, a machinist and an undertaker pulled off one of the greatest of World Cup sporting upsets when they beat England 1-0 at the World Cup in Brazil.

A new soccer push began with the creation of various new leagues in the 1960s and then a determined attempt to claim a place on the international stage. Crucial to the game's progress was the contribution of the women's national team who have dominated the international scene, winning three World Cups and four Olympic gold medals.

A bid to win host rights to the men's World Cup in 1986 was rebuffed but the lessons learned were crucial to landing the 1994 and 2026 finals. Team USA were ever-present at the finals between 1990 and 2014. Three times they reached the second round before failing, surprisingly to reach the 2018 finals.

United States Soccer Federation founded
1913

FIFA affiliated
1914

CONCACAF Gold Cup
1991
2002
2005
2007
2013
2017

➲ Clint Dempsey of the USA heads the ball clear as Daniel Van Buyten of Belgium looks on during the 2014 Brazil World Cup. Along with Landon Donovan, Dempsey is the most prolific USA goal scorer.

↑ New York City FC midfielder and Italian legend Andrea Pirlo fights for the ball against New York Red Bulls midfielder Sacha Kljestan at Yankee Stadium, New York.

MLS

Major League Soccer (MLS) is the successful outcome of all the lessons learned about how not to run domestic competition down the years. A tightly controlled, centralised management system has capitalised on US commercial acumen in the field of TV and sponsorship rights.

The consistent presence of the national team at the World Cup finals, the success of the women's game and general popularity among both sexes at grass roots level have all enhanced the sport's image. No longer is soccer considered an "ethnic" peculiarity.

The first serious attempt to create an elite national league was launched in 1967 with the founding of the North American Soccer League. Veteran stars such as Cosmos' Pelé and Franz Beckenbauer plus the likes of Johan Cruyff and George Best flitted across the stage before the NASL collapsed amid a mountain of debts in 1984.

MLS was launched in 1996 with a determination not to fall into the same traps. Beginning with 10 teams, the early years were tough as it faced hostility from other sports and sections of the media. Since then it has expanded steadily to 22 teams, with 19 in the US and three in Canada. A demand for teams to play in soccer-specific stadia also contributed to MLS establishing its own corporate and sporting "personality". The season runs from March to October with competition organised in Eastern and Western Conferences climaxed by a playoff series.

Los Angeles, with England veteran David Beckham in their ranks between 2007 and 2012, have been the most successful outfit with five MLS Cups to their name. They are followed by DC United from Washington (four) then San José Earthquakes, Sporting Kansas City and Houston Dynamo (two each).

Costs have been controlled by a salary cap which has been recognised by various court rulings. However an option permitting a "designated player" allows clubs to sign one star name whose salary is excluded from being limited by the regulatory caps.

MLS by the numbers

22
NUMBER OF TEAMS

1993
MLS LAUNCHED

5
MOST MLS CUP WINS: **LA GALAXY**

285
MILLION DOLLARS: VALUE OF **LA GALAXY**, THE MOST VALUABLE MLS CLUB

86%
DIFFERENCE BETWEEN MINIMUM PAY IN MLS SOCCER AND THE MORE LUCRATIVE NFL FOOTBALL

145
ALL-TIME GOALS: **LANDON DONOVAN** LA GALAXY AND SAN JOSÉ EARTHQUAKES

TOP TEAM FROM THE WESTERN CONFERENCE AND FROM THE EASTERN CONFERENCE, PLUS THE WINNERS OF THE MLS CUP, QUALIFY FOR THE CONCACAF CHAMPIONS LEAGUE

MOST CAPS
CLAUDIO SUAREZ
177

WIN PERCENTAGE
51

GOALS SCORED PER MATCH
2.10

TOP SCORERS
JAVIER HERNANDEZ*
*June 2017

48

Mexico

Mexico dominated central American international football to such an extent that the national team and clubs have sought more testing competition in South American competitions such as the Copa America and Copa Libertadores.

Playing high-standard opposition also helped "El Tri" maintain their remarkable World Cup record of having appeared in 15 of the 20 finals tournaments. They missed the opportunity to qualify in 1990 after being banned by FIFA for having breached Youth Cup age-limit rules. Mexico's finest World Cups were in 1970 and 1986, when they reached the quarterfinals. They have reached the second round in all the last seven World Cups, including Russia in 2018.

Mexico's clubs figure among the most financially sound in Latin America courtesy of powerful television interests that have also played a key role in securing hosting the World Cup finals in both 1970 and 1986. Mexico will become the first country to host matches in three World Cup finals tournaments as part of a 2026 co-hosting bid with the US and Canada.

Star players have included goalkeeper Antonio Carvajal, one of only two players to appear at five World Cups, 177-cap-record international Claudio Suarez, free-scoring centre-forward Hugo Sánchez and 2012 Olympic gold medal match-winning striker Oribe Peralta.

A key role in the development of football in Mexico was played by tin miners brought from Cornwall in south-west England to Pachuca in the state of Hidalgo after concessions were granted to three British companies in 1900. Alfred Crowle, son of one of the mining families, was a stalwart of first national champions CF Pachuca and later led Mexico to their first international success in the 1935 Central American and Caribbean Games.

Pachuca have won four CONCACAF Champions League titles and six domestic championships but have been far outstripped in terms of domestic honours by rivals such as Club América (12 titles), Guadalajara (11) and Toluca (10).

Mexicon Football Federation founded
1927

FIFA affiliated
1929

CONCACAF Championship/ Gold Cup Wins
1965 1971
1977 1993
1996 1998
2003 2009
2011 2015

Olympics Gold
2012

Mexico teammates sing their national anthem after receiving the gold medals that marked Mexico's victory over Brazil at Wembley Stadium in the London 2012 Olympics.

Costa Rica

↑ The Costa Rica team line up behind the national flag before their round of 16 match against Greece at the 2014 World Cup in Brazil. Costa Rica won 5–3 on penalties after extra time to go on to their first World Cup quarter-final.

Costa Rica have made enormous progress since the late 1980s, as their performances at the World Cup have demonstrated. The breakthrough came in 1990 under widely travelled coach, Bora Milutinović. The Ticos were the second of the five different teams the Serb managed at the finals. He took over very shortly before the finals in Italy yet, against all expectations, guided them to victories over Scotland and Sweden and into the second round before they fell to Brazil.

They narrowly failed to reach the second round in 2002 but had the honour and glamour of sharing the opening match in 2006, although they lost 4-2 to hosts Germany.

After missing out on the 2010 tournament in South Africa - after losing an intercontinental playoff against Uruguay - Costa Rica returned to the finals in style in Brazil in 2014. They topped a first-round group including a trio of former world champions in Uruguay, Italy and England. Both their knockout ties went to penalty shootouts: Costa Rica beat Greece, lost to Holland and flew home as national heroes. Two years later goalkeeper Keylor Navas went on to become the first Costa Rican to win the UEFA Champions League with Real Madrid.

The Costa Rica football federation, FEDEFUTBOL, was founded in 1921 with the creation of a league championship. Membership of FIFA followed six years later. Costa Rica joined the central and north American confederation in 1962, one year after its creation, and have competed regularly in all regional tournaments.

Thus far they have won three CONCACAF Gold Cups and eight central American titles while top clubs Deportivo Saprissa and LD Alajuelense have each lifted a hat-trick of CONCACAF club titles. They are considered the third most successful CONCACAF nation after Mexico and the United States, and look set to be one of the stars of the region for years to come.

Costa Rica Football Federation founded
1921

FIFA affiliated
1927

CONCACAF Championship Wins
1963
1969
1989

Canada

Canada Soccer Association founded 1912	
FIFA affiliated 1912	CONCACAF Championship/ Gold Cup 1985 2000

Football in Canada struggled to establish itself due to the size of the country and the popularity of ice hockey, baseball, American football and basketball. Yet the game has a long domestic history. In 1904 Galt FC from Ontario not only entered but won the football demonstration tournament at the St Louis Olympics. Since the 1970s, and the initial days of the North American Soccer League, leading Canadian clubs have competed in US-based tournaments. Hence, clubs from Vancouver, Toronto and Edmonton competed in the NASL, and a trio from Vancouver, Toronto and Montreal now feature in MLS. Not until 2000 did Canada secure their first senior trophy in beating Colombia to win the CONCACAF Gold Cup. In 2015, Canada hosted a successful Women's World Cup. The nearest a Canadian club have come to a major prize was Toronto FC's shootout defeat by Mexico's Guadalajara in the 2018 CONCACAF Champions League final.

↑ Honduras players sing their national anthem before a game at the 2016 Rio Olympics.
↓ Martin Nash (left) and Paul Stalteri (right) of Canada fight for the ball with Martin Zapata of Colombia in the final of the CONCACAF Gold Cup 2000 in Los Angeles. Canada won 2–0 to achieve their first Gold Cup success.
→ Jamaica's Gareth McCleary is tackled by El Salvador's Alexander Larin during a CONCACAF Gold Cup match in Toronto in 2015. Jamaica won 1–0 and went on to their first final, losing 3–1 to Mexico.

100 HOUR WAR
WAS A BRIEF WAR FOUGHT BY EL SALVADOR AND HONDURAS IN 1969. TENSIONS BETWEEN THE TWO COUNTRIES COINCIDED WITH RIOTING DURING TWO 1970 WORLD CUP QUALIFIERS. THE WAR BEGAN ON 14 JULY 1969, WHEN THE SALVADORAN MILITARY LAUNCHED AN ATTACK AGAINST HONDURAS.

Honduras

Honduras Football Federation founded
1935

FIFA affiliated
1946

CONCACAF Championship
1981

Honduras has been plagued by insurgency and guerrilla warfare. Indeed, Honduras and neighbours El Salvador went to war in 1969 over the outcome of a World Cup qualifying match. The game was run initially by the clubs and, although the national team made their debut in 1921, a federation was not set up until 1951. The national team qualified for the World Cup finals on three occasions. In 1982, they fell in the first round despite a 1–1 draw with hosts Spain; in 2010, they were eliminated after failing to score a goal; and in Brazil 2014, they lost all three matches to France, Switzerland and Ecuador.

One of the most outstanding footballers was Alfredo Hawit, who played for the Progreso, Olimpia and Motagua clubs and made his national team debut aged only 15. Later he became president of the federation and then head of the central and north American confederation. Hawit was later banned from football by FIFA over corruption allegations.

Jamaica

Jamaica Football Federation
1910

FIFA affiliated
1962

Jamaica made remarkable strides in the 1990s but then faded again, in terms of the international game. A great deal of credit was due to Brazilian coach René Simões. In 1995, Jamaica received a special award from FIFA as the most improved team in the world federation's international rankings. They went on to qualify for the World Cup finals, for the first and only time, in 1998. In France, the Reggae Boyz lost 3-1 to Croatia and 5-0 to Argentina - for whom Gabriel Batistuta scored a hat-trick - but redeemed themselves with a 2-1 closing win over Japan in Lyon. Midfielder Theodore Whitmore, who had spells in England with Hull City and Tranmere Rovers, scored both their goals.

Jamaica slipped into the doldrums in subsequent years. However, they reached the quarter-finals of the CONCACAF Gold Cup in 2003, 2005 and 2011 and were runners-up in both 2015 and 2017. In 2015 they lost 3-1 to Mexico, and in 2017 by 2-1 to their United States hosts in Santa Clara, California.

Trinidad & Tobago

Trinidad & Tobago FA founded
1908

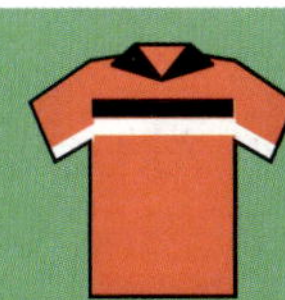

FIFA affiliated
1964

In 2006, the "Soca Warriors" became only the second Caribbean nation to reach the World Cup finals following a dramatic victory over Bahrain in an intercontinental play-off. They were held to a 1-1 draw at home but recovered to win 1-0 in Manama to book a place in the finals. As a result, Trinidad and Tobago became the smallest country to qualify for the FIFA World Cup.

Subsequently, the veteran Dutch coach Leo Beenhakker plotted a respectable campaign at the finals in Germany. A team starring Dwight Yorke, the Manchester United veteran, claimed a historic first point against Sweden. After that, however, Trinidad & Tobago lost 2-0 to both England and Paraguay. The pride and excitement of the campaign was dissipated in a decade-long row over match fees and bonuses between the players and the federation led by controversial FIFA vice-president, Jack Warner.

OCEANIA

Oceania is the poor relation of international football. Only Australia has ever had significant mainstream potential and it defected to join the Asian Confederation in 2006. An Oceania confederation was founded in 1965 but its fledgling reputation was damaged in 2000 when its long-serving president, Charles Dempsey, walked out on the FIFA executive in the midst of its deliberations over hosting rights to the 2006 World Cup. Not until 2001 did FIFA agree to grant Oceania a single guaranteed place at the World Cup finals. However, that guarantee was rescinded two years later. The Oceania qualifying winner was thus condemned to compete in an intercontinental playoff.

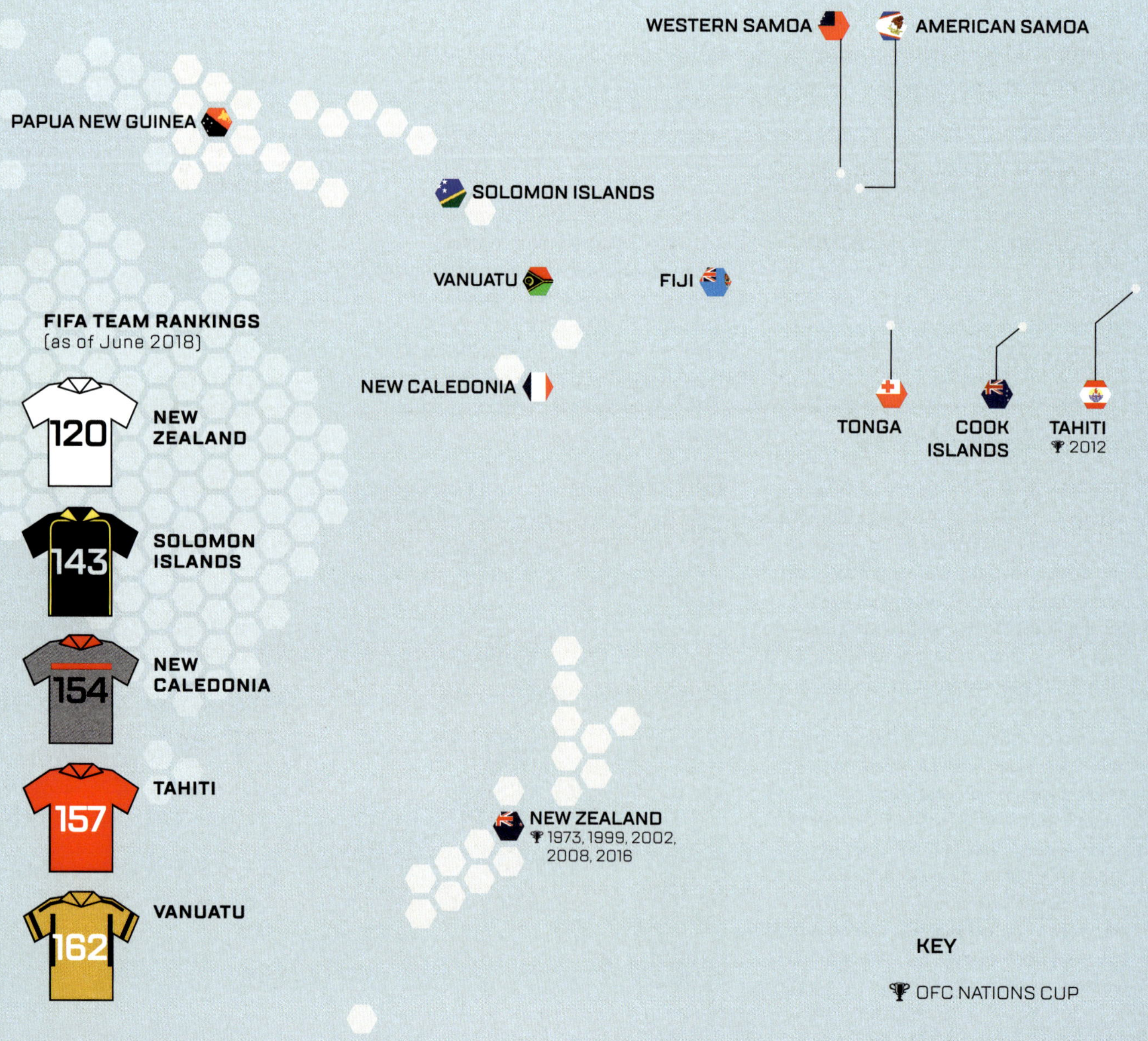

New Zealand's Shane Smeltz celebrates scoring the opening goal in a World Cup group match against Italy in 2010, in New Zealand's second World Cup.

New Zealand

New Zealand Football founded	
1891	
FIFA affiliated	**OFC Nations Cup**
1948	1973 1998 2002 2008 2016

New Zealand played second fiddle to Australia in Oceania ever since the NZ Soccer Association was founded in 1891. They did however win the inaugural Oceania Nations Cup in 1973 and then reached the World Cup finals for the first time in 1982. They lost all their matches in Spain, but those games launched the career of the All-Whites' star striker, Wynton Rufer. New Zealand did not return to the finals until 2010, after Australia's defection to Asia. A team tightly organised by Rufer's former team-mate, Ricki Herbert, drew all their games, against Slovakia, Italy and Paraguay, but finished one point behind the Slovaks in third place and were eliminated.

A major problem for New Zealand is that the domestic game is only semi-professional, so talented young players are quickly lured away to Australia, Europe or even Canada and the US.

The national team have won the Oceania Nations Cup five times, thus competing four times at the FIFA Confederations Cup. A New Zealand club also usually win the Oceania Champions League and thus compete at the FIFA Club World Cup every December.

30–0

TAHITI
SPOILED THE PARTY FOR THE COOK ISLANDS IN THEIR FIRST INTERNATIONAL GAME, IN 1971, WITH THIS 30–0 DRUBBING.

Tahiti

Tahiti Football Federation founded	
1989	
FIFA affiliated	**OFC Nations Cup**
1990	2012

The South Sea island, Tahiti, is best known to the outside world for the paintings of the post-impressionist Paul Gauguin. In the sporting world, it sprang a major surprise by competing in the Confederations Cup in Brazil in 2013. The French Polynesia team, which includes Tahiti, qualified for the World Cup warm-up tournament by winning the Oceania Nations Cup for the first time in 2012. Results in Brazil were predictably embarrassing as the players were overwhelmed by the pressure of playing on the great stages of the world game in Brazil's most famous stadiums. They lost 6-1 to Nigeria, 10-0 to Spain and 8-0 to Uruguay.

SOUTH AMERICA

Geographical and communications challenges in football's early years led to South America going its own way. CONMEBOL (the Confederacion Sudamericana de Futbol) was founded in 1916. The moving spirit was Uruguayan official, Hector Gómez, who had first proposed the body in 1912. That also led, in 1916, to the first official South American championship with Argentina and Brazil also founder members. Paraguay joined CONMEBOL in 1917, Peru in 1924, Bolivia in 1925, Ecuador in 1927, Colombia in 1940 and Venezuela in 1952. CONMEBOL grew in importance after the launch of the Copa Libertadores in 1960 to suit the continent's big clubs who wanted their equivalent to Europe's Champions Club Cup.

FIFA TEAM RANKINGS (as of June 2018)

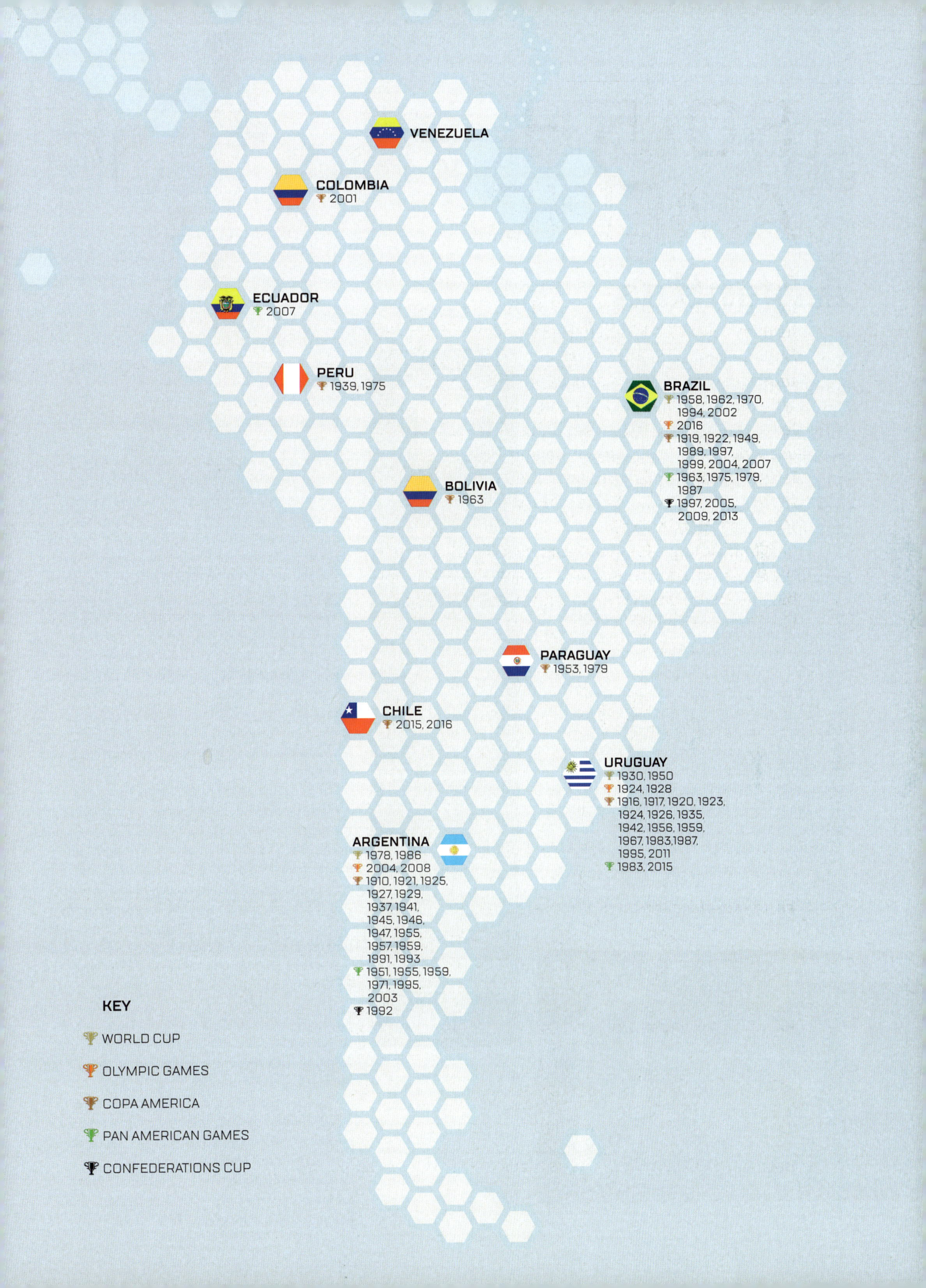
VENEZUELA
COLOMBIA
2001
ECUADOR
2007
PERU
1939, 1975
BRAZIL
1958, 1962, 1970, 1994, 2002
2016
1919, 1922, 1949, 1989, 1997, 1999, 2004, 2007
1963, 1975, 1979, 1987
1997, 2005, 2009, 2013
BOLIVIA
1963
PARAGUAY
1953, 1979
CHILE
2015, 2016
URUGUAY
1930, 1950
1924, 1928
1916, 1917, 1920, 1923, 1924, 1926, 1935, 1942, 1956, 1959, 1967, 1983, 1987, 1995, 2011
1983, 2015
ARGENTINA
1978, 1986
2004, 2008
1910, 1921, 1925, 1927, 1929, 1937, 1941, 1945, 1946, 1947, 1955, 1957, 1959, 1991, 1993
1951, 1955, 1959, 1971, 1995, 2003
1992
KEY
WORLD CUP
OLYMPIC GAMES
COPA AMERICA
PAN AMERICAN GAMES
CONFEDERATIONS CUP

GAMES PLAYED AGAINST SOUTH AMERICAN TEAMS
58%

WIN PERCENTAGE
54

GOALS SCORED PER MATCH
1.88

TOP SCORER
LIONEL MESSI
*May 2017
58*

Argentina

Argentina continues to produce some of the world's finest players, not only technically gifted but determined and hard-working. They have won the World Cup twice, finished runners-up three times and lifted the Copa America 14 times while their clubs have carried off the Copa Libertadores on 24 occasions throughout its five-decade history.

The British brought football to Argentina in the 1860s, and although at first it was exclusive to the British residents in Buenos Aires, by the turn of the century numerous clubs had been formed.

The Argentine Football Association was founded in 1891 by an Englishman, Alexander Hutton, and a league was formed the same year. Although the championship was not a truly national competition, as it contained only clubs from Buenos Aires, La Plata, Rosario and Santa Fé, their intense rivalry ensured that Argentina had a vibrant domestic scene from the outset.

The national side also made an early start and, in 1901, a representative side played neighbouring Uruguay in the first international match to be staged outside Great Britain. The seeds were sown for a rivalry that has grown into one of the most enduring and intense derby matches in the world.

Argentina FA founded
1893

FIFA affiliated
1912

World Cup
1978
1986

Copa América
1921 1925
1927 1929
1937 1941
1945 1946
1947 1955
1957 1959
1991 1993

Olympics Gold
2004 2008

⊖ Mario Kempes scores his and Argentina's second goal against Holland in the 1978 World Cup final.
⊕ Argentina captain, Diego Maradona, is in ecstasy after his team's 3–2 victory over West Germany in the 1986 World Cup final.

Professionalism was adopted in 1931, and River Plate and Boca Juniors soon emerged as dominant forces. River's starting team of the 1940s was the greatest of them all, with a forward line of Muñoz, Moreno, Pedernera, Labruna and Loustau, which became known as "La Máquina": a very well-oiled "machine" in the English translation.

The national side were runners-up to Uruguay in the 1928 Olympics and met their deadly rivals again two years later in the 1930 World Cup final. Although they lost 4-2, the impressive Argentine side was plundered by Italian agents - starting a draining process that has continued ever since.

To avoid repeating that fate, a third-rate side was sent to the 1934 tournament, and Argentina did not make a serious attempt on the World Cup again until the 1950s. Indeed, the 1950s saw the birth of an exceptional side, with another famous forward line of Corbatta, Maschio, Angelillo, Sívori and Cruz.

Little progress was made in the 1960s and 1970s, despite Independiente and Estudiantes having dominated the Libertadores Cup. Argentina had to wait until 1978 for their first World Cup success. On home soil, and with a side containing only one overseas-based player, Mario Kempes, Argentina deservedly won the tournament. They did so again in Mexico in 1986, inspired by captain and match-winner, Diego Maradona, who ranks as one of the greatest players the world has ever seen despite highly publicised problems off the pitch.

Maradona led Argentina to the 1990 World Cup final and defeat by West Germany. He was then sensationally banished from the 1994 finals after failing a dope test and his teammates, without him, fell in the second round.

The quarter-finals proved Argentina's limit in 1998, 2006 and 2010. Then they found a new superstar in Lionel Messi. But World Cup glory proved beyond even his record-breaking achievements. Argentina lost the 2014 final to Germany in extra-time, then tumbled out in the second round in Russia in 2018.

AFA

Argentina Primera

League football has been running in Argentina since 1891, launched at the impetus of Alex Lamont from the St Andrews Scotch School, which had been founded by Scottish immigrants to Buenos Aires in 1838.

Lamont rounded up four other clubs - Old Caledonians, Buenos Aires and Rosario Railways, Buenos Aires Football Club and Belgrano Football Club - for the first league created outside the United Kingdom. St Andrews, appropriately, were first champions.

The "league: imploded almost immediately but a successor, created by another immigrant teacher Alexander Hutton, was launched two years later. His English High School CA, later renamed Alumni, won the top division title 10 times between 1900 and 1911.

In 1913, the number of clubs jostling for inclusion led to the league being split into two sections. After the first round-robin series, the top 11 played again for the league and the bottom four in a relegation series. By now, Boca Juniors had joined the elite, to be followed in 1914 by River Plate. The two giants have dominated Argentinian football ever since. Their continent's "El Clásico" is one of the game's great derbies.

Boca Juniors player Cristian Chávez (left) tussles for the ball with Leonardo Ponzio, from River Plate, during a Buenos Aires derby game at the Monumental Stadium in 2012.

PRIMERA by the numbers

30
NUMBER OF TEAMS

1891
PRIMERA FOUNDED

36
MOST TITLE WINS: **RIVER PLATE**

3
THE ONLY KEEPER HAT-TRICK, SCORED BY **JOSÉ LUIS CHILAVERT** IN A GAME FOR VÉLEZ SARSFIELD IN 1999

15
AGE OF **SERGIO AGÜERO** ON HIS DEBUT FOR INDEPENDIENTE IN 2003

295
MOST GOALS: **ARSENIO ERICO** (1933–47)

TOP **5** TEAMS QUALIFY FOR THE COPA LIBERTADORES THE BOTTOM FOUR TEAMS ARE RELEGATED TO THE PRIMERA B NACIONAL

Between 1931 and 1934, two championships were played simultaneously, one among the traditionalist amateur clubs and one among the progressive professionals. Boca, in 1935, won the first unified championship.

Until 1966 one league championship was played per year, built around the Buenos Aires and Rosario clubs. In 1967, pressure from the provincial associations led to the addition to the calendar of a national championship including clubs from Córdoba, Mendoza and other cities. Although currently run as a year-long tournament with 30 teams each playing 30 games traditionally, since 1986, two all-inclusive championships have been staged each year: the Apertura (Opening Season) and Clausura (Closing Season).

River Plate hold the record of 36 titles followed, inevitably, by Boca with 33 and Racing of Avellaneda with 17.

Brazilian Serie A

Brazil is a vast country, roughly half the land mass of South America. Hence a unified national league championship on European lines was never a realistic prospect until the advent of jet travel.

The power of the domestic game was previously vested in more than 30 regional championships, organised by the provincial associations. Even so, the greatest focus of attention of fans, and later broadcasters and sponsors, was directed on the powerful rival leagues of São Paulo (Paulista) and Rio de Janeiro (Carioca).

Between 1959 and 1970, playoff competitions were organised between the top clubs of the two state leagues to designate a national champion. This was entitled the Torneio Roberto Gomes Pedrosa (after a former São Paulo FA president) from 1954 until 1967 and then, briefly, the Taça de Prata (Silver Cup), until 1970.

The next year saw the launch of the formal Campeonato Brasileiro. Its format has varied frequently to find a formula including clubs from around the country who wanted to join the party.

Its composition was also complicated by the propensity of relegation-threatened clubs to take court action, challenging rules and regulations and disciplinary decisions.

State championship attendances have slumped with the growing importance of the national championship. They take up the first half of the year with the national championship dominating the second half. Currently, the national championship comprises two divisions of 20 clubs and two further divisions, split regionally.

Rio and São Paulo clubs have won more than 30 national titles over four decades. Pelé's old club Santos boast 13 overall national titles since 1959 and 22 Paulista championships. Over the same period Palmeiras of Sao Paulo boast 14 and 24 while Sao Paulo FC claim seven and 21.

From Rio, Flamengo, probably Brazil's most popular club nationwide, boast six national titles and 33 Carioca championships compared with old rivals Fluminense's six and 31.

SERIE A by the numbers

20
NUMBER OF TEAMS

1959
SERIE A FOUNDED

9
MOST TITLE WINS: **PALMEIRAS**

14
RECORD RED CARDS IN ONE GAME – BETWEEN GOIÁS AND CRUZEIRO IN 1979

190
MOST GOALS: **ROBERTO DINAMITE** MAINLY FOR VASCO DA GAMA (1980–89)

65
GOALS SCORED BY **ROGÉRIO CENI** OF SÃO PAULO – THE RECORD FOR A KEEPER

TOP **6** TEAMS QUALIFY FOR THE COPA LIBERTADORES
BOTTOM **4** TEAMS ARE RELEGATED TO SERIE B

The Maracanã Stadium in Rio de Janeiro has played host to a number of Serie A clubs, including Flamengo and Fluminense.

Brazil

Brazil are the world's most admired football nation. They have won more World Cups than anyone else, five, and consistently produce players to impress and delight spectators at club and international matches all over the world.

Between 1958 and 1970, Brazil won the World Cup three times, with a team packed full of star players, including arguably the greatest in history, Pelé. Brazil are also the only country to have competed in every World Cup finals tournament.

Football was developed at the end of the 19th century, prompted by immigrant British students and workers. Leagues were soon established in Rio de Janeiro and São Paulo and the national team played their first formal international in 1914 against Argentina. In 1916, they entered the inaugural South American Championship, although the event has not been a rewarding one for them. Brazil have won it only eight times.

The World Cup proved another matter with a Brazilian golden age between 1950 and 1970. In 1950, they lost the final to Uruguay in front of their own shocked fans but in 1958 the advent of 17-year-old Pelé and Garrincha brought victory over the hosts, Sweden. In 1962, in Chile, an almost identical team triumphed again, this time over Czechoslovakia.

In 1966, a transitional side fell in the first round. However, newcomers such as Tostao, Gerson and Jairzinho were present in Mexico four years later when Brazil clinched a hat trick of World Cups, earning them the right to keep the Jules Rimet Trophy in perpetuity.

Brazil did not win again until their triumph over Italy after a penalty shootout in 1994. They reached the final again in France in 1998 with the emergence of powerful new centre-forward Ronaldo, who, together with the flair of Rivaldo, Cafu and Roberto Carlos, ushered in a new era.

Unfortunately, they fell to hosts France in a final shrouded in controversy. Ronaldo played, despite having suffered a convulsive fit on the morning of the game, but made no impression on a match that Brazil lost 3-0 in the Stade de France.

Four years later, Ronaldo made impressive amends by scoring both goals in the 2-0 final victory over Germany in Yokohama, Japan. He was also the tournament's eight-goal top scorer and thus equalled Pelé's Brazilian record of 12 goals in 14 finals appearances. Simultaneously right-back and captain, Cafu, became the first player to appear in the final of three consecutive World Cups.

Both stars were past their best when Brazil lost their crown in Germany in 2006, although Ronaldo did score the three goals which established him at the time as the World Cup's 15-goal all-time record marksman.

Fan fury after a quarter-final exit from the 2010 World Cup was nothing compared with the storm which exploded around the team's heads after humiliation on home soil in 2014. Brazil were favourites to carry off the World Cup for a sixth time. But, in the absence of injured new hero Neymar, their dreams exploded dramatically with a 7-1 semi-final defeat by Germany in Belo Horizonte.

Not until two years later were hope and belief rekindled, after Brazil, again as hosts, won Olympic football gold for the first time at the Rio de Janeiro Games. Neymar, living up to the responsibility of captaincy, converted the decisive winning penalty in Brazil's shootout victory over Germany in Maracanã.

Expectations were high for the 2018 World Cup. New coach Tite guided the Seleção to top the South American qualifying group and become the first nation to qualify for the finals. In Russia, however, Neymar & co were held 1-1 by Switzerland in their first match then knocked out by Belgium in the quarter-finals.

Ronaldo kisses the World Cup after Brazil's victory over Germany in 2002, in which he scored both goals.

Brazil Football Confederation founded
1914

FIFA affiliated
1923

World Cup
1958
1962
1970
1994
2002

Copa América
1919 1922
1949 1989
1997 1999
2004 2007

Olympics Gold
2016

MOST CAPS
CAFU
143

WIN PERCENTAGE
63

TOP SCORER
PELÉ
77

GOALS SCORED PER MATCH
2.20

⬆ Brazil players pose before playing England at the 1970 World Cup in Mexico. Is this the best Brazil team ever? Back: Carlos Alberto, Brito, Wilson Piazza, Felix, Clodoaldo, Everaldo; front: Jairzinho, Rivelino, Tostao, Pelé, Paolo César.

⬅ A jubilant Pelé is carried high by fans after Brazil's victory over Italy in the 1970 World Cup. Pelé is perhaps the most famous footballer of all time. He featured in four World Cups, the first, in 1958, at the age of 17. He won two winners' medals and was the youngest player to score in a final – netting the third and fifth goals in Brazil's 5–2 defeat of Sweden in 1958.

Chile

Chile are one of South America's original football pioneers. The sport was imported by British sailors landing at Valparaiso and taken up at local level with a federation being founded in 1895. They joined world federation FIFA in 1912 and launched a league in 1933.

Leading clubs are Colo Colo, Universidad de Chile and Universidad Católica, all based in the capital, Santiago.

Colo Colo, founded in 1925, have won a record 31 national championships and remain the only Chilean club to have lifted the Copa Libertadores. The colocolo is an Andean mountain cat but the club's nickname is "El Cacique", after an infamous Mapuche Indian leader who fought against the Spanish conquistadores.

In the Copa Libertadores in 1991, Colo Colo showed plenty of fighting spirit on the way to victory over Olimpia of Paraguay in the final. That was the first time a Chilean side had ever won a major honour. Previously, their greatest moments had come in hosting the World Cup finals in 1962. A fine team starring half-back Eladio Rojas and feisty left-winger Leonel Sanchez finished a best-ever third.

TOP SCORER
ALEXIS SANCHEZ

37

GOALS SCORED PER MATCH

1.43

WIN PERCENTAGE

39

YEARS CHILE WAITED FOR THEIR FIRST TROPHY (1910–2015)

105

Chile Football Federation founded
1895

FIFA affiliated
1913

Copa América
2015 2016

Before then, Chile had appeared only twice, and fleetingly, in the finals. Subsequently they fell in the group stage in 1966, 1974 and 1982. They were banned from the 1990 and 1994 World Cups after goalkeeper Roberto Rojas had feigned being hit by a firework during a qualifying match against Brazil in 1989.

Since then, however, the Chileans have cleaned up their act. In 1998, 2010 and 2014, they reached the World Cup's knockout stages before falling in the second round. In 2014, they came within a penalty shootout of knocking out hosts Brazil in front of their own fans.

Later, Chile found the winning formula in shootouts in the Copa América. They defeated Argentina on penalties in the finals of both the 2015 Copa and in a centenary tournament held a year later, ending their wait for a trophy of more than a century with not one, but two, major tournament victories.

Chile goalkeeper Claudio Bravo lifts the Copa América trophy at MetLife Stadium in East Rutherford, New Jersey, in 2016. This was Chile's second Copa América title.

Uruguay

Before the Second World War, Uruguay were undoubtedly the best team in the world. Today they are no longer a world power but are always dangerous opponents.

Montevideo's two great clubs, Peñarol and Nacional, have won more than 90 domestic championships between them. Both clubs have also enjoyed great success in the Copa Libertadores, Peñarol winning it five times, while Nacional boast three. Both have also won the Club World Cup on three occasions.

The national side dominated world football in the first half of the 20th century. Early successes in the South American Championship were followed by victory in the 1924 Olympics in Amsterdam. Uruguay repeated the success in 1928 in Paris, and two years later, as the host nation, swept to victory in the first World Cup.

The side of the 1920s and 1930s contained many of Uruguay's all-time greats: skipper José Nasazzi, the midfield "Iron Curtain" of José Andrade, Lorenzo Fernández and Álvaro Gestido, and outstanding forwards Héctor Castro, Pedro Cea and Héctor "The Magician" Scarone.

In 1950, Uruguay reclaimed their status on top of the world by defeating hosts Brazil 2–1 in the World Cup final in Rio de Janeiro's Maracanã. The side was inspired by inside-forward Juan Schiaffino, Uruguay's greatest player, along with wing-half Victor Andrade, captain and centre-half Obdulio Varela, plus match-winner Alcides Ghiggia at outside-right. Thus they remained unbeaten in the World Cup until finally losing 4–2 to the great Hungarian side in 1954 in Switzerland.

Subsequent World Cups proved largely disappointing despite the efforts of star forwards such as Fernando Morena and Enzo Francescoli. Finally, in 2010, the inspiration of forwards Diego Forlán and Luis Suárez lifted Uruguay back into the last four for the first time in 40 years. They reached the latter stages again in 2014 and 2018 but the only real success in that era was winning a record 15th Copa America in 2011.

Uruguay FA founded
1900

FIFA affiliated
1923

World Cup
1930 1950

Copa America
1916 1917 1920 1923 1924 1926 1935 1942 1956 1959 1967 1983 1987 1995 2011

Olympics Gold
1924 1928

Victorious Uruguay players hold aloft the Copa América trophy after defeating Paraguay 3–0 in the 2011 final, held in Buenos Aires. No other country has won the South American football championship more times than Uruguay.

The first winners of the World Cup: Uruguay 1930.

WIN PERCENTAGE
44

GOALS SCORED PER MATCH
1.58

15 RECORD NUMBER OF WINS IN THE COPA AMÉRICA

TOP SCORER **LUIS SUÁREZ***
*May 2017
48

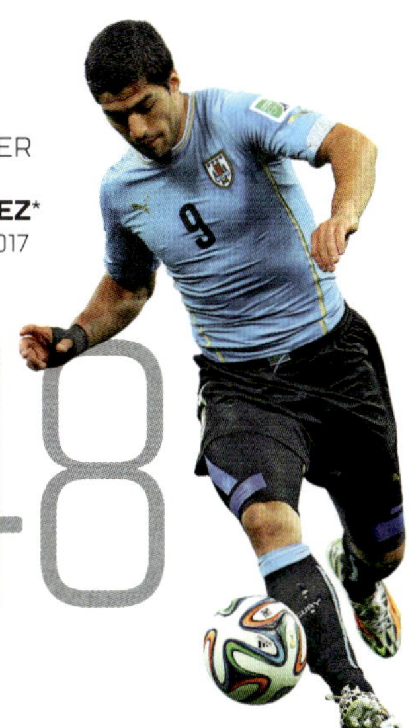

Bolivia

Bolivia Football Federation founded 1925	
FIFA affiliated 1926	Copa America 1963

Bolivia, since their first international outing in 1926, have been the perennial whipping boys of South American football. After direct progress to the World Cup finals in 1930 and 1950, they managed "proper" qualification only in 1994 when they shared the opening match glamour with defending title-holders Germany, losing 1-0 in Chicago.

South American rivals have complained in vain at the challenge of having to play Bolivia at an altitude of 12,000ft at the Estadio Hernán Siles in La Paz. Bolivia took significant advantage of local conditions to win the Copa América for the one and only time as hosts in 1963.

Colombia

Colombia Football Federation founded 1924	
FIFA affiliated 1936	Copa America 2001

Colombia's football history has been dominated by years of internal disputes, disruptions and turbulence. The most notorious was the creation in the late 1940s of a short-lived pirate league outside FIFA jurisdiction.

The Colombians made a modest World Cup debut in 1962 but, after withdrawing as host in 1986, did not appear in the finals again until 1990 and 1994. Playmaker Carlos Valderrama was a new hero then. He was succeeded in the star role by James Rodriguez when Colombia reached the quarter-finals for the first time in 2014. Their 2018 campaign ended in a shootout defeat by England in the second round.

Ecuador

Ecuador Football Federation founded 1925	
FIFA affiliated 1926	

Ecuador made history for themselves with a best-ever World Cup performance in 2006, when they reached the second round for the only time. Here they lost only 1-0 to England via a David Beckham free kick. This was the first time Ecuador had progressed so far, on only their second appearance at the finals, following a first-round elimination four years earlier in Korea and Japan. Players such as central defender Iván Hurtado and striker Agustín Delgado earned their nation a new footballing respect.

This was maintained when LDU Quito won the Copa Libertadores in 2008 and finished runners-up in the FIFA Club World Cup.

← Carlos Valderrama, known as much for his spectacular hair as his silky midfield skills, evades the tackle of a USA player at the 1994 World Cup. His 111 caps is a Colombian record.

↗ World Cup controversy flared up when it was suggested that Peru threw their game against eventual winners Argentina during the 1978 World Cup. Argentina needed to win by four clear goals to reach the final at the expense of their arch rivals, Brazil, and they promptly secured a 6-0 win.

Paraguay

Paraguay FA founded 1906	
FIFA affiliated 1925	Copa America 1953 1979

Paraguay's progress in "modern" World Cups has raised the country's international profile and the domestic game's self-confidence. One inspiration was charismatic goalkeeper José Luis Chilavert, who scored more than 60 goals in club and national team football from penalties and free kicks.

In 1998, 2002 and 2006, Paraguay reached the second round. In 2010, they appeared in the quarter-finals for the first time before losing 1–0 to Spain. They have won the Copa América twice, in 1953 and 1979. On the club front, Olimpia of Asunción have won the Copa Libertadores in 1979, 1990 and 2002 and been runners-up four times.

Peru

Peru Football Federation founded 1922	
FIFA affiliated 1924	Copa America 1939 1975

Football in Peru has been dominated by clubs from Lima, where the FA was founded in 1922. Peru's international debut came in 1927 in the Copa America, which they subsequently won at home in 1939. Their World Cup record was poor until stars such as defender Hector Chumpitaz and forward Teofilo Cubillas led them to the 1970 quarter-finals and 1978 second round. They also won the 1975 Copa America. Peru were absent from the finals for 36 years until falling in the first round in Russia in 2018. Twice tragedy has struck the game: in 1964 some 300 fans died in a stadium disaster at an Olympic qualifier against Argentina and in 1988 the Alianza team were wiped out in a plane crash.

Venezuela

Venezuela Football Federation founded 1926	
FIFA affiliated 1952	

Venezuela are the weakest of the 10 South American countries, but this is hardly surprising because the national sport is baseball. Originally members of CONCACAF, they made their international debut in 1938 and switched to CONMEBOL in 1958. The national team record offers only a handful of victories to celebrate in both the World Cup qualifying competition and Copa América, even though they enter both consistently.

"The Vinotintos" best outing was in 2007 when, as hosts, they reached the quarter-finals for the first time. None of Venezuela's clubs have ever even reached the final of the Copa Libertadores.

adidas
RMCF
18

FAMOUS CLUBS FROM AROUND THE WORLD

5

For any sports fan, there is little that inspires more passion than the local team. Since the formation of the very first clubs in the late 19th century, the domestic arena has been home to the most dramatic scenes and obsessive rivalries. These are the clubs who continue to inspire generations of dedicated fans.

UNITED KINGDOM

London may be the capital of England but it has never dominated the domestic game. London giants such as Arsenal, Chelsea and Tottenham have never had it all their own way in league or cups. The North West, a pioneer in professionalism, has remained a powerhouse of English football through the exploits and massive fan base of old rivals Manchester United and Manchester City, Liverpool and Everton. North East passion has propelled both Newcastle and Sunderland, while Midlands might has been represented through the decades by the likes of Aston Villa, Wolverhampton Wanderers and West Bromwich Albion.

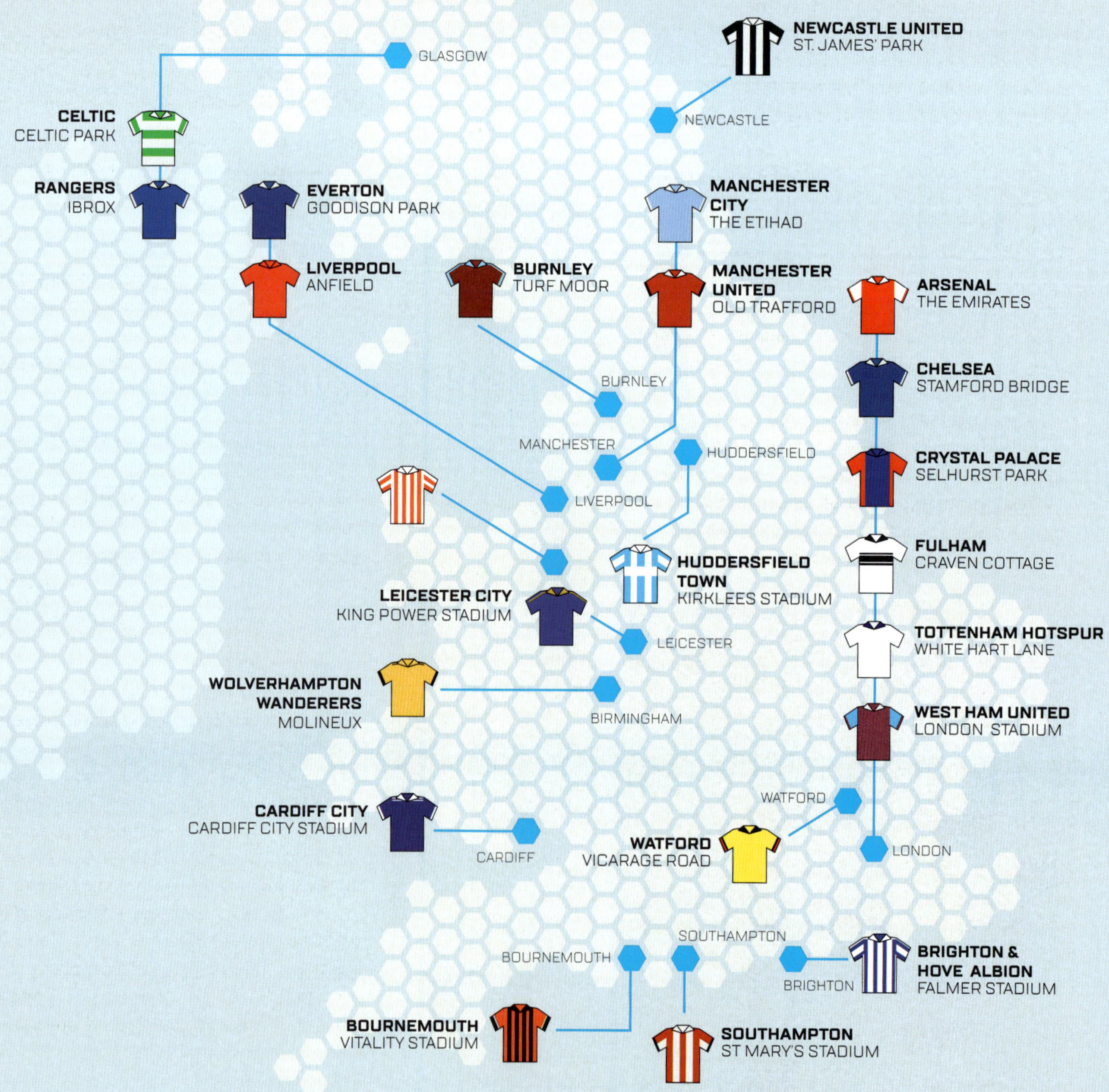

Chelsea

THE BLUES

Chelsea have been a focus of worldwide fascination since the 2003 takeover by Russian oligarch Roman Abramovich. His initial assault on English and European football reached a climax in May 2012 when the Blues fulfilled their owner's dream by winning the Champions League.

Founded
1905

Stamford Bridge
41 631

Premier League
6

FA Cup
8

League Cup
5

UEFA Champions League
2012

UEFA Europa League
2013

UEFA Cup Winners' Cup
1971
1998

UEFA Super Cup
1998

The Blues achieved the feat with a dramatic victory over Germany's Bayern on their home ground in Munich. A penalty shootout after a 1-1 extra-time draw saw Ivory Coast striker Didier Drogba write his name indelibly into Chelsea's history by scoring both their late equalising goal and the decisive penalty.

Chelsea should have been England's first competitors in the Champions Cup. They were invited to enter the inaugural competition in 1955-56 but withdrew on the orders of the Football League, which feared a fixtures snarl-up. It was 16 years before they made European amends, defeating Real Madrid in a Cup-winners' Cup final replay to win the club's first European trophy.

Within 10 years, however, Chelsea were in grave financial difficulties and it took all the business ingenuity new chairman Ken Bates could muster to turn the club around. By the mid-1990s Chelsea had become one of London's most fashionable clubs, attracting high-profile fans entertained by an imaginative transfer policy that brought in first Glenn Hoddle as player-manager then, in his wake, Ruud Gullit and Gianluca Vialli

The latter had barely been in management more than a few weeks before he was celebrating success, first winning the League Cup and then the Cup-winners' Cup.

Yet another Italian, Claudio Ranieri, steered Chelsea to fourth in the league in 2002-03. This was remarkable because Ranieri had no money to spend - in contrast to events after July 2003 when Abramovich paid £140m to buy 93 percent of the shares and wipe out their massive debts.

Suddenly Chelsea had the financial power to out-bid Manchester United, Arsenal and Liverpool in any transfer race.

Abramovich revolutionised the world market. He bought top English and world players plus the charismatic coach, José Mourinho. The "Special One", with a team backbone featuring captain John Terry and club record marksman Frank Lampard secured Premier League title success in 2005 and 2006. Mourinho was a winner for Chelsea again, after his second coming, in 2015.

Millions more were spent to support Mourinho and two further Italian managers. Carlo Ancelotti managed Chelsea's first league and FA Cup double in 2010, then stars such as Eden Hazard, Diego Costa and N'Golo Kante were available so Antonio Conte could win the league and FA Cup in 2017 and 2018.

The FA cup is held aloft by Chelsea skipper Ron Harris as he is chaired by teammates (left to right) Osgood, Hollins, Hutchinson, Houseman and Hinton after the FA Cup final replay at Old Trafford, Manchester, in 1970.

Frank Lampard, Chelsea's all-time top scorer with 211 goals, celebrates with the Champions League trophy following the 2012 final at the Allianz Arena, Munich.

Arsenal

THE GUNNERS

Arsenal are one of the most famous clubs in the game – as proved by the number of teams throughout the world who adopted that illustrious title in the hope it might bring them the same glory.

The Gunners' nickname owes everything to their original foundation in South East London, at the Woolwich Arsenal munitions works. In 1913, however, they moved to north London in the search for a greater supporter base.

The inter-war years were sensational. Legendary manager Herbert Chapman arrived from Huddersfield Town, where he had created a highly successful team in the early 1920s. Chapman guided Huddersfield to two successive championships before joining Arsenal in 1925. Using the new and innovative stopper centre half, they won the league championship five times, finished runners-up once, and won the FA Cup twice, again finishing runners-up once.

Great players of those days – wingers Joe Hulme and Cliff Bastin, centre forward Ted Drake plus attacking general Alex James and fullback captain Eddie Hapgood – remain legends of British football.

Chapman died in January 1934, as Arsenal were poised to win their third championship in four seasons. His work was carried on by secretary-manager George Allison, assisted by Joe Shaw and trainer Tom Whittaker. Under Whittaker's guidance, Arsenal won the league again in 1948 and 1953 and the FA Cup in 1950.

Fans had to wait 21 years for the next great achievement in 1970–71, when Arsenal became only the second English team of the 20th century to complete the celebrated double – winning both the league championship and the FA Cup in the same season. They beat Liverpool 2–1 after extra time at Wembley. Charlie George, who had grown up on Arsenal's doorstep, scored the Wembley winner.

A first European success had come in the Fairs Cup in 1970, when Arsenal beat Belgian club Anderlecht in the two-leg final. But the Belgian capital of Brussels was not a happy venue a decade later, when Arsenal lost the Cup-winners' Cup final to Spain's Valencia on a penalty shootout. That was Arsenal's fourth major final in three seasons, but they won only one, the 1979 FA Cup final against Manchester United.

Great players this time around included England's 1966 World Cup-winner Alan Ball, "double skipper" Frank McLintock, Irish playmaker Liam Brady and Northern Ireland's great goalkeeper Pat Jennings.

In the late 1960s and early 1970s, Arsenal had been guided in midfield by George Graham, who returned as manager in 1986 to reignite the flames of success. The most dramatic moment came in May 1989, when Arsenal became London's first league champions in 18 years thanks to a last-minute, final-day goal scored by Michael Thomas to deny Liverpool at a shocked Anfield.

Two years later, the wing magic of Sweden's Anders Limpar helped inspire another championship success before Graham parted company with the club after a controversy over transfer payments.

Graham had also led Arsenal to their second European success, a 1–0 win over Parma in the 1994 Cup-winners' Cup final. He was succeeded by Bruce Rioch who was himself replaced after just over a year in the autumn of 1996 by Frenchman Arsene Wenger.

Under Wenger's revolutionary leadership, Arsenal turned from being one of the most dour of sides into one of the most entertaining. Wenger

Founded
1886

Emirates Stadium
60 432

Premier League
13

FA Cup
13

League Cup
2

UEFA Cup Winners' Cup
1994

Fairs Cup
1970

13
FA CUP WINS – THE ALL-TIME RECORD

Arsenal, FA Cup winners 1930. Back: Baker, Lambert, Preedy, Seddon, Hapgood, John. Middle: Chapman (manager), Jack, Parker, James, Whittaker (trainer). Front: Hulme, Bastin.

49

GAMES UNBEATEN MAY 2003–OCTOBER 2004

DAVID O'LEARY
MOST APPEARANCES (1975–93)

722

brought a new approach to player management and capitalised on his knowledge of European football to import Frenchmen Patrick Vieira, Emmanuel Petit and Nicolas Anelka and Holland winger Marc Overmars. His reward, with Dutchman Dennis Bergkamp outstanding, was to win the club's second league and cup double in 1998.

Wenger's redesigned Gunners lost the UEFA Cup final of 2000 on penalties to Galatasaray and were beaten 2-1 by Liverpool in the 2001 FA Cup final. But his shrewd work paid rich dividends in 2001-02 with another league and cup double. Arsenal's mastery in 2003-04 was founded on a record-equalling unbeaten season enhanced by the goals of record marksman Thierry Henry. In eight years, the French World Cup winner scored 228 goals for Arsenal in all competitions.

UNAI EMERY
BECAME THE

19th

PERMANENT MANAGER IN ARSENAL HISTORY IN JULY 2018

Only one trophy remained elusive: the UEFA Champions League. Arsenal reached the final in 2006 but lost 2-1 to Barcelona in the Stade de France after threatening a remarkable victory despite the expulsion of goalkeeper Jens Lehmann.

That summer, Arsenal left cramped Highbury for an expansive new stadium, sponsored by Emirates Airlines, in nearby Ashburton Grove. However, the move, while improving the club's revenue stream and attracting a new American owner in Stan Kroenke, was not such a magnet in terms of title success and celebration. A comparatively luckless 14-year stretch from 2004 to 2018 brought regular appearances in the UEFA Champions League but 'only' four FA Cup wins. A need for change prompted the departure of long-serving Wenger in May 2018 and arrival of Spaniard Unai Emery.

Michael Thomas scores a last-minute goal as Arsenal, despite being labelled underdogs, beat Liverpool 2–0 at Anfield in May 1989. The victory gave Arsenal their ninth First Division title and denied Liverpool the chance of a second Double.

Manchester City

THE SKY BLUES

Manchester City have lived in the shadow of neighbours United for too long. That explains the great jubilation that greeted the Premier League title triumphs of 2012 and 2014, marking a newly enriched era under Abu Dhabi ownership.

Founded	1880
Etihad Stadium	55 097
Premier League	5
FA Cup	5
League Cup	4
UEFA Cup Winners' Cup	1970

Manchester City believe they lived in the shadows of neighbours United for far too long. Hence the jubilation which greeted the Premier League title treble of 2012, 2014 and 2018, which rewarded the massive financial investment of the club's Abu Dhabi ownership.

City won the FA Cup for the first time in 1904 (five years before United) but the league championship for the first time only in 1937 (by which time United had already been crowned twice). The most fabled of City's domestic triumphs, however, was in 1956 when they won the FA Cup final with German goalkeeper Bert Trautmann playing on despite a broken neck.

Trautmann was one of City's legends, along with heroes of the 1968 league championship-winning team such as right back (and later manager) Tony Book, midfielder Colin Bell, forward Neil Young, Mike Summerbee and Francis Lee (later chairman).

The management team of veteran Joe Mercer and innovative coach Malcolm Allison worked wonders with a team who went on to win the FA Cup in 1969 and the European Cup Winners' Cup in 1970. Young scored the winner against Leicester in the FA Cup final at Wembley and another in the 2–1 win over Poland's Gornik Zabrze in the European final in Vienna.

➊ Manchester City's Vincent Kompany embraces manager Pep Guardiola as he is substituted during a Premier League match at the Etihad Stadium, Manchester, in 2017.

A stream of big names came and went at Maine Road in subsequent years, including Scotland's Asa Hartford, England's Mike Channon and Poland's Kazimierz Deyna. But one solitary league cup victory in 1976 was the prelude to a seesaw existence before a final return to the Premier League in 2002.

A move the following year to the City of Manchester Stadium – a new venue taken over after the Commonwealth Games – did not provide the desired springboard to immediate success. Successive managers Kevin Keegan and Stuart Pearce struggled to keep City clear of the relegation zone despite costly acquisitions including French striker Nicolas Anelka and former England and Liverpool forwards Robbie Fowler and Steve McManaman.

In 2007, renewed hope was sparked by the extravagant promises of Thai politician and businessman Thaksin Shinawatra. He splashed out on former England manager Sven-Göran Eriksson and a squad-full of new players, but it soon transpired than Thaksin was more words than action. City's good fortune was that he was bought out in August 2008; the new proprietor was the Abu Dhabi United Group, owned by Sheikh Mansour bin Zayed Al Nahyan.

This takeover was followed by a spending spree that dwarfed the lavish expenditure of Chelsea's Russian oligarch, Roman Abramovich. Manager Mark Hughes set a £32.5m British transfer record in snatching Brazilian Robinho from Chelsea's apparent grasp. A year later, over £100m was spent on star names that included: Arsenal's Kolo Touré and Emmanuel Adebayor to strengthen both defence and attack, England midfielder Gareth Barry and the controversial Argentinian

➊ Manchester City captain Tony Book holds the 1969 FA Cup aloft as his teammates celebrate around him: (left to right) Glyn Pardoe, Francis Lee, Neil Young (half hidden), Mike Doyle, Harry Dowd, Colin Bell, Alan Oakes.

➋ The Premier League-winning Manchester City team line up for a group photograph before a Champions League match in 2017.

forward Carlos Tévez from neighbours United.

Still, no trophy had yet been secured and that prompted the replacement of Hughes, just before Christmas 2009, by Italian Roberto Mancini. Missing out on Champions League entry by one league place sparked yet more spending on world-class players, including Champions League winner Yaya Touré from Barcelona, Spanish World Cup winner David Silva and a hot-headed young Italian in Mario Balotelli from Mancini's old club, Internazionale.

The outcome: glory at last. City finished third in the league and, in the FA Cup, enjoyed beating Manchester United in the semi-finals and Stoke City 1-0 in the final.

↑ Sergio Aguero beats Taye Taiwo of Queens Park Rangers before scoring a last-gasp injury-time winner in the final game of the season to win the 2012 Premier League for Manchester City, their first title in 44 years.

The next target was to overthrow United as league champions. An early-season fall-out between Mancini and Tévez ultimately failed to derail a campaign that ended in thrilling drama in the last game of the 2011–12 season against Queens Park Rangers. City hit back to win from being down 2–1 with two stoppage-time goals. Argentinian Sergio Agüero was City's 23-goal leading marksman, including the winner against QPR, while Belgian club captain Vincent Kompany provided stability at the heart of defence.

Further title success followed in 2014 but City's owners were not content to rest on their laurels. Heavy investment continued to be undertaken and the managerial arrival of former Barcelona and Bayern manager Josep 'Pep' Guardiola brought further Premier success in 2018 in record breaking style with 106 goals and 100 points.

£1 BILLION

THE RICH LIST
SINCE 2008 AND THE ARRIVAL OF NEW OWNER SHEIKH MANSOUR, MANCHESTER CITY HAVE SPENT MORE THAN £1 BILLION ON NEW PLAYERS.

Manchester United

THE RED DEVILS

Manchester United fans revere Sir Matt Busby as the manager who laid the foundations of the modern era. But even his achievements pale by comparison with those of Sir Alex Ferguson, in an era that established United not only as commercial giants on the world stage but as England's record champions.

Founded as Newton Heath in 1878 by railway workers, the club evolved into Manchester United in 1902 and won the league twice and the FA Cup once before the First World War. Then they had to wait almost another 40 years before the spark of future greatness meant they emerged with a dramatic 4-2 FA Cup final victory over Blackpool.

This was the first outstanding team built by manager Busby, who had played for City before the Second World War. His second outstanding team were the so-called "Busby Babes", many of whom were developed through the club's youth system. United won the league championship in 1956 and 1957 while, in 1956-57, defying orders to become the first English side to enter the European Champions Cup. They opened their campaign with a 10-0 thrashing of Belgium's Anderlecht and never looked back - not even in the bleak days of February 1958, after eight players, including England internationals Roger Byrne, Tommy Taylor and Duncan Edwards, died in the Munich air disaster.

Munich deprived United of a golden generation. However, the sympathy felt for United after the disaster laid the foundation for the club's national, and later worldwide, fan base. In international terms it took United a decade to recover from Munich. Thus it was in May 1968 that United's European quest was rewarded as they defeated Benfica 4-1 in extra time at Wembley. Bobby Charlton, a Munich survivor along with defender Bill Foulkes and manager Busby, scored twice.

The club became synonymous with entertaining, attacking football as epitomised by the talents of Charlton, Denis Law and the wayward but mesmeric Northern Irishman, George Best. All three won the European Footballer of the Year award. Later came England's long-serving skipper Bryan Robson, who was still in a harness in 1993 when United, under Ferguson, regained the league title for the first time in 26 years.

The years between Busby's retirement as manager in 1971 and Ferguson's arrival in 1986 were bleak, and the new incumbent managed on a knife-edge in his early days. Only an FA Cup win in 1990 quietened fans demanding his dismissal. Further victory in the European Cup Winners' Cup in 1991 proved he was on the right lines.

Between 1993 and 1996, United won the league title three times in four seasons, including an unprecedented "double double" of league and FA Cup in 1994 and 1996. Goalkeeper Peter Schmeichel and forward Eric Cantona contributed the cosmopolitan icing to the most successful English club recipe of the 1990s.

Founded
1878

Old Trafford
75 643

Premier League
20

FA Cup
12

League Cup
5

FIFA Club World Cup
1999 2008

UEFA Champions League
1968*
1999
2008

UEFA Cup Winners' Cup
1991

UEFA Europa League
2017

UEFA Super Cup
1991

*European Cup

RYAN GIGGS
MOST APPEARANCES
963

ALEX FERGUSON
WIN PERCENTAGE
65%

⬆ Ole Gunnar Solskjær scores United's winner in the 1999 Champions League final. ⬅ Matt Busby lifts United spirits ahead of extra time in the 1968 European Cup.

Ferguson then pulled off a masterstroke, breaking up his title-winning squad and replacing it with a younger, even more impressive unit. As in Busby's days, the core was a remarkable group of homegrown players: Ryan Giggs, the Neville brothers, Paul Scholes and David Beckham. United were led too by another skipper with Robson's all-action qualities: hard-driving Irish midfielder Roy Keane.

United won another championship in 1997 and emulated that achievement in 1999 on becoming the only English club ever to win the "treble" of league title, FA Cup and European Cup. First they pipped Arsenal on the last day of the season to win the Premier League title then eased past Newcastle 2-0 at Wembley. In the Champions League final, United trailed 1-0 to Bayern Munich in Barcelona before turning the match on its head in the dying minutes with goals from Teddy Sheringham and Ole Gunnar Solskjær.

United dominated the Premier League for the next two seasons and again in 2002-03, courtesy of Ruud van Nistelrooy's phenomenal goal-scoring. Subsequent years saw United extend their title-winning and commercial reach. They secured a Premier League hat trick between 2006 and 2009 and – just to underline their pre-eminence – defeated Chelsea, albeit on penalties, to celebrate a third Champions League triumph in 2008.

British record signing Rio Ferdinand anchored defence with Cristiano Ronaldo and Wayne Rooney were the new attacking heroes whose brilliance apparently vindicated a controversial takeover by American sports entrepreneur Malcolm Glazier and his family.

In 2011, fans' concerns over the club's debts and the £80m sale of Ronaldo to Real Madrid were assuaged by a domestic record 19th league title, overhauling Liverpool's tally of 18. United extended the record to 20 in 2013 when Ferguson retired. Inevitably, his departure, after 27 trophy-packed years, left a managerial void which David Moyes and Louis Van Gaal struggled to fill before the appointment of José Mourinho in the summer of 2016, who led the club to their first Europa League trophy in 2017.

1000

FIRST TEAM TO SCORE 1000 PREMIER LEAGUE GOALS, APRIL 2016

Liverpool

THE REDS

Liverpool were league champions twice before the First World War, twice before the Second World War and once immediately after. But all of those paled into insignificance compared with what was to come when Bill Shankly's unrivalled enthusiasm took them to the first of their modern championships in 1964.

At the time the city of Liverpool surfed the waves of Beatlemania but the club went on to far outlast the "Fab Four". In the next 48 years, Liverpool were to win the league 13 times (adding up to 18), the FA Cup seven times (including one "double") and the League Cup on eight occasions.

Such drive proved relentlessly successful in Europe. Shankly and managerial successors Bob Paisley and Joe Fagan managed to create an approach that incorporated the physicality-based strengths of the English game with the more technical school of the best continental sides.

Five times Liverpool won the Champions League Cup. Borussia Monchengladbach, victims of the first of Liverpool's three UEFA Cup triumphs, were on the losing end again in Rome in 1977, when Kevin Keegan bowed out of the Anfield scene with the club's first Champions Cup secured. The following year, Brugge were beaten by Liverpool in the Champions Cup final at Wembley. The winning goal fell to Kenny Dalglish to score, after arriving from Scotland's Celtic for £440,000 to fill the gap left by Keegan's departure for Hamburg.

Dalglish will remain an Anfield legend, and not only for his achievements as a player in a career rewarded with 21 trophies. He took over as manager in the wake of the Heysel tragedy in 1985 and later had to bear the city's burden of pain after the 1989 Hillsborough disaster. At Heysel, 39 Juventus fans died; at Hillsborough, 96 Liverpool fans were crushed to death and 766 injured in the worst such tragedy in British sporting history.

A legacy of Heysel had been a five-year ban for English clubs from European competition. Once that suspension had been lifted, Liverpool secured the fifth and most dramatic of their Champions' triumphs. Istanbul was the stage in 2005 and saw Liverpool slumped 3-0 down to Milan at half-time. Then, in six sensational second-half minutes, inspirational captain Steven Gerrard fired them level and on to shootout success.

The league title continued to elude Liverpool. Finally, German manager Jurgen Klopp reinvigorated the team with his all-action 'Gegenpressing' style. First the Reds came within 90 minutes of success in the 2016 Europa League, then the astonishing goal-scoring accomplishments of Egyptian forward Mohamed Salah saw them reach the 2018 UEFA Champions League final.

MOST CLUB APPEARANCES IN ALL COMPETITIONS
IAN CALLAGHAN
857

Liverpool's players race to congratulate goalkeeper Jerzy Dudek after his penalty shootout saves had clinched their 2005 UEFA Champions League victory over Milan.

Founded
1892

Anfield
54 074

Premier League
18

FA Cup
7

League Cup
8

UEFA Champions League
1977* 1978*
1981* 1984*
2005

UEFA Cup
1973 1976
2001

UEFA Super Cup
1977
2001
2005

*European Cup

MOST GAMES MANAGED
BILL SHANKLY
783

STEVEN GERRARD
MOST APPEARANCES AS CAPTAIN
473

Tottenham Hotspur

SPURS/THE LILYWHITES

Tottenham, in 1960-61, were the first club in the twentieth century to win the league and FA Cup double. Not only that, they accomplished it with a style which set an almost unapproachable standard for their successors.

Danny Blanchflower was captain of a team featuring all-action Scotland left half Dave Mackay, a "will o'the wisp" inside right John White and, later, deadly goalscorer Jimmy Greaves. They reached the semi-finals of the Champions Cup in 1962 and became Britain's first European winners in the Cup Winners' Cup a year later, thrashing Atletico Madrid 5-1.

In 1972, at the expense of fellow English club Wolves, Spurs became the first holders of the new UEFA Cup. They were runners-up to old foes Feyenoord in 1974 but regained the UEFA Cup in 1984 after a penalty shoot-out victory over holders Anderlecht.

Along the way, Spurs electrified the game with an innovative transfer policy that included signing Argentinian World Cup-winners Osvaldo Ardiles and Ricardo Villa in 1978 and the acquisition of domestic heroes such as Glenn Hoddle, Chris Waddle, Paul Gascoigne and Gary Lineker.

For all their occasional successes in the FA Cup, Spurs remained as far away as ever from regaining the league title. That changed though after Harry Redknapp's arrival as manager. He took over in 2008 and within two years was leading Spurs in a lively Champions League challenge. Key players included Wales' Gareth Bale, Dutch forward Rafael Van der Vaart and central defender Ledley King. Bale, originally a wingback, earned an international reputation almost overnight with a Champions League hat trick against Internazionale of Italy.

Bale was sold to Real Madrid in the summer of 2013 for a then-world record £91m but Danish playmaker Christian Eriksen was the only success of the players bought with the money. Andre Villas-Boas and Tim Sherwood were short-lived managerial appointments until the arrival of Argentinian Mauricio Pochettino from Southampton in 2014.

Pochettino chose new signings wisely but found greatest success by delving into the club's own ranks. Centre forward Harry Kane, with the attacking support of another equally bright newcomer in Dele Alli, scored the goals that fired Spurs to third in the league in 2016 and 2018, and the runners-up spot inbetween.

Founded
1882

Tottenham Hotspur Stadium*
62 062

Premier League
2

FA Cup
8

League Cup
4

UEFA Cup Winners' Cup
1963

UEFA Cup
1972
1984

*Wembley Stadium 2017–18

Tottenham Hotspur's Dele Alli celebrates scoring his side's first goal against Arsenal during a 2-0 win at White Hart Lane in 2017. The victory meant Tottenham would finish above Arsenal in the Premier League for the first time since 1995.

JIMMY GREAVES
MOST GOALS
(1961–70)
266

Everton

THE TOFFEES

Premier League **9**

FA Cup **5**

UEFA Cup Winners' Cup **1985**

Founded **1878**

Goodison Park **39 571**

Everton, for all their proud history, have lived much of the past two decades in the domestic and European shadow of their neighbours, Liverpool. Yet the Goodison Park club had been Football League founder members in 1888 and number of the likes of free-scoring Dixie Dean, Tommy Lawton and Gary Lineker among a long line of outstanding attackers to grace "The School of Science". Everton hit the European heights in 1985 when they defeated Rapid Vienna in Rotterdam in the Cup Winners' Cup final under former midfield favourite Howard Kendall. A year later "The Toffeemen" won the league title for the ninth and last time to date.

Leicester City

THE FOXES

King Power Stadium **32 315**

Premier League **1**

League Cup **3**

Founded **1884**

Leicester City's only claim to major title fame had been three League Cup wins before they managed one of the great modern football fairy tales. Newly promoted, they just avoided relegation in 2015. Italian Claudio Ranieri was then brought in as manager and led them to an astonishing Premier League title. Key roles were played by goalkeeper Kasper Schmeichel, central defenders Wes Morgan and Robert Huth plus hard-working midfielder N'Golo Kante, winger Riyad Mahrez and 24-goal top-scorer Jamie Vardy. However, Leicester proved unable to maintain such success and Ranieri was sacked in the spring of 2017.

Newcastle United

THE MAGPIES

Premier League **4**

FA Cup **6**

Fairs Cup **1969**

Founded **1892**

St James' Park **52 404**

Newcastle United remain among the "greats" of the English game even though it is more than 60 years since they last landed the FA Cup in 1955 with fan favourite centre forward "Wor Jackie" Milburn. Later they won a European prize in the 1969 Fairs Cup but have had nothing more to celebrate, despite the presence of some outstanding attackers such as Malcolm Macdonald and Alan Shearer, plus skipper and later manager Kevin Keegan. Under Sir Bobby Robson they were third in 2003, but he was sacked a year later, ahead of tougher times under the controversial ownership of sportswear retailer Mike Ashley.

Southampton

THE SAINTS

St Mary's Stadium
32 505

FA Cup
1

Founded
1885

Southampton, nicknamed "the Saints" after their creation as the St Mary's church team, have been a consistent Premier outpost on the south coast for much of the last 40 years. In that time, their academy has developed a reputation for generating fine players, for example Theo Walcott, Gareth Bale and Adam Lallana. The high point in the Saints' history was a surprise FA Cup success over Manchester United in 1976 when they were still in the second division. Their highest league finish remains runners-up in the old First Division in 1984. Outstanding managers have included Ted Bates and Lawrie McMenemy plus, more recently, Mauricio Pochettino and Ronald Koeman.

Wolverhampton Wanderers

WOLVES

Premier League
3

FA Cup
4

League Cup
2

Founded
1877

Molineux Stadium
31 700

Another of the grand old names of English football, Wolves enjoyed their heyday in the 1940s and 1950s, when they won three league titles and two FA Cups under legendary manager Stan Cullis. In recent history they've been unable to consistently maintain their top-flight status, but a takeover by Chinese investors in 2016 has prompted a change in fortunes. The arrival of a clutch of Portuguese stars under manager Nuno Espirito Santo saw Wolves claim the Championship title in emphatic style, and earn a return to the Premier League in 2018.

West Ham United

THE HAMMERS

FA Cup
3

UEFA Cup Winners' Cup
1965

Founded
1895

London Stadium
57 000

West Ham are known as the "Football Academy" and never was the image better illustrated than in winning the Cup Winners' Cup at Wembley in 1965, beating Munich 1860 by 2-0. Hammers heroes back then included England World Cup-winning heroes Bobby Moore, Geoff Hurst and Martin Peters. Domestically, West Ham added to their 1964 FA Cup win with further triumphs in 1975 and 1980, and internationally they were 1976 runners-up to Anderlecht in the Cup Winners' Cup. The restrictive size of the Boleyn Ground held the club back financially, a problem resolved by a move in 2016 to the London Olympic Stadium.

34

ANDY COLE
THE STRIKER SCORED 34 LEAGUE GOALS FOR NEWCASTLE UNITED IN 1993–94, THE MOST IN A PREMIER LEAGUE SEASON – A RECORD SHARED WITH ALAN SHEARER, WHO MATCHED THE NUMBER FOR BLACKBURN ROVERS IN 1994–95.

Everton's Bill "Dixie" Dean directs a typically powerful header goalwards in a 1930 league match.
West Ham United celebrate with the European Cup Winners' Cup after their 2–0 win against TSV 1860 Munich in 1965. Bobby Moore (with cup) Martin Peters (to his left) and Geoff Hurst (to his right) went on to play in the England World Cup winning team of 1966.

FRANCE

The balance of power within French football changed with the new-era arrival of foreign investment, notably at Paris Saint-Germain and Monaco. Previously, the strength of French club football had been vested in the regions, notably in the 1950s and 1960s with Reims, Nice, Monaco and Nantes, then came Bordeaux and later Marseille. Saint-Etienne and Lyon generated revivalist reputations beyond France in the European club competitions. The successes of the national team in World Cup and European Championship in 1998 and 2000, respectively, also generated renewed enthusiasm and interest in the club game.

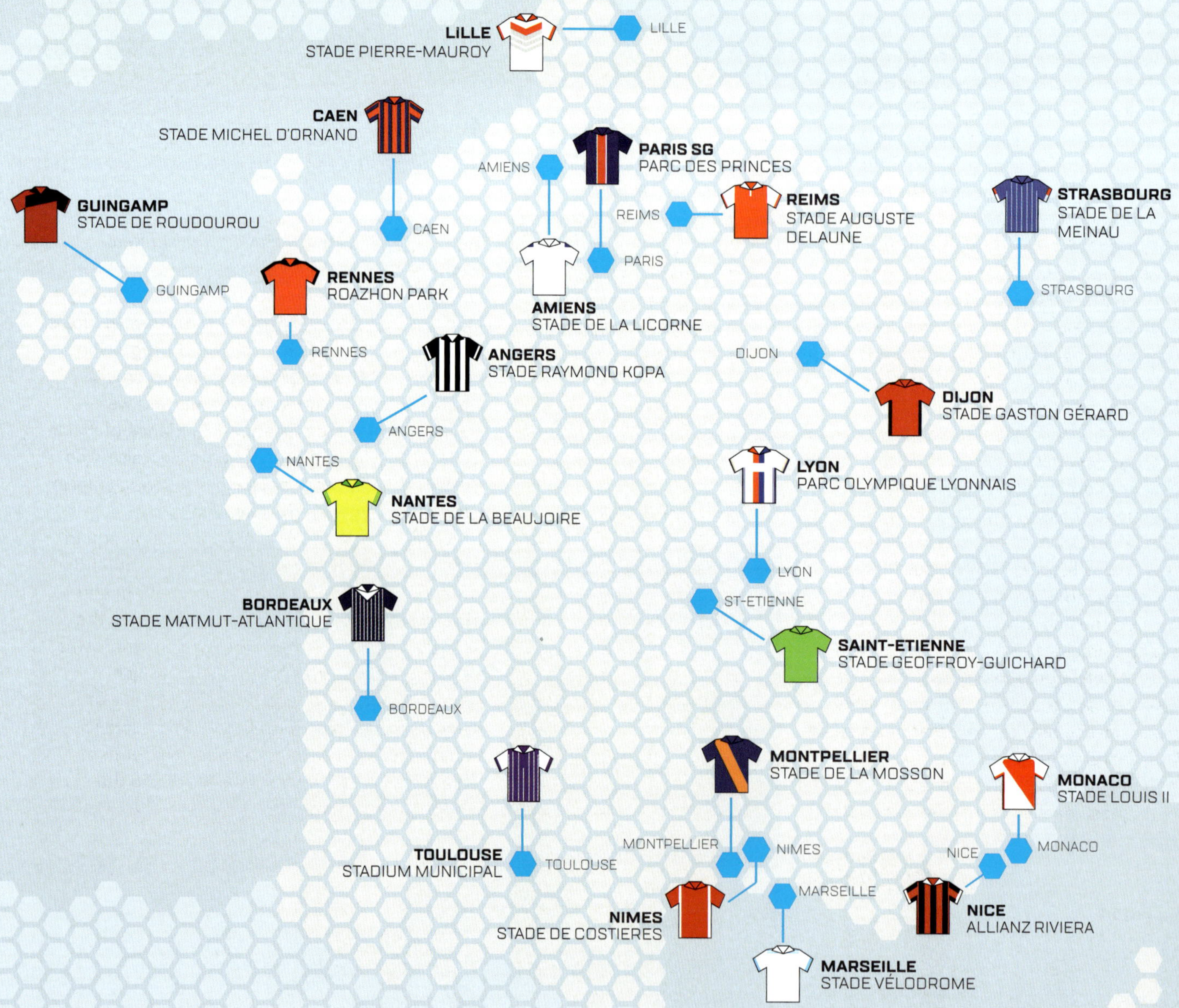

Paris Saint-Germain

THE PARISIANS

⬆ Paris Saint-Germain teammates jump for joy after beating Barcelona 4–0 in a UEFA Champions League first-leg match at the Parc des Princes stadium in 2017.

Paris Saint-Germain, remarkably, became the very first club from the French capital to win a European prize when they defeated Rapid Vienna 1–0 in the Cup Winners' Cup Final in 1996.

Yet PSG had been founded only 26 years earlier by fans anxious to fill the gap left by the collapse of professional football in the French capital. They did not turn fully professional until 1973, by which time they had risen to the brink of promotion to the French top division under the presidency of the couturier Daniel Hechter.

The trophy breakthrough arrived with French cup successes in 1982 and 1983 and was extended in 1986 when, under former English teacher Gerard Houllier, Paris won their first league title. This was the first time a Paris club had won the national championship since Racing Club 50 years earlier in 1936.

After Houllier's departure and a shake-up that involved new backing from TV channel Canal Plus, PSG reached European semi-finals in four successive seasons: losing in the UEFA Cup in 1993, the Cup Winners' Cup in 1994 and the Champions League in 1995, but this hurdle was finally cleared in the 1996 Cup Winners' Cup. PSG reached the final again the next season, only to lose to Barcelona.

That defeat preceded years of turbulence – leavened by occasional cup wins – before a multi-million investment by the Qatar Investment Authority promised to lift the club to new heights. Suddenly PSG's riches saw the club competing at the highest reaches of the international transfer market, in competition with the likes of Real Madrid and Manchester City.

PSG won the French league title four years in a row from 2013 to 2016, spearheaded by the goals of Sweden's Zlatan Ibrahimovic and Uruguayan Edinson Cavani. The 2013 triumph was crucial after a period of inconsistent results and was achieved under the managerial guidance of Italian Carlo Ancelotti. In this modern era PSG also won the French cup twice and league cup four years in succession between 2014 and 2017.

Along the way the club enhanced their squad with the additions of stars such as Brazil defender Thiago Silva, Italy midfielder Marco Verratti and Argentina winger Angel Di Maria. However, the ultimate ambition of the club's Qatari owners was to win the UEFA Champions League, which prompted the world record €222m signing of Brazil's Neymar from Barcelona in 2017. Even though PSG won all four trophies on offer in France they fell to holders Real Madrid in the European second round.

Founded
1970

Parc des Princes
48 712

Ligue 1
7

Coupe de France
12

Coupe de la Ligue
8

Trophée des Champions
7

UEFA Cup Winners' Cup
1996

NEYMAR
IN 2017, PARIS SAINT-GERMAIN PAID A SCARCELY CREDIBLE €222 MILLION TO SECURE NEYMAR'S TRANSFER FROM BARCELONA. THE INCREDIBLE PRICE MORE THAN DOUBLED THE PREVIOUS RECORD FEE.

96

HIGH POINTS
PSG WON LIGUE 1 IN 2015–16 WITH THE BIGGEST POINTS TOTAL EVER REGISTERED IN FRANCE'S TOP LEAGUE.

French striker Juste Fontaine beats a West German player at the 1958 World Cup, where he scored a record total of 13 goals. Fontaine made his name at Nice, scoring 43 goals in 69 league games.

Marseille players, including (left to right) Franck Sauzee, Basile Boli, Didier Deschamps and Eric Di Meco, celebrate their 1–0 victory over Milan in the 1993 Champions League with their chairman, Bernard Tapie.

With a squad of supremely exciting and talented young players, Monaco defied the odds to win their eighth Ligue 1 title in 2017.

Lyon

THE KIDS

Founded
1950

Parc Olympique Lyonnais
59 186

Honour	Titles
Ligue 1	7
Coupe de France	5
Coupe de la Ligue	1
Trophée des Champions	8

Olympique Lyonnais were the dominant club of the first decade of the 21st century in France. Ambitious owner Jean-Michel Aulas even forced a change in the law to allow French clubs to pursue finance on the stock exchange. Lyon were founded in 1950 from a merger between local rivals, Villeurbanne and FC Lyon. Within a year of becoming a professional club they secured promotion to the top division in 1951 but for years they were best known as a cup-fighting team; in the European Cup Winners' Cup they were both semi-finalists. A step upward came in 1993 with the appointment of ex-France midfielder Jean Tigana as manager-coach. Between 2002 and 2008, Lyon won a record seven consecutive league titles. They have also won the French cup on five occasions and made the semi-finals of the UEFA Champions League in 2010, as well as winning a joint record eight Trophee des Champions.

Marseille

THE PHOCIANS

- Founded: 1899
- Orange Velodrome: 67 394
- Ligue 1: 9
- Coupe de France: 10
- Coupe de la Ligue: 3
- Trophée des Champions: 3
- UEFA Champions League: 1993

Marseille are the only French club to have won the Champions Cup, though their success came amid scandal. Days after their cup-winning 1-0 win over Milan in 1993, it emerged that three players from Valenciennes had been bribed to ease up in a league game a week earlier. The club was barred from a European defence, stripped of their league title and relegated. Owner Bernard Tapie went to jail. The club, backed by their passionate group of fans, soon bounced back to regain the league title in 2010, a league cup hat-trick between 2010 and 2012 They were then overshadowed domestically by the rise of PSG, but still reached the final of the 2018 UEFA Europa League before losing to Atletico Madrid.

Monaco

THE RED AND WHITES

- Founded: 1924
- Stade Louis II: 18 523
- Ligue 1: 8
- Coupe de France: 5
- Coupe de la Ligue: 1
- Trophée des Champions: 4

The financial support of the royal family of Monaco supported the club for years while they drew among the smallest crowds in the top division. That did not prevent Monaco from winning eight league titles, five French cups and one league cup. But the post-Bosman change saw the club struggle and they slipped into the second division. In 2010, a majority stake was purchased by Russian billionaire Dmitry Ryboloviev. Expensive stars were signed; Colombian striker Radamel Falcao and Portuguese midfielders Bernardo Silva and Joao Moutinho combined with outstanding French newcomers Benjamin Mendy and Kylian Mbappe. In 2017 they won an eighth league title - their first in 17 years - and reached the semi-finals of the UEFA Champions League before losing to Italy's Juventus.

Nice

THE EAGLETS

- Founded: 1904
- Allianz Riviera: 35 624
- Ligue 1: 4
- Coupe de France: 3

Nice were French champions three times in the 1950s and twice provided testing opposition in the European Champions Cup for omnipotent Real Madrid. Famously Victor Nuremberg, Nice's Luxembourg inside forward, became one of the few players to score a hat trick against Madrid in Europe. Subsequently, however, the club lost their way and endured half a dozen spells in the second division, once by order of the authorities because of excessive debts. Their most recent trophy success was a rare, third French cup victory in 1997. The nearest they have come to a prize since then was in reaching the league cup final in 2006 when they lost 2-1 to Nancy. Their most famous former player remains Just Fontaine, the World Cup's 13-goal record scorer, whose lethal marksmanship fired Nice to league championship success in 1956 before he transferred to Reims.

GERMANY

The format of German club game has varied down the years with the twists and turns of history. Originally, the championship involved regional championships culminating in a title playoff series. Schalke and Nurnberg were dominant clubs in the inter-war years. After the Second World War, the regional system was maintained in West Germany until the early 1960s when the unified Bundesliga was created. Borussia Dortmund were the last champions of the old era, in 1963, and 1FC Koln their title successor in 1964. Bayern Munich, excluded from the launch league, were soon promoted to claim the first of their record 26 Bundesliga crowns in 1969.

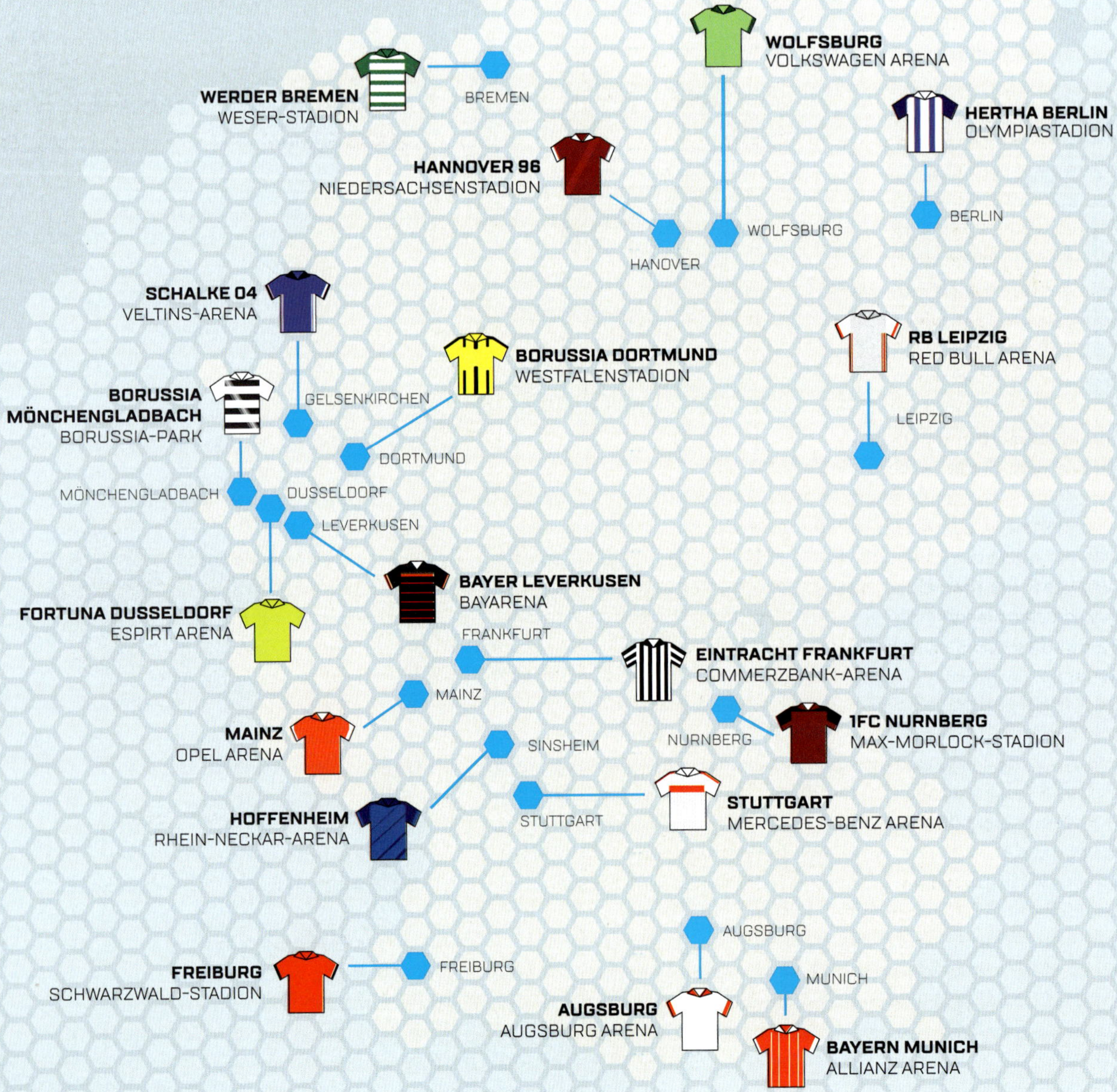

Bayern Munich THE REDS

Bayern Munich are Germany's greatest club and the only one to have climbed every peak: domestic championship and cup, Champions League, UEFA/Europa Cup, now-defunct Cup Winners' Cup, UEFA Super Cup and Club World Cup. Yet, until the late 1960s, their only prizes had been a national title in 1932 and a cup in 1957.

In 1967, Bayern won their first European trophy, the Cup Winners' Cup, with the nucleus of a team that would conquer the world – Sepp Maier in goal, Gerd Müller in attack and Franz Beckenbauer as a revolutionary attacking sweeper. This was the role from which he captained his country to victory in the 1972 European Championship and 1974 World Cup.

Bayern extended their domestic command into Europe when they won a hat trick of Champions Cups between 1974 and 1976. In 1974, Beckenbauer & Co. were at their brilliant best in defeating Atlético Madrid 4–0 in the only replayed final. Müller and Uli Hoeness both scored twice. Hoeness later became president of the club while Karl-Heinz Rummenigge, a European winner in 1976, rose to become chief executive.

Down the years, Bayern saw off all their domestic rivals. In the 1970s, their toughest rivals were Borussia Monchengladbach; in the 1980s, Hamburg and Werder Bremen; in the 1990s, Bremen and Bayer Leverkusen, and, since then, the most consistent challenge has come from Borussia Dortmund. However, Bayern's financial power – far beyond any other German club – has permitted them to buy the star players from all their rivals and win 12 Bundesliga titles in the 18 seasons of the new century.

Fan favourites among their later stars have included goalkeepers Oliver Kahn and Manuel Neuer, defender Philipp Lahm, midfielders Lothar Matthaus and Bastian Schweinsteiger, plus forwards Giovane Elber, Thomas Müller, Franck Ribery and Robert Lewandowski.

Title-winning coaches have included an international cast including Italians Giovanni Trapattoni and Carlo Ancelotti, Dutchman Louis Van Gaal and Spaniard Pep Guardiola. However one of the most popular was Jupp Heynckes who led Bayern to the league, cup and Champions League in 2013 before returning to win the Bundesliga again in 2018.

↑ Arjen Robben lifts the Champions League trophy after Bayern Munich's 2–1 victory over Borussia Dortmund in the 2013 final at Wembley Stadium.

Founded
1900

Allianz Arena
75 000

Bundesliga
28

DFB Cup
18

DFL League Cup
6

DFL Supercup
5

FIFA Club World Cup
1976 2001 2013

UEFA Champions League
1974* 1975* 1976* 2001 2013

UEFA Cup
1996

UEFA Cup Winners' Cup
1967

UEFA Super Cup
2013

*European Cup

365

GERD MÜLLER
THE STRIKER SCORED 365 GOALS IN 427 BUNDESLIGA MATCHES AND AVERAGED A GOAL PER GAME OR BETTER IN 6 OF HIS 14 SEASONS WITH BAYERN.

Borussia Dortmund's Paulo Sousa lifts the 1997 Champions League trophy after the Bundesliga team defeated Juventus 3–1 of Italy at the Olympiastadion in Munich.

Borussia Dortmund

THE BLACK AND YELLOWS

Founded 1909	DFB Cup 4
Westfalenstadion 81 360	UEFA Champions League 1997
Bundesliga 8	UEFA Cup Winners' Cup 1966
	FIFA Club World Cup 1997

Borussia hold a special place in history as Germany's first European winners - in 1966, when they beat Liverpool 2-1 after extra time to win the Cup Winners' Cup in Glasgow. Pride in that achievement extended to superstition when members of that team were flown by Dortmund to the away leg of their 1993 UEFA Cup semi-final against French club Auxerre. The "lucky charms" paid off again, though Dortmund subsequently lost to Juventus in the final. Revenge arrived in style four years later, when Dortmund beat Juventus 3-1 in the Champions Cup final in Munich. Two goals from Karlheinz Riedle and one from substitute Lars Ricken turned Dortmund into Germany's first European club champions since Hamburg 14 years earlier. In 2013, they reached the final again only to lose to Bundesliga rivals Bayern Munich in a memorable duel at Wembley. That was the closest Dortmund came to the top European prize as Klopp left and the club proved unable to prevent star players such as Mario Götze, Mats Hummel and Robert Lewandowski from transferring to perpetual champions Bayern Munich.

JÜRGEN KLOPP IN SEVEN SEASONS AS MANAGER OF BORUSSIA DORTMUND (2008–15), JÜRGEN KLOPP WON 56 PER CENT OF HIS GAMES.

24454

BIG BORUSSIA NUMBERS
THE SOUTH STAND AT BORUSSIA DORTMUND'S WESTFALENSTADION HOLDS 24 454 FANS, MAKING IT THE LARGEST FOOTBALL STAND IN EUROPE.

Michael Ballack celebrates after scoring for Bayer 04 Leverkusen in a 2001 Champions League 3–0 group match victory against Deportivo La Coruna.

Bayer 04 Leverkusen

THE WORKS TEAM

Bay Arena
30 210

DFB Cup
1

Founded
1904

UEFA Cup
1988

Bayer are the only mainstream German outfit permitted to benefit from a corporate label since the club were founded in 1904 by workers from the local pharmaceutical company. Surprisingly, given such corporate support, Leverkusen's only domestic success remains the German cup in 1993, albeit they have finished runners-up in the Bundesliga on five occasions, including four times between 1997 and 2002. Leverkusen have been regular contestants in European competition with almost 200 matches to their credit. They won the UEFA Cup in 1988 by defeating Espanyol of Barcelona in a penalty shootout. In 2002, a fine team starring penalty-taking goalkeeper Hans-Jorg Butt, Brazilian defender Lucio, German midfielders Michael Ballack and Bernd Schneider plus Bulgarian striker Dimitar Berbatov reached the Champions League final, only to lose 2-1 to Real Madrid in Glasgow.

Schalke 04

THE ROYAL BLUES
THE MINERS

Bundesliga
7

DFB Cup
5

Founded
1904

DFB League Cup
1

Veltins Arena
62 271

UEFA Cup
1997

Schalke rank among Germany's great clubs but have not won the league title since 1958. Schalke dominated German football in the 1930s; they overcame an illicit-payments scandal to win the national championship six times in nine years between 1934 and the cessation of domestic competition in 1942. Their only post-war league success was in 1958 when they beat the powerful Hamburg of Uwe Seeler 3-0 in the playoff final. Despite being European contenders over the years, Schalke boast only one trophy: the UEFA Cup, which they won in a penalty shootout against Internazionale in 1997. In the UEFA Champions League a team inspired by Spanish star Raúl González reached the semi-finals in 2011 before losing to Manchester United.

Wolfsburg

THE WOLVES

Bundesliga
1

DFB Cup
1

Founded
1945

DFL Supercup
1

Volkswagen Arena
30 000

Wolfsburg, supported and now owned by Volkswagen, have won Germany's three main prizes once each - the Bundesliga in 2009, the German cup in 2015 and the Supercup in 2015.

Founded in 1945, Wolfsburg were only promoted to the elite in 1997 and maintained their place courtesy of careful transfer dealings. Their most successful signings were strikers Grafite from Brazil and Eden Dzeko from Bosnia, who finished first and second in the league scoring rankings with 28 and 26 goals, in their title-winning season. Wolfsburg's most successful campaign in European club competition was in 2015-16, when they reached the quarterfinals of the UEFA Champions League before losing to eventual winners Real Madrid. They were also Europa League quarter-finalists in 2010 and 2015.

ITALY

Northern Italy has always commanded the roll of honour in the league and cup. History had its part to play. Genoa and Milan were the first cities in which football took root, while Juventus from Turin are record champions. Southern clubs such as Roma and neighbours Lazio plus Napoli further down the South West coast have managed only occasionally to interrupt the northern dominance. No Sicilian club have ever carried off a league title or cup, although Cagliari, from the island of Sardinia, did secure the Serie A Scudetto (shield) in 1970 thanks to the goal-scoring exploits of their record-breaking marksman, Luigi Riva.

Juventus

THE OLD LADY

Record Italian champions Juventus were founded by a group of students who adopted their famous black-and-white stripes after one committee member was impressed by the Notts County strip during a visit to England.

In the 1930s, Juventus laid the foundations for their legend as the "La Vecchia Signora" (The Old Lady), by winning the league championship five times in a row. Simultaneously they also reached the semi-finals of the Mitropa Cup on four occasions and supplied Italy's World Cup-winning teams with five players in 1934 and three in 1938.

Their own Gianpiero Combi was Italy's victorious captain in 1934, just as another Juventus goalkeeper, Dino Zoff, would be Italy's World Cup-winning skipper in Spain in 1982.

Post-war, the "Zebras" scoured the world for talent to match their import-led rivals. First came the Danes John and Karl Hansen then Argentinian favourite Omar Sívori and the "Gentle Giant" from Wales, John Charles. In 1971, they lost the Fairs Cup final to Leeds on away goals but, in 1977, beat Bilbao in the UEFA Cup final. Later they were strengthened by French inspiration Michel Platini and Poland's Zbigniew Boniek.

In 1982, no fewer than six Juventus players featured in Italy's World Cup-winning line-up, and Antonio Cabrini, Marco Tardelli, Gaetano Scirea, Claudio Gentile and Paolo Rossi helped Juventus to win the 1984 European Cup Winners' Cup and the 1985 Champions Cup. A decade later, seeking new magic, Juventus splashed out on Roberto Baggio and Gianluca Vialli. The latter captained Juve to victory in the Champions Cup final over Ajax.

ANDREA PIRLO

THE ARRIVAL OF ANDREA PIRLO AT JUVENTUS IN 2011 LED TO SUCCESIVE SERIE A TITLES IN 2012, 2013, 2014 AND 2015. IN 2016, PIRLO WAS SELECTED IN THE UEFA ALL-TIME EURO XI.

Founded	1897
Allianz Stadium	41 507
Serie A	34
Coppa Italia	13
Supercoppa Italiana	7
UEFA Champions League	1985* 1996
UEFA Cup Winners' Cup	1984
UEFA Cup	1977 1990 1993
UEFA Super Cup	1984 1996
FIFA Club World Cup	1985 1996

*European Cup

Fabrizio Ravanelli sets off on a trademark glory gallop after scoring for Juventus in the 1996 Champions League Final.

Juventus reached the Champions Cup final again in 1997 and 1998, only to lose on each occasion against Borussia Dortmund and then against Real Madrid in Amsterdam in 1998. A further painful defeat followed, on penalties, to Milan in the first all-Italian final, in 2003.

In 2006, "Juve" were punished with their first-ever relegation for their part in a major match-fixing scandal. They bounced back immediately and won seven Serie A league titles in a row between 2012 and 2018, under Antonio Conte and then Massimiliano Allegri. They were also runners-up twice in the UEFA Champions League in 2015 and 2017 to Barcelona and Real Madrid.

DINO ZOFF

IN 11 YEARS AT JUVENTUS, LEGENDARY KEEPER DINO ZOFF PLAYED IN EVERY SINGLE SERIE A MATCH (330 APPEARANCES) AND WON SIX SERIE A TITLES AND THE UEFA CUP.

Milan

THE RED AND BLACKS

Milan's domination of the European club game for almost two decades from the late 1980s was achieved by a futuristic matrix of sporting and commercial interests. The puppet-master was media magnate and later prime minister, Silvio Berlusconi, who had bought the club in 1986.

Milan had spent most of the inter-war years in the shadows of neighbours Internazionale. After the war they achieved spectacular success after buying abroad. Sweden had won 1948 Olympic gold thanks to the attacking skills of Gunnar Gren, Gunnar Nordahl and Nils Liedholm. Milan signed them en bloc then paid a world record £72,000 for Uruguayan World Cup-winner Juan Schiaffino.

The Rossoneri (red-and-blacks) were the first major rivals to Real Madrid in the new European Cup, losing to the Spanish club in the 1956 semi-finals then after extra-time in the 1958 final. That was also the year Milan discovered the teenaged Gianni Rivera, whose inside-forward genius inspired their first Champions Cup victory in 1963. His partnership with Brazilian centre forward José Altafini destroyed Benfica in the final so skipper and sweeper Cesare Maldini could raise the cup.

Rivera led Milan to the Champions Cup again in 1969 alongside the Cup Winners' Cup in 1968. But even his charisma could not save Milan from the scandals and financial disasters inflicted by a string of disastrous presidents.

This was where Berlusconi came in, providing both money and men – coaches Arrigo Sacchi and Fabio Capello, Dutch superstars Ruud Gullit, Marco Van Basten, Frank Rijkaard plus Italy's Franco Baresi and Paolo Maldini (son of Cesare) – to convert Milan into "new media" leaders.

Maldini Junior emulated his father as a Champions Cup-winning captain and claimed a fifth winner's medal after victory over Liverpool in 2007. He retired two years later before the end of an era was marked in 2017 when Berlusconi sold the club to a Chinese consortium.

Founded
1899

San Siro
80 018

Serie A
18

Coppa Italia
5

Supercoppa Italiana
7

FIFA World Club Cup
1969 1989
1990 2007

UEFA Champions League
1963* 1969*
1989* 1990*
1994 2003
2007

UEFA Cup Winners' Cup
1968 1973

UEFA Super Cup
1989 1990
1994 2003
2007

*European Cup

MARCO VAN BASTEN
MILAN LEGEND VAN BASTEN WAS NAMED FIFA WORLD PLAYER OF THE YEAR IN 1992 AND WON THE BALLON D'OR THREE TIMES, IN 1988, 1989 AND 1992.

Milan President Silvio Berlusconi (holding trophy) joins his players after their 2007 Champions League final victory over Liverpool.

Internazionale

THE BLACK AND BLUES

Internazionale were founded by dissenting, breakaway members of the Milan club in the early years of the century. That was not the end of the politics. In the 1930s, fascist laws forced Internazionale into a name change to rid the club of the foreign associations of their title. They took the name of the city's patron saint and became Ambrosiana. They led the way in continental club competition as one of the leading lights in the inter-war Mitropa Cup.

After the war, the club reverted to the Internazionale name and pioneered a tactical revolution. First, manager Alfredo Foni, a World Cup-winning full back before the war, won the league title twice by withdrawing outside-right Gino Armani into midfield; then Helenio Herrera conquered Italy, Europe and the world with the catenaccio defensive system.

Keeper Giuliano Sarti, sweeper Armando Picchi and man-marking defenders Tarcisio Burgnich, Aristide Guarneri and Giacinto Facchetti were as near watertight as possible. They were the foundation on which Spanish general Luis Suárez constructed the counter-attacking raids executed by Brazil's Jair da Costa, Spain's Joaquim Peiro and Italy's own Sandro Mazzola.

Inter won the European and World Club Cups in both 1964 and 1965 but could not soak up pressure indefinitely. In 1966, Real Madrid toppled Inter in the European Cup semi-finals while Celtic repeated the trick a year later in a memorable Lisbon final.

Not until the late 1980s could Inter recapture the magic when German midfielder Lothar Matthäus drove them to the 1989 league title, followed by a UEFA Cup hat trick in the 1990s. Later they regained domestic command following the relegation of Juventus after a matchfixing scandal. Inter won the Serie A crown five years in a row, first under Roberto Mancini and later under José Mourinho. The latter, having won league title success in a third major country, also guided Inter to their first European Champions' crown for 45 years, in 2010.

Founded
1908

San Siro
80 018

Serie A
18

Coppa Italia
7

Supercoppa Italiana
5

FIFA World Club Cup
1964
1965
2010

UEFA Champions League
1964*
1965*
2010

UEFA Cup
1991
1994
1998

*European Cup

In 2010, José Mourinho guided Internazionale to their first Champions Cup success in 45 years.

1

INTER FOREVER
INTERNAZIONALE ARE THE ONLY CLUB NEVER TO HAVE BEEN RELEGATED FROM ITALY'S SERIE A.

Fiorentina

THE PURPLES

Founded
1926

Stadio Artemio Franchi
43 147

Serie A
2

Coppa Italia
6

Supercoppa Italiana
1

UEFA Cup Winners' Cup
1961

Fiorentina have come back from the depths to rebuild a reputation for skilful football founded on the talents of stars such as Giancarlo Antognoni, Daniel Bertoni, Kurt Hamrin and Julinho. Yet the "Viola" owed their most notable league success, in 1955–56, to an ironclad defence which conceded a then record of only 20 goals in 34 games. They went on to reach the 1957 Champions' Cup final before losing 2-0 to Real Madrid in the Spanish capital. Fiorentina, however, had the consolation of being the first winners of the Cup Winners' Cup in 1961. Fiorentina reached a further European final when they lost to Internazionale in the UEFA Cup in 1990. Mismanagement then sent the club careering into bankruptcy in 2002. They had to "buy back" their old name and insignia as they battled up through the divisions and, eventually, into the Champions League.

$50 MILLION

FLORENTINE FALLOUT
WHEN FIORENTINA NOSE-DIVED INTO ADMINISTRATION AND NEAR OBLIVION IN 2002, THE FLORENCE CLUB HAD DEBTS ESTIMATED AT AROUND $50 MILLION.

Lazio

THE WHITE AND SKY BLUES

Founded
1900

Stadio Olimpico
70 634

Serie A
2

Coppa Italia
6

Supercoppa Italiana
4

UEFA Cup Winners' Cup
1999

UEFA Super Cup
1999

Lazio have endured turbulent times since they won a second Serie A title on a dramatic final day in 2000. That confirmed a double after they had also lifted the Coppa Italia. A year earlier they had triumphed in the last UEFA Cup Winners' Cup final. Further back, the club's great breakthrough had been in winning the league title for the first time in 1974, led by the goals of Giorgio Chinaglia. After the double of 2000, club president Sergio Cragnotti believed his club were poised to rise up among Europe's elite. But then coach Sven-Göran Eriksson left for England, Lazio slipped out of the Champions League and into debt and were caught up in a match-fixing scandal. They have yet to win the league again since 1999-2000, though they have secured three further Italian cups.

Napoli's Ciro Ferrara gets a celebratory hug from Diego Maradona during the 1989 UEFA Cup final.

Roma supporters unfurl banners of two of their heroes – longest-serving player Francesco Totti (left) and Agostino Di Bartolomei (right) – during a Serie A match against fellow Romans Lazio at the Stadio Olimpico in 2014.

Napoli

THE LIGHT BLUES

Founded **1926**

Stadio San Paolo **60 240**

Serie A **2**

Coppa Italia **5**

UEFA Cup **1989**

Napoli were, for many years, a club with more passion than purpose. Relegated in the penultimate pre-war season of 1942, Napoli spent much of the first 20 post-war years hopping between divisions. The "new era" began in 1965 and in the next decade Napoli established themselves as virtual ever-presents in the top four, albeit with only two Italian cups to show for it. The step up to European achievement demanded a coup – signing Maradona from Barcelona for a world record £5m. Within a fortnight, Napoli had recouped most of the fee in ticket sales. Maradona played to sell-out 85,000 crowds and inspired Napoli to win the league title twice, the UEFA Cup and the Italian Cup. After Maradona's dope-ban exit in 1991, Napoli crashed to the near-bankruptcy only to recover remarkably to regain Champions League status. Since 2012 they have enjoyed cup success three times.

Roma

THE YELLOW AND REDS

Founded **1927**

Stadio Olimpico **70 634**

Serie A **3**

Coppa Italia **9**

Supercoppa Italiana **2**

UEFA Cup **1961**

Roma, for all the headlines afforded the clubs of Milan and Turin over the years, were one of the first two Italian clubs to win a European trophy. That was in 1961 when Roma beat Birmingham City over two legs to win the Fairs Cup (now the UEFA Cup). Roma's team included two popular Argentinian forwards in Pedro Manfredonia and Antonio Valentin Angelillo and a fine Italian goalkeeper in Fabio Cudicini. Roma came closest to a European prize again in 1984. Led from midfield by Brazilian Paulo Roberto Falcao and in attack by Italy winger Bruno Conti, they were favourites to beat Liverpool in the Champions Cup final, but the match ended 1–1 after extra time and Roma lost on penalties. Since then, despite new American owners, they have managed only one further Serie A title.

Torino

THE MAROONS/THE BULL

Founded **1906**

Stadio Communale **27 958**

Serie A **7**

Coppa Italia **5**

Torino, for much of their existence, have been in the shadow of neighbours Juventus. The one era in which they took precedence ended in disaster. A fine team inspired by captain and inside-left Valentino Mazzola won the Italian league five seasons in a row either side of the second world war. But, weeks from the end of the 1948–49 season, the entire squad was killed in the Superga air disaster on their return from a friendly match in Lisbon. "Toro" never regained such dominance, being relegated several times and once going bankrupt. They did win the Serie A crown one further time in 1976, finishing two points ahead of Juventus. Centre forward Paolino Pulici was the league's 21-goal top scorer. Torino's last domestic success was in winning the Coppa Italia in 1993. In European competition, they were runners-up in the UEFA Cup in 1992.

NETHERLANDS

The twin centres of Dutch football were traditionally Rotterdam and Amsterdam. But the advent of professionalism and commercial interests opened the door to PSV from the "Philips city" of Eindhoven. Other clubs were also encouraged to raise their game after the excitement and popularity generated by the national team's World Cup achievements in the 1970s and the European successes of Ajax and Feyenoord. The most remarkable fact of all is that a country as small in size as the Netherlands has been able to establish itself as such a consistently powerful force within the world of international football.

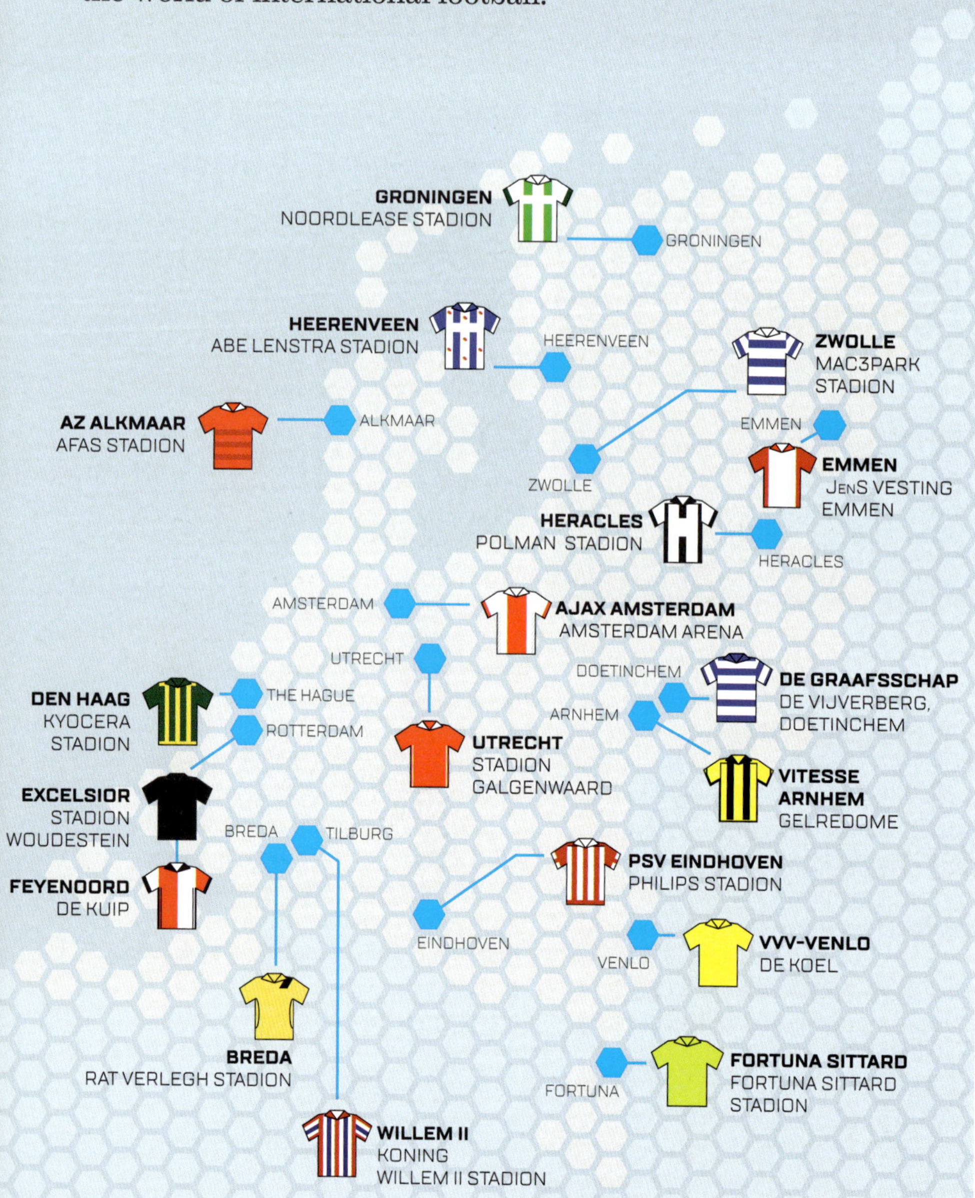

Ajax

SONS OF THE GODS

Founded
1900

Amsterdam Arena
53 748

Eredivisie
33

KNVB Cup
18

Johan Cruyff Shield
8

Champions League
1971* 1972* 1973* 1995

UEFA Cup Winners' Cup
1987

UEFA Cup
1992

UEFA Super Cup
1973 1995

FIFA Club World Cup
1972 1995

*European Cup

Ajax, on winning the 1992 UEFA Cup, became only the second club after Italy's Juventus to have won all the three then-existing European trophies and a full house of all seven titles available. The first hints of glory to come were seen in 1969 when they were runners-up in the Champions Cup. They then won Europe's top club prize three years in a row from 1971 to 1973. Peripatetic centre forward Johan Cruyff was the inspiration and leader of their "total football" revolution. Ajax won the Champions Cup a fourth time in 1996, reached the Europa League final in 2017 and boast a Dutch record 33 league titles.

122

AJAX ATTACK

IN 1966–67, AJAX SCORED 122 GOALS ON THEIR WAY TO THE EREDIVISIE TITLE. THIS DUTCH RECORD HAS NEVER BEEN BETTERED.

Feyenoord

THE CLUB OF THE PEOPLE

Founded
1908

Stadion Feijenoord (De Kuip)
51 177

Eredivisie
15

KNVB Cup
13

Johan Cruyff Shield
3

European Cup
1970

UEFA Cup
1974 2002

FIFA Club World Cup
1970

Feyenoord's most glorious domestic era was in the 1950s and 1960s when they won the league six times in 13 years, their 1965 and 1969 successes earning league and cup doubles. In 1970, led by Sweden striker Ove Kindvall, they became the first Dutch club to win the European Champions Cup and the World Club Cup. In 1974, Feyenoord added the UEFA Cup to their trophy room, a success later repeated in 2002. Years of disappointing domestic performances came to an end in 2017 when they won the Dutch league crown for the first time in 18 years. Veteran Dirk Kuyt hit a celebratory hat trick in the last game of the season before retiring.

PSV Eindhoven

THE PEASANTS

Founded
1913

Philips Stadion
35 500

Eredivisie
24

KNVB Cup
9

Johan Cruyff Shield
11

European Cup
1988

UEFA Cup
1978

PSV, despite their status as sports club of the Philips electronics corporation, were long outshone by Ajax and Feyenoord. That changed after a fine team featuring twins Willy and Rene Van de Kerkhof won the 1976 UEFA Cup. In 1988, they won their sole Champions Cup and provided key members of Holland's European title-winning team. An international outlook prompted the signing of top coaches such as Sir Bobby Robson and young Brazilian strikers Romário and Ronaldo. But financial restrictions within Dutch football prevented them holding stars long enough to emulate the glory days, though the Eredivisie triumph in 2018 was their third in four seasons.

43

PSV GOAL POACHER
STRIKER COEN DILLEN SCORED 43 GOALS FOR PSV IN THE 1956–57 SEASON, AN EREDIVISIE RECORD. THIS INCLUDED 20 GOALS IN ONE NINE-MATCH SPELL.

Feyenoord players show their joy at winning the 2017 Eredivisie in Rotterdam after a 3–1 win over Heracles Almelo in the final game of the season. It was also the final game for Dutch international Dirk Kuyt (centre) before retirement and he celebrated by scoring a hat trick.

PORTUGAL

Portuguese football has long been dominated by the "Big Three" of Benfica, Sporting Clube and FC Porto. They are the only three Portuguese clubs to have won European prizes. Though football is hugely popular throughout Portugal, few other clubs have ever threatened to upset the trio. Boavista from Oporto, and Belenenses from Lisbon are the only other two clubs ever to have broken the giants' stranglehold. Even then, they boast only one league title each to their name.

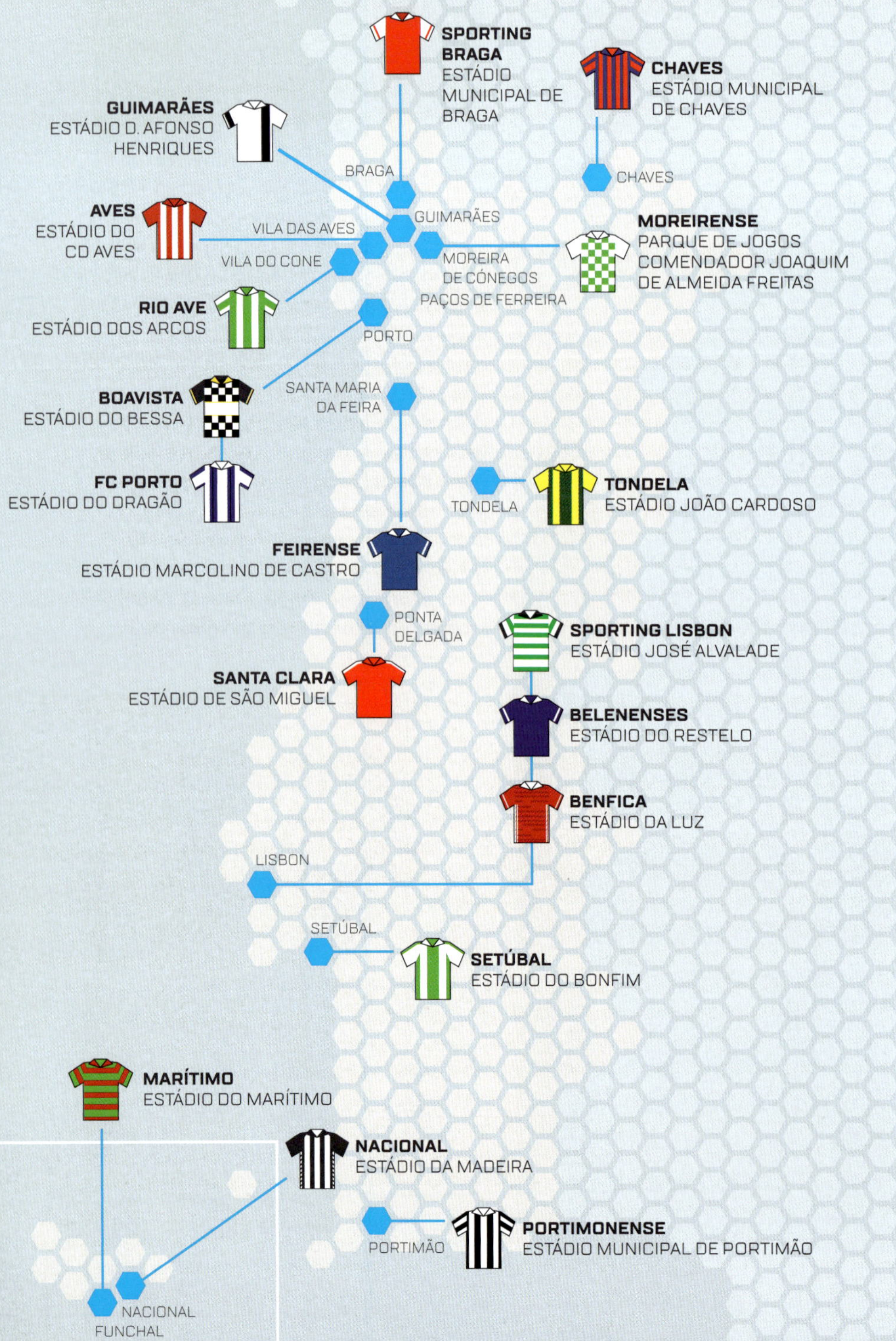

Benfica

THE EAGLES

- Founded: 1904
- Estádio da Luz: 64 642
- Primeira Liga: 36
- Taça de Portugal: 29
- Taça da Liga: 7
- Supertaça: 7
- European Cup: 1961, 1962

Benfica are a national institution with their huge stadium, rebuilt for the European finals of 2004, and a world record of 170,000 paying members. The Eagles of Lisbon have won the league a record 36 times, the cup on a record 29 occasions and take pride in their international reputation; Benfica won the Champions Cup in 1961 and 1962 when they introduced the finest Portuguese player of all time, Eusébio. He was the greatest of the many stars Benfica had discovered in the Portuguese colonies of Angola and Mozambique. A proud policy of using only 'Portuguese' players was scrapped in the mid-1970s after the colonies gained independence.

BENFICA ON TOP

NO OTHER TEAM IN PORTUGAL HAS ENJOYED MORE SUCCESS THAN BENFICA, WITH THE LISBON CLUB HAVING WON 81 DOMESTIC AND EUROPEAN TITLES.

81

➋ Eusébio of Benfica and Portugal heads the ball towards Nobby Stiles during the 2-1 win for England in the 1966 World Cup semi-final. The striker scored an amazing 473 goals in 440 games for Benfica.

➋ The Porto team take turns to kiss the trophy after their 3–0 victory in the 2004 Champions League final against Monaco in Gelsenkirchen, Germany.

Sporting Lisbon THE LIONS

Founded 1906	Primeira Liga 18
Estádio José Alvalade 50 095	Taça de Portugal 16
	Supertaça 8
	UEFA Cup Winners' Cup 1964

Sporting Clube do Portugal last reached a European final in 2005 when they finished as UEFA Cup runners-up to CSKA Moscow in front of their own fans in Lisbon. Hence their lone European success remains the Cup Winners' Cup in 1964. Sporting dominated domestic football in the 1950s when they won the championship seven times in eight years. In the 1960s, their back four of Morais, Batista, José Carlos and Hilario starred in the Portugal team that finished third in the 1966 World Cup finals in England. They have won the league 18 times and the cup on 16 occasions. Recently, they were notable for having discovered Cristiano Ronaldo.

Porto THE DRAGONS

Founded 1893	Supertaça 20
Estádio do Dragao 50 434	Champions League 1987* 2004
Primeira Liga 28	UEFA Cup 2003 2011
Taça de Portugal 16	UEFA Super Cup 1987
	FIFA Club World Cup 1987 2004

*European Cup

Porto were considered as only the number three team in the Portuguese hierarchy until their thrilling Champions Cup victory over Bayern Munich in 1987. Events then and since have ensured that, while their trophy count may not yet match that of Benfica, Porto have become an alternative centre of power with 28 league titles. Not only have Porto won the Champions Cup twice – the second time under José Mourinho – the UEFA Cup and the UEFA Super Cup, they also finished runners-up to Juventus in the Cup Winners' Cup in 1984. Star players down the years have included Peruvan Teófilo Cubillas, Moroccan Rabah Madjer and Portugal's own Fernando Gomes.

SPAIN

Madrid and Barcelona have been the twin centres of football in Spain, though the game's popularity, wealth and energetic rivalries have spanned the country – from Bilbao in the Basque north to Seville and Valencia in the south. The depth and breadth of a never-ending stream of playing talent is illustrated by the success down the years of other clubs, from Alaves to Zaragoza, in reaching European competition finals. Spanish clubs have won 55 major European trophies between them, more than any other country. For three years in a row, between 2014 and 2016, Spanish clubs won both the Champions League and the Europa League trophies.

Atlético Madrid

THE MATTRESS MAKERS

Atlético de Madrid have always existed in the shadow of neighbours Real but they still rank among the "Big Three" of Spanish football and boast a proud record at international level. They were runners-up to Real in the Champions League finals of both 2014 and 2016, on the first occasion after extra time and on the second occasion after not only extra time but also a penalty shootout.

Atlético were founded as an offshoot of Athletic Club of Bilbao and hence wear the same red-and-white stripes. They were founder members of the league in 1928–29 only to be relegated two years later. They regained the top flight only to finish in a relegation position before football was shut down by the Spanish Civil War.

After the end of hostilities, it took a merger with the air force club to keep Atletico in business but, as Atlético Aviación, they won the league title twice in succession in 1940 and 1941 and then again in 1950 and 1951. In 1959, they just failed to reach the Champions Cup final for the first time when Real beat them in a semi-final playoff. But European glory was not long in coming: in 1962, Atlético won the Cup Winners' Cup, defeating holders Fiorentina.

A move to a new home in the Estádio Vicente Calderon was followed by a Champions Cup runners-up finish to Bayern Munich in 1974, but Atlético's consolation was to then play, and win, the subsequent Club World Cup. Luis Aragonés, their Champions final goal scorer, had taken over as coach.

Atlético, under the ownership of controversial developer Jesús Gil, secured a league-and-cup double in 1996 before suffering their first modern relegation in 2000. They bounced back immediately to regain their elite status and win the Europa League in 2010 and 2012. New heroes included South American marksmen Sergio Agüero from Argentina, followed by Colombian Radamel Falcao.

However, the most outstanding contribution to Atlético's newfound fame and achievements was Argentinian trainer Diego Simeone. He had been a popular player in midfield for the club and was already a favourite with the fans on his return as coach. Simeone instilled an aggressive, highly disciplined style of football with which Atlético re-established themselves as a power both at home and abroad. After Atlético finished runners-up twice in the Champions League, stars such as France striker Antoine Griezmann and Uruguay defender Diego Godin led them to a third Europa League triumph in 2018.

Founded
1903

Wanda Metropolitano
68 000

La Liga
10

Copa del Rey
10

UEFA Cup Winners' Cup
1962

UEFA Cup/ Europa Lge
2010 2012 2018

UEFA Super Cup
2010 2012

FIFA Club World Cup
1974

↑ Atlético's squad celebrate winning the 1970 league trophy, secured with a 2–0 victory over CE Sabadell.
↓ Atlético Madrid players, legends and supporters greet the final match of La Liga 2016-17 season. This was also the final Atletico match to be played at the Vicente Calderon Stadium, the club's home since 1966.

Barcelona

BARÇA

Barcelona achieved a unique feat when, in 2009, they won the sextuple: the Spanish league and cup, Champions League, UEFA Supercup, Spanish Supercup and World Club Cup.

Founded in 1899 by a Swiss, Hans Gamper, Barcelona have a string of other successes to their proud name which go back, in international terms, as far as the Latin Cup of the immediate post-Second World War era. They count many glorious triumphs and great players but possibly the most impressive of all was the era from the 1950s and into the early 1960s.

In 12 years from 1948 to 1960, Barcelona won the Spanish league six times, the cup five times, the Fairs Cup twice and the Latin Cup twice. At one time, they boasted 20 internationals from seven different nations. That may not appear out of the ordinary in these post-Bosman times, but in the 1950s it was exotic. Two of those imports were Hungarian: Sándor Kocsis and Zoltán Czibor. A third was probably the club's greatest player of all time: Ladislav Kubala. When he lined up for his adoptive Spain in the mid-1950s he became the only player to appear for three countries, after winning earlier caps for both Hungary and Czechoslovakia. Later, Kubala had a long spell as boss of the Spanish national team.

Back in Kubala's playing days, Barcelona were first winners of the Fairs Cup. Later, they carried off

Founded
1899

Camp Nou
99 354

La Liga
25

Copa del Rey
30

Supercopa de España
12

FIFA Club World Cup
2009 2011 2015

UEFA Champions League
1992* 2006 2009 2011 2015

UEFA Cup Winners' Cup
1979 1982 1989 1997

Fairs Cup
1958 1960 1966

UEFA Super Cup
1992 1997 2009 2011 2015

*European Cup

74%

PEP GUARDIOLA
AS BARCELONA MANAGER (AUGUST 2008–MAY 2012), PEP GUARDIOLA WON 14 OUT OF A POSSIBLE 19 TROPHIES – A STRIKE RATE OF ALMOST THREE-QUARTERS.

Barcelona midfield generals Xavi (left) and Andres Iniesta each hold up four fingers to indicate that this 2015 Champions League trophy is the fourth win for both players.

LIONEL MESSI
2000
(13 YEARS OLD)

£0

FEES CONTRAST

LUIS SUÁREZ
2014
(27 YEARS OLD)

£64 980 000

the Cup Winners' Cup three times. But for years their European efforts in the Champions Cup seemed jinxed. First, in 1961, having apparently achieved the hard part by eliminating the title-holders and bitter rivals Real Madrid, they lost to Benfica in the final. Barcelona hit the woodwork three times, and lost 3–2 against the run of play.

In 1973, Barcelona's president, Josep Núñez, thought he had the key to Champions Cup glory when he paid a world record £922,000 for Johan Cruyff. He led them from relegation zone to championship but the closest they came to Champions Cup victory was the 1975 semi-final.

The jinx struck again, in even more galling circumstances, in 1986. Barcelona had been frustrated by two unsuccessful years with Diego Maradona as guiding light and only found success once he had left, just as Terry Venables was arriving as manager. Under Venables, Barcelona won the league, then reached the 1986 final of the Champions Cup. Controversially, he gambled on the fitness of long-time injured striker Steve Archibald to overcome the rank outsiders of Steaua Bucharest. Barcelona lost in a penalty shootout after a goalless draw.

Eventually, it took the return of Cruyff, this time as coach, to steer a new generation of

⬆ Barcelona players, including Johan Cruyff (front row, second left), pose for a photo before the European Cup semi-final first leg against Leeds United at Elland Road in 1975.
⬇ Michael Laudrup scored 93 goals in 288 games for Barcelona (1989–94) and was named the best Danish player ever after a public vote in 2006.

93

international stars – including Ronald Koeman, Hristo Stoichkov and Michael Laudrup – to long-overdue Champions Cup victory in 1992. Domestic success was a stable diet; Barcelona's 1994 league title was their fourth in a row.

Pep Guardiola, a midfield anchor under Cruyff, heralded a new era. He enjoyed an amazing first season as coach in 2008–09. Barcelona won everything possible, including a Champions League victory over Manchester United, becoming the first club to win a sextuple. New hero Leo Messi scored in that win and again in Barça's Champions League repeat against United in 2011. With Messi at the helm, and a host of supporting stars including forwards Neymar and Luis Suárez, their all-time most-capped player Xavi and fellow midfield playmaker Iniesta, Barcelona dominated La Liga between 2009 and 2016, claiming six championships in the eight years.

Simultaneously, Barça enjoyed success around the world, following the Champions League success in 2011 with another victory in 2015, as well as two UEFA Super Cups and two Club World Cups in the same years. Even a one-year transfer ban could not prevent them adding further titles, including the double in 2018 when they lost only once in the league and scored 99 goals.

Real Madrid

THE WHITES

Real Madrid are the richest and most successful club in the world. They stand as arguably the greatest thanks to a mixture of high-ego players, heavy transfer spending and a style of football which sometimes has proved too adventurous for their own good.

They are a record 13 time champions of Europe, a record 33 time champions of Spain and have also filled their vast trophy salons to bursting point with six Club World Cups, two UEFA Cups, four UEFA Super Cups and 19 Spanish cups. It all adds up to a football honours degree for the club originally founded by students as Madrid FC (the Real prefix, meaning Royal, was a title bestowed on the club later by King Alfonso XIII).

Madrid were among the founders of the Spanish cup and league competitions, and it was also the Madrid president, Carlos Padros, who represented Spain in helping launch FIFA in Paris in 1904. They were ambitious even then. In the late 1920s, they paid a then Spanish record fee of £2,000 for Ricardo Zamora, still revered as the greatest Spanish goalkeeper ever.

Civil War hostilities left Madrid's Chamartin stadium in ruins. At the time, the club had no money but boasted one of the greatest visionaries in European football history: Santiago Bernabeu, a lawyer who had been, in turn, player, team manager and secretary, and was now club president. Bernabeu launched an audacious public appeal that raised the cash to build the stadium that now bears his name. Huge crowds provided the funds to build a team who dominated the first five years of the new European Champions Cup – led by arguably the greatest signing in the club's history, that of Alfredo Di Stéfano in 1954.

Di Stéfano proved the star of stars, even though Bernabeu surrounded him with illustrious teammates like Hungary's Ferenc Puskás, France's Raymond Kopa, Uruguay's José Santamaría and Brazil's Didi. They won the European Champions Cup for all of its first five years and Di Stéfano scored in every final. Their peak was the 7–3 defeat of Eintracht Frankfurt in 1960.

A 32-year gap followed between Madrid's sixth and seventh wins, in 1966 and 1998. Then, led by homegrown striker Raúl, Real won the revamped Champions League, beating Juventus 1-0 in the final. Two years later they repeated the feat, destroying Valencia 3-0. Surprisingly, weeks later, president Lorenzo Sanz was ousted in elections by the property developer Florentino Pérez. He immediately honoured a crucial, alluring election pledge by breaking the world transfer record in paying Barcelona £35m for Portugal's Luís Figo.

FERENC PUSKÁS
1958

£3900

FEES CONTRAST

GARETH BALE
2013

£86000000

Founded
1902

Estádio Santiago Bernabeu
81044

La Liga
33

Copa del Rey
19

Supercopa de España
10

FIFA Club World Cup
1960 1998
2002 2014
2016 2017

UEFA Champions League
1956* 1957*
1958* 1959*
1960* 1966*
1998 2000
2002 2014
2016 2017
2018

UEFA Cup
1985 1986

UEFA Super Cup
2002 2014
2016 2017

*European Cup

CRISTIANO RONALDO
GOALS PER GAME FOR
REAL MADRID
* June 2018

1.027*

Ronaldo was head and shoulders above the rest: his only rival was Lionel Messi at Barcelona. Their rivalry appeared to spur them both on to more records. Ronaldo scored a single-season Champions League record of 17 goals in 2013–14 and, in 2018, established himself as the 152-goal all-time top scorer in European competition, and as Madrid's 438-goal record holder.

Along the way, the five-times FIFA World Player of the Year contributed a stream of goals as Madrid claimed four more European crowns and became the first club to win three titles in a row in the Champions League era. Yet in 2018 even Ronaldo had to share top billing with two-goal Gareth Bale in the victory over Liverpool in Kiev.

The first season under Pérez was revolutionary. Madrid not only won the league title but Pérez negotiated the reclassification of the club's "sports city" training ground so the land could be sold for development. This not only wiped the club's debt but provided further funds for transfer investment.

In 2001, Pérez struck again, signing French star Zinedine Zidane from Italy's Juventus for another world record of £45m. The following May, Zidane repaid the fee with the magnificent volley that provided Madrid's second goal as they beat Bayer Leverkusen 2–1 to regain the Champions League.

However, the subsequent arrivals of David Beckham and Ronaldo confused the mix. The "Galácticos" nickname became a derisory term for a team unbalanced between artists and artisans. Pérez quit as president in 2006 – only to return three years later to launch another league title-winning spending spree with an escalating series of world-record acquisitions. Brazil's Kaká cost £56m from Milan in 2009, Portugal's Cristiano Ronaldo £80m from Manchester United, then Welshman Gareth Bale a further world-record £86m from Tottenham Hotspur in 2013.

↑ Real Madrid, European champions 1960. Top: Del Sol, Canario, Dominguez, Santamaria, Marquitos, Di Stéfano, Gento. Front: Vidal, Zarraga.
↓ Real Madrid, Galacticos Class of 2003, with Ronaldo, Figo, Zidane, Roberto Carlos, Raul and Beckham.

Valencia

LOS CHE

	Supercopa de España 1
Founded 1919	UEFA Cup Winners' Cup 1980
Mestalla 55 000	UEFA Cup 1962* 1963* 2004
La Liga 6	
Copa del Rey 7	UEFA Super Cup 1980 2004

*Fairs Cup

Valencia are one of Spain's biggest clubs, their history sprinkled with success at both domestic and international levels. Founded in 1919, they have won La Liga on six occasions, most recently in 2004, and the cup seven times, most recently in 2008. In Europe, Valencia were one of Spain's first winners in landing the Fairs Cup, original forerunner to the UEFA Cup, in 1962 and 1963. They missed a hat trick after losing the next season's final to fellow Spanish outfit Zaragoza. In the now-defunct Cup Winners' Cup, Valencia won by defeating Arsenal on penalties in 1980. Twice they have ended as runners-up in the Champions League, against Real Madrid in 2000 in the first all-Spanish final, and Bayern Munich in 2001. Key players have included Spain inside forward Vicente Guillot in the 1960s then World Cup winners Mario Kempes (Argentina) and Rainer Bonhof (West Germany) in the late 1970s and early 1980s.

➔ Valencia celebrate a Spanish title success in 2002 as consolation for double disappointment in the Champions League finals of 2000 and 2001.

Athletic Bilbao THE LIONS

La Liga
8

Copa del Rey
23

Supercopa de España
2

Founded
1898

San Mames
53 289

Athletic – note the English form of the club's title – have not carried off a major trophy since winning the Spanish league and cup double in 1984. But they maintain a unique status courtesy of a Basque football pride first inspired by British seamen. That tradition has led to British coaches such as Arthur Pentland, Ronnie Allen and Howard Kendall. Bilbao were founder members of the top division in 1928 and have never been relegated. Star players included centre-forward Telmo Zarra and left-winger Piru Gainza in the 1940s then goalkeeper José Iribar in the 1970s. A teammate was midfielder Angel Maria Villar, later a senior official of FIFA and UEFA and head of the Spanish federation. Bilbao, despite their philosophy of Basque players only, have finished runners-up twice in the UEFA Cup, in 1977 and 2012. They have won the Spanish league title eight times and the cup an impressive 23 occasions.

Real Sociedad

THE WHITE AND BLUES

La Liga
2

Copa del Rey
2

Supercopa de España
1

Founded
1909

Anoeta
32 200

Real Sociedad were founded in northern Guipuzcoa as a cycling club and it was under the name of Club Ciclista San Sebastian that they won their first Spanish cup in 1909. In the league they struggled to establish a consistent presence in the top division until the late 1960s. By holding on to stars such as goalkeeper Luis Arconada, midfield general Jesús Zamora and forwards Jesús Satrústegui and Roberto López Ufarte, they succeeded in winning the league crown twice in a row in the early 1980s. Real's most successful subsequent season was 2002–03 when they finished runners-up to Real Madrid. In 2007, they were relegated after 40 years in the top flight. Recent stars include Dutch goalkeeper Sander Westerveld and Spain midfielder Xabi Alonso, while David Moyes was the club's sixth British coach during his time in office between November 2014 and November 2015.

Sevilla

LOS NERVIONENSES (THE ONES FROM NERVION)

Supercopa de España
1

UEFA Cup
2006
2007
2014
2015
2016

UEFA Super Cup
2006

Founded
1890

Estádio Ramón Sánchez Pizjuán
42 500

La Liga
1

Copa del Rey
5

Sevilla have forced their way into European football headlines by making a speciality of winning the UEFA Cup. In 2006 and 2007, they defeated Middlesbrough and then Spanish rivals Espanyol respectively. Later they returned to land a hat trick of Europa League titles at the expense of Benfica, Dnipro and Liverpool, after which coach Unai Emery was then lured away to Paris Saint-Germain. Sevilla had been founded in 1900 and landed their first domestic title in 1935 when they won the cup a year ahead of the outbreak of the civil war. They remained a power in the land after the fighting had subsided. They were runners-up in the league in 1940 and 1943 and then champions in 1947 for the first and so far only time. Their initial foray into the European Champions Cup was a disaster. Qualifying in 1958 as league runners-up to Real Madrid, they were drawn against their Spanish rivals and crashed to an 8-0 defeat.

Sevilla's Coke roars in delight after scoring one of his two goals in his team's 3–1 victory over Liverpool in the 2016 UEFA Europa League final.

EUROPEAN CLUB ROUND-UP

Anderlecht
BELGIUM

- Founded **1908**
- Constant Vanden Stock Stadium **28 063**
- Jupiler Pro League **34**
- Belgian Cup **9**
- Belgian Super Cup **13**
- UEFA Cup Winners' Cup **1976 1978**
- UEFA Cup **1983**
- UEFA Super Cup **1976 1978**

Anderlecht of Brussels were set on the path towards domestic domination by English coach Bill Gormlie in the post-war era. Next came Frenchman Pierre Sinibaldi, whose tactical acumen and astute use of the offside trap, alongside the talents of stars like Jef Jurion and Paul Van Himst, made them a power in Europe. too. Anderlecht reached their first European final in the Fairs Cup in 1970 then won the Cup-winners' Cup in 1976 and 1978. Van Himst, Belgium's greatest player, returned as coach to guide the club to UEFA Cup success in 1983. Their final European success came in 1990 when they reached the final of the Cup Winners' Cup, but lost to two extra-time goals from Sampdoria. Anderlecht have won the Belgian A league a record 34 times and the cup on nine occasions.

➔ The Anderlecht team, and some family members, celebrate after receiving the Juliper Pro League trophy in May 2017. The Brussels club have won the Belgian league title more than twice as many times as their closest rivals, Club Brugge.

➚ Celtic players acknowledge the cheers of their fans, delighted at the team's victory in the 2017 Scottish Cup, sealing the Glasgow club's fourth domestic treble-winning season.

Basel
SWITZERLAND

- Founded **1893**
- St Jakob-Park **38 512**
- Super League **20**
- Swiss Cup **12**

Basel dominated Swiss football in the 1970s and then again throughout the first decade of the 21st century. That is appropriate for one of the country's oldest clubs, founded after a newspaper advertisement appealing for enthusiasts in November 1893. Basel have competed in European competition ever since the start of the century and boast 20 league championships and 12 domestic cups. They were semi-finalists in the Europa League in 2013 but have yet to make any meaningful progress in the Champions League. Their redeveloped St Jakob-Park home was chosen by UEFA to host the 2016 Europa League final between Sevilla and Liverpool.

Besiktas
TURKEY

- Founded **1903**
- Vodafone Arena **43 500**
- Super Lig **15**
- Turkish Cup **9**
- Turkish Super Cup **8**

Beşiktaş are one of Turkey's three greatest clubs along with Fenberbahce and Galatasaray. Founded in 1903, they have never been relegated and have won the league title 14 times plus the cup on nine occasions. In Europe their furthest progress remains the quarter-finals in the Champions Cup in 1987 and UEFA Cup/Europa League in 2003 and 2017. Their most successful era, including three successive league titles, was achieved under Englishman Gordon Milne between 1987 and 1993. Stars have included Senegal's Demba Ba, Portugal's Ricardo Quaresma and Turkey's Oktay Derelioglu, the club's 14-goal top scorer in European competition.

Celtic

SCOTLAND

- Founded **1887**
- Celtic Park **60 411**
- Premiership **49**
- Scottish Cup **38**
- Scottish League Cup **17**
- European Cup **1967**

Celtic have been left unchallenged as Scotland's greatest club since the financial collapse of old rivals Rangers. They have won 49 league titles, a record 38 Scottish Cups and 17 league cups, encompassing the treble in both the past two seasons. Their greatest achievement was in becoming the first British club to win the European Champions Cup with a 2-1 triumph over Internazionale in Lisbon in 1967. They also won the domestic treble that season. Remarkably, the players of the team built by legendary manager Jock Stein all came from within 30 miles of Glasgow. Celtic were runners-up in the Champions Cup in 1970 and also in the UEFA Cup in 2003.

Dynamo Kiev

UKRAINE

- Founded **1927**
- NSC Olimpiyskiy **70 050**
- Premier League **15**
- Ukraine Cup **11**
- Ukraine Super Cup **6**
- UEFA Cup Winners' Cup **1975 1986**
- UEFA Super Cup **1975**

Kiev were founder members of the Soviet top division, yet had to wait until 1961 before becoming the first club outside Moscow to land the title. In 1975, Kiev, starring Oleg Blokhin, became the first Soviet club to win a European trophy, the Cup Winners' Cup. In 1986, they won it again and Igor Belanov, like Blokhin before him, was crowned European Footballer of the Year. Kiev emerged as the leading club in Ukraine upon the Soviet collapse; they won 13 league titles in the Soviet Union then 15 in Ukraine, plus nine Soviet cups and 11 in Ukraine.

Fenerbahçe

TURKEY

- Founded **1907**
- Sukru Saracoglu Stadium **50 509**
- Super Lig **19**
- Turkish Cup **6**
- Turkish Super Cup **9**

Fenerbahçe are the most powerful independent sports organization in Turkey, a fact which made the club a focus of political controversy during the turbulence of recent years. The club have won 19 league titles and six cups, and although they have never gone a season undefeated, they only lost one match in each of the 1959, 1964 and 1989 seasons. In European competition the furthest they have reached was the semi-finals stage in the 2013 Europa League. Leading players down the years have included goalkeeper Rustu Recber, Uruguayan defender Diego Lugano and Dutch striker Robin Van Persie. Coaches have included Brazil's 1994 World Cup-winner Carlos Alberto Parreira.

Olympiakos

GREECE

Founded
1925

Karaiskakis Stadium
32 115

Superleague
44

Greek Cup
27

Greek Super Cup
4

Olympiakos have achieved a monopoly in Greek football. The club have won the league title more than all their rivals put together. This success included the unique feat of seven championships won in a row between 1997 and 2003. In 2015, they became the first club in mainstream professional football across the world to have won five or more consecutive league titles five times, and along the way they have also won the Greek Cup 27 times. Free-scoring centre-forward Nikos Anastopoulos is a club legend, and four Olympiakos players were in the Greece squad that won a shock Euro 2004 success.

Rangers

SCOTLAND

Founded
1872

Ibrox Stadium
51 082

Premiership
54

Scottish Cup
33

Scottish League Cup
27

UEFA Cup Winners' Cup
1972

Rangers are the other half of the "Old Firm", their rivalry with Celtic dominating Scottish football until the club's collapse into bankruptcy in 2012. Yet Rangers still boast more league titles (54) than any other club in the world and were one of the first British teams to make a mark in Europe. The "Gers" were runners-up in the now-defunct Cup-winners Cup in 1961 and 1967 then won it in 1972. They were also runners-up in the UEFA Cup in 2008. Legendary personalities included managers Willy Struth and Scot Symon and players such as winger Alan Morton, halfback David Meiklejohn and club record marksman Ally McCoist.

Shakhtar Donetsk

UKRAINE

Founded
1936

Metalist Stadium
40 003

Premier League
11

Ukraine Cup
12

Ukraine Super Cup
8

UEFA Cup
2009

Shakhtar are the only club in Ukraine to raised a significant challenge to Kiev Dynamo in terms of both results on the pitch and political power and influence off it. The club were founded in the old Soviet era under the name of Stakhanovets in honour of a miners' leader in the industrial Donets Basin. The name change to Shakhtar (meaning "miner") was accomplished in 1951. Shakhtar won four Soviet cups and now boast 11 Ukraine league titles and 12 cups. The Russian military intervention in eastern Ukraine forced Shakhtar to flee their state-of-the-art Donbass Arena and move west to play in Kharkiv while keeping their name.

➔ The moustachioed Rangers squad of 1896–97 pose with their three trophies won that season: the Scottish Cup, the Glasgow Cup and the Glasgow Merchants' Charity Cup.

51%

RANGERS V CELTIC
IN SCOTLAND'S FIERCE 'OLD FIRM' RIVALRY, RANGERS CAN JUST ABOUT CLAIM TO HAVE THE EDGE OVER THEIR FELLOW GLASWEGIANS IN TERMS OF VICTORY PERCENTAGE.

Zenit St Petersburg players and coaching team show their delight at winning the club's first European trophy, after defeating Rangers of Scotland 2–0 in the 2008 UEFA Cup final.

Sparta Prague

CZECH REPUBLIC

- Founded 1893
- Generali Arena 19 416
- Czech First League 33
- Czech Cup 14
- Czech Supercup 2

Sparta are not only the most popular club in the Czech Republic but one of the oldest, founded in 1893. They were one of the great powers of central European football during the inter-war years. Twice they won the Mitropa Cup, the forerunner of today's European club competitions. Goal-scoring forward Oldrich Nejedly was among a Sparta nucleus who helped Czechoslovakia reach the 1934 World Cup final. For years, the team provided the majority of the national side - but although Sparta's primacy among Czech club sides remains undimmed, having won twice the number of titles of Slavia Prague, their closest rivals - in recent years the best Czech players have left Sparta to play overseas.

Viktoria Plzeň

CZECH REPUBLIC

- Founded 1911
- Doosan Arena 11 722
- Czech First League 5
- Czech Cup 1
- Czech Supercup 2

Viktoria, founded in 1911, reached the top division of Czechoslovak football in the mid-1930s. They also competed in the prestigious central European Mitropa Cup, albeit losing heavily to Italy's Juventus. After the Second World War, the club vacillated between the top two divisions and endured a number of name changes, including Skoda Plzen. Eventually, the club was bought by Italian investors at the turn of the century. Subsequently, they have become a truly leading force in Czech football. They won the cup for the first time in 2010 and then five league titles in eight seasons between 2011 and 2018. Outstanding recent players have included midfielders Jan Kopic and Tomas Horava and forward Michael Krmencik.

Zenit St Petersburg

RUSSIA

- Founded 1925
- Krestovsky Stadium 68 134
- Soviet/Russian Premier League 5
- Soviet/Russian Cup 4
- Soviet/Russian Super Cup 5
- UEFA Cup 2008
- UEFA Super Cup 2008

Zenit were founded originally as "Stalin" Leningrad (St Petersburg since 1991) but in the late 1930s officials decided it was no joke when a club with such a name was beaten. Thus they became Zenit in 1940. Zenit won the Soviet league and cup once each before the communist collapse. Subsequently, a controlling stake was taken by the Gazprom energy giant which helped fund the building of a new stadium for the Confederations Cup and then World Cup. Gazprom's investment also ran to new players. In 2008, they beat Rangers to win the UEFA Cup and followed up by defeating Manchester United to add the UEFA Super Cup to their roll of honour.

88%

SPARTA PRAGUE
SINCE THE CZECH REPUBLIC WAS FORMED IN 1993, SPARTA PRAGUE HAVE EITHER WON OR BEEN RUNNERS-UP IN 88 PER CENT OF THE CZECH FIRST LEAGUE SEASONS.

Al Ahly

EGYPT

Founded
1907

Cairo International Stadium
75 000

Egyptian Premier League
40

Egypt Cup
36

Egypt Super Cup
10

CAF Champions League
1982 1987 2001 2005 2006 2008 2012 2013

CAF Confederation Cup
2014

CAF Super Cup
2002 2006 2007 2009 2013 2014

Al Ahly are an Egyptian institution and the rivalry with Zamalek has dominated the nation's football. Al Ahly have had the upper hand, boasting both the record number of league and cup titles in the country. Indeed, from 1948 to 1962, Zamalek only broke Al Ahly's grip on the championship once, and the club went unbeaten from 1974 to 1977.

Al Ahly were also the first of the two clubs to win the African Champions Cup and now boast a record eight crowns plus one CAF Cup, and a record six African Super Cups. They are not only the most succesful African side, but also currently boast the second-most international club trophies of any side in the world, behind only Real Madrid. However, tragedy struck on February 1, 2012, at the end of a game between Al Ahly and hosts Al Masry in Port Said. Unrest linked to the "Arab Spring" boiled over and ended with 79 people dead and more than 1,000 injured.

CS Sfaxien

TUNISIA

Founded
1928

Stade Taïeb Mhiri
18 000

Ligue 1
8

Tunisian Cup
4

Tunisian League Cup
1

CAF Confederation Cup
1998 2007 2008 2013

Club Sportif Sfaxien, from the city of Sfax, were rated among the five top African clubs by the statistical specialists IFFHS at the end of the last century. Founded in 1928 as Club Tunisien, they upgraded to the present name in 1962, when they reached the top division.

Since then they have won the CAF Confederations Cup (formerly the CAF Cup), Africa's second club competition, on four occasions – in 1998 then 2007, 2008 and 2013 – making them the most successful club in that competition. They were also runners-up to Egypt's Al Ahly in the African Champions League in 2006. Notable coaches have included European Frenchman Philippe Troussier and German Otto Pfister. A star forward was Mohamed Ajid, who played for Tunisia at the 1978 World Cup but later died in mysterious circumstances. Differing versions suggest either he was killed by lightning during training or shot in a political assassination.

Espérance de Tunis TUNISIA

- Founded: 1919
- Stade de Rades: 60 000
- Ligue 1: 28
- CAF Confederation Cup: 1997
- Tunisian Cup: 15
- Tunisian Super Cup: 3
- CAF Champions League: 1994, 2011
- CAF Super Cup: 1995

Espérance Sportive from Tunis bear a proud record of success at home and abroad. They claim the largest domestic support and a distinctive gold and red strip which marks them out as characteristically Tunisian. They won their first league title in 1942 but it was not until the late 1980s that they started to make a consistent competitive mark.

They now lay claim to 28 domestic championships plus 15 cups and their greatest achievements were in 1994 and 2011 when they won the African Champions League Cup. They were also runners-up on four occasions between 1999 and 2012.

Espérance have won both the CAF Cup and CAF Super Cup once each. In 1995 Espérance were winners of the occasional Afro-Asian club crown and also boast two victories in the now-defunct Arab Champions Cup, in 1993 and 2009.

← Al Ahly fans light flares at the club's training stadium to mark the fourth anniversary of the riot at the Port Said Stadium in 2012 that left dozens of their number dead and hundreds injured..

↑ ES Setif players celebrate a goal in their victory over Western Sydney Wanderers in the match for fifth place during the 2014 FIFA World Club Cup.

ES Setif

ALGERIA

- Founded: 1958
- Stade 8 Mai 1945: 25 000
- Ligue 1: 8
- Algerian Cup: 8
- Algerian Super Cup: 2
- CAF Champions League: 1988, 2014
- CAF Super Cup: 2015

Entente Sportive from Sétif are one of only three Algerian clubs to have triumphed in the African Champions League. They achieved their breakthrough in 1988 with a 4-1 two-leg aggregate defeat of Nigeria's Iwuanyanwu Nationale, and then for the second time in 2014 with an away-goals victory over Vita Club of Congo Kinshasa. Their hero was former Metz forward El Hedi Belameiri, who was the competition's six-goal joint top scorer.

ESS were founded in 1958 and have won the professional championship eight times as well as the domestic cup on a record eight occasions. International successes include the CAF Super Cup, the Afro-Asian Club Championship and the Arab Champions League (twice).

Outstanding players have included goalkeeper Antar Osmanu, who helped Algeria win the African Cup of Nations in 1990 and then the Afro-Asian Nations title a year later.

Mamelodi Sundowns

SOUTH AFRICA

Founded 1970	Premier Soccer League 8
Lucas Moripe Stadium 28 000	Nedbank Cup 4
	CAF Champions League 2016
	CAF Super Cup 2017

Mamelodi Sundowns from Pretoria have outstripped the traditionally more popular Orlando Pirates and Kaizer Chiefs in recent years. They are also the only South African club to have played in the FIFA Club World Cup; Sundowns beat favourites Zamalek of Egypt to win the continental crown but lost 4–1 to Japanese hosts Kashima Antlers in the quarter-finals of the Clubb World Cup.

Their consolation was to go on and win the subsequent CAF Super Cup in 2017 by defeating TP Mazembe 1–0 at home in the Loftus Versfeld stadium in Pretoria, which had been one of South Africa's World Cup venues in 2010.

Four Sundown players had made it into that South African World Cup squad, including popular defender Matthew Booth. A fans' favourite was midfielder Teko Modise, who reportedly became South Africa's best-paid player after arriving from Orlando Pirates in 2011.

51%

MAMELODI SUNDOWNS
THE PRETORIAN TEAM HAVE THE HIGHEST WIN RATE IN THE SOUTH AFRICAN PREMIER DIVISION.

Raja Casablanca

MOROCCO

Founded 1949	Coupe du Trône 8
Stade Mohamed V 45 000	CAF Champions League 1989 1997 1999
Botola (league) 11	CAF Super Cup 2000
	CAF Confederation Cup 2003

Raja Casablanca made history as the first African club to appear in the FIFA Club World Cup when they competed in the experimental version of the tournament in 2000 in Brazil. They qualified after having won the African Champions League for a third time in a decade in 1999. Raja later became only the second African club to reach the Club World Cup final in 2013, when they lost 2–0 to Bayern Munich on home Moroccan soil in Marrakesh. At African international level Raja have also won the CAF Cup and Super Cup once each.

Raja rank among the richest and best-supported clubs in North Africa and rank third in terms of domestic league titles. Star players have included Abdelmajid Dolmy, who made 140 appearances in midfield for Morocco between 1973 and 1988, as well as Salaheddine Bassir, who scored 25 goals in 52 internationals between 1993 and 2002.

TP Mazembe

DR CONGO

Founded
1939

Stade TP Mazembe
18 500

Linafoot (league)
16

Coupe du Congo
5

CAF Champions League
1967 1968 2009 2010 2015

CAF Confederation Cup
2016 2017

CAF Super Cup
2010 2011 2016

Tour Puissant Mazembe made history in 2010 when they became the first African club to reach the final of the FIFA Club World Cup. They defeated Mexico's Pachuca and Brazil's Internacional before being overwhelmed 3-0 by Italy's Internazionale in the final.

The club was founded by students under the name of Holy St George. Later, they became Holy St Paul and then Englebert after the tyre company which became the club sponsor. "Tour Puissant" was added in 1966 after the club's initial championship success. Despite the club crest being a crocodile with a ball in its mouth, their nickname is "the Ravens".

Mazembe were a power in the early years of African club competition. They won the Champions League final twice in the late 1960s and later added three more crowns in 2009, 2010 and 2015. Other successes included the Confederations Cup in 2016 and the Super Cup in 2010, 2011 and 2016.

➚ Khama Billiat of Mamelodi Sundowns chases down the ball during a 2016 CAF Champions League match against Chicken Inn of Zimbabwe. Mamelodi's nickname, The Brazilians, reflects their choice of lookalike playing colours.

Wydad Athletic Club

MOROCCO

Founded
1937

Stade Mohamed V
67 000

Botola (league)
19

Coupe du Trone
9

CAF Champions League
1992 2017

Wydad, of Casablanca, the 2017 African champions, boast a proud history on which to build and rebuild title-challenging teams. The original WAC outfit was founded as an aquatics club in 1937 and a football section was not added for two years. Morocco was then a colonial territory under French control; Casablanca has not only been the cradle of top clubs such as Wydad, Raya and USM but was also the home town of Just Fontaine, the 13-goal record top scorer for France at the 1958 World Cup.

Wydad won the inaugural Botola championship in 1957 and now boast 19 titles plus nine cups. Their fifth Moroccan cup success in 1996 completed their first ever league-andup double. They progressed to win the Arab Champions League in 1989, their only African Champions Cup in 1992, the Afro-Asian Cup in 1993 and the now-defunct Cup Winners' Cup in 2002.

1

TP MAZEMBE
IN 2010, TP MAZEMBE BECAME THE FIRST CLUB FROM AFRICA TO APPEAR IN A FIFA WORLD CLUB CUP FINAL. THEY LOST 3–0 TO INTERNAZIONALE.

Zamalek

EGYPT

Founded
1911

Cairo International Stadium
75 000

Egyptian Premier League
12

Egypt Cup
26

Egypt Super Cup
3

CAF Champions League
1984 1986 1993 1996 2002

CAF Super Cup
1994 1997 2003

Zamalek Sporting Club have spent a large part of their history in the shadow of Cairo rivals Al Ahly but have still won the African Champions Cup five times and finished as runners-up twice. Their roll of honour also features the CAF Super Cup three times and the now-defunct Cup Winners' Cup once.

Zamalek were founded in 1911 as Qasr El-Neel and later the club's name was changed to the King Farouk Club, after the then King of Egypt. They took their present name from their home in the affluent western district of Cairo in 1952, after the Egyptian revolution.

In the early 1990s, Zamalek overtook Al Ahly to briefly become Egypt's top club, with a hat trick of league titles. They have won the league title on 12 occasions and the cup 26 times, but they have also known their fair share of tragedy. In 1974, some 48 fans died in a crowd stampede at a friendly game against Dukla Pragje, while, in 2015, at least 20 fans were killed by police while trying to enter the Cairo Air Defense stadium. Abdel Halim Ali is one of their many club legends, having become their top goalscorer before retirement in 2009.

ASIAN CLUBS

Al-Ahli SAUDI ARABIA

Founded
1937

King Abdullah Sports City
62 000

Saudi Professional League
3

Crown Prince Cup
6

King Cup
13

Super Cup
1

Al-Ahli, from Jeddah in Saudi Arabia, were founded in 1937 and have never been relegated from the unified national league championship which was launched in 1976 and is now hugely popular and commercially successful.

The club have won three league titles, and the kingdom's variety of competitions on a total of 26 occasions. The Saudi game has made a surprisingly minor impact at international level but Al-Ahli were Arab champions in 2003, as well as runners-up to Korean opponents in the Asian Champions League in 1985 (to Daewoo Royals) and 2012 (to Ulsan Hyundai).

Al-Hilal SAUDI ARABIA

Founded
1957

King Fahd International Stadium
68 752

Saudi Professional League
15

King Cup
8

Crown Prince Cup
13

Federation Cup
7

Super Cup
1

AFC Champions League
1991
2000

Al-Hilal, from Riyadh, lay claim to being Saudi Arabia's most successful and most popular outfit. Heading their roll of honour are two triumphs in the Asian Champions League Cup, in which they have been runners-up four times, most recently 2017. Al-Hilal claim two victories in each of the Asian Cup-winners Cup, Asian Super Cup and Arab Club Championships. Domestically, they have won the Saudi league on a record 15 occasions, and the various cups 30 times. The most outstanding player in their history is Sami Al-Jaber who scored more than 200 goals for the club.

Al-Sadd QATAR

Founded
1969

Jassim Bin Hamad Stadium
12 946

Qatar Stars League
13

Emir Cup
16

Qatar Cup
6

Qatar Super Cup
14

AFC Champions League
1989
2011

Al-Sadd are nicknamed the "Real Madrid" of Qatar, and also as "The Boss", as evidenced by the glittering array of trophies in their club HQ. The Al-Sadd stadium is also notable for using a prototype of the air-cooling system which the Qatari organisers of the 2022 World Cup promised in their successful bid to win host rights.

Al-Sadd have won the Qatari league 13 times and the assorted domestic cups on 36 occasions. They have also underlined Qatar's progress by winning the Asian Champions League twice, most recently in 2011 when they dramatically saw off Korean side Jeonbuk Hyundai Motors on penalties after a thrilling 2-2 draw.

1

AL-HILAL
IN 2009, THE INTERNATIONAL FEDERATION OF FOOTBALL HISTORY AND STATISTICS (IFFHS) VOTED AL-HILAL THE BEST ASIAN TEAM OF THE 20TH CENTURY.

Barcelona's Iniesta tussles with Al-Ahli's Fahad Hamad during a 2016 friendly in Doha, Qatar, which finished an eight-goal thriller. Barcelona eventually took the victory 5-3.

Guangzhou Evergrande players line up for a team photograph before a 2017 AFC Champions League group match against Kawasaki Frontale of Japan.

Buriram United

THAILAND

Founded
1970

I-Mobile Stadium
32 600

Thai League T1
6

Kor Royal Cup
4

Thai FA Cup
4

Thai League Cup
5

Buriram began life in 1970 as the Provincial Electricity Authority based in Ayutthaya. It wasn't until their move east to Buriram in 2010 that the club took off as the modern force in Thai football. In 2011, Buriram won the domestic treble of premier league, the Thai FA Cup and league cup - the first Thai club to ever do so - and set the national record of most league points in a season. This was outdone in 2013 when they secured the quadruple, also winning the Kor Royal Cup, only to be bettered once more in 2015 with a quintuple after victory in the Mekong Club Championship as well. Internationally, their furthest progress in the Asian Champions League was reaching the quarterfinals in 2013.

Guangzhou Evergrande

CHINA

Founded
1954

Tianhe Stadium
58 500

Chinese Super League
7

Chinese FA Cup
2

Chinese FA Super Cup
4

AFC Champions League
2013
2015

Evergrande have commanded Chinese football since the political nod of approval after years in which ball games were banned from public spaces. The original Tabao club had been founded in 1954, turned professional in 1993 and were purchased by the Evergrande Real Estate Group in 2010.

Big spending brought double success in the Asian Champions League in 2013 and 2015 and brought subsequent semi-final appearances in the Club World Cup both times. They won the much-hyped Chinese Super League seven years in a row between 2011 and 2017, inspired by club hero Gao Lin, their top goalscorer.

Jeonbuk

SOUTH KOREA

Founded
1994

Jeonju World Cup Stadium
42 477

K-League Classic
5

Korean FA Cup
3

AFC Champions League
2006
2016

Jeonbuk Hyundai Motors from Jeonju, backed by the South Korean automotive giant, became East Asia's first winners of the Asian Champions League Cup when they triumphed over Al-Karamah of Syria in 2006. They succeeded again in 2016, beating Al Ain of Abu Dhabi with goals from the inspired Brazilian Leonardo.

Jeonbuk, however, were then banned from defending their title by the Asian confederation because of a domestic match-fixing scandal that saw the club penalised with the loss of nine points and a fine of $90,000. An appeal was rejected by the Court of Arbitration for Sport.

Jeonbuk have won the domestic K-League on five occasions and the cup three times.

Kashima Antlers JAPAN

- J.League 8
- Emperor's Cup 5
- J.League Cup 6
- Japanese Super Cup 6
- Founded 1947
- Kashima Soccer Stadium 40 728

Kashima take their name from the deer of the Kashima Shrine and the "Antlers" horned in on the new era of Japan's three-year-old J.League to win their first league title in 1996. Their fans' early hero was Brazilian World Cup veteran Zico who later became coach of both the club and then the national team. The club extended their command of the J.League in 2000 with an unprecedented treble made up of the league, cup and Emperor's Cup. They boast a record eight championships, six J.League Cups and five Emperor's Cups. In 2016, they enjoyed a dramatic run in the FIFA Club World Cup, leading Real Madrid in the final before finally losing in extra time.

Muangthong United THAILAND

- Thai League T1 4
- Thai League Cup 2
- Thailand Champions Cup 1
- Founded 1989
- SCG Stadium 15 000

Muangthong United are one of the richest clubs in Thailand and have competed in the top league since 2009. One of their founding fathers was Worawi Makudi, a controversial ex-president of the Thai FA and long-serving member of the FIFA executive committee.

Initially known as Norgjorg Pittayanusorn, they took up the present identity after an ownership change in 2007. A year later they won the first of their four national league titles. United have also won each of the three domestic competitions but have yet to make any impression on the Asian club competitions, only reaching the last 16 of the Asian Champions League in 2017.

Sanfrecce Hiroshima JAPAN

- J.League 3
- Japanese Super Cup 4
- Founded 1992
- EDION Stadium Hiroshima 36 906

Sanfrecce Hiroshima were born in 1992 out of the former Toyo Kogyo works team, later Mazda SC, who had played in the old part-time Japanese Soccer League. The new name, for the J.League era, derived from a legend about the strength of three arrows and a conversion of the Italian term flecce (arrows).

They have won the J.League three times and reached the semi-finals of the FIFA Club World Cup in 2016 before falling to Argentinian River Plate. Star players include one-time J.League Player of the Year Hisato Sato. He is the all-time top scorer in the league and racked up more than 170 goals in 11 years with Sanfrecce, between 2005 and 2016.

← Kashima Antlers players pass round the congratulations after a 1–0 victory over Urawa Red Diamonds in a 2017 J1 League match.
↗ Oscar of Shanghai SIPG has his penalty saved by Shusaku Nishikawa of Urawa Red Diamonds in a 2017 AFC Champions League group match.

Seoul
SOUTH KOREA

Founded 1983	Seoul World Cup Stadium 66 704
	K League Classic 6
	Korean FA Cup 2

Seoul are backed by the GS Group after having been founded by the Lucky-Goldstar conglomerate in 1983. They are one of the most financially powerful clubs in South Korea and have won six league titles as well as five of the various domestic cups. They have been runners-up in the Asian Champions League on two occasions, most recently in 2013 when they fell to wealthy Guangzhou Evergrande on away goals.

One of their greatest players was striker Choi Yong-soo who was a regular in the national team and scored more than 50 goals for the club before later returning as coach. He also scored 27 goasl in 69 appearances for South Korea.

Sepahan
IRAN

Founded 1953	Naghsh-e Jahan Stadium 75 000
	Iran Pro League 5
	Hazfi Cup 4

Sepahan have been the leading club in Iran since the launch of the Iran Pro League in 2001. They have won five championships and four cups and, in 2007, became the only Iranian club to reach the final of the Asian Champions League. Foolad Mobarakeh Sepahan Sport Club (the club's full name) lost 3–1 on aggregate to Urawa Red Diamonds of Japan. Sepahan, owned by Mobarakeh Steel Company, owed much of their recent success to the coaching work undertaken by ex-Yugoslav international Zlatko Kranjčar. Two Sepahan players, goalkeeper Rahman Ahmadi and defender Ehsan Hajksafi, were in Iran's squad at the 2014 World Cup in Brazil.

Shanghai SIPG
CHINA

Founded 2005	Shanghai Stadium 56 842

Shanghai SIPG have taken over the mantle of the city's leading club from Shanghai Shenhua with heavy spending on foreign players. Imports have included Brazil's Hulk and Oscar as well as Portugal's Ricardo Carvalho. They convincingly demonstrated their financial might in January 2017 by signing midfielder Oscar from Chelsea for a league record £80m.

Expensively hired foreign coaches have included Sweden's Sven-Göran Eriksson and Portuguese Andre Villas-Boas. The club were created in 2005 as Shanghai Dongya by ex-international Xu Genbao and worked their way up the pyramid system to finish Super League runners-up in 2015, but have yet to see their financial investment rewarded with silverware.

OCEANIAN CLUBS

➔ Melbourne Victory fans show their colours during an A-League match against Brisbane Roar in 2017.
➔ Brisbane Roar players enjoy the sweet taste of a penalty shootout victory in an A-League Elimination FInal match against Western Sydney Wanderers in 2017.

Adelaide United AUSTRALIA

Founded 2003	A-League Premier 2
Coopers Stadium 16 500	A-League Champion 1
	FFA Cup 1

Adelaide United made history in 2008 as the first Australian side to compete in the FIFA Club World Cup after the country had transferred out of Oceania and into the Asian confederation. Adelaide lost to Gamba Osaka in the Asian Champions League final but, since the Japanese club were already assured a world slot as host team, Adelaide's status as runners-up earned them entry. Ironically they then lost 1-0 to Gamba in the quarter-finals.

Adelaide had been founded only five years earlier, in 2003, after the collapse of Adelaide City. They have won the A-League twice and the championship final once. The latter 2015–16 title triumph was remarkable in that Adelaide were bottom of the table without a win after eight games. After a revival run of 13 victories in 18 games they topped the table before beating Western Sydney Wanderers 3-1 in the grand final.

1880

AN AUSSIE FIRST
WANDERERS FC, FOUNDED IN 1880, IS THOUGHT TO HAVE BEEN THE FIRST FOOTBALL CLUB IN AUSTRALIA.

Auckland City NEW ZEALAND

Founded 2004	Premiership 8
Kiwitea Street 3 500	OFC Champions League 2006 2009 2011 2012 2013 2014 2015 2016 2017

Auckland City are one of the most consistently successful of New Zealand's clubs, with their international status enhanced by the opening up of Oceania competition to New Zealand national and club teams after Australia's defection to join the Asian confederation in 2006.

Auckland have won the Oceania Champions League on nine occasions, the national league eight times and the grand final six times. In 2014, they surprised the club game internationally by becoming the first Oceania club to reach the semi-finals of the FIFA Club World Cup in Morocco where they lost only after a penalty shootout to Argentina's San Lorenzo. An Auckland stalwart was defender Ivan Vicelich, who is New Zealand's record international with 88 caps, including starting appearances in each of the three group games at the 2010 World Cup.

Brisbane Roar AUSTRALIA

Founded 1957	Suncorp Stadium 52 500
	A-League Premier 2
	A-League Champion 3

Brisbane Roar took up their present title in 2009, the latest in a string of name changes. They were founded as Hollandia-India in 1957 by Dutch immigrant fans in Brisbane and were later transformed into Queensland Lions, then Queensland Roar in 2005, in time for the launch of the A-League.

An outstanding succession of big-name coaches, including the likes of Frank Farina, Ante Postecoglou, Frans Thijssen and John Aloisi, have overseen the club's progress. They won the A-League premiers league titles in 2011 and 2014 and the championship grand final in 2011, 2012 and 2014. At international level, Roar have qualified for the Asian Champions League four times, but have never made it out of the group stage. Defender Ivan Franjic and captain Matt McKay were both members of the Australian national team who appeared at the 2014 World Cup finals in Brazil.

ARCHIE THOMPSON
A MELBOURNE LEGEND, THOMPSON PLAYED A RECORD 262 LEAGUE AND CUP GAMES FOR VICTORY ACROSS 11 SEASONS, SCORING 97 GOALS. HE WAS AN EVER-PRESENT PART OF THE VICTORY TEAMS THAT WON SIX A-LEAGUE PREMIER AND CHAMPION TITLES.

Melbourne Victory AUSTRALIA

Founded 2004	A-League Premier 4
AAMI Park 30 050	A-League Champion 3
Etihad Stadium 53 359	FFA Cup 1

Melbourne Victory have been a member of the A-League since its creation, and have won four championships, three premiership prizes and one FFA Cup. They have also contested the Asian Champions League five times, but only made it to the round of 16 once, in 2016, losing to eventual winners Jeonbuk Hyundai Motors. One of their most outstanding players was New Zealand-born striker Archie Thompson, who set an international record in 2001 by scoring 13 goals in Australia's 31–0 victory over American Samoa, in a 2002 World Cup qualifying tie. Thompson scored 28 goals in 54 appearances for Australia and 90 goals in 224 A-League games for Victory between 2005 and 2016. In the 2007 A-League grand final, he scored five times in Victory's 6–0 thrashing of Adelaide United.

NORTH & CENTRAL AMERICAN CLUBS

Alajuelense
COSTA RICA

Founded 1919	Primera Division 29
Estádio Alejandro Morera Soto 17 895	Copa de Costa Rica 8
	CONCACAF Champions League 1986 2004

Liga Deportivo Alajuelense is, in central American style, a multi-sport club, but football is the central feature of an outfit founded in 1919. They won their first championship in 1928, inspired by the goals of Alejandro Morera, who later starred with Barcelona in Spain before the civil war. Morera returned to Alajuelense to lead them to more success as coach, and their home stadium is now named after him.

The club have won two CONCACAF Champions Leagues, in 1986 (against Transvaal of Surinam) and 2004 (thumping domestic rivals Deportivo Saprissa 5-1 on aggregate), and were runners-up on four occasions. At home they boast 29 league titles and a string of other domestic competition titles.

Defender Johnny Acosta was a member of the Costa Rican national team who lost unluckily to Holland on penalties in the quarter-finals of the 2014 World Cup in Brazil.

CD Olimpia
HONDURAS

Founded 1912	Liga Nacional 30
Estádio Tiburcio Carias Andino 35 000	Copa Presidente 3
	Super Copa 1
	CONCACAF Champions League 1972 1988

Club Deportivo Olimpia stand head and shoulders above every other club in Honduras in terms of both international and domestic achievement. Based in Tegucigalpa, they were founded as a basketball club in 1912 but within five years took up football. They now boast a domestic record 30 championships and are the lone Honduran club who can point to success in the regional CONCACAF Champions League.

Olimpia beat Robinhood of Surinam to win the 1972 title (although the two legs of the final were played in early 1973) and then Defence Force of Trinidad & Tobago in 1988. In the quarter-finals, Olimpia became the only Honduran club to win at Mexico's Estádio Azteca when they beat Cruz Azul there. Olimpia's record marksman is Wilmer Velasquez who totalled 196 goals in 392 appearances in three spells with the clubs between 1991 and 2009.

➔ Alajuelense players defend a free kick against DC United in the quarter-final of the 2015 CONCACAF Champions League. They went through 6–4 on aggregate but lost in the semi-final to Montreal Impact.

Club América's Miguel Samudio fires a shot towards the Guangzhou Evergrande goal during a 2015 FIFA Club World Cup match in Osaka, Japan. The Mexicans lost 2–1 to the Chinese team.

Club América

MEXICO

Founded
1916

Estádio Azteca
87 000

Liga MX
12

Copa MX
5

CONCACAF Champions Cup
1977 1987
1990 1992
2006 2015
2016

America are considered the greatest club in Mexico, founded in 1916 and owned since 1959 by the powerful Televisa media group, which also owns the club's 86,000-capacity home, the Estádio Azteca - stage for the World Cup final twice, in 1970 and 1986. The club have won the CONCACAF Champions League a record seven times, including twice in a row, in 2016 and 2016, and the Interamerican Cup twice as well. On the domestic scene America have won a record 12 professional championships and five cups. Top goalscorer is Zague (Luís Roberto Alves) who scored 189 goals in two spells between 1985 and 1998, followed by Cuauhtémoc Blanco and Octavio Vial, both with 152. Vial was later a title-winning coach with the club.

Cristóbal Ortega, who played in defence for Mexico at the 1978 and 1986 World Cups, holds the club record with 711 appearances.

DC United

USA

Founded
1994

RFK Stadium
45 596

MLS Cup
4

MLS Supporters' Shield
4

CONCACAF Champions League
1998

DC United were one of the great success stories of the youthful Major League Soccer. United made the perfect start, winning the inaugural MLS championship season in 1996 and three of the first four MLS Cups, while finishing runners-up in the other. Launch coach was Bruce Arena, who had previously built an outstanding record with the University of Virginia and later coached the United States to the quarter-finals of the 2002 World Cup.

Early heroes included their El Salvadoran leading scorer, Raul Diaz Arce, Bolivian midfielder Marco Etcheverry, US national captain John Harkes and goal-sharp Roy Lassiter. They have won the US Open Cup three times and, on the international stage, won the CONCACAF Champions League in 1998, a tournament they dominated by not conceding a single goal, and went on to beat Brazil's Vasco da Gama for the Interamerican Cup.

Deportivo Saprissa

COSTA RICA

Founded
1935

Estádio Ricardo Saprissa Ayma
23 112

Primera Division
34

Copa de Costa Rica
8

CONCACAF Champions League
1993
1995
2005

Deportivo Saprissa come from the city of San Juan de Tibas in the province of Costa Rican capital, San José. Saprissa were founded in 1935, named after one of their founder members, and have competed in the top division of the domestic league since 1949.

The "Purple Monster" have won a record 34 championships including a historic run of six titles in a row in the 1970s. Internationally, they have won the CONCACAF Champions League three times, most recently at the expense of Mexico's UNAM Pumas in 2005. That qualified them for the FIFA Club World Cup at which they reached the semi-finals before losing 3-0 to Liverpool. They went on to beat Al-Ittihad of Saudi Arabia 3-2 in the third place playoff.

The club's greatest player was Evaristo Coronado who scored a club record 148 goals in a further record 537 games between 1981 and 1995.

LA Galaxy

USA

Founded 1994	MLS Cup 5
StubHub Center 27 167	MLS Supporters' Shield 4
	CONCACAF Champions League 2000

⬆ David Beckham poses with the MLS Cup and his sons (left to right) Brooklyn, Cruz and Romeo after helping LA Galaxy to victory over Houston Dynamo in the 2012 final. This was the last of Beckham's 118 games for the club.

➡ Seattle Sounders players celebrate after their 5–4 penalty shootout win over Toronto FC in the final of the 2016 MLS Cup. Both teams were making their first appearance in an MLS final.

Los Angeles Galaxy made international sports headlines in the spring of 2007 when they clinched the signing of former England captain David Beckham from Real Madrid. The Los Angeles-based outfit took advantage of a change in Major League Soccer rules that allowed clubs to break the existing tightly imposed wage-cap to bring in star-names to boost the profile of the league. Brazil legend Pele said Beckham, the most iconic player of his era, had a promotional potential within the US game which matched his own in the mid-1970s.

But Galaxy were already a power before ex-World Cup defender-turned-director Alexi Lalas signed up Beckham and US World Cup skipper, Landon Donovan. They had won the CONCACAF Champions League in 2000 (beating Olimpia of Honduras) and now total five MLS championships as well as two US Open Cups.

Pachuca

MEXICO

Founded
1901

Estádio Hidalgo
27 512

Liga MX
6

CONCACAF Champions League
2002 2007
2008 2010
2017

$79.9
MILLION

MLS MONEY BAGS
ACCORDING TO *FORBES* MAGAZINE, THE 10 HIGHEST-PAID PLAYERS IN THE MLS EARNED $79.9 MILLION IN 2016, HEADED BY KAKÁ ON A COOL $9.4 MILLION.

Pachuca, from a city 60 miles north-east of Mexico City, are heirs to a great tradition. Football was introduced to the country by tin miners brought from Cornwall in England in the late 19th century.

The local club was founded in 1901, earning one of its nicknames as "The Cradle of Football". Hence, in 2001, CF Pachuca became the first Mexican club to celebrate a centenary of existence. Pachuca are now owned by millionaire local businessman, José Jesús Martínez Patiño.

Patiño's support in terms of both players and facilities has helped Pachuca win six championships, four CONCACAF Champions Cups and one Copa Sudamericana in 2006 (thus becoming the first CONCACAF team to win a CONMEBOL tournament).

Pachuca's finest player was Argentinian Gabriel Caballero, who scored 55 goals in 350-plus appearances for Pachuca in three spells between 1988 and 2009.

Seattle Sounders

USA

Founded
2007

CenturyLink Field
39 419

MLS Cup
1

MLS Supporters' Shield
1

Seattle Sounders are barely a decade old but have already made their considerable presence felt in Major League Soccer. They won the US Open Cup four times in six years between 2009 and 2014 and then stepped up to win the MLS championship cup itself in 2016.

Top scorer was United States striker Jordan Morris with 12 goals in a season which saw the club record a 40,000-plus average attendance for the fifth campaign in succession.

Sounders are the third club from the city to bear the name. The first Sounders were twice runners-up (in 1977 and 1982) in the doomed North American Soccer League; the second incarnation involved a Sounders side playing in the second-tier United Soccer Leagues between 1994 and 2008.

A new franchise was launched in 2007 by a consortium including businessman Adrian Hanauer and Microsoft co-founder Paul Allen.

PAUL ALLEN
THE MICROSOFT CO-FOUNDER AND SEATTLE NATIVE PART OWNS THE SEATTLE SOUNDERS AS WELL AS HAVING FULL CONTROL OF THE SEATTLE SEAHAWKS NFL TEAM.

Atlético Nacional
COLOMBIA

Copa Colombia	3
Superliga Colombiana	2
Founded	1947
Copa Libertadores	1989 2016
Estádio Atanasio Girardot	40 943
Primera A	16
Recopa Sudamericana	2017

Atlético Nacional of Medellin made history in becoming the first Colombian club to win the Copa Libertadores in 1989. Nacional, who provided the base of the Colombian World Cup team in the 1990s, had made their debut in the South American club cup in 1971 under Argentinian coach Osvaldo Zubeldía. He turned Nacional into Colombian champions three times in the mid-1970s and early 1980s. Zubeldía was followed by Luis Cubilla, at whose suggestion, in 1986, Nacional appointed Francisco Maturana as boss. In 1987 and 1988, they were championship runners-up and then beat Olimpia of Paraguay to lift the South American crown for the first time.

The club then became a subject of controversy due to links with notorious drugs baron Pablo Escóbar. After he was killed in 1993, his coffin was draped in a Nacional flag. Nacional restored their reputation in 2016 when they insisted that rivals Chapecoense be awarded the Copa Sudamericana after the Brazilian club's players and staff were killed in a plane crash on the way to play the final. Nacional had been pursuing the double after winning the Libertadores for a second time. Nacional enjoy a long-running rivalry with Independiente Medellin, with whom they share a stadium.

Barcelona SC
ECUADOR

Estádio Monumental Banco Pichincha	57 267
Founded	1925
Serie A	15

Barcelona are the leading club in Ecuador. They are based in Guayaquil, the commercial and industrial centre of the country and the city through which football was introduced by Uruguayans and Brazilians in the early years of the 20th century. Barcelona were founded in 1925 by a Spanish immigrant, Eutimio Pérez, who insisted the club be named after his favourite team back home in his native Catalonia. They won the last amateur championship in 1950 and the

first of the professional era a year later, and they now lay claim to a record 15 national championships.

In 1971, Barcelona became the first Ecuadorian club to reach the semi-finals of the Copa Libertadores with a team which included veteran centre forward Pedro Alberto Spencer, back home to finish his career after a record-breaking decade spent in Uruguay with Peñarol. After his retirement, Barcelona went almost a decade without success at home or abroad. However, a 1980s revival saw them reach the Copa Libertadores final in 1990, only to lose narrowly to Olimpia of Paraguay. In 1997, they reached the final for a second time but went down to Brazil's Vasco da Gama. They also won the league title that year before enduring a break of 14 years, before regaining it in 2012.

Fans of Atletico Nacional cheer on their team during the second leg of the Recopa Sudamericana final against Chapecoense of Brazil in May 2017. Atletico won the leg and the trophy, the first Colombian team to do so.

Boca Juniors

ARGENTINA

Founded 1905	Copa Argentina 3
La Bombonera 49 000	Copa Libertadores 1977 1978 2000 2001 2003 2007
Primera Division 33	Copa Sudamericana 2004 2005
Recopa Sudamericana 1990 2005 2006 2008	FIFA Club World Cup 1977 2000 2003

The legendary Boca Juniors striker Martin Palermo bids farewell to the fans after his final match at La Bombonera stadium, Buenos Aires, in 2011. He is the Argentinian club's highest ever scorer with 236 goals.

Boca are one of the two great clubs in the Argentine capital of Buenos Aires. They won the last Argentinian amateur championship in 1930 and the first unified professional one the next year. Two more titles followed in the next four years, thanks to some fine players, including the great Brazilian defender Domingos da Guia. In the 1940s and 1950s, Boca slipped into River Plate's shadow, re-emerging in 1963 when the goals of José Sanfilippo fired Boca to the final of the Copa Libertadores. They had to wait to win the title until the late 1970s. They then reached the final three years in a row, beating Cruzeiro in 1977 and Deportivo Cali in 1978 before losing to Olimpia of Paraguay in 1979.

Boca's rugged style, under Juan Carlos Lorenzo, proved controversial. Not one Boca player figured in Argentina's squad who won the 1978 World Cup even though, a year earlier, they had secured the first of their three world crowns. Boca rebuilt around Diego Maradona in 1981 but it was not until 2000 that they regained national and world prominence. They boast 22 international and 45 domestic trophies. All-time top scorer is Martin Palermo with 236 goals.

Bolívar

BOLIVIA

Founded 1925	Estádio Hernando Siles 41 143
	Liga de Futbol Profesional Boliviano 20

Bolívar are 20-times record champions of Bolivia since the start of the LPFB era in 1978, ahead of traditional rivals such as The Strongest, the other main club from their high-altitude home city of La Paz. They are the only Bolivian club ever to have reached the semi-finals of the Copa Libertadores, doing so in both 1986 and 2014. They also reached the final of the Copa Sudamericana, the continent's secondary competition, in 2004.

Bolívar were founded in 1925 and were champions of the original amateur tournament six times before the introduction of professionalism at the start of the 1950s. Star players down the years have included defender Marco Sandy, midfielders Luis Cristaldo and Carlos Borja as well as forward Marco Antônio Etcheverry. Borja spent all 20 years of his senior career with Bolívar, scoring 129 goals in more than 500 appearances.

Etcheverry, one of Bolivia's greatest players, played more than 100 games for the club either side of transfers that took him to Spain, Chile, Colombia and the United States. He was one of the products of the remarkable Tahuichi Academy, which has provided Bolivia with many other outstanding players.

Chapecoense

BRAZIL

Founded 1973	Arena Condá 22 600
	Copa Sudamericana 2016

Chapecoense, from Chapeco in the Brazilian state of Santa Catarina, gained worldwide attention in November 2016 when 18 of their players died in a plane crash in Colombia. The players were among 71 people killed as the club flew to play Atlético Nacional in the first leg of the final of the Copa Sudamericana, continental equivalent of UEFA's Europa League. The Colombians insisted on

➜ Chapecoense fans, filling the Couto Pereira Stadium in Curitiba, Brazil, in December 2016, pay tribute to the victims of the plane crash that a week earlier had robbed the club of most of its squad. The stadium would have hosted the second leg of the Copa Sudamericana against Atletico National.

➜ Alexis Sanchez shows his trademark determination in action for Colo-Colo during a Primera Division match in 2006. Sanchez spent one season at the Chilean club, on loan from Udinese of Italy, making his debut at 17, before moving to River Plate and then back to Udinese in 2008.

Chapecoense being awarded the trophy. "Chape" shared the $2m in prize money among families of the plane crash victims.

ACF Chapecoense were founded in 1973, from a merger of local rivals Atlético and Independente. They won the first of their six Santa Catarina state championships in 1977. In 2014, Chapecoense were promoted into the top division of the national championship from which they qualified in 2015 for the Copa Sudamericana. Their first appearance in international competition had ended in a quarterfinal defeat by River Plate of Argentina. In 2016, they reached the final by defeating Argentina's San Lorenzo de Almagro. Despite having been forced to rebuild their entire squad, Chapecoense won the 2017 Catarinense state championship.

Colo-Colo

CHILE

- Founded: 1925
- Estádio Monumental David Arellano: 47 347
- Primera Division: 31
- Copa Chile: 11
- Copa Libertadores: 1991
- Recopa Sudamericana: 1992

Colo-Colo were founded by five members of Magallanes FC, who broke away in a row over the appointment of a new club captain. Chief among them was David Arellano who was first captain of their new club and determined to build an international reputation. Within two years of Colo-Colo's foundation, they sent a team off to tour Spain and Portugal.

In 1933, Colo-Colo were among the founders of a professional league in Chile and, in 1941, they set another pioneering trend within the Chilean game by introducing a foreign coach in the Hungarian, Ferenc Platko – a one-time MTK and Barcelona goalkeeper. In 1948, they organised a South American club tournament that is considered a forerunner of the Copa Libertadores.

They are record 31-times league winners in Chile and the supreme transfer destination for most domestic players. Colo-Colo's finest achievement was in winning the 1991 Copa Libertadores, after they scored a 3-0 aggregate victory over Olimpia of Paraguay. Old stars included Misael Escuti, who kept goal when hosts Chile finished third in the 1962 World Cup, and striker Carlos Caszely a decade later.

1

COLO-COLO
THE SANTIAGO CLUB IS THE ONE AND ONLY CHILEAN REPRESENTATIVE TO HAVE WON THE COPA LIBERTADORES.

Corinthians

BRAZIL

	Copa do Brasil 3
Founded 1910	FIFA Club World Cup 2000 2012
Arena Corinthians 49 205	Copa Libertadores 2012
Serie A 7	Recopa Sudamericana 2013

Corinthians, from São Paulo, were founded as a result of the impact of a Brazilian tour by the famous English amateur club. The founding members were all Brazilians, one a house painter and the other four railway workers. Corinthians joined the São Paulo league in 1913 and won their first state title the following year during an era of strife over the advent of professionalism.

"Timão" won the first official Rio/São Paulo cup in 1950 and remain one of the country's most popular clubs. Corinthians have won the FIFA Club World Cup twice, including the original tournament in 2000 and then a second in 2012. They have been South American champions once and, domestically, claim six national chamionships and 28 Paulista state titles.

Star players over the years have included Gilmar, Brazil's 1958 and 1962 World Cup-winning goalkeeper, the 1970s hero Roberto Rivelino, as well as World Cup-winning centre-forward Ronaldo, who led them back from a brief relegation in 2007.

Corinthians play their home games in the Itaquera stadium, officially the Arena Corinthians, which was built anew for the 2014 World Cup and hosted the opening game in which Brazil beat Croatia 3–1.

Flamengo

BRAZIL

	Serie A 6
	Copa do Brasil 3
Founded 1895	FIFA Club World Cup 1981
Estádio Luso-Brasileiro 20 113	Copa Libertadores 1981

Flamengo are the most popular club in Brazil. Founded by dissident members of the Fluminense club and under the umbrella of the Flamengo sailing club, it now boasts more than 75,000 members. They first competed in the Rio league in 1912, winning the title

two years later. In 1915, they regained the crown without having lost a game.

A string of great names have graced the red-and-black hoops, among them defender Domingos Da Guia and the legendary centre-forward Leonidas da Silva. Known as the "Black Diamond", Leonidas played for Flamengo from 1936 to 1942, inspiring two state championship triumphs and earning a worldwide reputation through his brilliance in the 1938 World Cup finals in France.

Flamengo ran up a Rio state hat trick in the mid-1950s with their team nicknamed the "Steamroller" but did not reach the pinnacle of success until 1981. Riding high on the goals of a new hero in Zico - the so-called "White Pelé" - they won both the South American and World Club Cups. Zico was in a class of his own against Liverpool in the world final in Tokyo. He created all of Flamengo's goals in a 3-0 win. Flamengo have won six Brazilian championships and 34 Rio league titles.

Corinthians fans (left) and Flamengo fans (above) display the typical passions and sense of theatre that football brings out in Brazilians.

Nacional

URUGUAY

Primera Division
46

FIFA Club World Cup
1971 1980 1988

Founded
1899

Estádio Gran Parque Central
28 000

Copa Libertadores
1971 1980 1988

Nacional and Peñarol are the two great clubs of Uruguay and bitter rivals on both the domestic and international stages. Nacional were formed from a merger of the Montevideo Football Club and the Uruguay Athletic Club, and in 1903 were chosen to line up as Uruguay's national team against Argentina in Buenos Aires, with Nacional's men winning 3-2.

The club's domestic golden era is considered to be the years from 1939 to 1943, when they won the league each season under Scottish manager Williams Reasdale. Nacional's domestic domination was underlined by an 8-0 thrashing of old enemy Peñarol.

Later the club extended their status into the international arena. Nacional won the Copa Libertadores for the first time in 1971, when they also went on to secure the first of their three World Club Cup triumphs. They have also won the Copa Libertadores on three occasions, albeit the last one back in 1988, and three other Latin American international tournaments. Nacional have won the championship on 46 occasions and their roll of stars includes 11 of the Uruguayan teams who won Olympic gold in 1924 and 1928, nine members of the 1930 World Cup-winning squad and five of the 1950 winners. Their supporters also bagged a World Record when they unfurled the "biggest flag in the world" in 2013. It was 600 metres long.

Olimpia

PARAGUAY

Founded
1902

Estádio Manuel Ferreira
22 000

FIFA Club World Cup
1979

Primera División
41

Copa Libertadores
1979
1990
2002

Recopa Sudamericana
1991
2003

Olimpia have represented Paraguay at international level with both determination and success, the country's only outfit to have triumphed in both the Club World Cup and Copa Libertadores.

Dutch schoolteacher William Paats brought the first football to Paraguay in 1901 and his pupils created the club. Olimpia were founder members of the first division in 1906 and finished runners-up. Their first title arrived in 1912, and since then they have outstripped the rest. They put together league hat tricks from 1927–29 and 1939–41, won five times in a row in the 1950s and six times in succession between 1978 and 1983.

In the interim, Olimpia finished runners-up to Peñarol in the final of the inaugural Copa Libertadores in 1960. Twenty years later, they defeated favourites Boca Juniors of Argentina 2–0 on aggregate in the final and went on to beat Sweden's Malmo in the World Club Cup.

Key players were midfieders Hugo Talavera, nicknamed "The Architect", and Carlos Alberto Kiese. Further Copa Libertadores triumphs followed in 1990 and 2002. In addition to their world title and three Libertadores prizes, Olimpia have won 41 Primera Division titles and five other Latin American club trophies.

Peñarol

URUGUAY

Founded
1891

Estádio Campeon del Siglo
40 000

Primera Divison
49

Copa Libertadores
1960 1961
1966 1982
1987

FIFA Club World Cup
1961 1966
1982

Peñarol were the first club to win the World Club Cup three times, but their success is no modern phenomenon. They had been founded as the Central Uruguayan Railway Cricket Club in 1891 but changed their name in 1913 as the British influence waned. The railways sidings and offices were near the Italian Pignarolo district, named after the landowner Pedro Pignarolo, hence the Spanish name was adopted. Since then, Peñarol have been the pre-eminent power in Uruguayan football, along with old rivals, Nacional.

In 1950, they provided the nucleus of the Uruguayan national team, who

⬅ Peñarol's Alberto Spencer pressurises the Celtic keeper in 1967. Spencer holds the Copa Libertadores scoring record with 54 goals.
⬋ Peñarol players line up before a match against Cruz Azul of Mexico in 2001.
⬇ Racing Club captain Oscar Martin (right) clashes with Jimmy Johnstone of Celtic in the playoff for the 1967 Intercontinental Cup.

shocked Brazil in Maracana to win the 1950 World Cup. Peñarol provided goalkeeper Roque Maspoli – their World Club Cup-winning coach in 1966 – halfbacks Rodríguez Andrade and Obdulio Varela as well as centre-forward Oscar Miguez and goalscorers Juan Schiaffino and Alcides Ghiggia.

The club's international awakening came in 1960 in winning the inaugural Copa Libertadores, the first of their five. They were thrashed by Real Madrid in the first Club World Cup but made up for it the next year with victory over Benfica. Peñarol regained the world crown in 1966, at the expense of Real Madrid, and then again in 1982 when they beat Aston Villa in Tokyo.

Racing Club
ARGENTINA

Founded 1903	Primera Divison 17
	Copa Libertadores 1967
Estadio Presidente Peron 61 000	FIFA Club World Cup 1967

Racing stand as one of the traditionally great clubs of Argentinian football with the pinnacle of achievement coming in 1967 when they won the Copa Libertadores for the first and only time and then added the Club World Cup. Since then they have added only a handful of trophies to their roll of honour despite remaining a powerful influence within the organisation of the domestic game.

Racing were founded by French immigrants in 1903, entered the first division in 1920 and were champions three years later. The style of their successes in the early years earned their nickname of "The Academy" and, notably, they also won three championships in the 1940s otherwise dominated by River Plate's legendary "La Maquina" attack.

In 1967, it was under former international Juan José Pizzutti that they grasped continental and world titles. They could not maintain their command. In 1983, Racing were relegated for the first time. They bounced back to win the Copa Sudamericana in 1988 and claim league titles in both 2001 (despite declaring bankruptcy in 2000) and 2014.

Star players have included initial hero Alberto Ohaco, 1930s' top scorer Evaristo Barrera, 1960s' goalkeeper Agustin Cejas and 1986 World Cup-winning midfielder Julio Olarticoechea.

River Plate

ARGENTINA

Founded
1901

El Monumental
61 688

Primera Divison
36

Copa Argentina
2

Copa Libertadores
1986 1996 2015

Copa Sudamericana
2014

Recopa Sudamericana
2015 2016

FIFA Club World Cup
1986

River Plate are one of the two giants of Argentinian football, along with Boca Juniors. Traditionally, the club from the rich side of Buenos Aires, River were leaders in the development of professional football in the 1920s. In the 1930s, they boasted Bernabe Ferreyra, a legendary figure in local football; in the late 1940s, their high-scoring forward line was so feared and admired they were nicknamed "La Maquina" (The Machine).

Later, River developed more great players: Alfredo Di Stéfano, who would turn Real Madrid into possibly the greatest team of all time; Omar Sívori, who formed a wonderful partnership with John Charles after joining Juventus; and then 1978 World Cup winners Ubaldo Fillol, Daniel Passarella, Leopoldo Luque and Mario Kempes.

In 1986 they were joined in River's Hall of Fame by the likes of goalkeeper Nery Pumpido, centre-back Oscar Ruggeri and schemer Norberto Alonso, after victory in the 1986 Copa Libertadores provided formal confirmation of River's "millonarios" status. They not only beat América of Colombia but went on to win the Club World Cup for the first and last time to date. River have won 36 domestic championships and won the Copa Libertadores most recently in 2015.

1891

FOOTBALL PIONEERS

AN ARGENTINE FOOTBALL LEAGUE WAS FORMED IN 1891 – THE FIRST OUTSIDE EUROPE.

Santos
BRAZIL

- Copa do Brasil: 1
- Copa Libertadores: 1962 1963 2011
- Founded: 1912
- Estádio Urbano Caldeira: 16 068
- FIFA Club World Cup: 1962 1963
- Serie A: 8

Santos remain synonymous with Pelé, who played his entire mainstream career with the club. Santos had entered the São Paulo state championship in 1916 and became only the second Brazilian club to embrace professionalism in 1933, but it did not hit the headlines until the mid-1950s. Then, to guide a clutch of talented youngsters, they signed the 1950 World Cup veteran Jair da Rosa Pinto, and discovered the 15-year-old Pelé.

Santos harvested millions of dollars from friendly match tours around the world and reinvested heavily in surrounding Pelé with fine players. These included World Cup winners in goalkeeper Gilmar, centre back Mauro and wing-half Zito; an outside left with a ferocious shot in Pepe; and the precocious young talents of right-winger Dorval, schemer Mengalvio and centre-forward Coutinho, Pelé's so-called "twin".

Constant touring burned out many young players but Santos continued cashing in on Pelé's name until the early 1970s. Not until nearly 50 years later, in 2011, did they unearth a new superstar in Neymar and regain the Copa Libertadores. The world crown proved beyond Neymar's Santos, however: they lost 4–0 to his future club, Barcelona.

São Paulo
BRAZIL

- Serie A: 6
- FIFA Club World Cup: 1992 1993 2005
- Founded: 1930
- Copa Libertadores: 1992 1993 2005
- Morumbi: 67 053

São Paulo are one of only four clubs to have played in all the new-era Brazilian championships, along with Flamengo, Cruzeiro and neighbours Santos. They are the most successful Brazilian club at international level, boasting three Club World Cup successes in 1992, 1993 and 2005, as well as three victories in the Copa Libertadores and six other Latin American competitive titles.

São Paulo have triumphed in the Paulista state league on 21 occasions and won the national title six times. The club were formed from a merger between Paulistano and AA Palmeiras. A leading light was Paulo Machado de Carvalho, later a senior administrator behind Brazil's World Cup hat trick. The club's success prompted construction of the Morumbi stadium, which, on its opening in 1970, boasted a club world-record capacity of 140,000.

São Paulo reached their first South American club final in 1974, losing to Argentina's Independiente. It took the arrival of coach Telê Santana in the late 1980s to propel them to three state league titles in four years and then double successes two years in a row in the Copa Libertadores and World Club Cup. Star players included World Cup-winners in Cafu and Ronaldo, plus playmaker Rai.

↖ River Plate fans gather in the El Monumental stadium before a Buenos Aires derby game against Boca Juniors in 2008.
← A 19-year-old Pelé adjusts his kit during a match for Santos in 1960, a year in which he scored 33 goals in 33 games for the Brazilian club.

adidas
Fly
Emirates

6

GREAT PLAYERS

These are the men who have delighted fans over the years, not merely with their achievements, but with their personalities on the pitch – and occasionally off it. They draw spectators from far and wide, who are attracted beyond an attachment to a club or a national team.

⬆ Sergio Agüero celebrates after putting away a hat-trick goal for Manchester City against Tottenham Hotspur in 2014. He scored four in the match, making him City's top scorer in the Premier League.

Igor Akinfeev

NATIONAL TEAM Russia
BORN April 8, 1986
CLUB(S) CSKA Moscow

Akinfeev captained the Russia team that reached the quarter-finals of the 2018 World Cup as hosts. He was voted man of the match after the second round defeat of Spain on penalties. The goalkeeper has spent all his club career with CSKA Moscow, winning six league titles and six Russian cups.

Ademir Marques de Menezes

NATIONAL TEAM Brazil
BORN November 8, 1922, died May 11, 1996
CLUB(S) FC Recife, Vasco da Gama, Fluminense, Vasco da Gama

Ademir was the seven-goal leading scorer at the 1950 World Cup finals, totalling 32 goals in 37 internationals after starting out as a left-winger. He was a Rio de Janeiro state champion six times - on five occasions with Vasco da Gama and once with rivals Fluminense.

Sergio "Kun" Agüero

NATIONAL TEAM Argentina
BORN June 2, 1988
CLUB(S) Independiente, Atlético de Madrid (Sp), Manchester City (Eng)

Agüero, the son-in-law of Diego Maradona, made his name by helping Argentina win two World Youth Cups. A year later, he won Olympic gold with Argentina in Beijing. With Atlético Madrid, he won the 2010 Europa League before scoring 190-plus goals in seven years with Man City.

Flórián Albert

NATIONAL TEAM Hungary
BORN September 15, 1941, died October 31, 2011
CLUB(S) Ferencvaros

Albert was the first great player to emerge in Hungary after the dissolution of the great team of the early 1950s. He made his international debut at 17, was three times the domestic league's leading scorer and was enthroned as European Footballer of the Year in 1967.

José Altafini

NATIONAL TEAMS Brazil and Italy

BORN August 27, 1938

CLUB(S) Palmeiras, São Paulo, AC Milan, Napoli, Juventus, Chiasso (Swz), Mendrisio Star (Swz)

Altafini, an energetic and direct centre forward, was known in Brazil as "Mazzola" because of his resemblance to the 1940s Italian star. After the 1958 World Cup, he joined Milan, with whom he won the Champions Cup in 1963 by scoring a then record 14 goals. He also played for Italy.

Dani Alves

FULL NAME Daniel Alves da Silva

NATIONAL TEAM Brazil

BORN May 6, 1983

CLUBS(S) Bahia, Sevilla (Sp), Barcelona (Sp), Juventus (It), Paris Saint-Germain (Fr)

Dani Alves has proved one of the modern game's most outstanding attacking right backs. He won the UEFA Cup twice and the Spanish cup with Sevilla before moving for £20m in 2008 to Barcelona, with whom he won the treble of Champions League, La Liga and Spanish cup in his first season.

José Leandro Andrade

NATIONAL TEAM Uruguay

BORN November 20, 1898, died October 5, 1957

Club(s) Bella Vista, Nacional, Peñarol, Atlanta (Arg), Lanus (Arg), Wanderers

Andrade was an old-fashioned wing-half in the old 2-3-5 tactical system. He was a stalwart of the great Uruguayan teams of the 1920s and 1930s, winning football gold at the 1924 and 1928 Olympic Games and starring at the inaugural World Cup, which Uruguay won in 1930.

Osvaldo César "Ossie" Ardiles

NATIONAL TEAM Argentina

BORN August 3, 1952

CLUB(S) Hurácan, Belgrano, Instituto ACC, Tottenham Hotspur (Eng), Paris S-G (Fr), Tottenham Hotspur (Eng), Blackburn Rovers (Eng), Queens Park Rangers (Eng), Fort Lauderdale Strikers (US), Swindon Town (Eng)

Ardiles combined legal and football studies in the mid-1970s, when he earned his reputation as Argentina's playmaker under manager César Luis Menotti. After winning the 1978 World Cup, Ardiles joined Tottenham for £300,000, making him one of the great bargains of modern football.

22.9
MPH

GARETH BALE
THE WALES AND REAL MADRID STRIKER IS SAID TO BE THE CONSISTENTLY FASTEST FOOTBALLER ON THE PLANET, WITH HIS AVERAGE SPRINTING SPEED MEASURED AT 22.9 MPH (36.9 KPH) OVER A YEAR.

Roberto Baggio

NATIONAL TEAM Italy

BORN February 18, 1967

CLUB(S) Fiorentina, Juventus, Milan, Bologna, Internazionale, Brescia, Vincenza Calcio

Baggio became the world's most expensive footballer when Juventus bought him for £8m from Fiorentina, just before the 1990 World Cup. He helped Juve win the 1993 UEFA Cup and was voted World Player of the Year in 1994, despite missing a penalty in a World Cup final shootout against Brazil.

Gareth Bale

NATIONAL TEAM Wales

BORN July 16, 1989

CLUB(S) Southampton (Eng), Tottenham (Eng), Real Madrid (Sp)

Bale secured his status as Wales' most outstanding modern player by leading them to the Euro 2016 semi-finals. Cardiff-born, he made his name as a leftback with Southampton before moving up-field at Tottenham and then at Real Madrid with whom he won the Champions League four times.

Roberto Baggio starred for Italy in three World Cups, scoring nine goals in all.

FRANZ BECKENBAUER

1945– 1.81m (5ft 11 ½ in)

ONLY WINNER OF A WORLD CUP AS CAPTAIN AND THEN AS MANAGER

1

CLUB	INTERNATIONAL
BAYERN MUNICH NEW YORK COSMOS HAMBURGER	GERMANY
709 APPEARANCES	103 APPEARANCES
94 GOALS	14 GOALS
8 LEAGUE TITLES	67% WIN PERCENTAGE

1964
Makes his Bayern Munich debut – playing on the left wing

1965
Plays first match for West Germany, aged 20, in a 2-1 World Cup qualifying win against Sweden

1966
Stars in midfield, on the losing side, for West Germany in the 4–2 World Cup final defeat by England

1972
Captains West Germany to European Championship victory and leads Bayern to the second of four Bundesliga titles with Bayern

1974
Captains Bayern to victory in the European Cup final and then West Germany to victory in the World Cup

1976
Completes a record 103 appearances for West Germany before transferring to New York Cosmos

1980
Joins Hamburg and helps them to the Bundesliga title in 1982 before returning to New York Cosmos in 1983

1984
Appointed national manager of West Germany and goes on to win the World Cup in 1990

DER KAISER No other player has ever had a career that reached such tangible heights. As well as World Cup victories as both player and manager, "Kaiser Franz" won the European Championship in 1972, the Intercontinental Cup (1976), the European Cup (1974, 1975 and 1976), the UEFA Cup Winners' Cup (1967), as well as five Bundesliga titles and three North American Soccer League titles. However, Beckenbauer's great innovation as a player was in the revolutionary role of attacking sweeper, which he introduced in the late 1960s. Out on the pitch, he was graceful and elegant, combining an athlete's physique with a computer-like football brain. In an increasingly crowded modern game, Beckenbauer found that the sweeper role provided him with time and space in which to work his magical influence on a match. After retirement, he returned to Germany as national coach and, despite a lack of experience, masterminded their 1990 World Cup success. He then followed this up by leading Marseille to the Ligue 1 title in 1991 and Bayern Munich to the top of the Bundesliga in 1994.

Alan Ball

NATIONAL TEAM England

BORN May 12, 1945, died April 25, 2007

CLUB(S) Blackpool, Everton, Arsenal, Hellenic (SAf), Southampton, Vancouver Whitecaps (Can), Blackpool, Southampton, Floreat Athens (Australia), Eastern AA (HK), Bristol Rovers

Ball, son of a professional player and manager of the same name, was one of the hardest-working heroes of England's 1966 World Cup triumph. He made his name with Blackpool, collected a league championship medal with Everton in 1970, then later moved to Arsenal for a then record £220,000.

Gordon Banks

National team England

Born December 20, 1937

Club(s) Chesterfield, Leicester City, Stoke City, Ckeveland (US), Hellenic (SAf), Fort Lauderdale (US), St Patrick's Athletic (RI)

Banks set various England goalkeeping records on his way to World Cup success in 1966 and a nickname "as safe as the Banks of England". His then records included 23 consecutive internationals and seven clean sheets in a row, a run ended by a Eusébio penalty in the semi-finals.

Franco Baresi

NATIONAL TEAM Italy

BORN May 8, 1960

CLUB(S) Milan

Baresi was the finest in a line of superb Italian sweepers. He began as an attacking midfielder before providing the defensive foundation on which Arrigo Sacchi built Milan's all-conquering club team. He won two World Club Cups, three European Champions Cups and six league titles.

Jim Baxter

NATIONAL TEAM Scotland

BORN September 29, 1939, died April 14, 2001

CLUB(S) Raith Rovers, Rangers, Sunderland (Eng), Vancouver Royal (Can), Nottingham Forest (Eng), Rangers

Baxter's skill quickly established him as an Ibrox idol after Rangers signed him in June 1960. An attacking left half, "Slim Jim" won three Scottish leagues, three Scottish Cups and four League Cups. His profile was enhanced by selection for FIFA's World XI against England in 1963.

★ Franz Beckenbauer

See page 224

David Beckham

NATIONAL TEAM England

BORN May 2, 1975

CLUB(S) Manchester Utd, Preston NE, Real Madrid (Sp), LA Galaxy (US), Milan (It), Paris Saint-Germain (Fr)

Beckham was renowned even more as an international style icon and national ambassador than for what he achieved on the pitch. A high-earning, hard-working right-side midfielder, he led England at World Cup and European finals and won league titles in England, Spain, the US and France.

Karim Benzema

NATIONAL TEAM France

BORN December 20, 1987

CLUBS(S) Lyon, Real Madrid (Sp)

Benzema was a home-town discovery by Lyon who won four league titles with the club. In 2009, he turned down Manchester United because he had always dreamed of signing for Real Madrid with whom he subsequently won the UEFA Champions League four times and was French Player of the Year three times.

David Beckham, in Real Madrid colours, bends the ball like only David Beckham can in a 2006 Champions League match against Steaua Bucharest of Romania.

GEORGE BEST

1946–2005 1.75m (5ft 9ins)

CLUB

MANCHESTER UNITED
(and more than 10 others)

470
APPEARANCES (FOR MANCHESTER UNITED)

179
GOALS

0.38
GOALS PER APPEARANCE

INTERNATIONAL

NORTHERN IRELAND

37
APPEARANCES

9
GOALS

0
APPEARANCES IN A MAJOR TOURNAMENT

AGE WHEN BEST SCORED HIS FIRST GOAL FOR MANCHESTER UNITED

17

1961
Joins Manchester United as a 15-year-old apprentice

1964
The Best-Law-Charlton trio play together for United for the first time in a 4–1 win

1965
Gains first of two league championship medals – the second comes in 1967

1966
Scores two goals against Benfica in a European Cup game and is nicknamed "O Quinto Beatle" ("The Fifth Beatle")

1968
Scores in 4–1 European Cup victory over Benfica and becomes the one and only Irishman to win the Ballon d'Or

1974
Quits United after game against Queens Park Rangers. Top class career is effectively over

1983
Ends his football days after many comeback attempts

2005
Dies after losing fight with alcoholism. In 2006, Belfast City Airport is named after him

"THE FIFTH BEATLE" Best was the most gifted British player of his generation, but after his issues with drinking began, he walked out of Manchester United in 1974 at the age of just 26. He preferred to enjoy the high life, often fuelled by alcohol. Best attempted many comebacks and turned out briefly for a great number of clubs, before eventually hanging up his boots in 1983. At his peak, he was a force of nature: incredibly skilful, fast, two-footed and brave. He could tackle fiercely, had an eye for gaps that others never saw and conjured goals out of nothing. He stood out, even in a team that included such greats as Bobby Charlton and Denis Law, and his dribbling spectaculars are still shown on British TV, as is the outrageous lob he scored against Tottenham and the six goals he netted in one FA Cup tie against Northampton.

Dennis Bergkamp

NATIONAL TEAM Holland

BORN May 10, 1969

CLUB(S) Ajax Amsterdam, Internazionale (It), Arsenal (Eng)

Bergkamp, an Ajax youth product, made his European club debut the day after sitting school examinations. He starred for Holland at the 1992 European finals and went to Internazionale for £8m. Later sold to Arsenal, he played key roles in league and cup doubles of 1998 and 2002.

★ George Best

See page 226

Josef "Pepi" Bican

NATIONAL TEAM Austria, Czechoslovakia, Bohemia/Moravia

BORN September 25, 1913, died December 12, 2001

CLUB(S) Rapid Vienna, Admira, Slavia Prague, Vitkovice, Hradec Kralove, Dynamo Prague

Bican, for veteran Czechs, remains their greatest player more than half a century after his retirement with 800 goals to his career credit. Bican was a hero of the "Wunderteam" of the 1930s then starred for Czechoslovakia after Austria was swallowed up by the Anschluss.

Franz "Bimbo" Binder

NATIONAL TEAM Austria

BORN December 1, 1911, died April 24, 1989

CLUB(S) St Polten, Rapid Vienna

Binder, a prolific marksman, was the first European player to top 1,000 goals. He played 20 times for Austria and nine times for Greater Germany. His greatest achievement for Rapid was in the 1941 Greater German title playoff when he scored a winning hat trick against Schalke.

Laurent Blanc

NATIONAL TEAM France

BORN November 19, 1965

CLUB(S) Montpellier, Napoli (It), Nimes, Saint-Etienne, Auxerre, Barcelona (Sp), Marseille, Internazionale (It), Manchester United (Eng)

Blanc, among the finest central defenders in Europe, was first a winner in the 1990 French Cup with Montpellier. He missed the 1998 World Cup final through suspension but shared in the Euro 2000 win. Blanc played in Italy, Spain and England before becoming French national coach.

Holland's Dennis Bergkamp controls the ball before scoring the winning goal against Argentina in the 1998 World Cup quarter-final.

Danny Blanchflower

NATIONAL TEAM Northern Ireland

BORN February10, 1926, died December 9, 1993

CLUB(S) Glentoran, Barnsley (Eng), Aston Villa (Eng), Tottenham Hotspur (Eng)

Blanchflower, a tactically astute right half, was one of the major forces in Northern Ireland's valiant 1958 World Cup effort and Tottenham's outstanding team of the early 1960s. The league and cup double was followed by the FA Cup and then the European Cup Winners' Cup in 1963.

Oleg Blokhin

NATIONAL TEAM Soviet Union

BORN Nov 5, 1952

CLUB(S) Dynamo Kiev, Vorwärts Steyr (Aus), Aris Limassol (Cyp)

Blokhin, an outside-left, used his pace to electrifying effect in Kiev's Cup Winners' Cup triumph of 1975 when he was also voted European Footballer of the Year. Roles at the World Cups of 1982 and 1986 saw him become the first Soviet player to top 100 international appearances.

Pursued by David Beckham, Eric Cantona celebrates scoring the second goal for Manchester United in their 4–0 quarter-final victory over Porto in the 1997 Champions League.

Steve Bloomer

NATIONAL TEAM England
BORN January 20, 1874, died April 16, 1938
CLUB(S) Derby County, Middlesbrough, Derby County

Bloomer, England's most famous player before the First World War, established long-lasting records: his 352 league goals were not equalled until the 1930s; his 28 goals for England in only 23 games were not surpassed until the 1950s. He played for 22 years until the age of 40.

Zbigniew Boniek

NATIONAL TEAM Poland
BORN March 3, 1956
CLUB(S) Zawisza Bydgoszcz, Widzew Lodz, Juventus (It), Roma (It)

Boniek was arguably the greatest Polish football player of all time. He made his name at Widzew Lodz and a hat trick against Belgium in the 1982 World Cup persuaded Juventus to pay £1.1m. He scored their winner in the 1984 Cup Winners' Cup final and also won the Champions Cup a year later.

142

CAFU
THE 142 INTERNATIONAL CAPS WON BY THE FLYING DEFENDER ARE THE MOST ACHIEVED BY ANY BRAZILIAN.

Giampiero Boniperti

NATIONAL TEAM Italy
BORN July 4, 1928
CLUB(S) Juventus

Boniperti was the original golden boy of Italian football and a one-club man at Juventus where, ultimately, he rose to become president. A centre, then inside, forward, he played for FIFA's World XI against England in 1953 and won five Italian titles with Juventus, playing a record 444 league games over the course of his career.

Jozsef Bozsik

NATIONAL TEAM Hungary
BORN September 28, 1929, died May 31, 1978
CLUB(S) Kispest, Honved

Bozsik played right half in Hungary's 'Golden Team' of the early 1950s. An Olympics gold medal winner in 1952, his occasional goals included one from 30 yards in the 6-3 win over England in 1953. Bozsik stayed home after the 1956 revolution and combined a career as a footballer with that of an MP.

Gianluigi Buffon

NATIONAL TEAM Italy
BORN January 28, 1978
CLUB(S) Parma, Juventus, Paris Saint-Germain

Buffon, nephew of 1960s Italy keeper Lorenzo Buffon, cost Juventus a world record £33m fee for a goalkeeper, but it was money well spent. He won an Italian record 176 caps, a string of league titles and inspired Italy in both the 2006 World Cup win and run to the final of Euro 2012.

Cafu

FULL NAME Marcos Evangelista de Moraes
NATIONAL TEAM Brazil
BORN June 7, 1970
CLUB(S) São Paulo, Zaragoza (Sp), Palmeiras, Roma (It), AC Milan (It)

Cafu, an attacking right back, celebrated the climax of his career as captain of Brazil when they won the World Cup for a record fifth time in 2002. It was also his 111th appearance for his country and he is the only man to have played in three successive World Cup finals.

Eric Cantona

NATIONAL TEAM France
BORN May 24, 1966
CLUB(S) Martigues, Auxerre, Marseille, Bordeaux, Montpellier, Nimes, Leeds (Eng), Manchester United (Eng)

Cantona's career was a mixture of glorious success and disciplinary muddle. He clashed with coaches and officials in France before moving to England and winning the league five times - once with Leeds and four times in five years, including the double, with Manchester United.

Antonio Carbajal

NATIONAL TEAM Mexico

BORN June 7, 1929

CLUB(S) España, Leon

Carbajal set a record at the 1966 World Cup as the only man then to have appeared in five finals stages. He had already played for Mexico in the finals of 1950, 1954, 1958 and 1962. England was an appropriate farewell since he had made his international debut at the 1948 London Olympics.

Roberto Carlos

FULL NAME Roberto Carlos da Silva

NATIONAL TEAM Brazil

BORN April 10, 1973

CLUB(S) Palmeiras, Internazionale (It), Real Madrid (Sp), Fenerbahce (Tur), Corinthians, Anzhi Makhachkala (Rus), Delhi Dynamos (Ind)

Roberto Carlos earned fame not so much for his defensive skills and pace but for the remarkable ferocity of his free kicks. He was a key member of Brazil's World Cup-winning team in 2002 while helping Real Madrid win the Champions League in 1998, 2000 and 2002 and the Club Cup twice.

Iker Casillas

FULL NAME Iker Casillas Fernández

NATIONAL TEAM Spain

BORN May 20, 1981

CLUB(S) Real Madrid, Porto (Por)

Casillas ranks among the game's top goalkeeper-captains after leading Spain to their historic victorious treble in Euro 2008, Euro 2012 and World Cup 2010. He did not concede a goal in knockout matches in all three tournaments and went more than three hours unbeaten at Euro 2012.

Goalkeeper Iker Casillas stops a penalty on the way to Spain's 4–2 semi-final shootout victory against Portugal in 2012 Euros.

Edinson Cavani

NATIONAL TEAM Uruguay
BORN February 14, 1987
CLUB(S) Danubio, Palermo (It), Napoli (It), Paris Saint-Germain (Fr)

Cavani is among the most feared centre-forwards after scoring goals consistently in Uruguay, Italy and France. One of his country's top scorers, with 45 in more than 100 games, he has won the Copa America with Uruguay and 13 club titles with PSG in France, where he has been twice league top scorer.

John Charles

NATIONAL TEAM Wales
BORN December 27, 1931, died February 21, 2004
CLUB(S) Leeds (Eng), Juventus (It), Leeds (Eng), Roma (It), Cardiff, Hereford Utd

Charles, known as the "Gentle Giant", set a Leeds record of 42 goals in one season as a centre forward while also playing in central defence for Wales. He cost Juventus a then British record of £67,000 in 1957 and led them to three Italian Serie A titles with his 93 goals in 155 games.

John Charles watches the ball closely during a game for Juventus in 1957. In his first Serie A season, Charles scored 28 goals.

★ Bobby Charlton

See page 231

Giorgio Chiellini

NATIONAL TEAM Italy
BORN Augusy 14, 1983
CLUB(S) Livorno, Roma, Fiorentina, Juventus

Chiellini has been a rock at the heart of defence for Italy and Juventus, with whom he won seven successive Serie A titles from 2012 to 2018 as well as seven other domestic trophies. He helped Italy finish runners-up at Euro 2012 and third at the 2013 Confederations Cup in Brazil.

Ashley Cole

NATIONAL TEAM England
BORN December 20, 1980
CLUB(S) Arsenal, Crystal Palace, Arsenal, Chelsea, Roma (It), LA Galaxy (US)

Cole grew into one of the world's quickest and sharpest left backs after turning professional with Arsenal in 1998. He rapidly established himself as an England regular at World Cups and Euro finals before moving to Chelsea and setting a record of seven FA Cup winner's medals.

Mário Esteves Coluna

NATIONAL TEAM Portugal
BORN August 6, 1935, died February 25, 2014
CLUB(S) Deportivo Lourenço Marques, Benfica, Lyon (Fr)

Coluna was midfield general of Benfica's outstanding club side of the 1960s and the Portuguese national team which reached the 1966 World Cup semi-finals. Born in Mozambique, he scored spectacular long-range goals in both of Benfica's European Champions Cup final wins of 1961 and 1962.

Gianpiero Combi

NATIONAL TEAM Italy
BORN December 18, 1902, died August 12, 1956
CLUB(S) Juventus

BOBBY CHARLTON

1937– 1.73m (5ft 8ins)

THE PERFECT SPORTSMAN Bobby Charlton's name is synonymous with some of the greatest moments of the English game. Football was in the Charlton blood. Bobby and World Cup-winning brother Jackie were nephews of the 1950s Newcastle United hero Jackie Milburn, and Bobby fulfilled every schoolboy's dream when, at 17, he was signed by Manchester United. Charlton had established his first-team potential the season before the Busby Babes were lost when United's plane crashed in Munich. He was initially an inside-right, later switched to outside-left with England, and finally settled as a deep-lying centre-forward, using his pace out of midfield and thunderous shot to score some of English football's most spectacular goals. One such goal marked his England debut against Scotland, another broke the deadlock against Mexico in the 1966 World Cup finals, and dozens more inspired Manchester United's post-Munich revival. The European Cup victory at Wembley in 1968, when he captained United and scored twice, was his club highlight.

CHARLTON WAS BOOKED ONLY ONCE – AND EVEN THAT WAS NOT REPORTED BY THE REFEREE

1

CLUB

MANCHESTER UNITED
PRESTON NORTH END
WATERFORD

807 APPEARANCES

260 GOALS

0.32 GOALS PER APPEARANCE

INTERNATIONAL

ENGLAND

106 APPEARANCES

49 GOALS

0.46 GOALS PER APPEARANCE

1957
Wins his first league title and at 19 plays in the FA Cup final, losing to Aston Villa

1958
Survives the Munich air crash to play in another FA Cup final , losing this time 2–0 to Bolton

1963
Plays in his third FA Cup final, and is at last on the winning side as United beat Leicester City 3–1

1966
Stars for England in their World Cup victory against West Germany and is award the Ballon d'Or

1968
Scores two goals as United win the European Cup, defeating Benfica 4–1 at Wembley

1970
Plays his 106th and final game for England in the 3–2 defeat by West Germany at the World Cup finals

1973
Moves to Preston North End for two unsuccessful years as player-manager

1976
Joins League of Ireland side Waterford FC but plays only three games before hanging up his boots for good

1994
Becomes Sir Bobby after receiving a knighthood

JOHAN CRUYFF

1947–2016 1.80m (5ft 11ins)

1964
Signs his first Ajax contract at 16 and marks his debut with a goal

1966
Makes his debut for Holland in a 2–2 draw against Hungary and scores a last-minute equalizer

1971
Wins the first of three successive European Cups and is award the first of his three Ballons d'Or

1974
Captains and inspires Holland in the 1974 World Cup finals, where they lose 2–1 to hosts West Germany

1978
Retires from the national team before the World Cup finals, and leaves Barcelona to play in the United States

1982
Having returned to Ajax in 1980, wins his seventh Eredivisie title, followed by an eighth in 1983

1984
After falling out with Ajax, his playing swansong is to lead rivals Feyenoord to their first Eredivisie title in a decade

1992
Manages Barcelona to their long-awaited first victory in a European Cup final

THE TOTAL FOOTBALLER Cruyff made his first-team debut at Ajax at 17, his goalscoring international debut at 19 and went on to inspire Ajax and Holland through most of their golden 1970s. This was the era of "total football", of which Cruyff was the prime example. Nominally he played centre-forward. But his idea of centre-forward was about as orthodox as the squad number 14 he wore at Ajax. He was also to be found meandering through midfield and out on the wings, using his nimble, coltish pace to seriously unhinge defences. He saw the day when every player in a team would possess comparable technical and physical ability and would be able to interchange roles at will.
His finest moments included: single-handedly pulling Internazionale apart in the 1972 European Cup final, scoring both goals in Ajax's win; inspiring Barcelona to league victory in his very first season with them; and dominating the 1974 World Cup finals, the most notable wins coming against Argentina and Brazil, before the final which ended in defeat at the hands of West Germany.

INTERNATIONAL

HOLLAND

48 APPEARANCES

33 GOALS

0.69 GOALS PER APPEARANCE

CLUB

AJAX · BARCELONA
LOS ANGELES AZTECS
WASHINGTON DIPLOMATS
LEVANTE · FEYENOORD

661 APPEARANCES

369 GOALS

14 CRUYFF'S FAVOURITE SHIRT NUMBER, FOR CLUB AND COUNTRY

3 BALLON D'OR AWARDS 1971, 1973, 1974

65% CRUYFF'S WIN RATIO IN THE COLOURS OF HOLLAND

Combi was goalkeeper and captain of the Italian team who won the 1934 World Cup after being beaten seven times by Hungary on his debut in 1924. He kept goal for Juventus' four consecutive league title wins between 1931 and 1934, when he retired after Italy's World Cup triumph.

★ Johan Cruyff

See page 232

Teófilo Cubillas

NATIONAL TEAM Peru

BORN March 8, 1949

CLUB(S) Alianza, Basel (Swz), FC Porto (Port), Alianza, Fort Lauderdale (US), Alianza, S Florida Sun (US), Miami Sharks (US)

Cubillas was a key figure in Peru's entertaining appearances at the 1970 and 1978 World Cups. His 10 goals in those finals included a memorable goal against Scotland in 1978. He tallied 38 goals in 88 internationals and appeared for a World XI in a 1978 charity match on behalf of UNICEF.

Kenny Dalglish

NATIONAL TEAM Scotland

BORN March 4, 1951

CLUB(S) Celtic, Liverpool (Eng)

Dalglish's unique contribution to Liverpool as player and manager led to a stand at Anfield being named after him. Originally with Celtic, Dalglish won a total of 32 trophies, as well as becoming Scotland's joint record marksman and international with 30 goals in 102 games.

Bill "Dixie" Dean

NATIONAL TEAM England

BORN January 22, 1907, died March 1, 1980

CLUB(S) Tranmere, Everton, Notts Co

Dean began his England career at 20 by scoring more than once in his first five matches (two, three, two, two and three). He was still only 21 when he scored his record 60 league goals in one season for Everton, scoring two, four and three in the last three games of the season.

Kevin de Bruyne

NATIONAL TEAM Belgium

BORN June 28, 1991

➊ Kenny Dalglish (centre) is congratulated by his teammates after scoring the winning goal for Liverpool against Club Brugge in the 1978 European Cup final.

CLUB(S) Genk, Chelsea (Eng), Werder Bremen (Ger), Wolfsburg (Ger), Manchester City (Eng)

De Bruyne underlined his status as one of the game's finest playmakers with his central role in Manchester City's 2018 Premier League title win and Belgium' s run to third place in the World Cup. He was Belgium's Sportsman of the Year in 2015, when City bought him for a then-club record £54m.

★ Alfredo Di Stéfano

See page 235

Didi

FULL NAME Waldyr Pereira

NATIONAL TEAM Brazil

BORN October 8, 1928, died May 12, 2001

CLUB(S) Madureira, Fluminense, Botafogo, Real Madrid (Sp), Valencia (Sp), Botafogo, Sporting Cristal (Pe), São Paulo, Botafogo, Veracruz (Mex), São Paulo

Didi, as midfield general, was central to the success of Brazil's 4-2-4 and 4-3-3 systems at the 1958 and 1962 World Cups. He was the first to perfect the swirling "dead leaf" free kick, with which he baffled goalkeepers in scoring a dozen of his 31 goals in 85 games for Brazil.

➔ Didier Drogba jumps for joy after scoring Chelsea's third goal in a 3–0 victory over Arsenal in 2009.

Landon Donovan

NATIONAL TEAM United States
BORN March 4, 1982
CLUB(S) San Jose Earthquakes, Bayer Leverkusen (Ger), San Jose Earthquakes, LA Galaxy, Bayern Munich (Ger), Everton (Eng), LA Galaxy

Donovan was the finest United States player of the modern era. He won a record six Major League Soccer cups, and became the league's then all-time top scorer with 145 goals and all-time assists leader with 136. He was also the US 57-goal record marksman in his 157 internationals.

Didier Drogba

NATIONAL TEAM Ivory Coast
BORN March 11, 1978
CLUB(S) Levallois, Le Mans, Guingamp, Marseille (all Fr), Chelsea (Eng), Shanghai Shenhua (Chn), Galatasaray (Tur), Chelsea (Eng), Montreal Impact (Can)

Drogba, raised in France, exploded to fame with Marseille then, with Chelsea, became the only player to score in four separate FA Cup finals. Against Bayern Munich in the 2012 Champions League final, he scored both Chelsea's equaliser and their cup-winning last penalty in the shootout.

1.01

EUSÉBIO
IN A CLUB CAREER SPANNING MORE THAN 20 YEARS, EUSÉBIO AVERAGED JUST OVER ONE GOAL PER GAME. HIS RECORD FOR PORTUGAL OF 0.64 GOALS PER GAME WAS ALSO IMPRESSIVE.

Dragan Džajić

NATIONAL TEAM Yugoslavia
BORN May 30, 1946
CLUB(S) Red Star Belgrade, Bastia (Fr), Red Star Belgrade

Džajić was nicknamed the "Magic Dragan" by the British media after his left-wing skills helped take England apart in the semi-finals of the 1968 European Nations Championship. With Red Star Belgrade he was five times a national champion and four times a domestic cup winner.

Duncan Edwards

NATIONAL TEAM England
BORN October 1, 1936, died February 21, 1958
CLUB(S) Manchester United

Edwards was a young giant who is still revered by generations who never saw him play. Edwards was the most outstanding of Manchester United's Busby Babes. Having won 18 caps, he was expected to play a starring role in the 1958 World Cup before his death in the Munich air disaster.

Samuel Eto'o

NATIONAL TEAM Cameroon
BORN March 10, 1981
CLUB(S) Real Madrid, Leganes, Mallorca, Barcelona (all Sp), Internazionale (It), Anzhi Machachkala (Rus), Chelsea (Eng), Everton (Eng), Sampdoria (It), Antalyaspor (Tur)

Eto'o, a lively centre-forward, was African Player of the Year four times, scored more than 100 goals in five seasons with Barcelona and was only the second player ever to score in two Champions League finals. He was also Cameroon's all-time leading scorer with 56 goals in 118 games.

Eusébio da Silva Ferreira

NATIONAL TEAM Portugal
BORN January 25, 1942, died January 5, 2014
CLUB(S) Sporting Lourenço Marquez, Benfica, Boston Minutemen (US), Monterrey (Mex), Toronto Metro-Croatia (Can), Beira-Mar (Por), Las Vegas Quicksilvers (US), Uniao de Tomar, NJ Americans (US)

Eusébio was the first great African player to hit the world stage though, born in Colonial Mozambique, he scored his 41 international goals for Portugal. His thunderous shot won not only a

DI STÉFANO

Alfredo Di Stéfano

1926 – 2014 1.78m (5ft 10in)

THE BLOND ARROW Alfredo Di Stéfano is reckoned by many to be the greatest footballer of all. His greatness lay not only in his achievement in leading Real Madrid to victory in the first five consecutive European Cup finals but also because no other player so effectively combined individual expertise with an all-embracing ability to organize a team to play to his command. He began his career with River Plate in Argentina, making up part of a forward line nicknamed "La Maquina" (the Machine) for the remorseless consistency with which it took opposing defences apart. He later came to Spain and Real Madrid where, after only two weeks, he scored two in a 5-0 win against Barcelona. A legend was born. Madrid were Spanish champions in Di Stéfano's first two seasons and European Cup-winners in his next five. He scored in each of Madrid's European Cup finals, including a hat-trick against Frankfurt in 1960 in what has become one of the most admired performances of all time.

CLUB

RIVER PLATE
MILLONARIOS
REAL MADRID · ESPANYOL

665
APPEARANCES

484
GOALS

0.73
GOALS PER APPEARANCE

INTERNATIONAL

ARGENTINA
COLOMBIA*
SPAIN

41
APPEARANCES

29
GOALS

0.78
GOALS PER APPEARANCE

*4 caps not recognised by FIFA

WON 5 CONSECUTIVE EUROPEAN CUPS WITH REAL MADRID FROM 1956 TO 1960 – AND SCORED IN EACH OF THEM

5

1943
Makes his debut for River Plate, playing as a right-winger, aged 17

1949
Lured away, during the Argentine players' strike, to play for Millonarios in Colombia, winning three league titles

1953
Moves to Spain, where he joins Real Madrid

1956
Inspires Real to the first of five successive European Cup victories and makes his national debut for Spain

1960
Scores a hat-trick in Real's legendary 7–3 victory over Eintracht Frankfurt in the European Cup final

1963
Kidnapped – and later released unharmed – by urban guerrillas while on tour with Real Madrid in Venezuela

1964
Leaves Real for one last season with Espanyol, before becoming a coach in Argentina, Portugal and Spain

Champions Cup with Benfica but saw him top-score with nine goals at the 1966 World Cup.

Giacinto Facchetti

NATIONAL TEAM taly

BORN July 18, 1942, died September 4, 2006

CLUB(S) Trevigliese, Internazionale

Facchetti was a strapping centre forward with his local club in Treviso before he joined Inter and was turned into an attacking left back by coach Helenio Herrera. He scored a record 60 league goals before switching to sweeper, from where he captained Italy in the 1970 World Cup final.

Luís Figo

NATIONAL TEAM Portugal

BORN November 4, 1972

CLUB(S) Sporting Clube, Barcelona (Sp), Real Madrid (Sp), Internazionale (It)

Figo was the finest graduate of Portugal's "golden generation" from the early 1990s. A right winger then midfielder, he won a host of titles both at home and in Spain where he drew controversy by quitting Barcelona for Real Madrid. His choice was rewarded with Champions League success.

Tom Finney

NATIONAL TEAM England

BORN April 5, 1922, died February 14, 2014

CLUB(S) Preston North End

Finney was one of England's greatest players, his versatility matched by his skill. A right or left winger, he also played as a deep-lying centre-forward for his one club, Preston. Finney's 12-year England career brought him 76 caps, a then-record 30 goals and a knighthood.

Just Fontaine

NATIONAL TEAM France

BORN August 18, 1933

CLUB(S) USM Casablanca (Mor), Nice, Reims

Possibly Morocco's greatest export, Fontaine, despite the World Cup's expansion, still holds the record as its leading marksman with the 13 goals he scored in only six matches in leading France, as centre forward, to third place back in 1958. A European Cup runner-up with Reims in 1959, his career was cut short by injury.

Eyes glued to the ball, Luís Figo embarks on another penetrating run for Portugal, in a group game against Greece at Euro 2004.

Enzo Francescoli

NATIONAL TEAM Uruguay

BORN November 12, 1961

CLUB(S) Wanderers, River Plate (Arg), Matra Racing (Fr), Marseille (Fr), Cagliari (It), Torino (It), River Plate (Arg)

Francescoli, nicknamed "The Prince", was voted South American Footballer of the Year before transferring to France with Racing in 1986. He scored 11 goals in Marseille's championship season of 1989–90 before moving first to Italy, then back to River Plate to wind down his career.

Trevor Francis

NATIONAL TEAM England

BORN April 19, 1954

CLUB(S) Birmingham City, Nottingham Forest, Manchester City, Sampdoria (It), Atalanta (It), Rangers (Scot), Woollongong City (Australia), Queens Park Rangers, Sheffield Wednesday

Francis secured his place in British football history as the first £1m transfer when he left Birmingham City for Nottingham Forest in 1979. Months later, he scored their Champions Cup final winner against Malmo. Later, he took his attacking talents to Manchester City and on to Italy.

Arthur Friedenreich

NATIONAL TEAM Brazil
BORN July 18, 1892, died September 6, 1969
CLUB(S) Germania, Ipiranga, Americao, Paulistano, São Paulo FC, Atlético Mineiro, Flamengo

Friedenreich was the first great Brazilian footballer, and the first credited with more than 1,000 goals. "The Tiger" was also the first black player to break down early racial/cultural barriers in Brazilian football. He scored eight goals in 17 games for Brazil between 1914 and 1930.

Garrincha

FULL NAME Manoel Francisco dos Santos
NATIONAL TEAM Brazil
BORN October 28, 1933, died January 20, 1983
CLUB(S) Pau Grande, Botafogo, Corinthians, Portuguesa, Atlético Junior (Col), Flamengo, Olaria

Garrincha ranked alongside Pelé in Brazilian football in the 1960s. A teammate's deputation persuaded manager Vicente Feola to include him in the 1958 World Cup side in Sweden; he was a key figure in Brazil's success both then and at the 1962 finals, after an early injury to Pelé.

Paul Gascoigne

NATIONAL TEAM England
BORN May 27, 1967
CLUB(S) Newcastle, Tottenham Hotspur, Lazio (It), Rangers (Scot), Middlesbrough, Everton, Burnley, Gansu Tianma (Chn), Boston Utd

A powerful midfielder with a deft touch, Gascoigne's career was blighted by his own misfortune with injuries after starring in England's run to the 1990 World Cup semi-finals. A year later, "Gazza", having started with Newcastle, won the 1991 FA Cup with Tottenham. He later had successful spells at Rangers and Middlesborough.

Francisco Gento

NATIONAL TEAM Spain
BORN October 22, 1933
CLUB(S) Santander, Real Madrid

Gento was proof that Real Madrid's great team of the 1950s and 1960s was more than "just" Di Stéfano and Puskás. His pace at outside-left earned him the nickname of "El Supersonico". Gento is the only man to have won six European Champions Cups and he also amassed 12 league titles.

Steven Gerrard

NATIONAL TEAM England
BORN May 30, 1980
CLUB(S) Liverpool, LA Galaxy (US)

Gerrard's goal-scoring gifts marked him out as a world-class midfielder as he strode up from the Liverpool youth ranks in the late 1990s. Notably,

Paul Gascoigne screams his delight after scoring an audaciously skilful goal for England against Scotland at Euro 1996.

Ruud Gullit carries the European Cup in triumph after Milan's 4–0 victory over Steaua Bucharest, in which the Dutch attacking midfielder scored two goals.

he shared in Liverpool's magnificent five trophies in 2001 and inspired their legendary 2005 Champions League triumph against Milan in Istanbul.

Ryan Giggs

NATIONAL TEAM Wales
BORN November 29, 1973
CLUB(S) Manchester United

Giggs, the son of a rugby league player, became Wales' youngest-ever player against West Germany in October 1991 at 17 years and 321 days. His left-wing talent helped Manchester United win 13 league titles, four FA Cups and four League Cups. He was also twice a European club champion.

Jimmy Greaves

NATIONAL TEAM England
BORN February 20, 1940
CLUB(S) Chelsea, AC Milan (It), Tottenham Hotspur, West Ham

Greaves was an instinctive goal-scorer, whose speed in thought and deed for Chelsea and Tottenham made up for his lack of size and power. His 44 goals in 57 internationals for England included two hauls of four goals and four hat-tricks; his 357 goals in league games included three five tallies.

Antoine Griezmann

NATIONAL TEAM France
BORN March 21, 1991
CLUB(S) Real Sociedad (Sp), Atlético Madrid (Sp)

Griezmann, a hero for France with four goals at the 2018 World Cup, including a penalty in the final win, had been overlooked by several French clubs as a teenager because of his slight build. As a result, he built his career in Spain with Real Sociedad and, after a £23m transfer, with Atletico Madrid.

Ruud Gullit

NATIONAL TEAM Holland
BORN September 1, 1962
CLUB(S) HFC Haarlem, Feyenoord, PSV, Milan (It), Sampdoria (It), Chelsea (Eng)

Gullit was the world's most expensive player when Milan bought him from PSV for £5m in 1987. He repaid the Rossoneri by inspiring victories twice in the European Champions Cups and three times in Serie A. On top of all that Gullit captained Holland to success at Euro 1988.

Asamoah Gyan

NATIONAL TEAM Ghana
BORN November 22, 1985
CLUB(S) Liberty Professionals, Udinese (It), Modena (It), Rennes (Fr), Sunderland (Eng), Al Ain (UAE), Shanghai SIPG (Chn), Al Ahli (Dubai)

Asamoah Gyan rose to international fame when he claimed the fastest goal of the 2006 World Cup for Ghana after 68 seconds against the Czech Republic. He scored three goals at the 2010 finals before his penalty miss in the last minute of extra time cost a crucial victory chance against Uruguay.

Gheorghe Hagi

NATIONAL TEAM Romania
BORN February 5, 1965
CLUB(S) FC Constanta, Sportul Studentesc, Steaua Bucharest, Real Madrid (Sp), Brescia (It), Barcelona (Sp), Galatasaray (Tur)

Hagi was a top-flight league player at 17, an international at 18, and a year later was appearing in the 1984 European finals. He inspired Romania to the quarterfinals of the 1994 World Cup and the second round in 1998. The same year he led Turkey's Galatasaray to UEFA Cup glory.

Hakan Sukur

NATIONAL TEAM Turkey
BORN September 1, 1971
CLUB(S) Sakaryaspor, Bursaspor, Galatasaray, Torino (It), Galatasaray, Internazionale (It), Parma (It), Blackburn Rovers (Eng), Galatasaray

Hakan Sukur was a centre forward standard-bearer for Turkey's emerging national team in the 1990s. He was regularly Galatasaray's top scorer and, at the 2002 World Cup, scored Turkey's opening goal after a record 11 seconds in the third-place play-off defeat of the co-hosts, South Korea.

Ernst Happel

NATIONAL TEAM Austria
BORN June 29, 1925, died November 14, 1992
CLUB(S) Rapid Vienna, Racing Club of Paris (Fr)

Happel was a redoubtable centre-back with Rapid and Austria in the 1950s. He possessed a powerful shot and once scored a hat trick, with two free kicks and a penalty, in an early European Champions Cup tie against Real Madrid. Later became one of Europe's most successful coaches.

162

RYAN GIGGS
THE WELSH DYNAMO AND MANCHESTER UNITED STALWART HOLDS THE RECORD FOR THE MOST ASSISTS IN PREMIER LEAGUE HISTORY.

Eden Hazard

NATIONAL TEAM Belgium
BORN January 7, 1991
CLUB(S) Lille, Chelsea (Eng)

Hazard, an attacking midfielder or winger, began his career in France, winning a league and cup double with Lille. More success followed in England at Chelsea before he was hailed as one of the finest players at the 2018 World Cup, captaining Belgium to a best-ever third place.

★ Thierry Henry

See page 240

Nandor Hidegkuti

NATIONAL TEAM Hungary
BORN March 3, 1922, died Febeuary 14, 2002
CLUB(S) MTK Voros Lobogo

Hidegkuti was the centre forward whose deep-lying tactical trick provided the strategic fulcrum for the great Hungarian team of the early 1950s. He helped Hungary win Olympic Gold in Helsinki in 1952 and featured in the historic 6-3 win over England at Wembley in 1953.

Fernando Ruiz Hierro

NATIONAL TEAM Spain
BORN March 23, 1968
CLUB(S) Malaga, Valladolid, Real Madrid, Al Rayyan (Qtr), Bolton (Eng)

Hierro graduated to iconic status at Real Madrid after joining in 1989 from Valladolid. His greatest match was the 1998 Champions League final when his sure-footed tackling inspired victory over Juventus – the first of Hierro's three Champions League successes in five seasons.

Gonzalo Higuain

NATIONAL TEAM Argentina
BORN December 10, 1987
CLUB(S) River Plate, Real Madrid (Sp), Napoli (It), Juventus (It)

THIERRY HENRY

1977– 1.88m (6ft 2in)

VA VA VOOM! Henry was a different operator from other great strikers. He rarely scored the "little" goals – the close-range finishes, the simple headers – of other strikers. His trademark strike was spectacular. He dribbled in from the left at speed, dismissed a defender or two on the way, then unleashed a low, curling right-foot shot. His finishing with his left was handy too; he had the close control to tie markers in knots and he could be lethal with free kicks from 30 metres. His goals propelled Arsenal to the Premier League title in 2002 and 2004 and towards FA Cup wins in 2002, 2003 and 2005. Finishing as the Premier League's top scorer in 2002, 2004, 2005 and 2006, Henry also well surpassed Ian Wright's club goals record of 184. He continued his haul of trophies at Barcelona, winning La Liga twice (2009, 2010), along with the Champions League, UEFA Super Cup and FIFA World Club Cup, all in 2009. Like so many players, Henry ended his career in the MLS, lending his silky skills to the New York Red Bulls.

CLUB

MONACO · JUVENTUS
ARSENAL · BARCELONA
NEW YORK RED BULLS

792
APPEARANCES

360
GOALS

0.45
GOALS PER APPEARANCE

INTERNATIONAL

FRANCE

123
APPEARANCES

51
GOALS

59%
WIN PERCENTAGE

1994
Makes top division debut for Monaco two weeks after his 17th birthday

1997
Wins Ligue 1 with Monaco – scoring 9 goals in 36 games. Makes senior France debut

1999
Sold to Juventus in January but plays only 16 games and joins Arsenal in August for £11 million

2000
Scores 26 goals in all competitions in first season with Arsenal. Wins Euro 2000 with France

2002
Collects league and FA Cup medals with Arsenal "double" squad. Premier League top scorer with 22 goals

2006
Double runner-up: with Arsenal in the Champions League and then with France at the World Cup in Germany

2007
Joins Barcelona and helps them win La Liga and the Champions League in 2009

2010
Leaves Barcelona to join New York Red Bulls of the MLS. Wins Supporters' Shield with them in 2013

4

WINNER OF THE PREMIER LEAGUE GOLDEN BOOT IN 2002, 2004, 2005 AND 2006 – MORE TIMES THAN ANY OTHER PLAYER

Higuain is a cosmopolitan centre forward. He was born in France, plays national team football for Argentina and has scored most of his club goals in Spain and Italy. In the 2010 World Cup, he became, against South Korea, only the third Argentinian to score a hat trick in the finals.

Glenn Hoddle

NATIONAL TEAM England

BORN October 27, 1957

CLUB(S) Tottenham Hotspur, Monaco (Fr), Swindon, Chelsea

Hoddle's midfield exploits in the 1980s and early 1990s mean he remains an icon at Tottenham. Hoddle won the UEFA Cup and FA Cup before collecting a league title in France with Monaco under Arsene Wenger. Later, he managed England to the second round of the 1998 World Cup.

Geoff Hurst

NATIONAL TEAM England

BORN December 8, 1941

CLUB(S) West Ham United, Stoke City, Cape Town City (SAf), West Bromwich Albion, Cork City (RI), Seattle Sounders (US)

Hurst was a striker for the big occasion. Playing most of his career at West Ham, he scored the remarkable total of 46 goals in the League Cup, 23 in the FA Cup (including in the 1964 final) and three in the 1966 World Cup final. The feat later earned him a deserved knighthood.

Zlatan Ibrahimovic

NATIONAL TEAM Sweden

BORN October 3, 1981

CLUB(S) Malmo, Ajax (Hol), Juventus (It), Inter (It), Barcelona (Sp), Milan (It), Paris S-G (Fr), Manchester Utd (Eng) , LA Galaxy (US)

Ibrahimovic, qualified for Bosnia-Herzegovina and Croatia, chose to play for Sweden and soon became one of Europe's hottest properties. He won league titles in four different countries - Holland, Italy, Spain and France - before winning a League Cup in England with Manchester United.

Andres Iniesta

NATIONAL TEAM Spain

BORN May 11, 1984

CLUB(S) Albacete, Barcelona

Zlatan Ibrahimovic celebrates after scoring for Milan against Fiorentina at the San Siro in 2010. In just two seasons with Milan, the Swedish goal machine netted 56 times.

Iniesta was a playmaking key to the Barcelona team who, in 2009, landed six titles in a year. With Spain, he took a huge role in their historic triple triumph in European Championships and World Cup between 2008 and 2012. He scored the World Cup winning goal against Holland in 2010.

Jairzinho

FULL NAME Jair Ventura Filho

NATIONAL TEAM Brazil

BORN December 25, 1944

CLUB(S) Botafogo, Marseilles (Fr), Kaizer Chiefs (SAf), Cruzeiro, Portuguesa (Ven), Noroeste, Fast Club, Jorge Wilsterman (Bol), Botafogo, 9 de Octubre (Ec)

Jairzinho was heir to Garrincha's glory, both with Botafogo and with Brazil, and even played in the same squad as his hero at the 1966 World Cup. Four years later Jairzinho made history by scoring in every game in every round of the 1970 World Cup on Brazil's route to victory.

Mario Kempes of Argentina leaves two Dutch players for dead in the final of the World Cup in 1978.

Alex James

NATIONAL TEAM Scotland

BORN September 14, 1901, died July 22, 1979

CLUB(S) Raith Rovers, Preston (Eng), Arsenal (Eng)

James was the outstanding inside forward of the 1930s in British football. Initially a goal poacher, he changed style to become playmaker for Arsenal under legendary Herbert Chapman. James scored only 26 league goals in eight years but made countless others with his astute passing.

Pat Jennings

NATIONAL TEAM Northern Ireland

BORN June 12, 1945

CLUB(S) Newry Town, Watford (Eng), Tottenham Hotspur (Eng), Arsenal (Eng)

Jennings, a goalkeeper of immmense character, even bowed out of football in a big way by retiring at the 1986 World Cup after winning his 119th cap for Northern Ireland – on his 41st birthday – against Brazil. His 1,000-match career included four FA Cup finals – one win apiece with Tottenham and Arsenal.

Harry Kane

NATIONAL TEAM England

BORN July 28, 1993

CLUB(S) Tottenham Hotspur

Kane became only the second England player, after Gary Lineker, to win the Golden Boot as top scorer at a World Cup after scoring six in the 2018 finals in Russia. Captain of both Tottenham and England, Kane was Premier League top scorer in 2016 and 2017 and is already sixth in Spurs' all-time top scorers chart. Only Alan Shearer has reached 100 Premier League goals in fewer games than Kane's 141.

Roy Keane

NATIONAL TEAM Republic of Ireland

BORN August 10, 1971

CLUB(S) Cobh Ramblers, Nottingham Forest (Eng), Manchester Utd (Eng), Celtic (Sc)

Keane ranks among Old Trafford legends for captaining Manchester United aggressively to sustained success, particularly between 1998 and 2005. He won 11 domestic trophies with United but unluckily missed the 1999 Champions League victory over Bayern Munich through suspension.

Kevin Keegan

NATIONAL TEAM England
BORN February 14, 1951
CLUB(S) Scunthorpe, Liverpool, Hamburg (Ger), Southampton, Newcastle

Keegan, the only British player to win the European Footballer of the Year award twice, cost Liverpool a bargain £35,000 from Scunthorpe in 1971. He won two league titles before joining Hamburg after the Reds' 1977 Champions Cup triumph. He also scored 21 goals in 63 games for England.

Mario Alberto Kempes

NATIONAL TEAM Argentina
BORN July 15, 1952
CLUB(S) Instituto Córdoba, Rosario Central, Valencia (Sp), River Plate, Hercules (Sp), Vienna (Aus), St Polten (Aus)

Kempes first tasted World Cup football in West Germany in 1974. The success of his transfer to Valencia earned him a key role in hosts Argentina's World Cup squad in 1978. Kempes was the event's top scorer with six goals, including two in the 3-1 defeat of Holland in the final.

Ove Kindvall

NATIONAL TEAM Sweden
BORN May 16, 1943
CLUB(S) Norrkoping, Feyenoord (Hol), Norrkoping, IFK Gothenburg

Kindvall scored 126 goals in five seasons in Holland with Feyenoord. Three times he was top scorer in the Dutch league and he also scored the extra-time winner against Celtic in the 1970 Champions Cup final. Kindvall led Sweden's attack at the 1970 and 1974 World Cups.

Jürgen Klinsmann

NATIONAL TEAM Germany
BORN July 30, 1964
CLUB(S) Stuttgart Kickers, VfB Stuttgart, Internazionale (It), Monaco (Fr), Tottenham Hotspur (Eng), Bayern Munich, Sampdoria (It), Tottenham Hotspur (Eng)

Klinsmann was West Germany's Footballer of the Year during his first Bundesliga spell with Stuttgart. He then roamed successfully from Internazionale to Monaco to Tottenham before returning to Bayern Munich. Klinsmann was a World Cup and European title-winner in 1990 and 1996.

Jürgen Klinsmann of West Germany manages to get a shot away despite the attentions of Holland's Berry van Aerle in a round of 16 game at the 1990 World Cup.

Miroslav Klose

NATIONAL TEAM Germany
BORN June 9, 1978
CLUB(S) Kaiserslautern, Werder Bremen, Bayern Munich, Lazio (It)

Klose is the leading scorer in the history of the World Cup. The two strikes he contributed towards Germany's 2014 triumph lifted him ahead of Brazil's Ronaldo in the all-time list with 16 goals. He is also Germany's all-time leading marksman with 71 goals in 137 appearances.

Sándor Kocsis

NATIONAL TEAM Hungary
BORN September 30, 1929, died July 22, 1979
CLUB(S) Ferencvaros, Honved, Young Fellows (Swz), Barcelona (Sp)

Kocsis was a goal-hungry inside right for Honved and Hungary in the early 1950s. He scored 75 goals in 68 internationals and was the 11-goal leading marksman at the 1954 World Cup. He quit Hungary after the 1956 uprising and was a European Cup runner-up with Barcelona in 1961.

Vincent Kompany

NATIONAL TEAM Belgium

BORN April 10, 1986

CLUB(S) Anderlecht, Hamburg (Ger), Manchester City (Eng)

Kompany made his international defensive debut at 17 against France. His youthful maturity saw him appointed subsequently as captain of Belgium and then of Manchester City with whom, despite a number of injuries, he won three Premier League crowns, the FA Cup and three League Cups.

Raymond Kopa

NATIONAL TEAM France

BORN October 13, 1931, died March 3, 2017

CLUB(S) Angers, Reims, Real Madrid (Sp), Reims

Kopa, son of an immigrant Polish miner, starred first at Reims, with whom he was a loser in the first Champions Cup final in 1956. He then won the European crown three times with Real Madrid and set up the goals with which Just Fontaine shot France to third place at the 1958 World Cup. His great career ended in controversy around his outspoken fight for player's contract rights.

Johannes "Hans" Krankl

NATIONAL TEAM Austria

BORN February 14, 1953

CLUB(S) Rapid Vienna, Wiener AC, Barcelona (Sp), 1st Vienna, Rapid, Wiener SC, Kremser SC, Austria Salzburg

Krankl's greatest year was 1978. He scored 41 goals for Rapid Vienna, to win the Golden Boot as Europe's leading league marksman, and starred for Austria at the World Cup finals in Argentina. He then joined Barcelona and inspired their victory in the 1979 European Cup Winners' Cup.

Ladislav Kubala

NATIONAL TEAMS Czechoslovakia, Hungary, Spain

BORN June 10, 1927, died May 17, 2002

CLUB(S) Ferencvaros (Hun), Bratislava (Cz), Vasas Budapest (Cz), Barcelona (Sp), Español (Sp), FC Zurich (Swz), Toronto Falcons (Can)

Kubala fled west after playing as a centre or inside forward for both Czechoslovakia and Hungary in the late 1940s. He then became one of Barcelona's greatest players, being Spanish champion five times and twice winning the Fairs Cup. He also played for Spain's national team.

Frank Lampard of Chelsea celebrates in customary fashion after scoring one of his 32 Premier League penalties, this time against Manchester United at Stamford Bridge in 2001.

Ángel Amadeo Labruna

NATIONAL TEAM Argentina
BORN September 26, 1918, died September 20, 1983
CLUB(S) River Plate, Rampla Juniors (Uru), Rangers de Talca (Chile), Platense

Labruna, at inside left, was a key member of the legendary River Plate "Maquina" of the 1940s. He played for River Plate for 29 years and was 40 when he was recalled by Argentina for the 1958 World Cup finals to complete an international career which brought him 17 goals in 36 games.

Philipp Lahm

NATIONAL TEAM Germany
BORN November 11, 1983
CLUB(S) Bayern Munich, Stuttgart, Bayern Munich

Lahm ranks as one of European football's most reliable defensive players at fullback, on either flank or anchor. He possessed a vicious free kick, which he used to great effect. Lahm played almost all his club career for Bayern, whom he captained to the treble in 2010, as well as leading Germany to their World Cup success in Brazil in 2014.

Frank Lampard

NATIONAL TEAM England
BORN June 20, 1978
CLUB(S) West Ham United, Swansea City, Chelsea, Manchester City, NY City (US)

Lampard is Chelsea's all-time top scorer with 211 goals out of midfield. With mulitple league and cup trophies to his name already, he captained the Blues to victory in the 2012 Champions League and the Europa League a year later. His "phantom goal" against Germany at the 2010 World Cup prompted the lasting legacy of the introduction of goal-line technology.

Grzegorz Lato

NATIONAL TEAM Poland
BORN April 8, 1950
CLUB(S) Stal Mielec, Lokeren (Bel), Atlante (Mex), Polonia Hamilton (Can)

Lato was an outstanding striker who made his debut for Poland 1971 and won an Olympic gold medal in Munich a year later. Lato scored 46 goals in 104 internationals for his country, including a top-scoring seven goals at the 1974 World Cup, where Poland finished third. He remains the only Polish player to have won the Golden Boot.

Michael Laudrup

NATIONAL TEAM Denmark
BORN June 15, 1964
CLUB(S) Brondbyernes, Lazio (It), Juventus (It), Barcelona (Sp), Real Madrid (Sp), Vissel Kobe (Jap), Ajax (Hol)

Michael and brother Brian are international sons of former Danish international, Finn Laudrup. Michael won the World Club Cup with Juventus before moving on to win the European Champions Cup with Barcelona. He also starred at the 1986 World Cup finals in Mexico.

Denis Law

NATIONAL TEAM Scotland
BORN February 22, 1940
CLUB(S) Huddersfield (Eng), Manchester City (Eng), Torino (It), Manchester United (Eng), Manchester City (Eng)

Law, despite his medium height and slim build, scored many spectacular headed goals and was an incisive inside forward for Manchester United. He was 1964 European Footballer of the Year, won two league titles and the 1963 FA Cup, while scoring 30 goals in 55 games for Scotland.

Scotland's Graeme Souness keeps a close eye on Michael Laudrup in a group match at the 1986 World Cup as the Dane makes one of his characteristic mazy runs from midfield.

DIEGO MARADONA

1960– 1.65m (5ft 5in)

2

THE FIRST PLAYER TO BREAK THE WORLD TRANSFER RECORD TWICE

CLUB

ARGENTINOS JUNIORS
BOCA JUNIORS · BARCELONA
NAPOLI · SEVILLA
NEWELL'S OLD BOYS

588
APPEARANCES

312
GOALS

0.53
GOALS PER APPEARANCE

INTERNATIONAL

ARGENTINA

91
APPEARANCES

34
GOALS

16
RECORD NUMBER OF APPEARANCES AS CAPTAIN IN WORLD CUP MATCHES

1976
Makes league debut at 15 for Argentinos Juniors., and in 1977 makes debut at 16 for Argentina

1980
Sold to Boca Juniors for £1 million, a record at the time for a teenager

1982
Sold to Barcelona for £3 million and to Napoli in 1984 for £5 million

1986
Inspires Argentina to victory at the World Cup finals in Mexico and is chosen as Player of the Tournament

1987
Leads Napoli to a first-ever Serie A title and, a year later, to victory over Stuttgart in the UEFA Cup final

1990
Takes Argentina back to the World Cup final, but they lose 1–0. Fails a dope test in 1991 and is banned for 15 months

1992
Makes short comebacks with Sevilla and Newell's Old Boys. Banned again for 15 months after 1994 World Cup

1995
Returns to playing with Boca Juniors and retires in 1997

RECORD NUMBER OF TIMES MARADONA WAS FOULED DURING THE 1990 WORLD CUP

50

THE HAND OF GOD Maradona was not just the world's greatest player throughout the 1980s and early 1990s. He was also the most controversial and the most enigmatic. His goal against England in the 1986 World Cup when he collected the ball inside his own half and beat five defenders and the goalkeeper before sliding it home was hailed as the goal of the century. Maradona then went on to score the dramatic winner in the final. His great ability made his subsequent fall all the greater when a failed dope test and a 15-month ban from world football was aggravated by an arrest for cocaine possession. Even his 1994 World Cup comeback ended in the shameful ignominy of a further dope-test failure and playing ban. Maradona reappeared at the World Cup in 2010, this time as manager, bringing Argentina to the quarter-finals.

Tommy Lawton

NATIONAL TEAM England
BORN October 6, 1919, died November 6, 1996
CLUB(S) Burnley, Everton, Chelsea, Notts County, Brentford, Arsenal, Kettering Town

Lawton was one of England's great traditional centre forwards. He scored a hat trick on his senior debut at 16, was league top scorer two years in a row and won a title medal with Everton at 19 in 1938-39. But for the war, he would have scored far more than 23 goals in 22 England games.

Leonidas da Silva

NATIONAL TEAM Brazil
BORN November 11, 1910, died January 24, 2004
CLUB(S) Bonsucesso, Peñarol (Uru), Vasco da Gama, Botafogo, Flamengo, São Paulo

Leonidas was Brazil's 1930s superstar, but played only 23 times for his country. He invented the overhead bicycle kick, unveiling it to score twice on debut against Uruguay. He was eight-goal top scorer at the 1938 World Cup, including four in a 6-5 victory over Poland. Injury kept him out of the semi against Italy, which Brazil lost.

Billy Liddell

NATIONAL TEAM Scotland
BORN January 10, 1922, died July 3, 2001
CLUB(S) Liverpool (Eng)

Liddell, an accountant, Justice of the Peace and youth worker, was one of Liverpool's greatest players. He spent all of his career with the club, winning the league in 1947 and being an FA Cup runner-up three years later. He set club records with 492 league appearances and 216 goals.

Nils Liedholm

NATIONAL TEAM Sweden
BORN October 8, 1922, died November 5, 2007
Club(s) Norrköping, Milan (It)

Liedholm was an inside forward who evolved into a sweeper. He helped Sweden win the 1948 Olympic title then moved to Milan, scoring 60 goals as part of the celebrated GreNoLi trio, with Gunnar Gren and Gunnar Nordahl. "Il Barone" then captained hosts Sweden to runners-up spot at the 1958 World Cup.

902

PAOLO MALDINI
THE ULTIMATE ONE-CLUB MAN, MALDINI APPEARED 902 TIMES FOR MILAN IN ALL COMPETITIONS, FROM 1984 TO 2009.

Gary Lineker

NATIONAL TEAM England
BORN November 30, 1960
CLUB(S) Leicester, Everton, Barcelona (Sp), Tottenham Hotspur, Nagoya Grampus 8 (Jap)

Lineker landed all sorts of records in a goal-laden career in England, Spain, England again and Japan. He went within one goal of England's 49-goal scoring record, 10 coming in World Cup final tournaments. He won the FA Cup with Spurs, despite missing a penalty in the 1991 final.

Billy McNeill

NATIONAL TEAM Scotland
BORN March 2, 1940
CLUB(S) Celtic

McNeill was well suited by his nickname of "Caesar". In both size and style he was a big man, and was the hub of Celtic's defence during their great 1960s. He won a host of domestic medals and, in 1967, as captain of Celtic, became the first Briton to lift the European Champions Cup.

Paolo Maldini

NATIONAL TEAM Italy
BORN June 26, 1968
CLUB(S) AC Milan

Maldini was the son of Cesare, Milan's first Champions Cup-winning captain, and an even finer defender. He spent all his 25 seasons with the club, winning 26 trophies, including one Club World Cup, five Champions Leagues, seven Serie A titles and two Intercontinental Cups.

★ Diego Maradona

See page 246

Josef Masopust

NATIONAL TEAM Czechoslovakia
BORN February 9, 1931, died June 29, 2015
CLUB(S) Union Teplice, Dukla Prague, Crossing Molenbeek (Bel)

Masopust was the only man from the old Czechoslovakia to win the European Footballer of the Year award, which he collected in 1962 after the Czechs finished runners-up to Brazil. Masopust scored the opening goal in the final, which they ultimately lost 3-1. A versatile player, he played all over the pitch during his career.

MESSI

1987– 1.70m (5ft 7in)
Lionel Andrés Messi

RECORDS

MOST GOALS SCORED IN LA LIGA (383 – END 2017–18 SEASON)

MOST GOALS SCORED IN A LA LIGA SEASON (50)

MOST GOALS SCORED IN A CLUB FOOTBALL SEASON IN EUROPE (73 IN 2011-12)

MOST GOALS SCORED IN A CALENDAR YEAR (91 IN 2012)

MOST CONSECUTIVE GAMES SCORED IN (21)

CLUB	INTERNATIONAL
BARCELONA	ARGENTINA
637 APPEARANCES	128 APPEARANCES
552 GOALS	65 GOALS
0.82 GOALS PER APPEARANCE	

*July 2018

5

MESSI PLAYER IN HISTORY TO WIN FIVE BALLON D'OR AWARDS 2009, 2010, 2011, 2012, 2015

THE ATOMIC FLEA

Lionel Messi announced himself as one of the greatest players of all time when, in 2012, he set a record for the most goals scored in a calendar year on his way to making top-scoring history with both his club, Barcelona, and his country, Argentina. Born in the Argentinian city of Rosario, Messi joined the Catalan club at 13 from Newell's Old Boys after Barcelona offered to pay for growth hormone treatment. His dedication to the Catalan club has not gone unrewarded. The little Argentinian's prodigious pace and dribbling skills, combined with an uncannily precise finish, have helped Barcelona to nine La Liga titles, six Copa del Rey victories, four UEFA Champions League titles and three FIFA Club World Cups. In addition to having topped the scoring charts in almost every club competition, Messi can also boast an Olympic gold medal won in Beijing in 2008. The one title which has eluded him is the World Cup. The closest he came was in 2014, when Argentina finished as extra-time runners-up to Germany in Brazil. Messi's consolation was to be named as Best Player at the finals.

2005
Scores first Barcelona goal, against Albacete. Wins first La Liga title and first full international cap

2009
Helps Barça to the treble: La Liga, Copa del Rey and Champions League. Wins first Ballon d'Or

2010
Scores 100th goal for Barça and becomes the first player to score back-to-back La Liga hat-tricks

2011
Wins third Champions League. Passes Ronaldo's Barça record of 47 goals in a season

2012
Reaches 233 goals to become all-time top Barça scorer. Scores five in a Champions League game – a record

2014
Gets to a first World Cup final but loses 1–0 to Germany. Has the consolation of the Golden Ball award

2015
Wins seventh La Liga, fourth Champions League, and third Copa del Rey, UEFA Super Cup and FIFA World Club Cup

2016
Wins the FIFA Ballon d'Or for a record fifth time, wins Spanish league and cup double and scores 500th career goal

2017
Wins Spanish cup again and, with 37 goals, is top-scoring award-winner in not only Spain but Europe

2018
Wins Spanish domestic double and a record fifth European Golden Boot

Sir Stanley Matthews

NATIONAL TEAM England
BORN February 1, 1915, died February 23, 2000
CLUB(S) Stoke City, Blackpool, Stoke City

Matthews, the "Wizard of Dribble", was a football legend. A peerless outside right, he did not retire until the age of 50, famously won the FA Cup at 38 in 1953 in the "Matthews Final" and was the first European Footballer of the Year in 1956. His war-spanning England career earned him 54 caps.

➔ Stanley Matthews sets off on one of his trademark dribbles, playing for Blackpool in an FA Cup sixth-round game against Fulham in 1948.

Lothar Matthaus

NATIONAL TEAM West Germany
BORN March 21, 1961
CLUB(S) Borussia Monchengladbach, Bayern Munich, Internazionale (It), Bayern Munich, New York-New Jersey MetroStars (US)

Matthaus was Germany's outstanding leader in midfield and then sweeper from the early 1980s. His career reached its zenith in 1990 when he was West Germany's World Cup-winning captain. Matthaus won seven league titles in Germany with Bayern and one in Italy with Internazionale.

Kylian Mbappé

NATIONAL TEAM France
BORN December 20, 1998
CLUB(S) Monaco, Paris Saint-Germain

Mbappé was named Best Young Player at the 2018 World Cup in Russia after his four goals, including one in the final, helped fire France to glory. The previous year he had become the second most expensive player of all time when PSG agreed to pay Monaco a basic €150m fee.

Valentino Mazzola

NATIONAL TEAM Italy
BORN January 26, 1919, died May 4, 1949
CLUB(S) Tresoldi, Alfa Romeo, Venezia, Torino

Mazzola was a Milan-born inside left who starred at Venezia before joining Torino. He captained and inspired "Toro" to five consecutive league titles. However, before they could celebrate the fifth title, Mazzola and his team were all killed in the 1949 Superga air disaster.

150

LOTHAR MATTHAUS
BETWEEN 1980 AND 2000, MATTHAUS WON 150 CAPS FOR GERMANY, A NATIONAL RECORD. HE ALSO APPEARED IN 25 WORLD CUP GAMES – MORE THAN ANY OTHER PLAYER.

Giuseppe Meazza

NATIONAL TEAM Italy
BORN August 23, 1910, died August 21, 1979
CLUB(S) Ambrosiana-Internazionale, AC Milan, Juventus, Varese, Atalanta, Internazionale

Meazza was one of only two Italian players to win the World Cup in both 1934 and 1938, inside forward partner Giovanni Ferrari being the other. He scored a then league record 33 goals for Inter in the 1928–29 season, while his goal haul for Italy was an impressive 33 in 53 matches.

Billy Meredith

NATIONAL TEAM Wales
BORN July 30, 1874, died April 19, 1958
CLUB(S) Manchester City (Eng), Manchester United (Eng), Manchester City (Eng)

Meredith, Wales' legendary right winger, played his last senior game - a losing FA Cup semi-final - when he was nearly 50. He won 48 caps, with 11 goals, over 25 years and played 1,000 first-team matches despite missing a complete season after being involved in a match-fixing scandal.

★ Lionel Messi

See page 248

➜ Cameroon forward Roger Milla performs one of his unforgettable dances after scoring an extra-time goal against Colombia at the 1990 World Cup.

➜ Pavel Nedved, playing for Juventus, eyes up his opportunities in a Champions League group match in 2003. Nedved's powerful shooting abilities, with both feet, earned him the nickname "The Czech cannon".

Roger Milla

NATIONAL TEAM Cameroon
BORN May 20, 1952
CLUB(S) Leopards Douala, Tonnerre Yaounde, Valenciennes (Fr), Monaco (Fr), Bastia (Fr), Saint-Etienne (Fr), Montpellier (Fr), St-Pierroise (Reu), Tonnerre, Pelita Jaya (Indo), Putra Samarinda (Indo)

Milla (real name Miller) delighted crowds at the 1990 World Cup with his celebratory dances around the corner flags. His goals made him the first player to become African Footballer of the Year for a second time. In 1994, he became the oldest player to appear in the World Cup, at 42.

Luka Modrić

NATIONAL TEAM Croatia
BORN September 9, 1985
CLUB(S) Dinamo Zagreb, Zrinjski, Inter Zapresic, Dinamo, Tottenham (Eng), Real Madrid (Sp)

Modric was named as Best Player at the 2018 World Cup after inspiring Croatia to reach the final, where they lost to France. The playmaker built his reputation at Dinamo Zagreb and Tottenham Hotspur before winning four UEFA Champions Leagues with Real Madrid.

Luisito Monti

NATIONAL TEAMS Argentina and Italy
BORN January 15, 1901
CLUB(S) Huracán, Boca Juniors, San Lorenzo, Juventus (It)

Monti was an old-style attacking centre-half who won Olympic silver in 1928 with Argentina against Uruguay. He was on the losing side against the same opponents at the first World Cup two years later. Juventus, in 1931, brought Monti to Italy, with whom he won the World Cup in 1934.

Bobby Moore

NATIONAL TEAM England
BORN April 12, 1941, died February 24, 1993
CLUB(S) West Ham, Fulham, San Antonio Thunder (US), Seattle Sounders (US), Herning Fremad (Den), Carolina Lightnin (US)

Moore, England's World Cup-winning captain in 1966, also captained West Ham to success in the FA Cup and European Cup-winners Cup. Considered one of the greatest central defenders of all time, he won a then record 108 caps. In 2002 he featured in a BBC list of 100 Greatest Britons.

José Manuel Moreno

NATIONAL TEAM Argentina
BORN August 3, 1916, died August 26, 1978
CLUB(S) River Plate, España (Mex), River Plate, Universidad Católica (Chile), Boca Juniors, U Católicxa (Chile), Defensor (Uru), FC Oeste, Independiente Medellín (Col)

Moreno is rated by veteran Argentinians as their greatest footballer. An inside right, he began with River Plate with whom he was a league title winner four times while featuring in their legendary "Maquina" forward line of the late 1940s. Moreno scored 20 goals in 33 internationals.

Gerd Müller

NATIONAL TEAM West Germany
BORN November 3, 1945
CLUB(S) Nordlingen, Bayern Munich, Fort Lauderdale Strikers (US)

Not the archetypal striker, "Der Bomber" was short and muscular. In 62 internationals, he scored 68 goals, and was as prolific for Bayern with 365 goals in total. Trophies followed and he led his team to four domestic league and cup wins, as well as three European Champions Cup victories.

Thomas Müller

NATIONAL TEAM Germany
BORN September 13, 1989
CLUB(S) Bayern Munich

Müller is the latest star forward bearing the Müller name. Thomas exploded in 2009–10 as Bayern won the domestic double and reached the Champions League final. He matured into a World Cup winner in Brazil four years later.

José Nasazzi

NATIONAL TEAM Uruguay
BORN May 24, 1901, died June 17, 1968
CLUB(S) Lito, Roland Moor, Nacional, Bella Vista

Nasazzi was one of the great captains in football history. He led Uruguay to their victories in the 1924 and 1928 Olympic Games and then to the 1930 World Cup. Nasazzi was also a South American champion on four occasions in his 15-year, 64-game international career.

Pavel Nedved

NATIONAL TEAM Czech Republic
BORN August 30, 1972
CLUB(S) Sparta Prague, Lazio (It), Juventus (It)

Nedved, European Footballer of the Year in 2003, was the finest Czech player since the 1990s split from Slovakia. The playmaker won league titles at home with Sparta Prague and in Italy with Juventus. He also helped Lazio carry off the last European Cup Winners Cup, in 1999.

Oldrich Nejedly

NATIONAL TEAM Czechoslovakia
BORN December 13, 1909, died June 11, 1990
CLUB(S) Zebrak, Rakovnik, Sparta Prague, Rakovnik

Nejedly played inside left for the Sparta club that dominated the Mitropa Cup for much of the 1930s and for the Czechoslovak national team that reached the 1934 World Cup final. He was also the World Cup's leading marksman with five goals among his 29 in 44 internationals.

GREATEST OF ALL TIME Pelé's teenage exploits as a player with his local club, Bauru, earned him a transfer to Santos at the age of 15. He rapidly earned national and then international recognition. At 16 he was playing for Brazil; at 17 he was winning the World Cup, although not until his team mates had persuaded national manager Vicente Feola to throw him into the action. Santos were not slow to recognize the potential offered their club by Pelé. The directors created a sort of circus, touring the world, playing two and three times a week for lucrative match fees. The income from this gave the club the financial leverage to buy a supporting cast that helped turn Santos into Intercontinental Cup champions twice. But the pressure on Pelé was reflected in injuries, one of which restricted him to a peripheral role in the 1962 World Cup finals, and it was not until 1970 that Pelé shone brightest at a World Cup again, his performance the apotheosis of a great player at his very best, achieving the rewards he deserved. It says everything about Pelé's transcending genius that he was the one man able to set light to football in the United States in the 1970s. Although the North American Soccer League eventually collapsed, football was by that stage firmly established as a grass-roots American sport. Without Pelé's allure that could never have happened and the capture of host rights for the 1994 finals would never have been possible.

1956
Joins big-city club Santos scores four goals in his league debut

1957
Makes debut for Brazil against Argentina and becomes the youngest goalscorer in an international

1958
Becomes youngest-ever World Cup winner, scoring two goals in the final as Brazil beat Sweden 5–2

1962
Misses Brazil's 1962 World Cup win because of injury but wins the Intercontinental Cup with Santos

1970
Inspires Brazil to complete historic World Cup hat trick in Mexico

1975
Ends 18-month retirement to play for Cosmos of New York in the North American Soccer League

1977
Retires again after lifting Cosmos to their second NASL championship

1995
Appointed Minister for Sport in Brazil. Receives honorary British knighthood two years later

2000
Shares FIFA Player of the Century award with Maradona

CLUB

SANTOS
NEW YORK COSMOS

702
APPEARANCES

656
GOALS

0.93
GOALS PER APPEARANCE

INTERNATIONAL

BRAZIL

92
APPEARANCES

77
GOALS

74%
WIN PERCENTAGE

92
WORLD RECORD NUMBER OF CAREER HAT TRICKS

PELÉ

Edson Arantes do Nascimento
1940 – 1.73m (5ft 8in)

Manuel Neuer makes yet another save for Bayern Munich, in a 2011 Bundesliga game against Nuremberg.

Günter Netzer

NATIONAL TEAM West Germany

Born September 14, 1944

CLUB(S) Borussia Mönchengladbach, Real Madrid (Sp), Grasshopper (Swz)

Netzer, a supreme midfield general, was at his best in the West German side that won the 1972 European Championship. He lost his place to Wolfgang Overath after joining Real Madrid. Netzer was twice a West German champion with Borussia, twice a Spanish champion with Madrid.

Manuel Neuer

NATIONAL TEAM Germany

BORN March 27, 1986

CLUB(S) Schalke, Bayern Munich

Neuer has set new standards for a modern, enterprising style of goalkeeping, described as a "sweeper-keeper". He won the 2014 World Cup with Germany as well as an award for being the best keeper in the tournament. Remarkably for a goalkeeper, he was third in the 2014 FIFA World Player ballot.

Neymar

NATIONAL TEAM Brazil

BORN February 2, 1992

CLUB(S) Santos, Barcelona (Sp)

Neymar showed superstar status in leading Brazil to the semi-finals of the 2014 World Cup, then a first Olympic football gold in Rio in 2016. Raised at Pele's old club Santos he cost Barcelona £61m and then, after winning the Champions League, cost Paris S-G a world record €222m in 2017.

Wolfgang Overath

NATIONAL TEAM West Germany

BORN September 29, 1943

CLUB(S) Köln

Overath, an old-style inside left, was among the most admired members of the West German sides at the World Cups of 1966 and 1970 and in winning the crown in 1974. Overath played his entire senior club career for Köln and scored 17 goals in 81 internationals between 1963 and 1974.

Antonin Panenka

NATIONAL TEAM Czechoslovakia

BORN December 2, 1948

CLUB(S) Bohemians Prague, Rapid Vienna (Aus)

Panenka was a skilled midfield general who spent most of his career in the Czech shadows with Bohemians before emerging at the 1976 European Championship. Panenka struck the decisive blow in the final against West Germany with a cheeky penalty chip that decided the shootout and the title.

Daniel Passarella

NATIONAL TEAM Argentina

BORN May 25, 1953

CLUB(S) Sarmiento, River Plate, Fiorentina (It), Internazionale (It)

Passarella is the only Argentinian player to have won two World Cups, as the hosts' captain in 1978 and as a squad member in 1986. A rugged defensive halfback, he starred for River Plate before moving to Italy to establish himself as a goal-scoring defender with Fiorentina and Inter.

★ Pelé

See page 252

Silvio Piola

NATIONAL TEAM Italy

BORN September 29, 1913, died October 4, 1998

CLUB(S) Pro Vercelli, Lazio, Torino, Juventus, Novara

Piola was a powerful centre forward who scored 30 goals in 24 games between a two-goal debut against Austria in 1935 and a 1-1 draw with England in 1952. Over this period, Piola

55%

MANUEL NEUER
THE BAYERN MUNICH STOPPER KEEPS HIS GOAL INTACT IN MORE THAN HALF HIS GAMES. NEUER REACHED 100 BUNDESLIGA CLEAN SHEETS IN RECORD TIME IN FEBRUARY 2017 – AFTER ONLY 183 MATCHES.

celebrated becoming a World Cup-winner in 1938 after scoring twice in a 4-2 defeat of Hungary in the final.

Andrea Pirlo of Juventus succeeds in outwitting Barcelona's Andres Iniesta and Sergio Busquets during the Champions League final in 2015.

Gerard Pique

NATIONAL TEAM Spain

BORN February 2, 1987

CLUB(S) Barcelona, Manchester Utd (Eng), Zaragoza, Barcelona

Pique, the "Catalan Beckenbauer", was allowed to join Manchester United in 2004. After four years, he returned home to share in Barcelona's unique title "six-pack" in 2009. Subsequently, he won the 2010 World Cup and the 2012 European Championship with the Spanish national team.

Andrea Pirlo

NATIONAL TEAM Italy

BORN May 19, 1979

CLUB(S) Brescia, Internazionale, Reggina, Milan, Juventus, NY City (US)

Pirlo established himself as one of the most perceptive of modern playmakers, starring for Italy at successive World Cups and European finals. With Milan he won two Champions Leagues and two Italian titles before guiding Juventus to four more domestic crowns between 2012 and 2015.

František Plánička

NATIONAL TEAM Czechoslovakia

BORN June 2, 1904, died July 20 1996

CLUB(S) Slovan Prague, Bubenec, Slavia Prague

Plánička was Central Europe's finest goalkeeper of the 1930s, starring in the World Cups of both 1934 - when Czechoslovakia lost the final 2-1 to Italy - and 1938. He was a domestic league champion nine times with Slavia, won the domestic cup six times and Mitropa Cup in 1938.

Michel Platini

NATIONAL TEAM France
BORN June 21, 1955
CLUB(S) Nancy, Saint-Etienne, Juventus (It)

Platini was the greatest French footballer after Kopa and before Zidane. He scored a then record 41 goals for France, for whom he was nine-goal top scorer in inspiring the hosts' 1984 European title win. Platini was top scorer three years in a row in Italy after joining Juventus in 1982.

Paul Pogba

NATIONAL TEAM France
BORN March 15, 1993
CLUB(S) Manchester Utd (Eng), Juventus (It), Manchester Ut (Eng)

Pogba cost Manchester United a world record £90m when they bought the midfielder back from Juventus in 2016. He had played for United as a teenager but moved to Italy after failing to make a breakthrough. Pogba lived up to his status with his fine displays in France's 2018 World Cup win.

Ferenc Puskás

NATIONAL TEAM Hungary and Spain
BORN April 2, 1927, died November 17, 2006
CLUB(S) Budapest Honved, Real Madrid (Sp)

A symbol of the legendary "Magic Magyars" who dominated the 1950s, he possessed one of the most lethal left foots the game gas ever seen. He made his debut for Hungary at the age of 18, and after four undefeated years reached the World Cup final in 1954. Puskás played injured, and the gamble failed when Hungary lost at the moment it mattered most. He later joined Real Madrid where, with Di Stéfano, he formed one half of one of the all-time great striking partnerships.

Carles "Charly" Puyol

NATIONAL TEAM Spain
BORN April 13, 1978
CLUB(S) Barcelona

Puyol was a one-club defender who rose through the Barcelona ranks to become club captain in 2004. He won 14 domestic club prizes plus three Champions Leagues, two UEFA Super Cups and two Club World Cups. He was also a world and European champion with Spain in 2010 and 2008.

0.99

FERENC PUSKÁS
THE HUNGARIAN FOOTBALLING GENIUS SCORED AT VERY NEARLY A GOAL PER GAME (84 IN 85) FOR HIS COUNTRY.

Helmut Rahn

NATIONAL TEAM West Germany
BORN August 16, 1929, died August 14, 2003
CLUB(S) Rot-Weiss Essen, Koln, Enschede (Hol), Meiderich SV Duisburg

Rahn's shooting power from outside right was immense, as Hungary found to their cost in the 1954 World Cup final. Rahn struck West Germany's equalizer at 2-2 and then the late winner. He could not repeat himself in 1958 but still totalled 21 goals in 40 international matches.

Raúl Gonzalez Blanco

NATIONAL TEAM Spain
BORN June 27, 1977
CLUB(S) Real Madrid, Schalke (Ger), Al Sadd (Qtr), NY Cosmos (US)

Raúl was one of the greatest of Real Madrid players but his career was just too early for him to enjoy Spain's World Cup and Euro glory years. He is Madrid's second all-time top scorer with 323 goals and won six leagues, one world title, three Champions Leagues and four Spanish cups.

➔ Captain of Barcelona, Carles Puyol, lifts the Champions League trophy after defeating Arsenal 2-1 in 2006 at the Stade de France.

Franck Ribéry

NATIONAL TEAM France
BORN April 7, 1983
CLUB(S) Boulogne, Ales, Brest, Metz, Galatasaray (Tur), Marseille, Bayern Munich (Ger)

Ribéry shot to fame with his sparkling performances on the wing for France in their run to luckless runners-up spot in the 2006 World Cup. At club level he won the league and cup double with Bayern to become the first player voted Footballer of the Year in both France and Germany.

Frank Rijkaard

NATIONAL TEAM Holland
BORN September 30, 1962
CLUB(S) Ajax, Sporting Lisbon (Por), Zaragoza (Sp), AC Milan (It), Ajax

Rijkaard was one of the most versatile stars of the 1990s. He turned professional under Johan Cruyff at Ajax and played in Portugal and Spain before joining Milan, with whom he won the European Cup and World Club Cup twice apiece. In 1995, he won another Champions Cup with Ajax.

Luigi Riva

NATIONAL TEAM Italy
BORN November 7, 1944
CLUB(S) Legnano, Cagliari

Riva, orphaned in childhood, was adopted by all of Italy after shooting the Azzurri to the 1970 World Cup final. He scored three times in quarter and semi-final wins over Mexico and West Germany. Weeks earlier his formidable left foot had fired Cagliari to a shock league title success.

Rivaldo

FULL NAME Vitor Borba Ferreira
NATIONAL TEAM Brazil
BORN April 19, 1972
CLUB(S) Mogi-Mirim, Corinthians, Palmeiras, Deportivo La Coruña (Sp), Barcelona (Sp), Milan (It), Cruzeiro, Olympiakos (Gr), AEK (Gr), Budyonkor (Uzb), Washington Phoenix (US)

Rivaldo joined Barcelona for a club record fee of £16m from Spanish rivals Deportivo La Coruña in 1997 to replace fellow Brazilian Ronaldo. He was Brazil's best forward when they finished runners-up at the 1998 World Cup and his five goals helped propel Brazil to success in 2002.

23
MPH

ARJEN ROBBEN
THE FLYING DUTCH WINGER MADE THE FASTEST EVER RECORDED FOOTBALL SPRINT OF 23 MPH (37 KPH) IN THE 5–1 WORLD CUP DRUBBING OF SPAIN IN 2014.

Gianni Rivera

NATIONAL TEAM Italy
BORN August 18, 1943
CLUB(S) Alessandria, AC Milan

Rivera was Italy's Golden Boy in the early 1960s. As a creative inside forward with Milan, he was twice a winner of the World Club Cup, the European Champions Cup and the Italian league, as well as three times an Italian Cup-winner and once European Footballer of the Year, in 1969.

Arjen Robben

NATIONAL TEAM Holland
BORN January 23, 1984
CLUB(S) Groningen, PSV Eindhoven, Chelsea (Eng), Real Madrid (Sp), Bayern Munich (Ger)

Robben's pace and power off right or left wing earned him a transfer to Chelsea at the age of 20. He won two league titles but, after injury issues, sought a new start in Spain. He stayed barely a year at Real Madrid before finding a happier haven at Bayern Munich, whom he fired to the Champions League final in both 2010 and 2012.

Romário da Souza Faria

NATIONAL TEAM Brazil
BORN 29 January, 1966
CLUB(S) Vasco da Gama, PSV Eindhoven (Hol), Barcelona (Sp), Flamengo, Valencia (Sp), Flamengo, Vasco da Gama, Al Saad (Qtr), Fluminense, Vasco da Gama, Fluminense

Romario was the finest striker in the game in the 1990s. Discovered by Vasco da Gama, he was transferred to PSV Eindhoven, where he struck 98 league goals in five years. A move to Barcelona was followed by a five-goal World Cup campaign that saw Brazil triumph in the US in 1994.

Ronaldinho

FULL NAME Ronaldo Assis de Moreira
NATIONAL TEAM Brazil
BORN March 21, 1980
CLUB(S) Gremio Porto Alegre, Paris Saint-Germain (Fr), Barcelona (Sp), Milan (It), Flamengo, Atlético Mineiro

Ronaldinho was a throwback to the style of earlier Brazilian stars who enjoyed indulging both their own technical virtuosity on the pitch and lifestyle off it. He contributed an outrageous floated goal to Brazil's quarterfinal win over England on the way to a 2002 World Cup triumph.

RONALDO

Cristiano Ronaldo
1985 – 1.85m (6ft 1in)

BRAND CR7 Sir Alex Ferguson brought a teenage Ronaldo to Manchester United for a remarkable £12 million that was later seen as a bargain. He quickly developed judgement, confidence with his left foot and power in the air, qualities that inspired United to three Premier League titles and a Champions League win. In 2009, Real Madrid paid a world-record £80m transfer fee for Ronaldo. As well as leading Real Madrid to multiple trophies in La Liga, the Champions League and other club competitions, he capped a remarkable international career when, despite limping off in the final, he inspired Portugal to victory in the 2016 European Championships, the first major trophy in the nation's history. In 2018, he established himself as the 152-goal all-time top scorer in European competition, and as Madrid's 438-goal record holder. Along the way, the five-time FIFA World Player of the Year contributed a stream of goals as Madrid claimed four more European crowns. In 2018, Ronaldo decided to undertake one further new adventure in Italy with Juventus.

CLUB

SPORTING LISBON
MANCHESTER UNITED
REAL MADRID
JUVENTUS

761
APPEARANCES

573
GOALS

0.75
GOALS PER APPEARANCE
*July 2018

INTERNATIONAL

PORTUGAL

154
APPEARANCES

85
GOALS

25
RECORD NUMBER OF INTERNATIONAL GOALS FOR CLUB AND COUNTRY IN A CALENDAR YEAR (SHARED WITH MESSI AND VIVIAN WOODWARD)

350
FASTEST PLAYER TO 350 GOALS FOR A SINGLE CLUB IN ANY MAJOR EUROPEAN LEAGUE – IN 335 GAMES FOR REAL MADRID

2003
Signed from Sporting Lisbon by Manchester United and helps new club win the FA Cup

2008
Scores in United's Champions League triumph over Chelsea and wins Ballon d'Or and FIFA World Player of the Year

2009
After helping United to a third successive Premier League title and League Cup, joins Real Madrid

2012
Wins La Liga and Supercopa de España with Real and is joint top scorer at Euro 2012

2014
In a golden year for Real, wins Copa del Rey, Champions League, UEFA Super Cup and FIFA World Club Cup

2016
Leads Portugal to first major silverware at Euro 2016 and helps Real to Champions League victory

2017
Becomes first player to score 100 Champions League goals and helps Real to a first La Liga in five years

RONALDO

Ronaldo Luís Nazário de Lima

1976 – 1.83m (6ft)

THE PHENOMENON At 18, a lack of experience meant Ronaldo was never in the running for a starting role at the 1994 World Cup but that did not deter PSV Eindhoven, weeks later, from paying £6.5 million for him. After 54 goals in 57 games for PSV, Barcelona paid £13.2 million to introduce Ronaldo to Spanish football. The result was a triumph: Barcelona won the UEFA Cup Winners' Cup, the Copa del Rey and the Supercopa de Espana. A further move to Internazionale for £19.5 million added a UEFA Cup medal to his honours list. Then came the 1998 World Cup in France. Ronaldo scored against Morocco, Chile (two) and Holland in the semis to lead Brazil to the final against their French hosts. Frustratingly, on match day, he suffered a convulsive fit and Brazil crashed to a 3–0 defeat. Ronaldo was injured for much of the next four years but then produced a top-scoring eight-goal campaign to inspire Brazil's record-extending fifth World Cup win. Four years later, in Germany, Ronaldo forgot a controversial spell with Real Madrid long enough to claim three more goals for an aggregate of 15, bettered only by German striker Miroslav Klose in 2014.

CLUB

CRUIZEIRO · PSV · BARCELONA
INTERNAZIONALE · REAL MADRID
MILAN · CORINTHIANS

518 APPEARANCES

352 GOALS

0.68 GOALS PER APPEARANCE

INTERNATIONAL

BRAZIL

98 APPEARANCES

62 GOALS

70% WIN PERCENTAGE

1993
Plays first game for Cruzeiro and scores 12 goals in 14 games to earn a debut for Brazil in 1994

1995
Rewards PSV Eindhoven for a £6.5m outlay with 35 goals in 36 games

1996
Scores "only" 12 goals in 13 games in an injury-hit season, then joins Barcelona for a club record £13.2m

1997
Scores the UEFA Cup Winners' Cup final winning goal for Barcelona. Moves to Internazionale

1998
Scores 25 Serie A goals and wins the UEFA Cup with Internazionale. Finishes World Cup runner-up

2002
Scores eight as Brazil win World Cup. Joins Real Madrid and wins a third FIFA World Player of the Year award

2003
Top scorer in La Liga with 23 goals to win the first league title of his career

2007
Transfers from Real Madrid to Milan

2009
Joins Corinthians and wins the Copa do Brasil. Plays final Brazil game in 2011 and retires

19.5
(million pounds)
WORLD RECORD TRANSFER IN 1997 FROM BARCELONA TO INTERNAZIONALE

★ Cristiano Ronaldo

See page 257

★ Ronaldo Luiz Nazario de Lima

See page 258

Wayne Rooney

NATIONAL TEAM England
BORN October 24, 1985
CLUB(S) Everton (Eng), Manchester United, Everton

Rooney was an apprentice when he hit the headlines with a brilliant first Premier goal against Arsenal in October 2001. Later came a £25m move to Manchester United, a record 53 England goals in 119 games, plus one Champions League, one Club World Cup and nine domestic trophies.

Paolo Rossi

NATIONAL TEAM Italy
BORN September 23, 1956
Club(s) Prato, Juventus, Como, Lanerossi Vicenza, Perugia, Juventus, AC Milan

Rossi's story is one of triumph over adversity. He was discarded by Juventus after knee trouble, then banned for three years after a betting scandal. Only three matches after his ban, Italy took him to the 1982 World Cup and he was top scorer with six goals, collecting a winner's medal.

Karl-Heinz Rummenigge

NATIONAL TEAM West Germany
BORN September 25, 1955
CLUB(S) Lippstadt, Bayern Munich, Internazionale (It), Servette (Swz)

Rummenigge was one of the greatest bargains in German football history. Bayern paid Lippstadt £4,500 for their winger in 1974 and sold him a decade later for more than £2m. In the meantime, he won the World Club Cup and European Cup and twice had been hailed European Footballer of the Year.

Ian Rush

NATIONAL TEAM Wales
BORN October 20, 1961
CLUB(S) Chester (Eng), Liverpool (Eng), Juventus (It), Liverpool (Eng), Leeds United (Eng), Newcastle United (Eng)

Rush was a goal-scorer supreme in modern British football. The Wales centre-forward was only 18 when he cost Liverpool £300,000 from Chester City and he went on to break scoring records for club and country, as well as in FA Cup finals, with five goals in three winning appearances.

Mohamed Salah

NATIONAL TEAM Egypt
BORN June 15, 1992
CLUB(S) El Mokawloon, Basel (Swz), Chelsea (Eng), Fiorentina (It), Roma (It), Liverpool (Eng)

Salah enjoyed a sensational season in 2017-18. He scored 44 goals in all competitions for Liverpool and was the Premier League's 32-goal top marksman. The forward scored both of Egypt's goals at the 2018 World Cup in Russia, despite having only just recovered from a shoulder injury suffered in the Champions League final defeat by Real Madrid.

Hugo Sánchez

NATIONAL TEAM Mexico
BORN June 11, 1958
CLUB(S) UNAM, Atlético Madrid (Sp), Real Madrid (Sp), Club América, Rayo Vallecano (Sp)

Hugo Sánchez was top league goal-scorer in Spain five seasons in a row in the late 1980s and

A jubilant Wayne Rooney celebrates after scoring an equaliser for England against Uruguay in a group match at the 2014 World Cup.

Peter Schmeichel, in action for Manchester United in 1995, was a towering presence in goal during the club's run of five Premier League titles in the 1990s.

early 1990s. His 230-plus goals were all followed by a celebratory somersault. Sánchez won two league titles in Mexico with UNAM and five in Spain with Real Madrid, plus the UEFA Cup.

Nílton Santos

NATIONAL TEAM Brazil
BORN May 16, 1927, died November 27, 2013
CLUB(S) Botafogo

Santos played left back in the Brazil team that won the World Cup in 1958 and 1961 (and was no relation to right-back partner Djalma Santos). He played 83 times for his country between 1949 and 1963 and was nicknamed "The Encyclopedia" by teammates and fans, who held him in high respect.

Juan Alberto Schiaffino

NATIONAL TEAM Uruguay and Italy
BORN July 28, 1925, died November 13, 2002
CLUB(S) Peñarol, Milan (It), Roma (It)

Schiaffino, an inside or centre-forward, reached a peak in 1950 when he scored Uruguay's equaliser at 1-1 in their shock victory over Brazil in the World Cup decider at the Maracaná. After the 1954 finals, he was sold for a world record £72,000 to Milan with whom he won three league titles.

Peter Schmeichel

NATIONAL TEAM Denmark
BORN November 18, 1963
CLUB(S) Hvidovre, Brondbyerenes (Den), Manchester United (Eng), Sporting Clube (Por), Aston Villa (Eng), Manchester City (Eng)

Schmeichel was a hero of Denmark's astonishing triumph at the 1992 European Championship, with crucial saves against Holland in the semi-final and Germany in the final. With Manchester United he won the league and cup double twice before securing the treble in 1999.

Paul Scholes

NATIONAL TEAM England
BORN November 16, 1974
CLUB(S) Manchester United

Scholes, locally Salford-born, may have lacked the charisma of a Beckham or Giggs, but few players brought as much to their Manchester United team. Scholes won 66 caps before his England retirement in 2004, with appearances at the 1998 and 2002 World Cups and Euro 2000.

Uwe Seeler

NATIONAL TEAM West Germany
BORN November 5, 1936
CLUB(S) Hamburg

Seeler, son of a former Hamburg player, made his senior debut in a 3-1 defeat by England at Wembley in 1954 at the age of 18. He returned to captain West Germany in their World Cup final defeat in 1966, but took revenge with a back-headed goal when Germany won 3-2 in a dramatic 1970 quarter-final.

Sergio Ramos

NATIONAL TEAM Spain

BORN March 30, 1986

CLUB(S) Sevilla, Real Madrid

Ramos joined Madrid as a fullback but won the 2010 World Cup and Euro 2008 and 2012 in central defence for Spain, and many international and national club titles. Key goals include Madrid's dramatic stoppage-time equalizer against Atlético in the 2014 Champions League final.

Alan Shearer

NATIONAL TEAM England

BORN August 13, 1970

CLUB(S) Southampton, Blackburn Rovers, Newcastle United

Shearer starred first at Southampton before leading Blackburn to a surprise league win in 1995. Later he went home to Newcastle to set a club record of 206 goals. Shearer scored 30 goals in 63 England games, and tallied 283 league goals with a record 11 Premier hat tricks.

Andriy Shevchenko

NATIONAL TEAM Ukraine

BORN September 29, 1976

CLUB(S) Dynamo Kiev, Milan (It), Chelsea (Eng), Dynamo Kiev

Shevchenko made his international mark by converting a decisive penalty to bring Milan a shootout victory over Juventus in the 2003 Champions League final. He was twice top scorer in Italy's Serie A after having previously celebrated being five times a Ukraine champion with Kiev.

Peter Shilton

NATIONAL TEAM England

BORN September 18, 1949

CLUB(S) Leicester, Stoke, Nottingham Forest, Southampton, Derby, Plymouth Argyle, Bolton Wanderers, West Ham United, Leyton Orient

Shilton was only 20 when first capped, and 40 when he made his 125th and last appearance for England at the 1990 World Cup. He conceded only 80 goals. At club level, with Nottingham Forest, he won the Champions Cup twice and the UEFA Super Cup and English league once each.

Nikita Simonian

NATIONAL TEAM Soviet Union

BORN October 12, 1926

CLUB(S) Kirilia Sovietov, Spartak Moscow

Simonian, one of the few Armenian football players to have succeeded in the Soviet game, scored a record 142 goals in 265 league matches in the 1950s. Three times he was leading scorer in the Soviet Supreme League, and his 1950 haul of 34 goals set a record that stood until the 1980s.

Matthias Sindelar

NATIONAL TEAM Austria

BORN February 18, 1903, died January 23, 1939

Club(s) FC Hertha Vienna, FK Austria

Sindelar, nicknamed the "Man of Paper" for his slim build, was the centre-forward inspiration of the Austrian "Wunderteam" of the 1930s. He scored 27 goals in 43 internationals, led Austria to the World Cup semi-finals in 1934 and won the Mitropa Cup twice with FK Austria.

Enrique Omar Sívori

NATIONAL TEAM Argentina and Italy

BORN October 2, 1935, died February 17, 2005

CLUB(S) River Plate, Juventus (It), Napoli (It)

Sívori was nicknamed "Big Head" by fans because

Andriy Shevchenko enjoys the moment after scoring for Milan against Sparta Prague in the 2014 Champions League. In seven years with Milan, the Ukranian striker scored 175 goals.

of his technical skills. An inside left with talent but a temper, he cost Juventus a world record £91,000 in 1957 and brought them three league titles. He played for both Argentina and Italy and was 1961 European Footballer of the Year.

Luis Suárez celebrates scoring the first of his two goals for Uruguay during the 2–1 defeat of England in a group match at the 2014 World Cup in Brazil.

Sócrates Brasileiro Sampaio de Souza Vieira de Oliveira

NATIONAL TEAM Brazil
BORN February 19, 1954, died December 4, 2011
CLUB(S) Botafogo SP, Corinthians, Fiorentina (It), Flamengo, Santos, Botafogo SP

Sócrates, nicknamed "The Doctor" for his medical qualifications, was a playmaking centre-forward for the fine Brazil team considered back home as "moral winners" of the 1982 World Cup. Also a political theorist, he scored 22 goals in 60 games for Brazil between 1979 and 1986.

Jürgen Sparwasser

NATIONAL TEAM East Germany
BORN June 14, 1948
CLUB(S) Magdeburg

Sparwasser was one of East Germany's few outstanding players. In the 1974 World Cup, he scored the historic goal that beat hosts West Germany in the first and last meeting between the two. He totalled 15 goals in 77 internationals and won a Cup Winners' Cup medal with Magdeburg in 1974.

Hristo Stoichkov

NATIONAL TEAM Bulgaria
BORN August 2, 1966
CLUB(S) CSKA Sofia, Barcelona (Sp), Parma (It), Barcelona (Sp), CSKA Sofia, Kawisa Reysol (Jap), Chicago Fire (US), DC United (US)

Stoichkov joined Barcelona in 1990 on the personal recommendation of coach Johan Cruyff. He led them to their long awaited first Champions Cup victory in 1992. Stoichkov also inspired Bulgaria's fourth place finish at the 1994 World Cup and won European Footballer of the Year.

Luis Suárez

NATIONAL TEAM Uruguay
BORN January 24, 1987
CLUB(S) Nacional, Groningen (Hol), Ajax (Hol), Liverpool (Eng), Barcelona (Sp)

Suárez, a magnet for controversy, raced up the international club ladder with Nacional, Groningen, Ajax, Liverpool and Barcelona – despite three biting incidents and a row over a racist comment. He was a world and European club champion in 2015 and Europe's 40-goal league top scorer in 2015-16.

Francesco Totti

NATIONAL TEAM Italy
BORN September 27, 1976
CLUB(S) Roma

A one-club man in a mercenary era, Totti was the spirit of Roma. He won one Serie A and two Coppa Italias with the club, and as their leading goalscorer and most capped player, not to mention the youngest captain in Serie A history, he was a true club legend. Totti also achieved with Italy, first as European Championship finalist in 2000, then as a World Cup winner in 2006.

Colombia's captain, Carlos Valderrama, holds off the challenge of a USA defender during a group game at the 1994 World Cup. Valderrama went on to win 111 caps – a Colombian record.

Yaya Touré

NATIONAL TEAM Ivory Coast

BORN May 13, 1983

CLUB(S) Beveren (Bel), Metalurh Donetsk (Ukr), Olympiakos (Gr), Monaco (Fr), Barcelona (Sp), Manchester City (Eng)

Touré was brought to Europe by Belgium's Beveren in 2001 then won the Champions League with Barcelona in 2009 before joining Manchester City. He was voted African Footballer of the Year in 2011 after scoring the winning goal in the FA Cup final to end City's 35-year trophy drought.

Carlos Valderrama

NATIONAL TEAM Colombia

BORN September 2, 1961

CLUB(S) Santa Marta, Millonarios, Atlético Nacional, Montpellier (Fr), Valladolid (Sp), Medellin, Atlético Junior Barranquilla, Tampa Bay Mutiny (US), Miami Fusion (US)

Valderrama was voted South American Footballer of the Year in 1987 after guiding Colombia to third place at the Copa America. He stood out for his all-round skills – as well as frizzy hairstyle – and enjoyed South American Cup glory with Atlético Nacional before brief spells in France and Spain. He returned to Colombia and was once again South American Footballer of the Year in 1994.

Marco Van Basten

NATIONAL TEAM Holland

Born October 31, 1964

Club(s) Ajax, AC Milan (It)

Van Basten contributed one of the all-time great international goals when he volleyed home a long cross in the 1988 European Championship final against the Soviet Union. A prolific scorer and multiple trophy-winner with Ajax and Milan, with whom he won World Footballer of the Year, his career was eventually cut short by ankle injuries.

⊕ Robin Van Persie unleashes an outrageous flying header to score Holland's first goal in their 5–1 defeat of Spain at the 2014 World Cup in Brazil.

Paul Van Himst

NATIONAL TEAM Belgium
BORN October 2, 1943
CLUB(S) Anderlecht, RWD Molenbeek, Eendracht Aalst

Van Himst was Belgium's greatest player. With Anderlecht he was domestic champion eight times, a cup-winner four times and league top scorer three times. Van Himst scored 31 goals in 81 internationals, including the 1970 World Cup and a third-place finish as European hosts in 1972.

Robin van Persie

NATIONAL TEAM Holland
BORN August 6, 1983
CLUB(S) Feyenoord, Arsenal (Eng), Manchester United, Fenerbahçe (Tur), Feyenoord

Striker Van Persie became Arsenal club captain after Cesc Fabregas's exit in 2011 and responded magnificently to become the Premier League's 30-goal top scorer in 2011–12. However his major trophy haul remained just one UEFA Cup with Feyenoord plus one FA Cup with Arsenal. With Holland he was a World Cup runner-up in South Africa in 2010.

Obdulio Varela

NATIONAL TEAM Uruguay
BORN September 20, 1917, died August 2, 1996
CLUB(S) Deportivo Juventud, Wanderers, Peñarol

Varela was captain of the Uruguayan team that shocked Brazil by beating their hosts in Rio's Maracaná stadium in the 1950 World Cup decider. He was an old-style attacking centre-half and a captain who led by example. He also spearheaded Uruguay's success in the Copa America - twice.

Patrick Vieira

NATIONAL TEAM France
BORN June 23, 1976
CLUB(S) Cannes, Milan (It), Arsenal (Eng), Juventus (It), Internazionale (It), Manchester City (Eng)

Arsene Wenger signed Vieira from Milan and the £3 million fee soon looked a bargain; Vieira drove Arsenal to the league and cup double in 1998 and 2002. With France, he was a reserve for the 1998 World Cup win but first choice by the time of the Euro 2000 victory, and a finalist in the 2006 World Cup. He also captained Arsenal to seven league and cup victories in eight seasons.

Rudi Völler

NATIONAL TEAM Germany

BORN April 13, 1960

CLUB(S) Kickers Offenbach, TSV 1860 Munich, Werder Bremen, Roma (It), Marseille (Fr), Bayer Leverkusen

Völler joined Werder Bremen from TSV 1860 Munich in 1982 and, in his first season, was league top scorer with 23 goals, Footballer of the Year and won his first cap. He was a World Cup runner-up in 1986 and a winner in 1990. Later he became national manager, guiding Germany to the 2002 World Cup Final against all the odds.

Fritz Walter

NATIONAL TEAM Germany

BORN October 31, 1920, died June 17, 2002

CLUB(S) Kaiserslautern

Walter and brother Ottmar were inside-left and centre-forward stars with Kaiserslautern in the 1940s and early 1950s - and also World Cup-winners together against favourites Hungary in 1954. Walter scored a hat trick on his debut against Romania in 1940 and tallied 33 goals in 61 games.

George Weah

NATIONAL TEAM Liberia

BORN October 1, 1966

CLUB(S) Young Survivors, Bongrange, Mighty Barolle, Tonnerre (Cam), Monaco (Fr), Paris Saint-German (Fr), Milan (It), Chelsea (Eng), Manchester City, Marseille (Fr), Al-Jazira (UAE)

Weah made history in 1995 when the Liberian striker became the first winner of the European Footballer poll after a rule change that opened up the award to players of any nationality. He dedicated the award to Arsene Wenger, under whom he won the French league title at Monaco.

Billy Wright

NATIONAL TEAM England

BORN February 6, 1924, died September 3, 1994

CLUB(S) Wolverhampton Wanderers

Wright was a wing-half who moved successfully into the centre of defence on his way to a then world record of 105 caps for England. He captained not only England but also the highly successful multiple league championship-winning Wolves team of the late 1950s.

George Weah celebrates scoring a goal for Paris Saint-Germain. He won the 1993–94 Ligue 1 title with PSG before making a high-profile move to Milan in Italy.

ZINEDINE ZIDANE

1972– 1.85m (6ft 1in)

2001 WORLD RECORD TRANSFER FEE FROM JUVENTUS TO REAL MADRID (million euros)

75

FIFA WORLD PLAYER OF THE YEAR 1998, 2000, 2003

3

CLUB

CANNES · BORDEAUX
JUVENTUS
REAL MADRID

506 LEAGUE APPEARANCES

95 GOALS

13 TROPHIES WON

INTERNATIONAL

FRANCE

108 APPEARANCES

31 GOALS

3 GOALS SCORED IN WORLD CUP FINALS (JOINT RECORD WITH VAVA, PELE AND GEOFF HURST)

1989
Makes his debut for Cannes in Ligue 1 and joins Bordeaux in 1992

1996
Euro 96 semi-finalist with France and transfers to Juventus, winning the UEFA Super Cup

1998
World Cup winner with France and a second Serie A championship with Juventus

2000
Wins the European Championship with France and is voted FIFA World Player of the Year for the second time

2001
Signs for Real Madrid for a world-record breaking fee of around 75 million Euros

2002
Wins Champions League and UEFA Super Cup in first season with Real Madrid

2003
La Liga champion and voted FIFA World Player of the Year for a record-equalling third time

2006
Scores in World Cup final, but France loses and his career ends with a sending-off in extra time

ZIZOU Zidane's greatest moment was picking up a World Cup winner's medal after France's 3–0 win over Brazil in 1998, when he scored two of the goals. His career took off at the age of 20, when he was snapped up by Bordeaux and inspired them to the UEFA Cup final in 1996 before Juventus came calling. Among Zidane's achievements in Italy were two Serie A titles, one UEFA Super Cup and one Intercontinental Cup. Two years after his 1998 World Cup-winning performance, Zidane also guided France to victory at Euro 2000. The 2006 World Cup, though, was not as kind to Zidane, most notably the doomed final defeat by Italy when he was sent off. In 2001, Zidane had joined Real Madrid, the highlight of his time there coming in May 2002, when he volleyed one of the most masterful winning goals ever seen in the Champions League in a 2–1 win over Bayer Leverkusen.

Lev Yashin makes a flying save to keep out Italy's Sandro Mazzola during the Soviet Union's 1–0 victory in a 1966 World Cup group match at Roker Park, Sunderland.

Xavi

FULL NAME Xavier Hernández i Creus
NATIONAL TEAM Spain
BORN January 25, 1980
CLUB(S) Barcelona, Al Sadd (Qtr)

Xavi enjoyed unprecedented success between 1999 and 2015. Barcelona's Catalan playmaker won the World Cup and two European titles with Spain, plus 17 domestic titles, two Club World Cups, four Champions Leagues and two UEFA Super Cups. Possibly his most successful year, in a truly glittering career, came in 2009, when he helped Barcelona to a clean sweep of six trophies at home and abroad. He was himself man of the match in the Champions League final victory.

Lev Yashin

NATIONAL TEAM Soviet Union
BORN October 22, 1929, died March 20, 1990
CLUB(S) Moscow Dynamo

Yashin, rated by many as the greatest goalkeeper of all, was also an ice-hockey star. He made his Soviet debut in 1954 and, two years later, won Olympic gold in Melbourne. In 1960, he inspired the Soviet Union's inaugural European title win. Overall, he earned 78 caps and was the 1963 European Footballer of the Year.

Zico

FULL NAME Artur Antunes Coimbra
NATIONAL TEAM Brazil
BORN March 3, 1953
CLUB(S) Flamengo, Udinese (It), Flamengo, Kashima Antlers (Jap)

Zico, youngest of three footballing brothers, marked his Brazil debut in 1975 by scoring with a speciality free kick. In the World Cup, Zico was at his best in Spain in 1982. Months earlier, he had inspired Flamengo's superb demolition of Liverpool in Tokyo in the World Club Cup.

★ Zinedine Zidane

See page 266

Dino Zoff

NATIONAL TEAM Italy
BORN February 28, 1942
CLUB(S) Udinese, Mantova, Napoli, Juventus

Zoff played a then record 112 times for Italy, of which the 106th was the World Cup final defeat of West Germany in Madrid in 1982. In 1973–74, he set a world record of 1,143 international minutes without conceding a goal. He won European trophies both as player and coach with Juventus.

Index

Picture Credits

The publishers would like to thank the following sources for their kind permission to reproduce the pictures in this book.

Key, T: top, B: bottom, L: left, C: centre, R: right.

Action Images: /Andy Couldridge: 189BR

Alamy: /Lordprice Collection: 10

Colorsport: 11, 12BL, 112C; /Andrew Cowie: 161; /Stuart MacFarlane: 44; /Pica: 34; /Wilkes: 156

Getty Images: /Shaun Botterill: 177; /Jean Catuffe: 108; /Alexandr Fedorov/Pressphotos: 117; /Jeff Gross: 264; /J A Hampton/Topical Press Agency: 18BL; /Karim Jaafar/AFP: 89; /Jasper Juinen: 103B; /Keystone: 17TR; /Art Rickerby/ The LIFE Picture Collection: 252; /Topical Press Agency: 15BR

PA Images: 9T, 15TL, 17BC, 17BR, 20BL, 22BL, 23BR, 33T, 57T, 124BR, 155TR, 160BR, 165, 187T, 208T, 231, 267; /ABACA: 106TR, 183BR; /AFLO: 85; /Jack Abuin/Zuma Press: 62BC; /Oliver Acker/ DPA: 62T; /Matthew Ashton: 25BC, 25BR, 27BC, 40, 41, 48-49T, 54T, 54BL, 64BR, 128, 136BR, 266; /Balkis Press/ABACA: 88; /Gavin Barker/Sports Inc.: 75B, 80, 132BR; /Baumann/DPA: 16BL; /Ron Bell: 36; /Bildbyran: 127; /Claudio Bresciani/TT News Agency: 123TR; /Geraldo Bubniak/Zuma Press: 212; /Marco Buzzi/Buzzi: 238; /Peter Byrne: 160TR; /Lynne Cameron: 222; /Derek Cattani: 183TL; /David Cheskin: 24BC; /Paul Chiasson/The Canadian Press: 68; /Barrington Coombs: 97B; / CORDON: 185R, 186TR, 213; /Jose Luis Cuesta/ CORDON: 152; /DPA: 121BC, 143, 151, 168TL, 178, 221T, 221B, 250, 257, 263; /David Davies: 125; /Adam Davy: 28BL, 43, 84, 134B, 139, 145, 163, 176BL; /Sean Dempsey: 234; /David Ebener/ DPA: 67; /Mike Egerton: 26B, 28BC, 30BL, 33B, 46, 56, 57B, 61, 87BL, 94, 97T, 109T, 111B, 116BR, 162BR, 186BR, 195, 225, 244; /Thomas Eisenhuth/ DPA: 73, 191, 254; /EMPICS Sport: 13, 14BC, 14BR, 16BR, 31BL, 132TR, 149BL, 149BR, 164; / Maxi Failla: 218; /Matthew Fearn: 95T; /Alejandro Fernandez: 26T; /Paulo Fonseca/EFE: 70TL; / Fotoarena/SIPA USA: 136T; /Nigel French: 31BC; / GES-Sportfoto/DPA: 229; /Li Ga/Xinhua: 107T; / Federico Gambarini/DPA: 50BR, 99B; /Ed Garvey/ Manchester City FC: 159T; /Daniel Garzon/Zuma Press: 210; /Andreas Gebert/DPA: 101, 153B, 175BL; /Joe Giddens: 118B; /Tim Goode: 6-7, 96; /Laurence Griffiths: 228; /Jonas Güttler/DPA: 172BR; /Lionel Hahn/ABACA USA: 209BR; /Jeff Holmes: 193; /Owen Humphreys: 60B, 155BL; / Dave Hunt/AAP: 205B; /Massimo Insabato/IPA MilestoneMedia: 47BL; /Matsu Kawamori/AFLO: 64BL; /David Klein/Sportimage: 105BL; /Dmitry Korotaev/Kommersant/Sipa USA: 79; /Leo La Valle/ EFE: 144; /LaPresse: 18BR; /Brian Lawless: 124BL; /Virginie Lefour/Belga: 192; /Christian Liewig/ ABACA: 30BC, 50BL, 78, 92T; /Marcio Machado/ Zuma Press: 197, 207; /Paul Marriott: 157B; /Tony Marshall: 27BR, 45, 47TR, 87BR, 118TL, 148BL, 150, 215, 216BL, 236, 261; /Kenzaburo Matsuoka/AFLO: 201, 203; /Maxppp: 167BL; /Miguelez/CORDON: 190; /Paul Miller/AAP: 51; /Chema Moya/EFE: 66; /Chuck Myers/ABACA USA: 206; /Daisuke Nakashima/AFLO: 104, 105T; /Tracey Nearmy/ AAP: 204, 205TL; /Phil Noble: 162BL; /NurPhoto/ SIPA USA: 167TR, 186BC, 248; /Phil O'Brien: 39, 187B, 265; /Kirk O'Rourke/Rangers FC: 102; / Panoramic: 107B, 168BL, 272BL; /Gabriel Piko/ Piko Press: 30TR, 71, 129, 211; /Nick Potts: 4, 29B, 95B, 114B, 135, 160BL, 188BL, 189TR, 258, 259, 262, 272TL, 272TR; /Peter Power/The Canadian Press: 53; /Antonio Pozo/Media Expre/Zuma Press: 185B; /Presse Sports: 58, 235; /Duncan Raban: 22BR, 272L; /Rauchensteiner/Augenklick/DPA: 172T; /Revierfoto/DPA: 103TR, 171TR; /Chris Ricco/ Sports Inc.: 42T; /Martin Rickett: 28BR, 30BR, 109C, 158TR, 159BL; /Peter Robinson: 21TR, 21BL, 21BR, 22T, 22BC, 23BL, 24TR, 32, 37, 38TR, 38BL, 60T, 75T, 99T, 111TL, 121TL, 121BL, 123L, 142BL, 147T, 162L, 223, 226, 232, 233, 242, 243, 245, 246, 272R; /Fabio Rubinato/DPA: 214; /S&G and Barratts: 12TR, 15BL, 18BC, 18T, 20BR, 23BC, 120, 157TR, 158BL, 162TR, 188C, 249; /SMG: 14BL, 70BR, 122T, 194, 216TR; /Amr Sayed/Zuma Press: 196; / Shajor/PikoPress: 149TR; /Valery Sharifulin/TASS: 31BR, 119; /Samuel Shivambu/Sports Inc.: 198; Sven Simon: 8, 146B; /Sven Simon/DPA: 9B, 147BL, 171BR, 173, 175BR, 224, 253; /Neal Simpson: 24BL, 24BR, 92BL, 93, 113, 146TR, 175TR, 176TR, 237, 255, 260, 272BC; /Mark Smith/Zuma Press: 74, 133, 148BR; /Michael Steele: 227; /Studio Buzzi SRL: 241; /Henri Swarc/ABACA: 169; /Topham Picturepoint: 16T, 19T, 19BR, 59, 72, 188-189, 217, 230; /Jun Tsukida/AFLO: 202; /VI Images: 42B, 63, 112BL, 153T, 179, 181, 186BL, 220; /Aaron Vincent Elkaim/The Canadian Press: 137; /Brooks Von Arx/Zuma Press: 142TR; /John Walton: 27BL, 29T, 106BL, 115, 157TL, 251; /Aubrey Washington: 25BL; /Bernd Weissbrod/DPA: 98BC; /Werek/DPA: 110, 272BR; /Witters: 20BC, 100, 219; /Valeria Witters/Witters: 126; /Wilfried Witters/Witters: 98BR; /Xinhua/SIPA USA: 48BL, 52, 62BL, 86, 114TR, 134TR, 200, 208-209; /Chris Young: 240; / Wu Zhuang/Xinhua: 55L

Shutterstock: 11B, 12BR, 116TR

Every effort has been made to acknowledge correctly and contact the source and/or copyright holder of each picture and Carlton Books Limited apologises for any unintentional errors or omissions, which will be, corrected in future editions of this book.